MARCO

NORWAY

www.marco-polo.com

Sightseeing Highlights

The beauty of Norway lies above all in its natural landscapes, but the harbour towns and fishing villages are delightful too, not to mention the exotic-looking stave churches. We have listed the sights that are on no account to be missed here.

©BAEDEKER

❶ ✶✶ Nordkapp
Much spectacle around the dark, forbidding cliffs
page 312

❷ ✶✶ Kjerringøy
Exciting open-air museum in an old trading centre
page 175

❸ ✶✶ Lofoten
Resembling the spines of dragons, these bizarre island peaks rising up out of the sea reach heights of 1000m/3280ft.
page 285

❹ ✶✶ Trondheim
Norwegian kings are crowned in Nidaros Cathedral.
page 417

❺ ✶✶ Røros
The old mining settlement is on the UNESCO World Cultural Heritage List.
page 362

❻ ✶✶ Trollstigen
An ascent for car drivers with nerves of steel
page 359

❼ ✶✶ Geirangerfjord
The number one Norwegian fjord
page 199

❽ ✶✶ Briksdalsbreen
Icy blue glacier tongue terminating in a crystal clear lake
page 308

❾ ✶✶ Jostedalsbreen
A trip to the largest glacier on the European mainland
page 250

Do You Feel Like...

...Norway tailored to your personal interests? Then these ideas may help.

WILDLIFE EXPERIENCES

- **Bird cliffs in the far south**
  During summer, the island of Runde is firmly in the hands of thousands of ocean-going birds.
  pages 148 and 150
- **Musk ox** ►
  Encounters with musk ox are possible while hiking on the Dovrefjell. **pages 186 and 188**
- **Sperm whales ahead**
  The Vesterålen Islands are ideal for whale-spotting tours.
  pages 436 and 440

SPORT

- ◄ **Speedy zodiac trips**
  The foaming waters of the Sjoa are ideal for rafting tours.
  page 206
- **Cycling the Rallarvegen**
  The former supply route for the Bergen railway line is one of Norway's most beautiful cycling routes. **page 237**
- **Over the Besseggen**
  The route for the mythical Peer Gynt's hellish ride over the Besseggen is actually one of the most beautiful alpine hikes.
  page 258

PLACES TO STAY

- **Ready for the lighthouse**
  At Skudeneshavn, you can stay in the harbour lighthouse (boat included). **page 243**
- **Cosy in the ice** ►
  The Ice Hotel is rebuilt annually at Snorrisniva near Alta. **page 154**
- **Fjord luxury**
  The Kvikne Hotel looks straight out over the Sognefjord.
  pages 373 and 376

BACKGROUND

Trollstigen, a spectacular road

ENJOY NORWAY

TOURS

Bryggen quarter in Bergen is listed as UNESCO World Heritage

SIGHTS FROM A TO Z

PRICE CATEGORIES
Restaurants
(main dish without a drink)
££££ = over 300 NOK
£££ = 230 – 300 NOK
££ = 150 – 230 NOK
£ = up to 150 NOK
Hotels (Preis für ein DZ)
££££ = over 1400 NOK
£££ = 1000 – 1400 NOK
££ = 600 – 1000 NOK
£ = up to 600 NOK

Note
Billable service telephone numbers are marked with an asterisk: *0800…

Contents • CONTENTS

BACKGROUND

Concise, to the point, ideal for quick reference: here are the things you need to know about the land of fjells and fjords, about the oil boom, the monarchy and the proud Sami People. Come to Norway and discover Europe's far north!

A Land of Fjords

Nature is rarely as tangibly and closely experienced as it is in Norway. There are the great fjords: valleys plunging vertically down into the earth, filled with deep blue seawater. There are the fjells: uninhabited mountain regions across which run the migration routes of musk ox and elk. The midnight sun turns night to day and those in search of solitude will find their paradise in Norway, yet so will sun-seekers looking to stretch out on the beach.

Restless souls will quickly find peace in Norway. The hectic pace and stress of life are soon forgotten during a journey around this country, where progress is always slow on the narrow serpentine roads. Bit by bit, a new equanimity finds its way into the traveller's mind and the life's joys are rediscovered in a landscape whose beauty has few rivals in Europe. Three quarters of the country consists of mountains, and hiking and mountaineering number among the most popular outdoor activities. The landscape is also characterized by its coast and the skerries: a swarm of rock islands and islets, on some of which stand solitary huts painted in bright colours. Norwegians as well as visitors love to spend their holidays in such a »hytta«. Yet Norway does not only promise solitude: the scenery is characterized by wood-frame farms; on the coast, meanwhile, stand colourful fishermen's cabins. The cities provide a contrast to the nature holiday: Oslo for example, with its promenades, nightlife districts and famous Vigeland Park; the historic Hanseatic town of Bergen, considered the secret capital of Norway; and, of course, the old royal city of Trondheim with its monumental Nidaros Cathedral. And from there, the gateways to the north open up.

Bizarre skyline of the Nordland coast

BEYOND THE ARCTIC CIRCLE

The Arctic Circle sits around the country's slim neck like an invisible necklace. During the summer months, darkness never falls, even at the level of Trondheim, while beyond the Arctic Circle the summer sun never sets at all. Some travellers report that this excess of light makes them positively euphoric. With a little luck, the visitor at this time of year will experience the type of light that gives an atmosphere of unreality, seeing the landscape glow in warm colours and even discovering an unfamiliar sense of freedom. Suddenly it is no longer important when to set off on the hike or where to pitch the tent. On the other hand, those who come in the winter will see the aurora borealis: hovering curtains of colour that silently dance across a profoundly black sky.

OIL, ELK AND REINDEER ROAST

Fish, endless forests and natural resources of all kinds: Norway is indeed a blessed country. However, the wealth of the nation with one of the highest standards of living in the world comes mostly from the

oil that rises from the seabed off its coasts. The Norwegians have invested their petrodollars – which, in the meantime, run into the billions – in a special fund, saving for the time when the oil wells run dry. The country rightly looks towards that day with trepidation, for oil and gas account for a third of its export income. Talking of money, the visitor to Norway will also experience the movement of currency: namely the Norwegian krone flowing out of his or her pocket! It is not only the astronomical prices charged

With luck, you may meet the Sami people and their reindeer

for alcohol that empty the wallet either. Eating out, accommodation, petrol – everything is significantly more expensive here than in the rest of Europe. For that reason, many travellers arrive in camper vans fully stocked with provisions from home. One of the most beautiful ways to travel the country is of course by a Hurtigruten ferry: the trip, »the most beautiful ocean journey of the world«, takes five days to pass along the endlessly jagged coast, from Bergen right up as far as distant Kirkenes. Along the way, the spiky mountain summits of the Lofoten Islands are passed, as well as the mighty plateau of Nordkapp and idyllic fishing villages. Talking of fish: in Norway you can catch them yourself in the numerous fjords and rivers. Salmon, halibut, fjord trout and cod are on the menu at many restaurants. So are elk sausage and reindeer roast, perhaps even traditionally prepared in a wood-fired oven in the style of the Sami. All this makes a holiday in Norway unique. Experience has proved that those who visit the country once are more than happy to come back.

Facts

Nature and Environment

Thousands of fjords cut into the backbone of Europe's longest country. Elk, reindeer and whales can be spotted moving from the southern tip up to Nordkapp and, depending on the time of year, the midnight sun or the unearthly spectacle of the aurora borealis can be marvelled at.

EUROPE'S LONGEST COUNTRY

No other European country is as long as Norway. The port of Kristiansand in the far south is around 2500KM/1553mi from Nordkapp. That is equal to the distance from Kristiansand to Florence. Together with all the mountains and the fissured coast line, this represents a considerable challenge to transport. From east to west, the country measures no more than 432km/268mi at its widest point (between the southern Norwegian Kappstad and the Swedish border). At the level of Narvik, the east-west axis shrinks to 2km/1mi. Norway is largely a mountainous country. More than half of its land lies at elevations of over 500m/1640ft and a further quarter rises above 1000m/3281ft. Considering the extreme northern latitude, this feature is of defining significance as regards the possibilities of forestry and agriculture. Flatter landscapes can only be found in the land surrounding the Trondheimsfjord and the Oslofjord, as well as to the south of Stavanger. The **Scandinavian Mountains** are predominantly comprised of ancient sediment and volcanic stone, as well as of gneiss. Morphologically, they are fold mountains, which fused with the far older stone mass of the Baltic Plate to the east in prehistoric times to form the bulk of Sweden and parts of Finland. This approximately 400-million-year-old mountain range has been greatly eroded over the course of millennia.

Sharp relief

> **?** MARCO ⊕ POLO INSIGHT
>
> *Nature records*
>
> Norway's nature is spectacuklar. Europe's deepest lake and highest cliff are both in Norway. Hornidalsvatnet near the Nordfjord is 514m/1686ft deep, while not far from the mouth of the Nordfjord the mountain cliff Hornelen rises spectacularly from the water, towering 860m/2820ft in the air.

During the Ice Age all of Norway was covered by the giant, inland ice blanket that extended across Scandinavia, millions of square Ice Age miles wide. It is believed that during the coldest phase of the Ice Age

The Power of ice

Briksdalsbreen in western Norway

the ice reached a depth of up to 3500m/11,483ft. This mighty ice sheet exerted enormous pressure on the underlying rock stratum: the pressure generated at an **ice thickness of 3000m/9843ft** would have been 2700t/sq m. As soon as the ice sheet began to melt, the slow rising process of the continental shelf commenced, a process that continues to this day. At present, the section rising fastest is along the Finnish Bay, at a rate of about 1cm/0.4in per year. The coastal levels of the skerries have also risen, while expanses of water in valleys and hollows have silted up.

Coasts and skerries No other coast on earth is as **markedly fissured** as Norway's. Its 2532km/1573mi coastline extends to 25,148km/15,626mi if the numerous fjord outlines are included. Countless skerries, tips of rocks and small islands that rarely reach a height of more than 50m/164ft above sea level, rise up out of the smooth water. Their number is estimated at between 50,000 and 150,000, though only around 2000 of them are inhabited. These rocky protuberances rising out of the sea are the offshore part of the coastal plate extending from the mountains. Today, the lowest points of the plate lie up to 50m/164m below the surface of the water. The region between the coast and the skerries is a popular area for amateur sailors with their motorboats and yachts, and numerous freight and passenger boats also travel within the protected channels created by the skerries.

The fjords: world class valleys Inland, the flat coastal strip is joined by the steeply rising bulk of the Scandinavian mountains, with summits reaching close to 2500m/8202ft. The mountains are edged by individual deeply cut fjords. The two most beautiful »emblems of Norway« have been under UNESCO protection since 2005: the **Geirangerfjord** and the Nærøyfjord, the most spectacular side-arm of the **Sognefjord**. Fjords, some of which cut up to 200km/125mi inland, are pre-Ice Age

Fjord formation

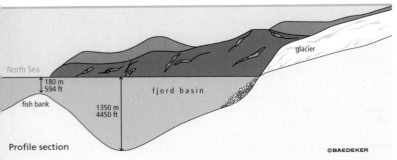

North Sea

180 m
594 ft

fish bank

fjord basin

glacier

1350 m
4450 ft

Profile section

©BAEDEKER

river valleys that were deeply eroded during the ice flows down to the sea during successive ice ages, and which then filled with sea water. They are often U-shaped in cross section, with extremely steep sides above and below the water. There is an almost complete absence of banks along the water's edge and human settlement could only take place where the confluence of side valleys caused a mound of sediment to accumulate. Depths of up to 1200m/3937ft (Sognefjord 1308m/ 4291ft) mean even ocean-going ships can travel all the way to the end of fjords. Some side valleys open into a fjord via a clear step and such openings are often recognisable as a »foss« (waterfall) crashing down from a great height. A seabed lip or fish bank usually seals the fjords morphologically from the coastal shelf.

Of course it is hard to develop overland routes near the fjords. Only where there are larger settlements at the end of fjords does a twisting road ascend the steep end of the valley in countless curves (for example the Trollstigveien near Åndalsnes or the Ørneveien near Geiranger) to reach the undulating highland plateau of the mountains mountains – the so-called fjell that lies at 800m/2620ft–1000m/3280ft above sea level. In the Scandinavian region, the word »fjell« describes all land that lies above the tree line. The Norwegians call the extensive and monotonous plateaus »vidda« (as in Finnmarksvidda and Hardangervidda). Due to the rising level of the Scandinavian landmass, rivers flowing from the edges of the vidda regions cut deep valleys into the highland plateaus. Thus the watershed towards the south and southeast of the fjells is characterized by broad, flattened out valleys, the so-called East Norwegian farming valleys, such as Østerdal, Gudbrandsdal, Valdres, Hallingdal, Numedal, Setesdal and Sirdal. These valleys too were broadened out by retreating ice sheets, but not nearly as deeply as the fjords to the west. Typical vidda landscapes are in the districts of Trøndelag (Dovrefjell reaches elevations of up to 2286m/7500ft above sea level), Telemark, Hedmark and Akershus.

Fjell and vidda

Alpine characteristics, such as ridges, cirques and sheer walls, dominate the high mountain ranges of the Lofoten and Jotunheimen. This is also where the highest elevations in Norway (and Scandinavia as a whole) can be found, such as the glaciated **Galdhøppigen** (2469m/ 8101ft) and **Glittertind** (2452m/8045ft). Prior to the ice ages, the summits of the Jotunheimen(like those of the Lofoten) were rounded, but steep ridges and peaks were created by glacial erosion during the ice ages.

Alpine mountains

Despite the fact that Norway's glaciers have diminished in volume over the past two centuries – just as those of the European Alps – and that the area covered in ice has shrunk, the country still boasts **Europe's largest ice-covered area**. The largest glacier in the coun-

Shrinking glaciers

try is the **Jostedal Glacier** or Jostedalsbreen, lying at an altitude of around 1500m/5000ft–1700m/5600ft. It extends to the west from the Jotunheimen mountain range between the interiors of the Nordfjord to the north and the Sognefjord to the south. Its total area has shrunk in recent decades, going from more than 1000 sq km/400 sq mi to around 487 sq km/188 sq mi at present. With their many fingers trailing off, the glaciers are reminiscent of a mass of overflowing porridge.

Lowlands In addition to these mountainous landforms, Norway also contains smaller lowland regions, which have been settled and intensively farmed since time immemorial. These are the regions around the Oslo basin and the Trondheimsfjord, as well the coastal landscape of Jæren to the south of Stavanger. The Oslo basin, stretching all the way to Lake Mjøsa, the country's largest lake, is part of the huge tectonic rift valley that cuts through Europe. The Oslofjord is therefore not truly a fjord. A flat bank has formed from marine sediment around the southern and eastern shore of the Trondheimsfjord, a cultural area that reaches altitudes of up to 200m/656ft due to the rising Scandinavian landmass. In Jæren the picture changes dramatically: the climatically mild Jæren plain south of Stavanger more resembles the Danish Jutland peninsular or southern Sweden.

?

MARCO ⊕ POLO INSIGHT

Mineral water

Although Norway has a lot of water, it has just one natural source of mineral water. The sulphuric salty spring called Kong Håkons kilde (King Håkon's well) bubbles up in the Oslofjord near Larvik and would attract spa guests from both home and abroad at the end of the 19th century. Today its waters are sold under the name »Farris«

CLIMATE

Gulf Stream Norway's geographical location, its huge length from north to south and the mountainous nature of its landscape ensure there is great variation in weather and climate (climate table p. 461). No country at a similar latitude has such a mild climate as Norway, a fact caused by the extensions of the Gulf Stream, which act as a »radiator« for the entire coast, keeping it ice-free right up to the extreme north even during the most severe of winters. They also ensure that most of Norway enjoys a maritime climate with moist, cool summers and mild winters. In contrast, to the east of the mountains that act as a weather divide, the climate is continental, and features great variation in temperature, depending on the times of year and day, and also less rainfall.

Norway's weather is better than its reputation. Though the west coast belongs to Europe's rainiest regions, precipitation declines rapidly east of the mountains, where there is also ever more sunshine. The reason for this typical west to east difference lies in the westerly winds that always bring clouds from the Atlantic, which deposit their rain on the mountain ranges. When this happens, there is dry high pressure weather on the rain shadow side of the mountains to the east. The highest precipitation and snowfall occurs in the southern fjord region, which has up to 3000mm/118in rainfall per year. The highest recorded levels of up to 5000mm/197in are only recorded in the most westerly glacier region. Generous amounts of rain also fall in the Saltfjell mountains and in the Lofoten. Those who hate rain should avoid the old Hanseatic town of Bergen, in which it frequently buckets down with rain (2250mm/89in per year on 202 days). The regions around Oslo, Finnmarksvidda and the Gudbrandsdal valley enjoy much more pleasant weather, and even have to rely in part on artificial irrigation for their agriculture.

Where does it rain the most?

Spring starts late after a long dark winter. Polar winds ensure that temperatures only increase gradually before the beginning of May, and even during the few summer weeks, the weather normally remains quite cool. In July and August, however, the thermometer is capable of recording temperatures of up to 30°C/86°F. When this happens, a positively Mediterranean atmosphere blossoms in the southern valleys of Norway and the normally ice-cold lakes transform into waters ideal for bathing with temperatures reaching up to 25°C/77°F. Traditionally, July is the warmest month and February the coldest. With an annual median of around 7.7°C/45.8°F, the coast between Stavanger and the Sognefjord is considered the warmest region in Norway and fruit and vegetables flourish here. The coldest temperatures are reached in Finnmarksvidda, where the annual average is –3.1°C/26.4°F.

Occasional Mediterranean temperatures

In the valleys of southern Norway the temperatures between mid-June and mid-August normally hover between 18°C/64°F and 22°C/71°F, during prolonged heatwaves even reaching 30°C/86°F. Along the coasts the temperature is normally two to four degrees cooler. During the night temperatures drop to between 8°C/46°F and 12°C/54°F. For central and northern Norway, average maximum daily temperatures of 15°C/59°F–17°C/63°F are normal, though they can also be slightly higher in southern Finnmark. Along the coast and in the Lofoten mountains warm clothing is essential, as it rarely gets warmer than 12°C/54°F–15°C/59°F.

Summer

Winter commences after a short autumn, as early as mid-September in northern Norway. Away from the coasts, severe and snowy weather predominates from November to April, with temperatures be-

Winter

tween -6°C/21°F and -25°C/-13°F. It gets the coldest in Finnmark where, on 6 February 1998, a temperature of -55°C/-67°F was recorded in Kautokeino. Severe winters also characterize the valleys and highlands of southern Norway, with a continuous freeze-up of between -5°C/23°F and -10°C/14°F during the day and -10°C/14°F and -15°C/5°F during the night. With the exception of the coasts, Norway disappears under a thick blanket of snow during the winter, which reaches its greatest depth between March and April, when it can be between 50cm/20in and 2m/7ft thick. In northern Norway and in the mountains, this white wonderland lasts from mid-October to the beginning of June (over 200 days), while in the valleys of southern Norway it remains from mid-November to the beginning of May. In Lapland it can even snow in the summer.

Sunshine   The sun shines most frequently along the »Norwegian Riviera« between Kristiansand and Oslo, and in the Gudbrandsdal valley (1600hrs–1900hrs per annum). These figures equal Central Europe's top levels and, in Kristiansand during June, they can even exceed them with an average of 280 hours of sunshine (10hrs per day). But if the sun is shining in the east, the west coast is usually rainy. The best chances to experience the fjords in good weather exist between April and May or when there are easterly winds that disperse the clouds, creating high pressure. Towards the north, Atlantic lows increasingly challenge the sunshine, although even coastal cities like Trondheim, Bodø or Tromsø can offer reasonable averages of 200hrs of sunshine per month between May and June. There is a great deal of bad weather and frequent coastal fog in Nordkapp precisely when the largest number of visitors come to the area in July, which obstructs views of the breathtaking landscape and the midnight sun.

MAGICAL POLAR LIGHTS

Veils of Light   The delicate dance of the polar lights is one of nature's most memorable spectacles. Named after the Roman goddess of the dawn, they are known as the **»aurora borealis«** in the northern hemisphere and the »aurora australis« in the southern hemisphere. Many people visit Norway, and especially Tromsø, during winter, with the sole purpose of witnessing the northern lights just once in their lifetimes. The shimmering veils of light display all kinds of patterns: shaped sometimes as wisps or bands, sometimes as broad curtains of light that illuminate the firmament. These light phenomena occur at between 100km/62mi and 300km/187mi altitude and can be viewed from many places at the same time, even thousands of miles apart. At one time the northern lights were understood as harbingers of war, catastrophes or times of economic hardship. Now that more scien-

(► MARCO POLO Insight p.22)

You'll need a little luck to see the aurora borealis in such magnificence.

tific explanations are favoured it is believed that the northern lights are the result of astrophysical and geophysical processes. The effect is produced when the rays of the sun hit the outer layers of the earth's atmosphere, known as the ionosphere, where charged particles are then drawn in the direction of the magnetic poles. There they collide with electrons – among others with atoms of nitrogen and oxygen – setting off vibrations, and the result of this collision is the illumination of the atoms. Nitrogen atoms give off a somewhat red light, while the oxygen atoms glow blue and green. With luck, if the charged particles from the sun are particularly dense (normally once in an eleven-year cycle), the northern lights can even be seen in as far south as Ohio in the USA and southern Germany in Europe.

IN THE LAND OF THE MIDNIGHT SUN

Where the sun never sets

At the equator it is always day for twelve hours and night for twelve hours. The rest of the world experiences changeable lengths of day and night because the earth's axis is slightly tilted with respect to its plane of orbit. The Arctic and Antarctic Circles are found at 66.5° at the northern and southern latitude respectively. At the Arctic Circle to the north (»polsirkelen« in Norwegian) the sun never sinks below the horizon during the summer; instead the so-called midnight sun shines. Known as the polar day this phenomenon can be observed at the precise latitude of the Arctic Circle **alone during the summer solstice**, on 21 June. On that date the presumed orbit of the sun reaches its greatest

Aurora Borealis

Aurora borealis or northern lights in the colours white, yellow, green are not uncommon at the Polar Circle. These illuminated paintings in the sky always appear when there is increased solar activity.

▶ **Where do the northern lights come from?**
Polar lights appear at both of the earth's magnetic poles at the same time. On clear nights the conditions for watching polar lights are ideal in the months September, October and March.

Dipolar axis

Earth's axis

geographic North pole

magnetic North pole

— field lines —

geographic South pole

magnetic South pole

▶ **How are polar lights formed?**

©BAEDEKER

① After strong eruptions on the sun electrically charged particles flow as solar wind towards Earth.

Solar wind

Sun

Polar light
in Norway (film)

A phenomenon at great heights

200km/120mi —

Polar lights appear at an altitude
of 100 – 400 km (60 – 240 mi)

Thermosphere
up to 500km/300mi

100km/60mi —

·· 80km/50mi

Mesosphere

·· 50km/30mi

Stratosphere

·· 10km/6mi

Troposphere

2

Magnetosphere

2 After some days the particles hit Earth's
magnetic field at high speeds. The fields
keep dangerous radiation away from
the Earth.

3

3

Magnetic
field
(Van Allen belt)

Earth

3 Some of the particles penetrate the upper
layers of the atmosphere in the polar
regions, where they encounter gases like
nitrogen and oxygen. Lights of various
colours appear in the sky.

northern declination on the Arctic Circle, though there are also places south of the circle where it does not get dark, dusk excepted. As the dates for the midnight sun are drawn from astronomical data depending on sea level, there is a good chance of seeing the phenomenon from the tops of hills even in places a little to the south of the Arctic Circle. The further north you go, the longer the polar day lasts during summer. At the North Pole itself the polar day ought to last precisely half a year, but in fact lasts a little longer due to the curving of light rays in the earth's atmosphere. At that point the sun rises at the beginning of spring on 21 March and sets at the beginning of autumn on 23 September, a total of 187 days. The polar night of winter is therefore correspondingly reduced. The Scandinavian regions north of the Artic Circle, the actual »Land of the Midnight Sun«, is referred to as the »North Calotte«.

Flora and Fauna

Although around a quarter of Norway is covered by forest, the country is relatively species poor in terms of flora. The country's southern fauna, on the other hand, is richer than in Central Europe. The lord of the northern forests is the elk, while the reindeer roams in the barren tundra. The country's most famous fish is the salmon, and the cliffs of the jagged coastline are home to countless marine birds.

The plant world of northern Europe is rather species poor, since summers are short and cool. Only mountain flora less sensitive to cold

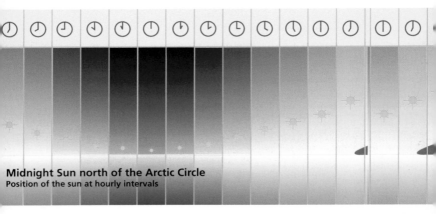

Midnight Sun north of the Arctic Circle
Position of the sun at hourly intervals

survived during the ice ages, and then only in the region of the west coast warmed by the Gulf Stream, as far as the Lofoten Islands. In contrast, the animal world is far more diverse than in Central Europe, due to the low population density of humans, and the variety of land-scapes made up of forests, highland plateaus, mountains and rivers, as well as a coastline characterized by its fjords, islands and skerries.

FLOWERS IMPERVIOUS TO FROST: NORWEGIAN FLORA

Around a quarter of Norway is covered in forest. In many areas of the country, however, the high mountains mean that forest is more or less limited to the sheltered valleys. There is little in the way of forest on the Atlantic coast. The skerries are normally pure rock and suffer significant erosion due to rainfall. **Many kinds of berries** (blueberry, cranberry and cloudberry) grow in the forests, as well as numerous mushroom species (for example, porcini and chanterelle). In the nature reservations of the Jotunheimen and Rondane mountains, the tree line is at 1000m/3281ft above sea level; by the Arctic Circle, the tree line has come down to 500m/1640ft, and the further north you go, the lower it sinks, until it reaches sea level itself.

Trees and berries

Mixed deciduous forests cover the southern regions of the country in particular. Red beech, oak, winter linden, ash, alder, elm, birch and a diverse variety fruit trees, such as cherry, are all common. Beech trees can be found right up to the mountains. Oaks can be found far into the north, as far as Trondheim. The further north you get, however, the more deciduous forest is replaced by coniferous forest.

Deciduous forest in the south

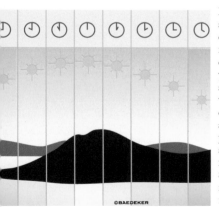

Extensive moors and dense spruce and pine forests are characteristic for central and northern Norway. Along the coast they reach right up beyond the Arctic Circle. In southern and eastern Norway Norwegian spruce predominates, while in western and northern Norway the pine is the most common species. The tree line of these forests reaches from 800m/2625ft in the Tele-mark and Hardangerfjord regions, to just 450m/1476ft

Coniferous forest in the north

©BAEDEKER

Too cold: no trees grow on the highlands of Jontunheimen

in Finnmark. Here, in the north, only slim spruce and solitary pines are found.

Unique birch habitat

Low birch forests characterize the transitional zone of the pine trees in the arctic habitat. Fjell birch raise the tree line by 100m/328ft–200m/656ft in mountainous areas. This birch zone, typical for all of Scandinavia, is unique on earth. The mountain valleys are greened by birch forests and willows, which are occasionally so thick as to be impenetrable. Ground cover in these northern forests is characterized by berry bushes and, in drier places, by Icelandic moss (despite its name a lichen).

Short summers in the tundra

Those who want to experience the tundra do need to travel very far north, for example to Spitsbergen or the Bear Islands. The extremely short **growth period of no more than three months** does not enable tree growth. The species-poor tundra can only sustain hardy dwarf birch and bushes, heather, moss and lichen.

Real alpine meadows can only be found in Norway's southern mountain region. The variety of flowering plants ranges from orchids to dry bushes, juniper and heather. Further north, the fjell highlands are similar to tundra: the landscape is characterized by bushes and heather, as well as mosses. At higher elevations, mosses, lichen and a few willow species predominate. Attentive mountain hikers will notice the numerous types of saxifrage (stone breaker). Annual plants are rarely found as their development is curtailed by the very short growing period. Because it is so cold on the Norwegian fjells, there are also very few pollinating insects, and most plants therefore have rather insignificant blossoms. The snow bed willow has proved itself to be especially adaptable. It grows very slowly and only achieves a height of a few centimetres during the course of five decades. Individual plants have adapted to their inhospitable environments in very interesting ways. Some develop sugary botanical juices not dissimilar to anti-freeze in their leaves and buds. The intense UV light on the fjell highlands inhibits the vertical growth of plants. Instead many plants here form rosettes, pads or even entire carpets, by that means taking advantage of the limited warmth emanating from the ground and also offering less surface area to wind. Very common flowering plants include primroses and, during summer in particular, the purple foxglove.

Meadows and heaths

REINDEER, WOLF AND ELK – THE ANIMAL KINGDOM

Two climate and vegetation zones are of defining importance for Norway's animal kingdom. The forests of the southern regions belong to the temperate zone and are principally inhabited by the same species as in the forests of Central Europe: these include roe deer, red deer, foxes, rabbits and badgers. However, thanks to the low human population density and the limited cultural and industrial changes to the natural environment, Norway's variety of animal species is actually greater than that of Central Europe, and animals can often be found here that have long been marginalized or become extinct elsewhere.

Southern fauna

The northern regions of Norway belong to the arctic alpine zone. There is naturally a smaller number of animal species here and the fauna is characterized by superb adaptation to the toughest living conditions.

Northern regions

The most common animal is the reindeer (►MARCO POLO Insight p.264). The snow grouse and arctic rabbit are also typical of this region along with the highly endangered species of otter, wolverine, wolf, and arctic fox.

Elks   The uncontested **king of the northern forests** is the elk, which can weigh up to 800kg/1760lb and grow to a length of almost 3m/10ft and a height of 2m/7ft. Elks are rarely seen as they are extremely shy animals. On the other hand, an elk may stumble in front of your car at dusk, even around Oslo. The consequences are often fatal. A consistent conservation policy over the past decades has increased the elk population, so that hunting is now permitted to the tune of more than 30,000 animals annually.

Reindeer   Norway's most widespread animal species is the reindeer, which grazes the barren north in huge herds. The indigenous Sami people keep reindeer for their milk, meat and furs. The nuclear catastrophe of Chernobyl (1986) was a particular disaster for the reindeer, as the largest part of their grazing habitat was contaminated by radioactive rain. Many animals had to be put down. After the Second World War, Greenland musk ox were repeatedly released into the wild in Norway and a significantly sized herd can now be observed on the Dovrefjell.

Goats, sheep, cattle and horses   Sheep and goats are very important suppliers of wool, milk and meat. In climatically suitable regions, cattle are also farmed. The rather small but tough and very nimble fjord horse was once a self-sufficient working animal and is now becoming ever more popular for horse-riding.

Lemmings   Lemmings, rodents around 8cm/3in–15cm/6in in length, with a stunted tail, are members of the vole family that live in the arctic regions of Norway. Herbivorous, they are mostly active at dusk and during the night, when they create extensive underground dens. During winter, they live under the snow blanket and do not hibernate. There are several lemming species. The most common in Norway is the mountain lemming which has a strong tendency to mass reproduction: a fertile female mountain lemming can produce three dozen young per year. This massive increase in population triggers two major annual migrations. In the spring the males, especially, seek out new summer quarters en masse. During autumn all lemmings set off in search of new habitats. At the beginning of a good lemming year there is a variety of plentiful food available for these animals, but massive overgrazing leads to food

The lemming: a member of the vole family

shortages and the lemmings are forced to seek new homes. During the course of this effort they traverse streams, rivers and lakes; many perish during these mass migrations. A popular but erroneous myth is that they willingly seek out death by throwing themselves over cliffs into the sea. Such »good« lemming years are, of course, also advantageous for the population of their natural predators, in particular owls, buzzards and the south polar skua.

The coastal waters of Norway are home to diverse species of seal and sea lion, as well as whales (including the minke whale and the sperm whale; ▶ MARCO POLO Insight, p. 438). So far, the only sea mammal that enjoys official protection is the dolphin. The coastal waters and the fjords are particularly rich in salmon, ocean trout and char. Out on the open seas, huge shoals of herring are sometimes encountered and large numbers of mackerel frequent the waters around the south and southwest coasts during summer. About one fifth of the fish that occur in the waters of Norway are cod. Their livers are highly prized as delicacies. However, the formerly huge stocks of cod, halibut, ocean salmon and herring have been badly decimated by over-fishing during recent decades. Numerous crustaceans can be found along the coast, in particular diverse prawn and crab species, as well as lobster.

Norway's most famous fish is without a doubt the salmon that can only be caught under certain conditions (Enjoy Norway, Active Holidays). The largest specimen so far caught by fly-fishing weighed in at 34kg/75lb. Each of the roughly 400 salmon rivers in Norway contains its own family of salmon, each distinct in terms of size and markings from all others. What counts for the passionate salmon fisherman is the battle with the fish, as it returns from many years in the Atlantic and climbs up the driving waters of its native river, never shrinking from any obstacle in order to reach its goal: the spawning grounds at the river's source. Additional Norwegian freshwater fish include the rainbow and river trout, as well as char, perch, whitefish, pike and eel. The deeply fissured cliffs of the Norwegian coast still offer protected breeding grounds to innumerable seabirds. Species include the guillemot and the endangered common murre, as well as other species that have become rare or extinct in Central Europe, such as the

Freshwater fish

? *Around the world*

MARCO ⊕ POLO INSIGHT

The coastal tern flies a distance of 40,000km/25,000mi annually. It breeds in the northern arctic, migrates to the southern hemisphere during winter and spends two months there, after which it sets off for the long journey north once more. No other birds covers such distances and no other life form enjoys so much light, because these animals benefit from the midnight sun twice a year.

Location:
Western edge of the Scandinavian Peninsula

Area: **386,598 sq km/149,266 sq mi**

Population: **5,2 mil.**

Population density:
13 per sq km/35 per sq mi

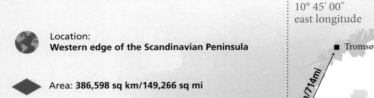

Norway

10° 45' 00"
east longitude

■ Tromsø

11150km/714mi

59° 54' 36"
north latitude

Oslo

839km/521mi

1155km/717mi

■ London   ■ Berlin

▶ Geographical data

Distance north to south:
1756 km/1097mi
Mainland coast: **25,148 km/15,717mi**
Most northern point:
Knivskjelodden (71° 11' 9" north)
Most southern point:
Kap Lindesnes (57° 58' 43" north)
Largest glacier:
Jostedalsbreen (487 sq km/118 sq mi)
Largest lake: **Mjøsa (362 sq km/
139 sq mi)**
Highest mountain: **Galdhøpiggen
(2469m/8101ft)**

▶ Government

Parliamentary monarchy
Head of state: **King Harald V**

Prime Minister:
Erna Solberg (Conservative)

Official languages: **Bokmål** (book tongue)
und **Nynorsk** (New Norwegian)

▶ Population

Minorities: **Sami** (Laps) and
Kvener (Kwen)
Foreign immigrants: **10.2 %** (especially
from **Sweden, Pakistan, Denmark**)
Population growth: **1.3 %** per year

▶ Cities

Capital: **Oslo**

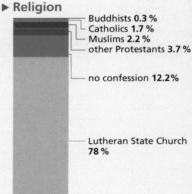

▶ Religion

Buddhists **0.3 %**
Catholics **1.7 %**
Muslims **2.2 %**
other Protestants **3.7 %**

no confession **12.2%**

Lutheran State Church
78 %

Oslo 623,300
Bergen 267,800
Trondheim 179,600
Stavanger 129,200

©BAEDEKER

Economy

Land in agricultural use:
approx. 3 %

Employment:

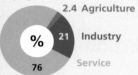

2.4 Agriculture

21 Industry

76

Service

GDP
(2013): **£313 bil.**
GDP per capita: **£63,300**

Unemployment: **2.9%** (2013)
Inflation: **1.2 %** (2013)

Oil production: **1.8 mil.**
barrel per day (2013, **over 50%**
of Europe's production)

Gas production:
108,7 bil. cubic metres

▶ Climate in Oslo

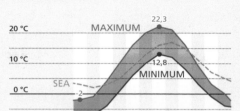

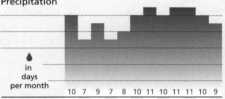

Precipitation

in
days
per month

| | | | | | | | | | | | |
|10|9|7|9|7|8|10|11|10|11|11|9|

in
hours
per day

| 1 | 3 | 4 | 6 | 7 | 8 | 8 | 7 | 5 | 3 | 5 | 1 |

J F M A M J J A S O N D

▶ Norwegian coast and fjords

	Length	Depth
Romsdalsfjord	**88km/55mi**	**500m/1640ft**
Geirangerfjord	**15km/9mi**	**600m/1968ft**
Nordfjord	**110km/68mi**	**590m/1936ft**
Sognefjord	**204km/127mi**	**1308m/4291ft**
Aurlandsfjord	**17km/11mi**	**500m/1640ft**
Nærøyfjord	**17km/11mi**	**500m/1640ft**
Hardangerfjord	**179 km/111mi**	**800m/1625ft**
Lysefjord	**40km/25mi**	**500m/1640ft**

Approx. 50,000 islands
Coast line incl. fjords and islands: **approx.
57,000km/35,400mi**

Length of coastline for other countries:

— Canada **202,200km/125,500mi**
— Indonesia **55,000km/34,100mi**
— Philippines **37,000km/23,000mi**
— Australia **35,000km/21,000mi**
— Japan **30,000km/18,600mi**

Romsdalsfjord

— Geirangerfjord
— Nordfjord
— Sognefjord

Aurlandsfjord
Næroyfjord

— Hardangerfjord

Length of fjords

200km/124mi

Lysefjord

15km/9mi

gyrfalcon, the white-tailed eagle, the fish eagle, and the golden eagle. There are also those on the red list of endangered species, such as the cotton teal, the peregrine falcon, and the lesser black-backed gull. The Atlantic puffin has also come under threat in recent decades. The primary cause is over-fishing, as Atlantic puffins principally feed on sand eels, skippers, capelin and herring.

Population · Politics · Economy

Densely populated in the southern coastal regions and far less so in the north, modern Norway ranks as one of the richest countries in the world due to the oil boom. The constitutional hereditary monarchy does not belong to the European Union, but it is party to the Schengen Accord. The Sami People make up the largest minority and predominantly live in the most northern regions of the country, where they now preside over their own parliament.

Paradise for hermits   The country's impassability and rough climate has allowed for the creation of significant population densities only in a few places. Almost half of Norway's population lives in the favourable settlement areas around the Oslofjord. The least populated region is Finnmark, where there are barely two inhabitants per square kilometre.

The transition of a society of fishermen and farmers into a modern industrial nation, which occurred at the end of the 19th century, initially took place peacefully and without the development of class divisions. For some time now, however, social change has not been being achieved without conflict. The country's development strategy is challenged by a marked imbalance between the centre and the periphery. Expensive infrastructure and subsidy programmes have had to be provided – especially for agriculture and fishing – to persuade the inhabitants of the sparsely populated and poorly served regions of western Norway's interior and all of northern Norway to remain where they are.

The oil boom   The structural changes that have appeared as a result of the exploitation of oil and gas deposits along the Norwegian coast since the 1970s have created new challenges for the state planners. Coastal settlements and cities such as Stavanger, Bergen and Trondheim have grown very rapidly, which has not only resulted in significant adaptation problems for their inhabitants, but has also led to environmental problems.

Norway is traditionally a country that people leave. In the second half of the 19th century almost one million Norwegians emigrated, including to North America. However, in the last ten years the number of immigrants has almost doubled. Today, almost 10% of the population come from other countries, the majority from Sweden, Pakistan and Denmark.

Increasing immigration

The approximately 40,000-strong **Sami** population – which forms the most significant minority among Norwegian inhabitants and predominantly resides in the northern territories – meanwhile has its own parliament, entrusted with representing the interests of this ethnic group. Every Norwegian must be able to speak the two official languages: »Bokmål« which is similar to Danish; and »Nynorsk«, which is an amalgam of 19th-century Norwegian dialects. Additionally, the Sami are now also offered their own language, also called »Sami«, as a school subject (for more on the Sami ▶MARCO POLO Insight p. 34 and p. 264). A second significant minority in terms of numbers are the approximately 12,000 descendants of the **Kven**, immigrants from the Baltic and Finland.

MARCO POLO TIP

! *Easter with the Sami*   **Insider Tip**

The liveliest experience of Sami culture and tradition can be enjoyed during Easter week in Kautokeino and in Karasjok. That is when many Sami marry, and on Easter Saturday Samit from Norway, Sweden and Finland come together in colourful festive costumes for competitions including races on reindeer sleighs and snowmobiles, as well as putting their lassoing skill to the test. The cultural highlight during easter festivities is the Sami Garnd Prix in the large hall on the edge of Kautokeino, when the best joik singers are celebrated.

STATE AND SOCIETY

Norway has been a **constitutional hereditary monarchy** since 1814. The king – Harald V since 1991 – nominates the executive with the help of the council of state (government), which is dependent on the support of parliament. The king can veto parliamentary decrees which can be resolved by electing a new parliament, which issues a new decree. Laws are made by the Storting (parliament), whose 165 members are elected for four-year terms. Proposed legislation is initially debated in the Odelsting (lower house) before being passed to the Lagting (upper house), to which a quarter of all parliamentarians belong.

A king at the helm

A Norwegian administrative anomaly is formed by Svalbard in the Arctic Ocean. This administrative entity includes Spitsbergen and

Svalbard, a special case

The Marsh People of the High North

The Sami people migrated to northern Scandinavia from the Ural region as early as four thousand years ago. They consider themselves the indigenous population in Norway, Sweden and Finland, yet they are an ethnic minority there today. Only a few still keep reindeer like their forefathers did, but Sami language and culture is maintained: joik singing still survives and the beautiful Sami costume is worn during traditional festivals.

The inhabitants of northern Norway call themselves the »Marsh People« (Sámi, Sapme, Sámit, Samen). The number of people with more or less Sami blood is estimated to be around 40,000, of which around half are settled in Norway and a quarter respectively in Finland and Sweden. As early as AD 100, Tacitus mentioned this reindeer herding, hunting people who walked using snow shoes, and the Sami also feature in the Icelandic sagas.

Religion and Language

Originally the Sami were hunters and herders with an animist religion. A shaman mediated between people and the gods with his drum, the Noaidi. An increasingly strong Scandinavian colonization of Sami territories took place from the 16th century onwards. Christianization, territorial disputes and a gradual settlement of the high north marginalized the Sami, their way of life and their shamanism-infused culture ever more. This process also led to the gradual decline of the Sami language, a development that was only halted in the 1960s. Since then, teaching Sami – a language that is not related to the Germanic group, but to the Finno-Ugric group – at schools has been permitted. The indigenous language is an important facet of growing up with a Sami identity. Norwegian and Sami were given equal status as official languages in various north Norwegian provinces in 1990. In this way the Sami were granted the right to maintain their culture once more.

The Sami Today

As a result of the many centuries of assimilation, most Sami now live from agriculture or fishing, like other Norwegians, and even follow careers as school teachers and bus drivers.Less than one tenth of Norwegian Sami people still travel through the land of Sámpi or Sámi-id eanan (Land of the Sami) as reindeer herders, as of yore. But it is this tenth, in particular, who maintain the Sami cultural heritage. Most Sami only live in their small wooden or earth huts or in tents with an opening for smoke at the top during the summer. Occasionally, during winter, the boat-shaped reindeer-drawn sleigh, known as a »pulk«, is still used for transport. Quite a few Sami cultural goods are also very popular with tourists. Reindeer furs and pewter works are popular purchases, as are colourful ribbon weavings, carpets, carved horn and

A forest of antlers – reindeer remain the basis of life for many Sami.

bone, as well as birch bark items. Sami traditional costume is a knee-length skirt with red and yellow borders and tight cloth trousers. A cloth hat is also part of the ensemble which, for Norwegian Sami men, has several points. Shoes are made of soft leather and end with a turned-up point. More than anything, the joik is an important element of Sami tradition. The monotonal, but very rhythmic, harmonic singing describes places, people and landscapes. Its roots probably reach back as far as Stone Age. The Christian church prohibited joik singing at the beginning of the 17th century, fearing devilish magic. This proscription was only lifted in the 1980s, since which time it has also been permitted during music lessons in the Sami lands.

Confident and Proud

The world was made aware of the Sami around 1980, when the Norwegian government drew up plans for the building of a dam along the north Norwegian Altaelv river that would have flooded a large area. Together with environmentalists, the Sami resisted this prestige project for years, and it was eventually realized on a much smaller scale than originally proposed. This success fomented a new solidarity among the Sami, and a new-found pride in their own culture and tradition. As a result a Sami parliament was established in Karasjok. Those employed in this and other institutions now have better opportunities to ensure that their interests receive a fair hearing in the Norwegian government.

Bouvet Island. Norway has had sovereignty over this island group since the 1920 Svalbard Treaty. However, there are also many Russian citizens living here.

Parliament and government

The red-green coalition government lost its majority in the parliamentary elections of 2013. A new minority government was formed between the conservative Høyre Party and the rightist Progressive Party. Høyre leader Erna Solberg became prime minister

Administrative provinces and regions

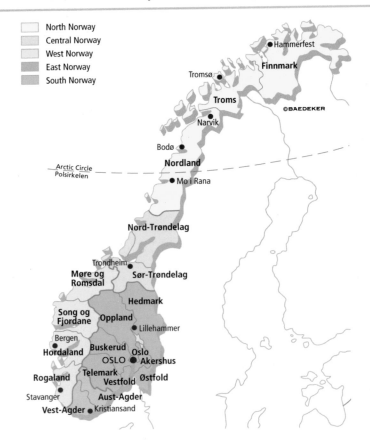

Legend:
- North Norway
- Central Norway
- West Norway
- East Norway
- South Norway

©BAEDEKER

Hammerfest

Finnmark

Tromsø

Troms

Narvik

Bodø

Nordland

Arctic Circle / Polsirkelen

Mo i Rana

Nord-Trøndelag

Trondheim

Møre og Romsdal

Sør-Trøndelag

Hedmark

Song og Fjordane

Oppland

Lillehammer

Bergen

Hordaland

Buskerud

Oslo

OSLO

Akershus

Rogaland

Telemark

Vestfold

Østfold

Stavanger

Aust-Agder

Vest-Agder

Kristiansand

The state owns, in whole or in part, numerous major industries. The tremendously important energy industry is controlled by the state, with a dedicated oil and energy ministry underlining the significance of this industrial sector. The monopoly of control over public services vital to society, along with the massive subsidy programmes for the fishing and agriculture sectors, has further contributed to the concentration of power in the state's hands – one of the reasons for the high level of taxes in Norway.

A great force

Norway's foreign policy focuses on the United Nations. As a result of its experiences during the Second World War, Norway renounced its traditional neutrality and became a founding member of NATO in 1949.

Foreign policy

The Norwegian parliament voted to accept the constitution of the European Economic Area (EEA) in 1993, and in that respect the states of the European Free Trade Association (EFTA) and the European Union (EU) were able to come to an understanding regarding the formation of the European Economic Area (EEA. However, the Norwegian population voted **against full membership of the European Union** in 1972 and in 1994. As a member of the European Economic Area the country has to accept all decisions made by the European Union, but as a non-member of the EU exerts limited influence over these decisions. Norway's international policy is developed in line with the Nordic Council, whose members also include Sweden, Denmark and Finland.

The position of women has traditionally been very strong in Norway, one of the first countries in the world to give women the right to vote, back in 1913. In 1981 Gro Harlem Brundtland (▶Famous People) became Norway's first woman prime minister, and a further eight women joined her cabinet.

The role of women

Stoltenberg's socialist 2007 government had a female majority for the first time, and a comprehensive childcare enables three quarters of Norwegian women to be in full or part-time work. From 2005 on, the boards of Norway's companies have been required to meet a quota of 40% women, which also applies to state-run businesses, and a stated political goal is for the rule to apply to shareholding companies in future.

Children are highly valued in this society, a fact that is evident not only on 17 May (a national holiday), when thousands of singing children parade past the royal family. A »children's ombudsman« is entrusted with ensuring conditions for a good and safe childhood, for example by improving the position of families with children. The holder of this post is also charged with protecting the rights of children at school or in the playground.

Children

North Sea Oil and Natural Gas

Lucky Norway! The country has huge underwater oil and natural gas reserves off-shore, but since it gets almost 95% of its power from hydro-electricity, it can sell its oil. Norway is the 14th largest oil producer and the 7th largest gas producer.

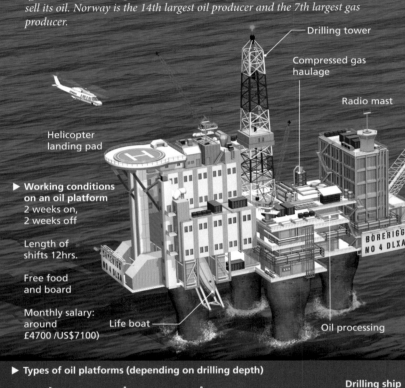

Drilling tower

Compressed gas haulage

Radio mast

Helicopter landing pad

BÖRERIGG NO 4 DLXA

▶ **Working conditions on an oil platform**
2 weeks on, 2 weeks off

Length of shifts 12hrs.

Free food and board

Monthly salary: around £4700 /US$7100)

Life boat

Oil processing

▶ **Types of oil platforms (depending on drilling depth)**

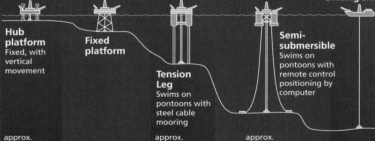

Drilling ship

Hub platform
Fixed, with vertical movement

Fixed platform

Tension Leg
Swims on pontoons with steel cable mooring

Semi-submersible
Swims on pontoons with remote control positioning by computer

approx. 120 m/400ft– 170m/ 550ft

up to 500m/1600ft

approx. 150 m/500ft– 1500m/5000ft

approx. 50m/160ft– 3000m/9400ft

up to 3600m/ 11,800ft

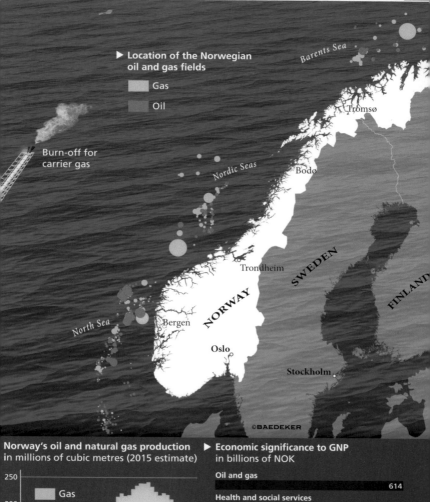

▶ Location of the Norwegian oil and gas fields

Gas

Oil

Burn-off for carrier gas

Barents Sea

Tromsø

Nordic Seas

Bodø

Trondheim

SWEDEN

FINLAND

NORWAY

North Sea

Bergen

Oslo

Stockholm

©BAEDEKER

Norway's oil and natural gas production
in millions of cubic metres (2015 estimate)

Gas

Oil

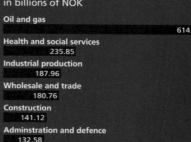

▶ **Economic significance to GNP**
in billions of NOK

Oil and gas — 614

Health and social services — 235.85

Industrial production — 187.96

Wholesale and trade — 180.76

Construction — 141.12

Adminstration and defence — 132.58

Credit and insurance — 106.35

ECONOMY

A strong economy With GDP at 89,400 US dollars per person (2013), Norway is one of the richest countries in the world. Oil and gas, shipping and fishing are the most important economic sectors. Norway's economic strength is largely thanks to North Sea oil. Almost half of Norway's exports originate from the oil industry and its supply industries. The shipping and fisheries sectors, in contrast, have been suffering from tough conditions in recent times. Norwegian employment costs are the highest in the world and no other country in the world has less working hours per year. Everything is very expensive in Norway, and taxes are high (a fact relevant for tourists, too).

Oil, gas Even though exploration in the Norwegian North Sea in search of oil only began in 1963, oil and gas extraction now plays a dominant economic role. Globally, Norway ranks 14th as oil producer and seventh as natural gas producer (►MARCO POLO Insight, p. 38); in terms of GDP, Norway even ranks as third among the oil and gas producing nations. The financial blessings provided by the oil industry are controlled by the state. Almost one quarter of tax income flows to the state coffers, while the rest goes to an oil fund intended to finance the pensions of future generations. The largest oilfield, known as the **Troll field**, covers a seventh of European demand for oil. The Ekofisk field 240km/150mi southwest of Stavanger is also of great economic significance, as are the Frigg field to the west of Bergen, the Statford field at the level of the Sognefjord estuary, and the Snøhvit (Snow White) and Goliath fields near Hammerfest. Ekofisk, which was the first to be developed, is now listed as a national monument. In the meantime, exploration and extraction activities have extended north to the Artic Sea, which according to American scientists could conceal a quarter of worldwide oil and gas reserves. The largest natural gas field in the world is the **Stockmann field** on the Russian border.

Dangerous work The oil platforms and accommodation platforms, alongside the processing ships, loading terminals and pipeline junctions together form regular cities on the ocean (►MARCO POLO Insight, p. 38). Having dealt with complex off-shore and transport conditions Norway's technological expertise is in high demand around the world, yet the dangers inherent in off-shore industries remain significant, not least from the permanent risk posed by oil spills, with all its inherently catastrophic consequences. In 1979, for example, the Bravo Platform anchored off the Ekofisk oil field broke loose and it was only due to the dedicated intervention by Texan oil well fire fighter Red Adair and his men that a major environmental disaster was averted. Three years later, the Alexander Kielland Platform was ripped off its anchorage by a ferocious North Sea, claiming over 100 lives.

Faced by depleted reserves in its traditional oil fields, Norway is looking for new sources and the search is being focused around the 373 sq km/144 sq mi area of the island of Jan Mayen, 900km/559mi north-west of Norway. Initial drilling has already begun off the island that is two thirds covered by glaciers. If successful, commercial drilling could begin in 2020. Gas is also believed to be present off Jan Mayen. In the meantime, oil and gas exploration has advanced as far as the polar seas, as American scientists believe the Arctic Ocean possibly contains a quarter of the world's oil and gas reserves. Furthermore, the largest natural gas field in the world lies close to the Russian border, at Stockmann. Norway and Russia agreed upon the exact course of their border and future co-operation in the exploitation of the fish and gas reserves of the Barent Sea, in 2010.

New sources

Technological developments and altered market conditions have led to once significant industrial sectors, such as shipping, wood, glass production and food products losing out; Norway has so far not succeeded in establishing greater economic diversification and reducing its dependency on two sectors: North Sea oil and gas, and the fishing industry. The most important centres of shipbuilding today are in Stavanger, Bergen and Trondheim, where this traditional economic sector has greatly benefited from the oil boom. The strong demand for offshore equipment, such as drilling platforms and tank equipment, has resulted in dynamic development. Norway has also proved itself to be a pioneer in this sector: Norwegians were the first to build oil tankers with double hulls. However, the demand for Norwegian ships is presently on a steady downward spiral.

Dependent on oil

Norway is an extremely important seafaring nation. It maintains **one of the world's largest merchant navies**. International passenger shipping, especially the lucrative cruise market, is dominated by Norwegian shipping companies. Norwegian luxury liners travel all the world's oceans and major Norwegian shipping companies also dominate the American market. There are plans to become the pre-eminent force in the European market for cruises.

Traditional seafaring nation

Norway's wealth of cheap hydro-power has led to a flourishing aluminium industry, which requires high levels of energy. Other branches of the Norwegian steel and the paper industry have greatly profited from this plentiful source of energy.

Aluminium

Despite Norway's massive natural oil and gas resources, thermal power stations are only of limited significance. Thanks to high mountains and plentiful water, Norway is able to meet almost 95% of its electricity needs from hydroelectric facilities (▶MARCO POLO Insight p. 380).

Hydroelectric power

Agriculture High mountains, fjell landscapes and barren soil mean that only 3% of the nation's territory can be exploited for agriculture. These areas are found, for example, in the fertile lime and clay fields around the Oslofjord, the Trondheimsfjord and Lake Mjøsa, as well as in the region south of Stavanger. To the west, agriculture is limited to the 40km/25mi–60km/37mi-wide coastal area, as well as to narrow strips along the lower fjord valleys. Cereals, potatoes and greenhouse vegetables are cultivated here. In the region around the Hardangerfjord, fruit cultivation also has a role to play. The extremely short growing season in the north is also a limiting factor – only 140 days per year in northern Norway for example. Arable agriculture therefore gives way to animal husbandry moving further north. North of the Arctic Circle, therefore, only reindeer herding, sheep farming and the breeding of animals for fur have any economic significance. 80% of foods and semi-luxury foods have to be imported. Norwegian agriculture today can only be kept alive by means of high subsidies.

Forestry In contrast to the neighbouring countries of Finland and Sweden, Norway's forestry sectors are in decline. Norway is therefore keen to develop long-term afforestation programmes to increase its forest areas.

Fish farming After natural oil and gas, fish and fish products are Norway's most important export items. The largest markets are France and Russia. More than half the export income in this sector comes from farmed salmon and trout produced by fish farms. The **salmon business**, in particular, is booming and Norwegian salmon is in high demand in Britain, Germany, Poland, Russia, Japan and even Sweden. Norway is the world's foremost producer of farmed Atlantic salmon, which is very popular (►MARCO POLO Insight p. 102). Fish farming in massive aqua farms has expanded at a tremendous rate over recent decades, especially for salmon and trout. Modern fish farming is considered an innovation in Norway. There are now around 1200 such businesses, producing more than the market consumes. The collapse in the prices for salmon and serious marketing problems brought economic ruin for many fish farmers. The monoculture of mass fish keeping, uncontrolled use of antibiotics and use of beta-carotene to increase the red colour of salmon meat all combined to bring aqua farming into disrepute. These days, antibiotics are hardly used. Furthermore, farming in narrow fjords is avoided, in order to avoid overfertilized waters. Nevertheless, biotechnological research continues. A new type of farmed fish is the arctic char and, in the meantime, halibut, Dover sole and a variety of crustaceans and mussels are also farmed.

Fishing Norway is also Europe's most significant fishing nation. The main species caught at present are capelin (a type of salmon), cod (►MAR-

CO POLO Insight, p. 88 and p. 292), mackerel, shellfish and coley. The fish processing industry's main products are fishmeal, fish oil and tinned fish, though the number of fish processing factories has declined by almost one third in the past two-and-a-half decades. Coastal fishing is in decline, especially in the region of the Lofoten. Herring and cod have also lost significance. Due to international pressure, **whaling** (▶MARCO POLO Insight, p. 438), which Norway resumed in 1993, is becoming less tenable. Despite this, however, the national whaling quota for 2011 was set at 1286 for minke whale, although less than half this number was actually caught, because the cool storages are full of unwanted whale meat from previous years. Hardly anyone in Norway still wants to eat whalemeat.

Tourism

Back in the 18th century, it was salmon that attracted the first tourists to Norway – mostly those members of the British nobility that were not frightened by the challenging journey. Today the journey is much easier and Norway enjoys great popularity as a tourist destination. The British are the fourth most significant visitor group after the Swedes, the Germans and the Danes, and contribute 8% of Norway's tourist visitors annually. Additional employment is created by tourism, especially in the regions of central and northern Norway with weak infrastructure. At present, tourism accounts for 7% of all Norwegian jobs and contributes around 4% to the national GDP. In an effort to promote tourism in rural areas, a new tourism strategy was developed in 2007, to promote active holidays, especially trekking, canoeing, kayaking, sailing and winter sports, as well as holidays close to nature.

Salmon from the aquaculture industry has flooded the market and caused prices to collapse

Welcome to Everyday Life

Here you will find some special tips and opportunities for getting to know Norway beyond the tourist crowds and for meeting »real« people.

KING GAZING

Although the Norwegian Royal Household is close to civilian life, you are unlikely to see the king himself. Unless, that is, you happen to be in Oslo on 17th May, which is Norway's National Holiday, when the entire Royal family spends many hours on the palace balcony or steps, waving to flag-bearing school children. Arrive early, and you have a good chance of seeing the king and his family close-up.

SAMI ENCOUNTERS

It is a long journey to snow-bound Lapland, but the effort is well-rewarded, especially at Easter, when the Sami People of Kautokeino and Karasjok celebrate Easter Week. This is a time, when the Sami of Norway, Sweden and Finland all don their colourful traditional costume and many couples tie the knot, so it is the only occasion when outsiders can gain real insight into the country's indigenous culture. Plenty of other fun is also available, such as snow mobile races, reindeer races, and lassoing contests. Another highlight is the Sami Grand Prix at Kautokeino, where a great deal more than the best joik song is celebrated.
www.samieasterfestival.com

WORKING IN NORWAY

Working in Norway is not only an opportunity to get to know the land and its people; the wages are also very attractive. The Norwegian Labour and Welfare Administration (NAV) is the place for jobseekers to start their search, and a number of their services are also available abroad. All employment offices within the European Union exchange information on working and living conditions in EU Countries and co-ordinate their services within the European Network known as EU-RES (European Employment Services). They also have a database of jobs available within the EU. Those with Norwegian language skills can also scan the Norwegian Yellow Pages for the addresses of Norwegian firms offering work.

www.nav.no, www.ec.europa.eu/eures, www.gulesider.no

WORKING HOLIDAYS ON NORWEGIAN FARMS

As a farm-stay guest, you are expected to work up to 35 hours a week, helping with the hay harvest, milking, feeding, or with fruit and vegetable crops. In return, you get free board and lodging, as well as a weekly (taxed) stipend of around £75. Applications are open to all 18-30-year-olds and farming or gardening experience is an advantage, but not essential. Norwegian language skills are not required as English is an acceptable working language.

www.atlantis.no

History

From the Stone Age to the Oil Boom

Ice Age hunters roamed the tundra, Vikings ruled the waves, but then the country had to bow to its neighbours: for many centuries Norway remained under the control of Denmark and Sweden and it only became an independent country in 1905. Now however, shored up by petrodollars, Norway takes a very self-confident stand in Europe.

HUNTERS, FARMERS AND GERMANIC TRIBES

10000–2500 BC	Hunter-gatherers in Norway
from 2500 BC	First farmers
1800–500 BC	Bronze Age: rock paintings
AD 200	Runic writing is invented

As the ice of the glaciers retreated, the first humans migrated to the area. Archaeological finds of fishing and hunting tools prove that man lived along the Norwegian coast as early as 10,000 years ago. While the interior of the Scandinavian Peninsula was still under ice, the settlement areas along the coast reached all the way up to Finnmark. It is unclear if these hunter-gatherers were ancestors of the Sami people (once known as the Lapps or Laplanders). — Stone Age

There are also significant finds dating from the Nordic Bronze Age (Nordic Circle) originating in southern and western Norway. The **rock paintings**, found predominantly along the west side of the **Oslofjord** and along a strip of land heading into Sweden to the east of Trondheim, date from this time. Animals hunted for food, such as reindeer, deer and fish are portrayed, as well as occasional images of humans and boats. The **burial mounds** also date from this epoch, complete with elaborate tombs for the dead of chieftain families. — Nordic Bronze Age

In Norway, the Germanic tribes spread all the way to the Arctic Circle during the **Ice Age**. Kinship groups, headed by chieftains, emerged in the fjord valleys. The era of the **great migrations** (AD 400 – AD 550) appears to have been an unsettled time for Norway, because many tribes created defensive systems, some of which were — Germanic tribes

Three swords near Stavanger recall the battle of 872, when Harald Fairhair vanquished the minor kings at the Hafrsfjord

The Vikings are Coming!

This call inspired fear and loathing all over Europe for over three hundred years. The Vikings extensive war and looting campaigns have been the foundation of their reputation to this day. However, they were also traders, explorers and talented boat builders.

The Vikings made their first bloody entry into the history books in AD 793, when they attacked the English monastery of Lindisfarne. In 845 they conquered Paris, in 862 Cologne and in 882 they ransacked the city of Trier. The great era of the Vikings (from the old Norse »vik« = bay), as the northern Germanic tribes of the early Middle Ages are referred to today, spanned the 8th to 11th centuries. The »Nortmanni« (Northmen), as contemporary reports refer to the northern Germanic people, left their Nordic homeland and penetrated into the rest of Europe and far beyond.

The First in America

The so-called »Rus« (probably the Finnish word for the eastern Northmen, or the Swedes), headed southeast to trade with the Slavic tribes, and they also settled in this region. They founded a new »Rus(s)ian« state and expanded their sphere of influence as far as Constantinople and Bagdad. The western Northmen (Norwegians) moved to the southwest, settling in almost uninhabited regions of Scotland, as well as on the Shetland Islands, the Orkneys and the Hebrides. From there they attacked Ireland and England. For decades they exacted tribute payments from the inhabitants of the French northwest coast, until the French king gave them the land in fief and it became known as Normandy (»the land in which the Normans rule«). They attacked Spain and Italy and pushed on as far as Antioch; they settled Iceland, which had been uninhabited until then, and brought northern Germanic culture to its greatest flowering there. Their sense of adventure pushed them ever further. Erik the Red discovered Greenland while based in Iceland, and many Norwegians soon settled there. Leif Eriksson, his son, left Greenland in 992 heading west, and landed in Newfoundland, now the easternmost province of Canada. The Vikings therefore discovered America 500 years before Columbus.

Setting off into the World

What suddenly impelled the Northmen to head off into the world, having lived relatively peacefully for a long time? An important feature of agricultural Nordic society was inheritance. The oldest son inherited the estate while the other sons had to make their own way. Furthermore, the climate became warmer towards the end of the 8th century, which meant fields could be better exploited. More cereal crops meant less hunger and accelerated population increases. However, as the expansion of agricultural resources was unable to keep pace with the population increase, many Northmen were forced to seek their fortune abroad, either as traders and colonists, or as feared soldiers and looters.

Brilliant Seafarers

The Vikings ability to conquer the world so successfully lay first and foremost in their superiority at sea. They were at home on the worlds oceans, they proved themselves to be outstanding seafarers and their long, yet manoeuvrable dragon boats were the most seaworthy craft of their day. The 20m–25m/66ft–82ft-long and 3m–5m/10ft–16ft-wide hull had an identical bow and stern which allowed for forward and backward steering with equal ease. These light yet tough wooden boats did not lie deep in the water and could quickly be pulled to shore or even across land. Superior boat-building technique alone, however, does not quite explain the Vikings military success. Ideology may have been a deciding factor. All of Scandinavia had remained heathen until far into the Middle Ages. Odin, the god of poetry and war, ruled in the Northmens celestial heavens. He decided who would die on the battlefield and took the bravest to join him in paradise, or Valhall (Walhalla). The Vikings therefore positively sought out battle and death by the sword, so that they might reach Valhall where they would join the gods in one last battle against the dark forces of the cosmos.

»Leif Erikson discovers America«, a painting by Christian Krohg (1893) exhibited in the Seafaring Museum in Oslo

virtual fortresses. Even today, the remains of fortifications can be seen spread over 50km/30mi along the eastern shore of Lake Mjøsa. During the Iron Age, **iron extraction** from bog ore became ever more widespread. In particular the techniques of weapon production were improved. The art of writing also caught on and, from AD 200, **runic inscriptions** became common on jewellery and tools. Around the 4th century AD, people in Norway also began to carve runic script into stone, among other places into rock walls, standing stones and onto tomb covers. While the name »Scandinavia« was first used by Pliny the Elder (around AD 75), and Tacitus also mentioned Swedes (Suiones) and Finns (Fenni), ancient songs give no evidence of a common name for the Norwegian tribes. The later word »Norvegr« simply means »the way to the north«.

THE CREATION OF NORWAY

around 872	Harald Fairhair unifies the country
8th–11th century	Vikings spread fear and horror.
10th–11th century	Violent Christianization of the population
around 1250	Norway reaches the height of its power under Håkon Håkonsson

Dozens of small kingdoms were created up to the 8th century AD. But around the year 872 Harald Hårfagre (»Fairhair «; 872–930), who came from an old Oslofjord ruling dynasty, conquered all the other minor kings and united western and southern Norway under his rule. After his death, however, the minor kingdoms partly revived. During this same period, the **Vikings** also undertook their spectacular warring campaigns and raids, penetrating into distant parts of western and central Europe, as well as into the Atlantic region.Norway's First TownArchaeologists recently discovered the remains of Norway's first town, called Skiringssal, at Kaupang in the Fylke Vestfold. A total of 10,000 items were found, including the remains of houses, wells and latrines, as well as jewellery and ceramics. The site was discovered with the help of reports commissioned by England's King Alfred, towards the end of the 9th century, when he received a visit from the Viking seafarer Ohthere of Hålogaland. Skiringssal is described as a trading port and settlement, with resident sea pilots and craftsmen.

One all-powerful ruler

It took about two centuries before the entire heathen population had accepted the Christian faith. The minor kings (Jarle) of Trondheim, who wanted to keep their ancient traditions, proved to be particu-

Christian-ization

The Saga Column at Elveseter presents Norwegian history you can touch, beginning in 872

larly stubborn opponents of the missionary work that began at the end of the 10th century. Yet with a firmness that often bordered on the brutal, King Olav Haraldsson (1015–30) established both unification and **Christianity**. He fought against the Danes and the Trondheimers and was exiled in 1028. Attempting to return, he fell at the **Battle of Stiklestad** in 1030. Soon afterwards, he was honoured as a martyr and raised to the status of a Norwegian national hero, as well as being made a saint. He went down in history as **Saint Olav**, Norway's eternal king. His body was brought to Nidaros (the present-day Trondheim) and buried there. **Nidaros Cathedral**, the largest medieval construction in Scandinavia, was erected over his tomb. Shortly before 1100, the first bishoprics emerged in the kingdom, including the bishopric of Nidaros that became an archbishopric in 1152 and took the lead in establishing a national church. The power of the church soon grew to such an extent that it was able to demand the right to grant land in fief.

Håkon
Håkonsson

Under Håkon Håkonsson (1217–63) the Norwegian kingdom achieved the height of its power, having secured itself as a hereditary monarchy. The crown controlled the nobility, administration was reorganized, the population increased, towns and cities were built or developed further, and Norway achieved its **greatest territorial gains** with the annexation of Iceland, Greenland, the Faroe Islands, the Hebrides, and parts of Sweden.

UNDER DANISH RULE

1319	Norway initially falls to Sweden
1397	Kalmar Union unites Norway, Denmark and Sweden
1387–1814	Norway belongs to Denmark
1536	Reformation

Loss of
independence

Having already been under Danish rule for a short period in the 11th century, Norway entered into a personal union with Sweden after the extinction of its royal lineage in 1319. According to royal inheritance, the Swedish crown prince **Håkon VI** (1340–80) was the rightful heir to the Norwegian Crown. In 1349, the plague reduced Norway's population by two thirds. As a result, the country was in a severely weakened state when Håkon VI married **Margrethe of Denmark**, daughter of the Danish king Waldemar IV Atterdag. It was therefore child's play for Margrethe to take control of Denmark, Sweden and Norway after her husband's death in 1389. Queen Margrethe created the constitutional basis for this union of states, during which Norway finally lost its independence, by establishing the **Kalmar Union** in 1397, which was intended to unite the Nordic countries against the German Empire.

Akershus fortress in Oslo was built in the 1660s

Unlike Sweden, Norway remained tied to Denmark until 1814. The dissolution of the Norwegian state council took place in 1536, and a **Danish governor** ruled in Norway from 1572 onwards. The **Reformation** spread from 1536 onwards, and in the succeeding era Danish became the official state language, including in church and school. The old Norwegian language only survived in dialects. Economically, Norway experienced an upturn. However, trade in the 15th and 16th centuries was almost entirely dictated by the German **Hanseatic League**. Mining was of increasing importance from 1624 onwards, for which miners from the German-speaking lands were also brought in. Silver mining was begun near Kongsberg, and copper was mined in Røros from 1644 onwards. Revolt against Danish hegemony only emerged at the beginning of the 19th century. The continental blockade against England established by **Napoleon I** in 1806 resulted in a counter-blockade of the Norwegian coast by the British, which inhibited seafaring and soon caused economic hardship in the country. Understandably, Norway sought to disassociate itself from Denmark, which was aligned with Napoleon. After Napoleon I's defeat, Denmark had to cede Norway to Sweden in the **Treaty of Kiel**. Copenhagen was only allowed to keep the Faroe Islands, Iceland and Greenland. The Norwegian islands of Orkney and Shetland had already been pawned to Scotland by the Danish King Christian I, in the 15th century.

A Danish province

UNION WITH SWEDEN

1814	Norway writes itself a liberal constitution on 17 May (a national holiday)
1814–1905	Personal union with Sweden
1854	Railway link between Oslo and Eidsvoll

Independent constitution

The Norwegians did not accept the Treaty of Kiel, however, declaring independence and giving themselves a liberal constitution at Eidsvoll on 17 May 1814, now a national holiday . Norwegians were only persuaded to accept the personal union with Sweden after **Swedish troops invaded** their country, but they were allowed to keep their constitution.

Upswing in the economy

Norway experienced a general upturn in the economy from the beginning of the 1830s. The first textile factories and machine workshops were founded in the 1840s, which formed the foundation of Norway's modern industries. Norway also rose to become an important **seafaring nation** between 1850 and 1880, thanks to its ever-expanding merchant fleet.

Norway becomes independent

Sweden granted Norway home rule. The Norwegian national assembly (the »Storting«) was empowered to nominate the government and pass laws, though these could always be vetoed by the Swedish king. In 1880, though, the Storting successfully campaigned to have the Swedish right of veto annulled and only the union's foreign policy continued to be dictated by Stockholm alone. But when the now mighty seafaring nation of Norway demanded to have its own economic consulates abroad and the Swedes rejected their wishes, the Storting threatened a split in **1905**, and Stockholm responded by demanding a **popular referendum** that was to decide the future of the union. 368,392 Norwegians voted for the dissolution of the Union, while only 184 voted for its continuation, and Sweden granted Norway its **independence** without further objection. In a further referendum the Norwegians voted to keep the monarchy and shortly afterwards Prince Karl of Denmark took the name of Håkon, after having been elected Norwegian King. Håkon ruled from 1905 to 1957.

THE WORLD WARS

1911	Roald Amundsen is the first to reach the South Pole.
1913	Female suffrage is established.
1914–18	Norway remains neutral during World War I.
1940	Norway is occupied by German troops.
1945	King Håkon VII returns from exile.

Norway was enjoying an economic upturn at the time of the union's dissolution. It had cheap energy through hydroelectric power, foreign investment was flowing into the country, and electro-chemical and electro-metallic factories were established for the first time. Politically, Norway also developed into one of the most advanced and liberal nations in Europe.

Pre-war era

Norway remained **neutral** during the First World War, though it suffered greatly from the **submarine war** waged by the Germans in the North Atlantic. The merchant fleet, vital for the supply of goods to the nation, was halved with losses of over 800 ships to submarines and mines. But the Norwegians also made a great deal of money from the wartime economy: their fish and ores (especially copper) were highly prized by the warring nations.

First World War

Norway also attempted to remain neutral during the Second World War. However, both the Germans and the Allies had a strong interest in controlling the Norwegian coast. There was a particular focus on the port of Narvik , from which iron ore was shipped to Germany via Swedish Kiruna.

Second World War

After British forces had **mined Norwegian waters**, an ambush-style occupation of Norway followed by German troops in April 1940, who were intent on pre-empting a British landing. The Norwegian army offered considerable resistance, despite withdrawing, and was supported by British, French and Polish expeditionary corps. Particularly costly battles took place around the **iron ore port of Narvik** and, in June 1940, the Norwegian forces capitulated. The royal family and the government fled into **exile in London**, where the exiled Norwegian government set up shop. From then on, **Vidkun Quisling**, the leader of an insignificant fascist association, was imposed as prime minister of a puppet regime by the Germans. Quisling – who was to be condemned by the Norwegian courts after the war and executed – was soon replaced by a state governor, again appointed by the Germans.

Large sections of the Norwegian population offered fierce resistance from early on in the war, but the German occupying forces held the country in a firm grip. Nevertheless, when compared to other countries subjected to the Nazi terror, Norway emerged more or less unscathed from the Second World War. The German troops were forced to withdraw from Norway at the end of 1944 and their final capitulation took place on 8 May 1945. A total of 10,262 Norwegians were killed in battle during the war or lost their lives as prisoners. Many cities and municipalities were destroyed in bombing raids or by fire. The Norwegian King Håkon VII, returned from his London exile as early as June 1945.

Resistance

INTO THE 21ST CENTURY

from 1946	Swift reconstruction and upturn
1969	The legendary Ekofisk oil field is discovered
1972/1994	Norway says no to membership of the EC/EU
1981	Gro Harlem Brundtland is the first woman to become prime minister
August 2001	Crown Prince Håkon marries Mette-Merit Tjessem.2011 The rascist Anders Behring Breivik is responsible for the unbelievable bloodbath that occurred in Oslo and on the island of Utøya.

Welfare state and oil nation

Reconstruction after the war was unexpectedly rapid. By 1946 industrial production and gross national product were already higher than in 1938, which enabled the development of a welfare state based on the Swedish model. The oil age began in 1969, when natural oil and gas was discovered at the Ekofisk field in the North Sea (►MARCO POLO Insight p.38).

Norway and Europe

In terms of foreign policy, Norway exhibited extreme restraint during the early years after the war. However with the onset of the Cold War and the increasing tension between East and West, a new stand was taken. A founding member of the United Nations , it joined the North Atlantic Treaty Organization (NATO) in 1949. Unlike in Sweden and Finland, the Norwegian people voted against full membership of the European Community in 1972 and then of the European Union in 1994. It seems this small nation's fear of unions of any kind was just too strong. Many also feared that Europe would use the country's oil wealth as a ready source of contributions.

Monarchy in the firing line

When Håkon, the Norwegian heir to the throne, announced his plans to marry Mette-Marit Tjessem Høiby in 2001, there were cries of outrage. But it was not the fact that his chosen bride was a commoner that made the Norwegian people hot under the collar – after all, King Harald himself had also once chosen a non-royal. It was more Mette-Marit's earlier life: wild parties, and an illegitimate child by a playboy with criminal convictions. »Someone like that«, according to many Norwegians, should definitely not become queen. But when the wedding took place in August 2001, all was forgiven and forgotten: the rejoicing by the Norwegian people knew no limits. Her Royal Highness Princess Ingrid Alexandra was born on 21 January 2004. Since absolute primogeniture was established in Norway in 1990, Princess Ingrid Alexandra could one day follow her father onto the Norwegian throne, a fate denied to Princess Märtha Louise, the present King Harald V's first-born child. The Norwegian Crown Prince's second child, Prince Håkon Sverre Magnus, was born 3 December 2005.

On wedding day all the trouble about the former life of Mette-Marit was forgotten

Until the reforms of 2012, King Harald V was also the head of the Norwegian Church. World Class Sailor The Norwegian Olympic and World Champion Sailor Siren Sundby earned the sailing world's highest accolade in 2003, when she was named 'World Sailor of the Year.' Culture Oslo's spectacular new opera house was inaugurated in 2008, designed to recall a mountain of icebergs. Furthermore, Stavanger was nominated European Capital of Culture. Bloodbath The Norwegian rascist Anders Behring Breivik perpetrated an unimaginable bloodbath on 22 July 2011, when he caused eight people to die in a bomb attack in Oslo's parliamentary district, and then shot 69, mostly young people, taking part in a summer camp on the island of Utøya. The shock for Norwegians could not have been greater, given they were used to living in a peaceful country with relatively low criminality, until then. The Norwegian Prime Minister Jens Stoltenberg's response was therefore all the more astonishing, when he announced »We will respond to this outrage with even more democracy, even more openness.« The public interest in Breivik's trial that was carried out with great diligence in 2012, was tremendous. The result, in August 2012: Breivik was condemned to 21 years for the murder of 77 people, and to be sectioned indefinitely thereafter.

Art History

Norway's pre-historic rock art in the Arctic Circle, its Viking ships and stave churches are unique.

ANCIENT ART

The era of the early Stone Age , during which the transition from hunting and gathering to settled agriculture took place, occurred in Scandinavia around 1800 BC. The **rock paintings** of the Arctic Circle were created at that time. Many of these rock paintings display images of game animals, with relatively few pictures of humans. Some researchers have interpreted the images as **magical paintings** that were somehow intended to bring good fortune when hunting, but the true motivation that inspired the archaic artists will probably never be known.

Germanic art in Scandinavia spans almost three millennia, from the Bronze Age , which lasted from 1800 BC to 600 BC in this region, all the way to the first century AD. The Bronze Age **Bronze Age** is characterized by technical innovation: the extraction, smelting and working of **bronze**. The weapons, tools and jewellery that were made of stone during the Stone Age were now made of metal; expressive art from the Bronze Age has also survived in the form of **rock paintings**, with schematic cultural illustrations of such events as festive processions, ritual war games and sleigh processions, as well as images of boats and pilgrims. **Early history**
Germanic art flowered when the originally rather sober illustrations developed into lively zoomorphic (animal) ornamentation. There is a penchant for filigree art from early history right up to around AD 350, and fibulas or clasps are embellished with granular gold and silver wires. Later, the technique of **chip carving in bronze and silver** was popular until the 6th century. This style of art involved making intricate decorative indentations into the metal with a sharp point. Originally, this technique probably came from wood carving and has survived in folk art to this day. Abstract **zoomorphic ornamentation** and ribbon-like tracery predominate from the 6th century to around 800. The »**Animal Style**« of various regions is characterized by a development from highly abstract animal forms to intricate ornamental compositions. A tip for those trying to recognize the animal in any one of these decorative works: if you first find the easily identified eye, the rest can be deciphered much more easily.

Early Stone Age

Germanic art

Kings are crowned in the Nidaros Cathedral in Trondheim

Viking art   Viking art (approx. 800–1100) is also characterized by zoomorphic ornamentation. The Viking's greatest technical achievement was replacing the old rowing boats with ocean-going **keel boats**, which had reinforced hulls, masts and a keel. It was this superior ship construction that made possible the Viking's great success. An impressive example of this innovative type of vessel is the **Oseberg ship** (in the Viking Boat Museum in Oslo), used as a burial ship for a **Norwegian princess** (►MARCO POLO Insight p.346) in AD 834. Another clinker-built ship is the **Gokstad ship** from the grave mound of Kongshaugen, located near Sandar in the district of Vestfold (today also in the Viking Ship Museum, Oslo). The 24m/79ft-long boat contained (among other things) the grave of a dressed man lying on a magnificent bed accompanied by a wealth of burial objects. When Christianity finally superseded the Germanic heathen religions, zoomorphic ornamentation also disappeared. The last examples date from around 1100 and can be seen, for example, in the **stave church at Urnes** (around 1090).

ROMANESQUE AND GOTHIC (11TH–15TH CENTURY)

Romanesque   Christianization, which took place around AD 1000, marks the end
Stone   of the Germanic and Viking artistic heyday. Building using bricks
churches   was established around 1160. Churches built of stone signified the **power of the new religion** and are now the best-preserved architectural monuments from the Romanesque era, chalk and granite being the favoured building materials. The stone buildings from the Romanesque era, including **Stavanger Cathedral** (around 1130) and the **Lyse monastery church** (around 1146) were modelled on English examples.

Stave   Wood is Norway's traditional building material and craftsmen exhib-
churches   ited great artistry very early on. The **influence of shipbuilding techniques** can be seen in the stave churches (►MARCO POLO Insight p.179 and p. 406), whose walls are made up of vertically placed posts in the stave building style. One of the oldest wood churches, the **stave church of Urnes**, dates from around the year 1090. Most of the stave churches still surviving today can be found in the triangle between Oslo, Bergen and Trondheim.

GOTHIC ARCHITECTURE (13TH–15TH CENTURY)

Architecture   The architectural style of Norway's Gothic churches often follows the Franco-Spanish examples. Several sacred buildings also recall German **red-brick Gothic** church building. The influence of the English style in that era also left a lasting impression, as can be seen, for example, in Trondheim Cathedral (new building phase from 1152).

Norwegian painting and sculpture from the Middle Ages displays very little originality and is predominantly preserved in the form of church frescoes. **Historic Germanic ornamentation techniques** have survived in the carvings of the stave churches. During the late Middle Ages, paintings, winged altars and alabaster reliefs were imported from the Netherlands, Lübeck and England.

Gothic Painting and Sculpture

RENAISSANCE AND BAROQUE (16TH–18TH CENTURY)

Only a few examples of Renaissance architecture can be found in Norway, but there are significant Baroque buildings. Cities are still dominated by their Baroque fortifications today, their military significance a dim and distant memory. Outstanding examples of Baroque fortress building include the **Akershus** in Oslo, built in 1660; the **Kristiansten** fortress of 1681 in Trondheim; the **Håkonshalle** in Bergen, built in 1700; the **Vardøhus** (northern Norway) built in 1738; and the **Fredriksten** fortress in Halden (southern Norway). A complete 17th-century garrison town can be seen in the historic centre (Gamlebyen) of **Frederikstad**.

Fortress architecture

With the **invention of the band saw** at the end of the 16th century, it became possible to divide tree trunks into individual boards. In this way wood cabins could be given a protective shield against the weather and their design could also follow styles for façades from other parts of Europe. Thus wooden houses were created in the 17th and 18th centuries that mirrored the formal designs of stone buildings in their detail. Much-discussed examples that can still be seen today are the old wooden houses of the mining town of Røros, as well as the Hanseatic merchant homes on the Bryggen at Bergen. Norway's largest wooden building, the **Trondheim Stiftsgården**, displays an extremely impressive copy of what would be a Baroque stone façade elsewhere.

Wooden architecture

ART IN THE 19TH AND 20TH CENTURIES

A large array of public buildings was created in the Classical style after the dissolution of the union with Denmark. H.F.D. Linstow built the royal palace at Kristiania (today Oslo) between 1824 and 1848, and also redesigned the Karl Johansgate, the main thoroughfare of

Classical art

the Norwegian capital. The university buildings were built in 1852 according to designs by Christian H. Grosch. Romantic German castle building also made an impression here, its influence particularly noticeable in the market hall next to the Oslo cathedral, designed by Christian H. Grosch in 1849.

Swiss style   The so-called Swiss style spread throughout Norway in the second half of the 19th century, although transformed by Nordic motifs it did develop into the Norwegian **Dragon style**. One of the most beautiful examples of this building style is the **»Frognerseteren«** restaurant, built on the Holmenkollen hill by Holm H. Munthe in 1890.

Sculpture   Renowned representatives of the younger generation of Norwegian artists include the sculptors **Stephan Sinding** (1846–1922), **Ingebrigt Vik** (1867–1927; ▶Hardangerfjord, Øystese) and, in particular, **Gustav Vigeland**, whose sculptures attract many visitors to Vigeland Park in Oslo.

Painting   Impressive works can also be found in Norwegian painting . The Romantics Johann Christian Dahl (1788–1857) and his pupil Thomas Fearnley (1802–42) were at work in the 19th century. The artists Johan Fredrik Eckersberg (1822–70) and Hans Gude (1825–1903) belong to the so-called Düsseldorf School, while Gerhard Munthe (1849–1929), Erik Werenskiold (1855–1938) and Christian Krohg (1852–1925) modelled their work on French art. **Edvard Munch** (▶Famous People), who is considered to be one of the founders of **Expressionism**, is of international significance.

MODERN ART

Cultural landscapes   Modern art includes numerous established Norwegian artists, such as Unni Askeland, Ludvig Eikaas, Mathias Feldbakken, Sverre Wuller, Ane Graff, Vibeke Tandberg and many more, who are renowned beyond Norway's borders. Cultural landscapesThe country has chosen 20 »cultural landscapes« that uniquely combine natural beauty and agricultural significance. A list of these can be found on the Norwegian government's, whereby each not only reflects its agricultural role, but also its specific art historical character that makes it a feature of Norway's natural and cultural heritage.FOLK ARTWoodcarvingThe art of wood carving goes back to the Vikings. Their famous ships were decorated with carved animal heads, usually dragon heads, and other figures from the bow to the waterline. Domestic items and tools were also decorated with carvings. In the 12th century, by which time the country had been Christianized, church building began in Norway, and the new stave churches (▶MARCO POLO Insight p.179 and

p. 406) provided wood carvers with a wealth of surfaces to work on. Some of the most beautiful examples of this medieval handicraft are seen on the carved doorways and window frames of farmhouses, and this art form in particular has survived right up to the present day. Wooden houses, including newly erected ones, are usually embellished with carvings on their exterior walls. A particularly beautiful example is the Frognerseteren restaurant built in the hills above Oslo in 1891 (▶p.351).

Another major folk art form is so-called »rosemaling« or rose painting , a form of rural painting that involves decorating parts of houses, furniture and everyday domestic items. Rose motifs and variations thereof do occur but, in addition, geometric patterns, portraits and landscapes are also featured. The oldest surviving paintings of this form date from the 17th century. Every settlement developed its own style due to the remoteness of the valleys, and these differences in style are so marked that experts today are able to give very precise information on the age and origin of rose painting works. Pieces of furniture adorned with rose painting are among the most desirable items in the Norwegian antiques market.

The third great artistic form in Norwegian folk art is costume-making and the wearing of traditional costumes is still popular today. Whatever the occasion, Norway's traditional garb is always guaranteed to be acceptable attire. Costumes are handed down through the generations, the silver belt traditionally being presented to daughter-in-laws, a gift from their husband's parents.

Folk costumes

The sculptures in Oslo's Vigeland Park always inspire conversation

Literature

Those who want something special to take home can stock up on plays by Henrik Ibsen and dramatic crime novels by Norwegian authors, not forgetting the renowned philosophical novel, *Sophie's World*, by Jostein Gaarder.

Old Norse poetry

Early Old Norse poetry takes three well-known forms: the pagan Eddaic poems, the sagas, and skaldic verse. Most of these works were composed in Norway, centred around the Norwegian royal court. Iceland was settled during the Viking period, where a rich culture soon developed, and this lies at the root of the close relationship between Old Norse and old Icelandic literature.

Danish period

During the personal union with Denmark between 1387 and 1814, Danish became the official language of state, church and school, and Norwegian only survived in rural dialects. The century of the Reformation signified the loss of the national language. Churches and

Olav Haraldsson (995 – 1030) is a literary figure in sagas, legends and in the modern *Saint Olav Drama*, which is performed in Verdal

monasteries were looted, and valuable manuscripts, including many sagas, fell victim to the flames. The Norwegian language was put to the test, and only humanismrevived consciousness of Norway's native roots and culture. National poetry experienced a heyday with the works of Claussøn Friis (1545–1614) in the 16th and 17th centuries. He also translated *Heimskringla*, the medieval stories of the Icelandic writer Snorri Sturluson, which was Norway's most-read book next to the bible during the 18th century.

A central figure in Norwegian as well as Danish literature is Ludvig Holberg (1684–1754). The comedies he wrote for the newly established Danish theatre in Copenhagen were soon performed outside Denmark and remain the foundation of the repertoire of Danish comic plays to this day.

Ludvig Holberg

After liberation from Danish hegemony in 1814, the foundations of Norwegian literature could be laid. This occurred at the time of the Romantic epoch. The most important proponent of Norway's literature was Henrik Wergeland (1808–45), who remains Norway's most famous lyricist to this day. His poems, dramas and essays reflect his deep commitment to cultural independence.

Henrik Wergeland

Norway's great epoch of literary realism, its golden age of literature, began at the end of the 19th century. Norwegian realism's outstanding works were written by the »Big Four«: **Jonas Lie** (1833–1908); **Alexander Kielland** (1849–1906); **Bjørnstjerne Bjørnson** (1832–1910); and **Henrik Ibsen** (1828–1906; ▶Famous People).

The Big Four

Knut Hamsun (▶Famous People) was honoured with the 1920 Nobel Prize in Literature for his novel Growth of the Soil (1917). **Sigrid Undset** (1882–1949; ▶Famous People) is among the greats of Norwegian literature and received the Nobel Prize for her trilogy Kristin Lavransdatter in 1928.

Nobel Prize in Literature

As far as contemporary Norwegian literature is concerned, a book for teenagers has achieved the greatest success: **Jostein Gaarder**'s (born 1952) *Sophie's World*, a novel on the history of philosophy , became a bestseller that has so far been translated into forty languages. Some of Norway's most famous authors today include Erik Fosnes Hansen, Herbjørg Wassmo and Lars Saabye Christensen, while Norwegian crime writers like Jo Nesbø also enjoy great popularity.

Contemporary literature

Famous People

ROALD AMUNDSEN (1872–1928)

The great polar explorer Roald Amundsen conducted research on both the northern arctic zone and the South Pole region. From 1897 to 1899 he took part in a Belgian expedition to the region of the South Pole. After scientific studies in Germany, where he specifically focused on techniques associated with measuring the earth's magnetism, he explored the northern magnetic pole. From 1903 to 1906, Amundsen was the first to sail the North West Passage, the shortest link between the Atlantic and Pacific Oceans cutting through to the north of North America. He then participated in the race to reach the South Pole. In January 1911 Amundsen landed on the Antarctic coast at the Ross Barrier and penetrated the ice pack by dog sled, and on 14 December 1911 he became the first man to reach the South Pole. When his British rival, Robert F. Scott, reached the South Pole, the Norwegian flag was already flying there. Between 1918 and 1920, Amundsen successfully travelled the North East Passage which also links the Atlantic and Pacific Oceans, but which leads north of Siberia; he was the second to do so, after Adolf Erik from Nordenskiöld. His real goal had been the ice floes at the North Pole, which he failed to reach. On 12 May 1926, he flew over the North Pole with two companions in the airbus »Norge«. Roald Amundsen disappeared during a flight to Spitsbergen in June 1928. An extensive search for his remains was unsuccessfully mounted in 2004, and the Norwegian navy tried again in 2009, but they also failed to find the two engine shafts of his plane, which are believed to lie at a depth of 400m/1,312ft, on the floor of the Barents Sea.

Polar explorer

BJØNSTJERNE BJØRNSON (1832–1910)

Born in Kvikne (Østerdalen), Bjørnstjerne Bjørnson had already begun writing reviews and articles during his studies in Christiania (Oslo today) and was the »literary speaker of his generation«. Bjørnson was one of the great realists of Norwegian literature and was a proponent of the artistic idea that nature and poetry should be seen as one entity, far from false aestheticism and radicalism. His bucolic stories, such as *Synnøve Solbakken* (1857; also known in English as *A Girl of Solbakken*), *Arne* (1859) and *En glad gut* (1860; *A Happy Boy*), were very successful and influenced literary trends elsewhere. His epics, such as *Arnljot Gelline* (1870), recalled the old sagas and were a popular read. As a journalist, he was just as committed to Norway's independence from Denmark's cultural influence as he was to Norway's move away from Sweden's political influence, and he was an energetic campaigner for an independ-

Writer

The actress Liv Ullmann became famous mostly through her roles in films directed by Ingmar Bergman

ent republic of Norway. He made passionate speeches for world peace, as well as for the freedom and independence of the individual and of nations. The text of Norway's national anthem was written by Bjørnstjerne Bjørnson: »Ja, vi elsker dette landet« (»Yes, we love this country«). He was honoured with the Nobel Prize in Literature in 1903. Bjørnson died in Paris in 1910, having spent a lifetime travelling and having spent many years in Germany, Italy, France and America.

GRO HARLEM BRUNDTLAND (BORN 20 APRIL 1939)

Politician

The politician Gro Harlem Brundtland was born in Oslo and had already joined the social-democratic Norwegian Labour Party as a schoolgirl. She studied medicine and after completing her first medical degree she attended Harvard, the elite American university, for two years in 1963. She was elected Norwegian Minister for the Environment in 1974 and party chairwoman of the workers' party in the following year; in 1977, she was called to serve in the Storting, the Norwegian parliament. She achieved great recognition as president of an international commission for environment and development. When the Norwegian central-right coalition government was forced to step down, she became the prime minister of the minority government headed by the Labour Party. She caused a stir – even in the relatively emancipated Norway – by appointing no less than eight women (from a total of 18) to serve in her cabinet. After 15 years in government, Brundtland resigned unexpectedly from her post in 1996.

ERIK THE RED (APPROX. 950–1007)

Discoverer of Greenland

The Vikings, also known as Normans or Northmen, spread from Scandinavia throughout Europe's coasts as pirates, merchants and conquerors between the 8th and 11th centuries. A Norwegian Viking, Erik the Red reached the island of Greenland during his voyage to Iceland in 982, which he named »Grönland« (»green land«). He established the first settlement with his followers in the southwest of the island in 985, and Greenland submitted to the authority of the Norwegian king in 1261. Today the island is an autonomous region belonging to Denmark.

EDVARD HAGERUP GRIEG (1843–1907)

Composer

Born in Bergen, the composer Edvard Grieg studied music at the Leipzig Conservatory before continuing his studies with N. Gade in

Copenhagen, who was then the leading Danish composer. He received defining inspiration from Richard Nordraak, through whom he discovered Nordic folk music. In 1866 in Christiania, the present-day Oslo, Grieg gave his first concerts of his own compositions of piano and violin sonatas, as well as songs. He met Franz Liszt in

Rome and, after his return, he joined a circle of young musicians and writers who wanted to create a national art movement. In his reworking of folk songs, Grieg established world renown for Norwegian music by combining native musical forms with his era's compositional forms. He composed piano music, chamber music and orchestral works (the *Holberg Suite* is a celebration for the 200th anniversary of the playwright Ludvig Holberg's birthday). Along with his orchestral pieces for Bjørnstjerne Bjørnson's *Sigurd Jorsalfar* (1872), his music for Henrik Ibsen's *Peer Gynt*, composed on the playwright's request between 1874 and 1876, is of particular significance. The music reflects the atmosphere in the high mountains, the rage of the wedding guests when the bride is stolen and, finally, Peer Gynt's dramatic homecoming and the peace of life with Solvejg, who has waited for him: *Solvejg's Song* is one of the most famous songs in the Norwegian musical repertoire.

KNUT HAMSUN (1859–1952)

Knut Hamsun (actually Pedersen) was the son of poor tailors of rural origin. The family moved to the Hamsund farming estate in Hamarøy across from the Lofoten Islands in 1862, and it is from here

Author

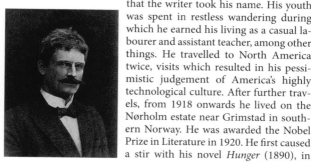

that the writer took his name. His youth was spent in restless wandering during which he earned his living as a casual labourer and assistant teacher, among other things. He travelled to North America twice, visits which resulted in his pessimistic judgement of America's highly technological culture. After further travels, from 1918 onwards he lived on the Nørholm estate near Grimstad in southern Norway. He was awarded the Nobel Prize in Literature in 1920. He first caused a stir with his novel *Hunger* (1890), in

RA II

which he describes the privations experienced by a young writer seeking success, which lead to physical and emotional exhaustion. Hamsun's works exhibit a profound feeling for nature and the belief in an all-pervading life force. He frequently portrayed the irrational in the actions of his characters and his literary work is seen as an attempt to overcome naturalism. Hamsun remains a controversial figure to this day, because he welcomed the German occupation of Norway in 1940. Furthermore, he published articles in Nazi-collaborator Vidkun Quisling's party newspapers. After the Second World War the author was arrested and sentenced to pay a fine, leaving him financially ruined.

THOR HEYERDAHL (1914–2002)

The zoologist and ethnologist Thor Heyerdahl made it his goal to prove that early trans-oceanic contact between peoples had been possible. For this purpose he crossed several oceans in simple boats. He sailed alone and used only ocean currents and winds. For his first expedition in 1947, Heyerdahl bravely crossed the Pacific on a raft called Kon-Tiki. He set off from the coast of Peru and finally reached Polynesia (Tahiti) after 101 days, having covered 8000km/5000mi. In 1955–56 he researched the culture of Easter Island. Between 1969 and 1970, his expedition entitled »Ra« led him from Morocco to the Caribbean island of Barbados. In 1977–78, he travelled through the Persian Gulf from Basra to Djibouti on a reed boat called Tigris, modelled on Sumerian craft. In 1983, he discovered the remains of an ancient sophisticated culture in the Maldives. Thor Heyerdahl recounted his expeditions in several books.

Explorer

HENRIK IBSEN (1828–1906)

Henrik Ibsen , Norway's greatest playwright, was born in Skien and died in Christiania (Oslo). After completing basic schooling he began a pharmacy apprenticeship in Grimstad, his father having become impoverished. In 1850 he began studying medicine, but from 1851 Ibsen worked as playwright at the theatre in Bergen. Afterwards he was employed as the artistic director of the theatre in Christiania. Ibsen left Norway in the spring of 1864 under a cloud and spent many years living abroad, mainly in Rome, Dresden and Munich. Ibsen, who had already written plays as a young man, began his career with the Roman play *Catilina* in 1850. The plays that were created in the following years were written under the pervading influ-

Playwright

A reconstruction of »Ra II« in the Kon Tiki Museum in Oslo

ence of Norwegian national Romanticism, whose conservative tendencies Ibsen criticized. Following on from his historical dramas and theatre of ideas, Ibsen created a new type of theatre with »realis-

tic drama«, whose radical criticism of social conditions marked the beginning of modern drama. In his piece *Pillars of Society* (1877) and following works, Ibsen illustrated life's illusions and the often hidden fragility of human relationships in stories from the everyday lives of ordinary people. Ibsen achieved world fame with his marital drama entitled The Dolls House (1879), in which the woman claims equal status in the partnership. This play, as well as the later marriage drama *The Ghosts* (1881), caused violent discussions in the Nordic countries, but both are still popular today. Ibsen's work had a powerful influence on the drama of the outgoing 19th century and the beginning of the 20th century. Edvard Grieg composed his Incidental Music for the play *Peer Gynt* (1867), which he wrote in Italy but is set in Gudbrandsdal and the highlands of Norway.

KNUD KNUDSEN (1831–1915)

Pomologist and photographer

Presumably half of Norway still bites into the Hardanger apples that Knud Knudsen cultivated. Knudsen travelled as far as Swabia in Germany in 1862, to pursue his passion as photographer, basket weaver and apple tree fanatic. It is not known what inflamed Knudsen's passion for pomology (the study of fruit trees), but he did grow up in a corner of Norway whose climate is uniquely suitable for growing fruit: the Hardangerfjord region. Born in Odda in 1831, he initially completed a sales apprenticeship in Bergen, and then trained as a basket weaver. Afterwards he repeatedly returned to his parent's farm where he planted an apple tree nursery – a novelty in those days – which he stocked with foreign fruit varieties. He quickly enjoyed success. In 1860, he won the prize for the greatest species variety in a fruit exhibition in Bergen. The state granted the talented young man who promised to develop innovative ideas a stipend to study abroad. So Knudsen went to Reutlingen in Germany, to one of the most famous fruit growing institutes of the time. His luggage will have raised some eyebrows. For, along with his photographic apparatus (very bulky in those early days), it also included a giant tent for use as a dark room, and countless glass plates for creating images. Knudsen studied at the institute for six months and in his free time took the first ever photographs of Reutlingen. Back at home, Knudsen chose not to tend to his fruit orchards but to open a photographic studio in Bergen instead. Nobody knows why he so resolutely turned his back on his beloved apple trees. Perhaps the two bad harvest years that followed his return permanently disillusioned him. However, he went down in Norwegian history as the founder of the first fruit plantations in the country, and Reutlingen, too, is grateful to him to this day, for providing invaluable historic photographic documentation of their town.

LEIF ERIKSSON (APPROX. 975 – APPROX. 1020)

The Norwegian seafarer Leif Eriksson , whose father was ►Erik the Red, was blown off course during his journey to Greenland in around 100. He ended up reaching the coast of North America. Presumably he landed in the area of Nova Scotia, a peninsula that today belongs to Canada. Leif Eriksson, who discovered America before Columbus and therefore counts as the first European who set foot in the New World, called the land he found on the east coast of North America »Vinland« (fertile, meadow country).

Discoverer of the Americas

EDVARD MUNCH (1863–1944)

Scandinavia's greatest painter Edvard Munch was born in Løten near Hamar, and died in Ekely near Oslo. He spent his childhood in Oslo (then called Christiania); his mother died of tuberculosis when he was five years old. With occasional breaks, Munch lived in Paris from 1885 onwards, where he was influenced by Vincent Van Gogh and Paul Gauguin. Later, he spent a good deal of time in Germany, especially Berlin. In 1909, he suffered a nervous breakdown and returned to Norway, where he created the frescoes for the University of Oslo in 1916. During his final years, which were marred by an eye problem, the painter frequently stayed in Åsgårdstrand. The coast and the sea are the setting for many of his paintings. Munch created paintings, drawings, lithographs and woodcuts that occasionally reflect influence from the art nouveau and Symbolism movements. In his landscapes, whose shapes he created in simplified, darkly glowing areas of colour, an early Expressionist art form is recognizable. His portraits of people are usually grim and express universal human experiences, such as fear, death and erotic love. Numerous themes exist in several versions. Munch began his cycle entitled *The Frieze of Life*, which consists of twelve paintings, for Max Reinhardt's Berlin Chamber Theatre in 1893. His most famous pictures include *The Sick Child* (1885–86), *The Scream* (1893), *Dance of Life* (1899–1900) and *Girl on*

Painter

Lost and found: *The Scream*

the Bridge (1900). In later life, he turned away from the portrayal of the darker side of life to more positive picture themes. In his will, Munch left his entire estate of 1000 paintings, 15,400 prints, 5400 watercolours and drawings, and six sculptures to the city of Oslo. Today most of these artworks can be viewed in the Oslo Munch Museum, as well as in the National Gallery. The Nazis, by the way, had no time for Munch: around 80 of his paintings were labelled »perverted art« by the National Socialists in 1937 and removed from public collections. On 22 August 2004 armed and disguised robbers stole *The Scream* and *Madonna* from the Oslo Munch Museum. Two years later six of the assumed seven culprits were arrested. They were all members of the Norwegian answer to the Mafia, the Tveita gang, named after a quarter of Oslo. During his appeal proceedings, one of the criminals, David Toska, offered to return the paintings to the police in exchange for remission of his 19-year prison sentence. On 31 August 2006 both paintings were seized in a raid. But the robbery left its traces: The Scream in particular has been so badly damaged by damp that it is impossible to restore it fully.

FRIDTJOF NANSEN (1861–1930)

Polar explorer

Polar explorer Fridtjof Nansen was born on a farm near Christiania (Oslo). In 1888 he and fellow Norwegian Otto Sverdrup (1854–1930) became the first men to cross Greenland from its east coast to its west coast on skis and by sleigh. In 1893, Nansen set off on a scientific expedition on his ship the Fram (»Ahead!«) through the North Polar Sea, departing from the north Siberian islands of »Nowaja Semlja«. In 1895, he reached a northern latitude of 86° 14' during an attempt to reach the North Pole, setting off by sleigh from the Fram. A year later Nansen returned to Norway via Franz Josef Land. He became a professor of zoology in 1896, and of oceanography in 1897. He led several expeditions into the North Atlantic between 1900 and 1914 and he wrote about his experiences in numerous books, including Farthest North, In Northern Mists and The First Crossing of Green-

land. His scientific exploration ship, the Fram, is today exhibited in the museum of the same name on the peninsula of Bygdøy near Oslo. Nansen also held political office in later life. In 1920, he oversaw the return of prisoners of war from Russia; in 1921–23, as High Commissioner for the League of Nations, he organized emergency aid to the starving in Soviet Union. On Nansen's instigation, a travel document was established for Russian refugees without papers, later known as the »Nansen passport«, which was also used for other refugees. In 1922 Fridtjof Nansen was honoured for his committed work with the Nobel Peace Prize.

BIRGER RUUD (1911–98)

Birger Ruud, born in Kongsberg, is a legendary figure in international skiing. The younger brother of Sigmund Ruud, who won silver at the Olympic Winter Games of 1928 in St Moritz, Birger Ruud was a talented ski jumper and downhill racer. He won Olympic gold at Lake Placid in 1932, achieved the same feat in Garmisch-Partenkirchen in 1936, and took the silver medal in the Olympics at St Moritz in 1948. An outstanding sports personality, Ruud made Nordic and Alpine skiing, including ski jumping, famous throughout the world. Wearing highly fashionable, dark ski pants along with Norwegian knitted gloves and hat, he took off from the Olympic ski jump on parallel skis with his arms outstretched before him. As if all that were not enough, he also won downhill ski races.

Skier

LIV ULLMANN (BORN 1938)

Norway's great actress Liv Ullmann first saw the light of day in Tokyo. After studying theatre in London and Stavanger, she began her career in the theatre and as of 1957 joined film productions too (▶photo p.66). Her first major role in film was as Elisabeth Vogler in *Persona*, directed by Ingmar Bergman, with whom she made a whole series of films. Bergman and Ullmann were together for years and have a daughter, the writer Linn Ullmann. Liv Ullmann has frequently portrayed women who only give the appearance of being psychologically grounded, and who are exposed to great challenges. The actress has appeared in over 60 films and has twice been nominated

Actress

for an Oscar. She has enjoyed great success in the USA, not just in Hollywood but also on Broadway. Meanwhile, she is also an award-winning director. In 1995, for example, she filmed the Norwegian literary classic *Kristin Lavransdatter* by Sigrid Undset, which tells the dramatic story of a woman in medieval Norway. She has also made a name for herself as a writer, with respected works such as *Changing and Choices*. Liv Ullmann has also involved herself in political and social issues and became a UNICEF Goodwill Ambassador in 1980. In her memoirs, which at the time of writing have yet to be published in the UK, she describes an enigmatic but glittering life, complete with personal crises and professional challenges.

SIGRID UNDSET (1882–1949)

Writer The author Sigrid Undset originally came from the Danish town of Kalundborg, and grew up in Oslo from the age of three. She was forced to abandon her studies after the premature death of her father, and worked as a secretary. She was married to the painter A.C. Svarstad from 1912 to 1925. Having warned against National Socialism in the 1930s, she fled to America in 1940. One of her sons was active in the resistance against Hitler. Undset returned to Norway in 1945. In her fiction, she created deeply intuitive, realistic portrayals of apparently uncomplicated, average people. She was particularly fascinated by the question of whether women should seek their life's happiness in work, in erotic love, or as mothers. After her conversion to Catholicism in 1925, she herself found human fulfilment in a campaigning life based on faith. Sigrid Undset began her literary career with novels and short stories portraying contemporary life. Later she turned to the style of old Icelandic sagas and her novels took their themes from the Norwegian past. It is these works that gained her international fame. Her trilogy *Kristin Lavransdatter* was written between 1920 and 1922, and in 1925 and 1927 she wrote *Olav Audunssøn i Hestviken* and *Olav Audunssøn og hans børn* respectively. She received the Nobel Prize in Literature for her life's work in 1928.

ADOLF GUSTAV VIGELAND (1869–1943)

Sculptor Adolf Gustav Vigeland first saw the light of day in the southern Norwegian settlement of Mandal. The artistically highly talented young man received his training in Oslo, Copenhagen, Paris, Rome and Florence. Vigeland created portraits and especially busts. During his early period, he was greatly influenced by Auguste Rodin. This is most apparent in one of his best known busts, the study of N.H. Abel made in 1905. During his later working life, Vigeland turned to a more classically influenced style of work. Among his most famous works from this later period are the monumental sculptures in Oslo's Frogner Park, for which he made around 100 symbolic figural groups and reliefs of granite and bronze. Vigeland died in Oslo in 1943, after which his studio was opened to the public as a museum.

ENJOY NORWAY

What specialties should you definitely try? Which festivals are not to be missed? What sport can you do in Norway and where is it most fun for children? Find the answers here.

Accommodation

Something For Everyone

Hotels in Norway are of a high standard and often offer value-for-money family rooms. The alternative is to choose a pension. In rural areas, there are cabins and holiday houses, as well as youth hostels and campsites. An increasingly popular option is also a »farmstay« holiday.

Huts and holiday homes

For many Norwegians, what life is really about is the splendid isolation of a cabin in the mountains, by a fjord or in the forest, with your very own little lake in front of the door. Even while more and more like to jet off to hotter climates these days, not many pass up at least a few days a year in the wilderness. Either people head for their own cabin, or they know someone who lets them use theirs. Creature comforts are not relevant during these trips and many cabins have neither electricity nor running water, which needs to be carried from a well or the nearby river. But many Norwegians also appreciate their holiday houses these days, which vary from Spartan **fishing huts** (rorbu) and simple **mountain cabins** (fjellhytte), to **campsite cabins** and luxurious pads. The standard choice though, is between **holiday villages** and isolated houses. The prices for visitors depend on the time of year, facilities and size, but you can be pretty sure that a holiday cabin is going to be cheaper than a hotel.

Countless **holiday home agencies** are available and early reservations can often result in finding a dream holiday house. For example, try Norbooking (www.norbooking.com)

Farmstay holidays

The farmstay holiday sector is still in its infancy in Norway, but the number of farms offering rooms with or without meals, as well as self-catering apartments and cabins has risen to over 200 in recent years. Many farms still keep animals and there are often horse-riding opportunities. A farmstay holiday is often an affordable alternative for families, compared to the relatively expensive holidays provided by hotel accommodation or holiday parks. The medieval farmsteads of the Gudbrandsdal region are especially atmospheric. A brochure on all options available for farmstay holidays is updated annually (www.nbt-nett.no).

B&Bs and pensions

In some towns and regions heavily frequented by tourists rooms with breakfast are offered at reasonable prices. Information is supplied by the regional tourist offices. Roadside signs indicating private rooms

Kvikne's Hotel in Balestrand was built in 1894, and is right on the Sognefjord

available can often be spotted, and either say »rom« or »overnatting«. Another option that is slightly cheaper than hotels is provided by pensions and guest houses that call themselves anything from pensjon, gjestgård, gård, fjellstue, gjestgiveri or turistheim. A brochure entitled The »Norway Bed & Breakfast Book« containing current addresses and prices for all of Norway, can be purchased in book shops or online at www.bbnorway.com.

Hiking Cabins   The approximately 100 Norwegian youth hostels, called vandrerhjem, are no longer the Spartan dormitories of the past and are not just for young people either. All either belong to the international associations of Hostelling International or VIP Backpackers Resorts International. More information can be found at www.hihostels.com and www.vipbackpackers.com. Norwegian youth and family hostels are a good alternative for travellers looking for affordable options. Singles, four-bed rooms and family rooms are all available and members of the various associations enjoy discounts.

Hotels   Norwegian hotels match the international standards of comfort and service in comparable price ranges. Luxurious hotels can be found in the large towns and cities, but many smaller places also offer excellent accommodation. Even the high north has good hotels and comfortable pensions to offer. There is no star system for rating accommodation, but the standard is generally high. Numerous hotels offer value for money family rooms with three to five beds, by the way. Some mountain lodges are not open all year round, but only during the summer and winter seasons. Many Norwegian hotels are adapted to the needs of disabled travellers, and some even have special facilities for allergy sufferers. Accommodation beyond human settlements is generally called a turisthotell or a høyfjellshotell. Small hotels are called pensjonater and an inn or guest house is called a gjestgiveri.

? MARCO ⊕ POLO INSIGHT

Price categories

The hotels in this guide book are divided into the following price categories:
££££ = over 1400 NOK
£££ = 1000 – 1400 NOK
££ = 600 – 1000 NOK
£ = up to 600 NOK
These are the average price for a double room with breakfast; for cabins etc, the price is per cabin or campsite, usually for 4 people.

Room reservations and discounts   Norwegian hotels are very expensive. However, many first-class hotels have special offers during the summer season or even all year round at weekends. To take advantage of the discounts offered by the hotel chains, a hotel pass or hotel cheque is required; for example, the Fjordpass (www.fjord-pass.com). Some discounts are valid throughout Scandinavia, among others, the Nordic Hotel Pass (www.gonor-

Holidays in a mountain cabin are usually quite a bit cheaper than in a hotel, but also a lot more remote...

way.no/go/choice.html). Hotel cheques must be validated in your country of residence prior to arrival in Norway. Many of the country's hotels belong to major international hotel chains, such as Best Western, Choice, Radisson/SAS and Rica. It is advisable to book ahead for hotel rooms during the Easter and summer holidays. An up-to-date list of accommodation is published by the Norwegian Tourist Board (▶Practical Information, p. 454).

There are roughly 1400 campsites in Norway that are divided into five categories (1–5 stars). In addition, there are a large number of unclassified campsites, which sometimes turn out to be nothing but a farmer's field. At any rate, the number of stars is not necessarily a decision-maker, because many very simple camp sites are in fabulous locations. Most campsites are equipped with the usual sanitary facilities, such as showers and washrooms, as well as cooking facilities. The larger sites also have shops and cafeterias. Furthermore, many have cabins (simple wooden huts with 4-6 bunks) that are also available for the day. The tourist offices, automobile clubs and camping organizations all publish an annually updated campsite listing, with information on location, size, facilities and quality. Camping card any stay at a campsite now requires visitors to have the new Camping Card known as the Camping Key Europe (that replaced the Camping Card Scandi-

Camping

navia). The new card is a joint initiative by the combined Scandinavian camping associations and by Europe's two largest automobile clubs: the Dutch ANWB and the German ADAC.

🛈 www.camping.no; www.nafcamp.com, www.campingkeyeurope.com

Camping wild

Note: camping in nature reservations and on military training grounds is prohibited. Those who wish to camp in the open countryside should always ask permission from the owners of the nearest private properties. Along the coast and at fjords it is recommended to position tents so that entrances are facing out of the wind. In the northern regions, a mosquito net is essential.

Insider Tip

Caravans and mobile homes

Not all roads are open to caravan-towing vehicles. Mobile homes can only be a maximum of 2.3m/7.5ft wide. Towing vehicles with a caravan cannot be longer than 18.5m/60.70ft and the caravan must not be wider than the car, and in all cases it must not be wider than

Norwegian campsites offer a great deal more comfort than the simple, but beautiful Sami tents

2.5m/8.2ft. The Norwegian transport authorities publish a map specifically for holidaymakers with mobile homes that indicates all prohibited routes for trailers, caravans and mobile homes. Furthermore, this map shows all sanitary posts for mobile home and caravan owners. The map can be ordered at www.statkart.no. The increasing number of visitors travelling with mobile homes is posing a challenge for the traditionally generous concept of open access (see below). Pollution and irresponsible behaviour by tourists has resulted in serious conflicts between landowners and campers, so it is highly advisable to stick to officially demarcated mobile home parks and campsites.

In Norway, everyone has the right to use beaches, shorelines, forest and meadows, even if they are privately owned. This is based on an ancient and universally respected traditional right whose limits are flexible. To avoid causing offence, however, camping on other people's property should always be preceded by a polite request; the same goes for making fires. Mobile homes, camper vans and tents must never be positioned less than 150m/164yd from any building or hut, and the site must be vacated after 48 hours. No sewage or rubbish should be left at the site. Sadly, thoughtless campers and mobile home owners have made themselves very unpopular in many places in recent years. The result is that while an entire network of sanitary posts has been developed and the number of campsites increased, there have also been an increased number of fines issued by the authorities to inconsiderate holidaymakers.

Open access

Outdoor fires near forests are prohibited from 15 April to 15 September. Severe fines are imposed for ignoring this rule.

Outdoor fires

Children in Norway

Paradise For Children

Norway is known to be an extremely child-friendly country. Appropriate facilities at accommodation and leisure facilities, as well as the gorgeous natural environment and the innumerable activities it offers all add up to happy holidays for kids.

Those who travel with children – of whatever age – would do well not to head for Nordkapp, unless they have at least a month to spare. Long car journeys and especially those on the many serpentine roads often result in car sickness and bad tempers on the back seat! If the question »are we there yet?« is not to be repeated too often, a family would ideally choose a specific region to explore and stick to relatively short, peaceful, day trips. That way, everyone will get the best from their Norway holiday, especially given the countless options for sport and leisure in the great outdoors.

Choose a small area

Whatever the family enjoys – excursions on foot, by bicycle or boat; days fishing or simply at the beach, the younger generation always has something to do. Even if the weather does not co-operate, there is always the option of visiting an animal enclosure or a leisure park. Even the capital city of Oslo has numerous child friendly activities, ranging from the Children's Art Museum to swimming.

Nature, fun and culture

Attractions for children

ÅLESUND
Atlantahavsparken
Visitors can marvel at the variety found in the Atlantic coastal waters at one of the country's largest aquariums, in Ålesund. The underwater show during which divers feed the large fish by hand is spectacular. The outdoor penguin enclosure is also popular (►p. 147).
www.atlanterhavsparken.no

HALLINGDAL
Langedrag
This sprawling mountain farm between Bergen, Oslo, Numedal and Hallingdal lies at 1000m/3281ft above sea level and is home to 350 animals. A special attraction are the five wolves in a large enclosure. The milk produced by the 50 goats is turned into cheese on site (►MARCO POLO tip p.215).
www.langedrag.no

Lakes or other outdoor activities: Norway's nature and countryside has many options for families with children

Vassfaret Bjørnepark

The stars of the park are the elk cow »Elfine«, which has even been featured in a TV programme, and the mighty brown bear »Rugg«. Other animals to admire close-up include lynx, fox and deer. The latest attraction is a large adventure playground.
www.bjorneparken.no

KONGSBERG
Sølvruvene

The silver mining town of Kongsberg lies 80km/50mi from Oslo and has a long history. A mine train takes visitors 2km/1mi into the old mining shaft (►p.270).
www.visitkongsberg.no

KRISTIANSAND
Kristiansand Dyreparken

The main attraction at this amusement park is the zoo with its monkey jungle and Nordic animals; as well as Kardemomme Town and Captain Swordtooth's Empire, designed by the Norwegian children's author Torbjørn Egner; and the water park. Plenty to do for an entire day (►p.276).
www.dyreparken.no

LILLEHAMMER
Lilleputthammer

Lilleputthammer is a model of the Storgata in Lillehammer, as it was in the 1930s (scale 1:4), where children can feel like giants, join drawing and craft-making activities, don fancy dress, or watch a film. There is also a climbing tower, trampolines and jump mats, as well as obstacle races. Especially fun for children under eight years old (►p.204).
www.lilleputthammer.no

MO I RANA
Grönligrotta

This is one of the few caves in Norway open to visitors, located near Mo i Rana. A guided tour leads to winding passages, glacier moulins and underground streams. An adventurous option for older children is a visit to the nearby Setergrotta (►p.302).
www.gronligrotta.no
www.setergrotta.no

OSLO
Bogstad Gård

A country estate outside Oslo where children can enjoy close encounters with sheep, cows, horses, pigs, rabbits and chickens. Frequent special family activities, such as riding, stable visits or sheep shearing. Adults appreciate the café, shop and art gallery.
www.bogstad.no

Det Internasjonale
Barnekunstmuseet

The Children's Museum in Oslo is not just a pleasure for children, but also for adults, who can see the world through children's eyes. See art by children and youths from all over the world. Art and music workshops are also on offer ((►MARCO POLO tip p.343).
www.barnekunst.no

Norsk Teknisk Museum

This Oslo museum offers a playful introduction to science, medicine and technology. Interactive experiments can be done in the science experience centre and activities for the whole family are provided during weekends (►p.341).
www.tekniskmuseum.no

Oslo Reptilpark

See around 100 different kinds of reptiles, from giant snakes to geckos. Tuesday is feeding day. www.reptilpark.no

TusenFryd

Norway's largest amusement park is south of Oslo, on the E18. Discover carousels, Viking Land, a large waterpark, and helter skelters. The only low are the high prices that are only worth it, if you stay all day (►p.352). www.tusenfryd.no

TELEMARK

Bø Sommarland

Norway's largest water park is in the Telemark region and tempts children with several water slides and other water activities (p.404). www.sommarland.no

Midsummer and Other Events

Norwegians like to party, be it to mark independence from Denmark on their National Day, or to celebrate the longest day of the year at midsummer. Particularly worth seeing is the colourful Easter Festival of the Sami People in the Finnmark region.

Norway's National Holiday is on 17 May and for many a very special celebration. Ceremonial processions are mounted throughout the country, characterised by much waving of the national flag. The most action occurs on Karl Johan gate, in Oslo. People line this fine boulevard from the early hours of the morning, proudly waving their Norwegian flags and glowing with patriotic joy. They particularly remember 1814 on this occasion, the year when Norway established its national law and 400 years of Danish rule were at an end.

17 May National Day

More than anything Norway's National Day has traditionally been an important **family celebration**, and children are at the centre of all events. They parade and march to the sound of drums and school marching bands, waving their Norwegian flags at the delighted crowds. In Oslo they march past the royal palace and, naturally, the **royal family** waves from the balcony for many hours.

National Day is not just about traditional and respectful celebrating, however, for this is also the highlight of the **»Russfeiring«**, the graduation parties for Norwegian high school students. Each type of college, from academic to technical, has its own colours and these school processions are much wilder and more exuberant and often include the consumption of huge amounts of alcohol.

A welcome occasion for celebration is midsummer, the shortest night of the year. Everyone looks forward to this day, because the **summer season** has definitely arrived by then. The last of the snow has melted, even in the mountains, and everywhere is in full blossom. Great **fires** are lit throughout the country on midsummer night – occasions when people sit around the fire together, eating and drinking and enjoying a very sociable event. Some get a little melancholy too, because the days will get shorter from now on and the coming winter is not so far away. Yet everywhere will be celebrating till then and not a single town or village is without its summer festival. A very popular option are the **music festivals**, which can be anything from jazz to blues to classical.

Midsummer

Action in the snow: in Kautokeino and Karasjok the Sami People hold reindeer races during Easter

Easter   One of the most colourful festivals in Norway is the **Easter Celebration of the Sami People** in Finnmark and the long journey to the high north is definitely worth it at this time. Nowhere else will you see so many colourful traditional costumes as during Easter in Kautokeino. In the old days, when the Sami People were still predominantly nomads and herding their reindeer across Scandinavia, Easter was one of the rare occasions when the dispersed community of family and friends could meet. Not only were the dark days of winter over, which was already enough reason to celebrate, but this was also a time when couples could marry at last and children could be baptised. The official Sami Easter Festival was established in 1972, and includes reindeer **sleigh races**, during which the normally sedate animals are inspired to race at breathtaking speeds. The cultural highlight is the **Sami Grand Prix**, when the top Sami musicians get together for their annual meeting in Kautokeino.

Christmas   The most important celebration for all Norwegians is Christmas, which is almost exclusively enjoyed in the private family sphere. Yet tourists can enjoy the pre-Christmas atmosphere easily enough and many squares are decorated with candle-lit **Christmas trees** and the streets are hung with garlands and lights. Christmas beer **(juleøl)** is brewed weeks before Christmas arrives; a sweet Christmas bread, similar to »stollen« is sold everywhere and restaurants offer opulent Christmas buffets. Atmospheric **Christmas markets** also characterise this traditional time of year.

The Midnight Sun is celebrated with great bonfires all over the country

Holidays and festival calendar

OFFICIAL HOLIDAYS
1 January (New Year)
Palm Sunday
Maundy Thursday
Easter Friday
Easter Sunday
Easter Monday
1 May (Labour Day)
17 May (National Day)
Ascension
Whitsunday
Whitmonday
25 and 26 December (Christmas)

SUMMER HOLIDAYS
The school holidays normally begin in the last week of June and end around mid-August. Businesses often shut down during the last three weeks in July. At these times, a great many Norwegians are travelling around their country and cabins and hotels tend to be full.

FESTIVALS AND EVENTS
A highly detailed guide is listed at www.norwayfestivals.com

JANUARY
Tromø International Film Festival
www.tiff.no

Tromø Festival of Northern Lights
ncluding music ranging from classical to contemporary composers www.nordlysfestivalen.no.

FEBRUARY
Røros winter market
www.rorosmartnan.no

MARCH
Holmenkollen Ski Festival
in Oslo, with World Cup races in cross-country skiing, Nordic skiing, and ski jumping
www.holmenkollen.com

International Birkebeiner cross-country ski races
between Lillehammer and Rena (www.birkebeiner.no).

Finnmarksløpet
Europe's longest huski race, covers a distance of around 400km/249mi across the Finnmark; www.finnmarkslopet.no

MARCH/APRIL
Easter Festival of the Sami People

Insider Tip

in Kautokeino and Karasjok. The reindeer races are the highlight, in which tourists can also participate. It is also a good time to hear their traditional joik singing
www.samieasterfestival.com

MAY/JUNE
The Bergen Festival
begins at the end of May, when renowned artists of both classical and modern music as well as painters and performance artists attend; www.fib.no

JUNE
Nordkapp Festival
in Honningsvåg
www.nordkappfestivalen.no.

The Great Endurance Test
is a cycle race covering 540km/ 335mi between Trondheim and

Oslo. There are also shorter races of 60km/37mi, 135km/84mi, 190km/118mi and 350km/217mi possible (►MARCO POLO Insight, p.118)
www.styrkeproven.no/trondheim-oslo.

Midnight Sun
On 23 June the entire country celebrates with great bonfires.

Harstad North Norway Festival
includes music, theatre, dance and art exhibitions
www.festspillnn.no

Oslo Bislet Games
is when the world's best athletes chase world records
www.diamondleague-oslo.com

Tromsø Midnight Sun Marathon
www.msm.no

JULY
Kongsberg Jazz Festival
www.kongsberg-jazzfestival.no

Molde Jazz Festival
Molde hosts Norway's largest jazz festival, including major artists from around the world.
www.moldejazz.no

Spelet om Heilag Olav
Verdal near Trondheim hosts a re-enactment of the Battle of Stiklestad in honour of St Olaf.
www.stiklestad.no

Riddu Riddu Festival
Kåfjord/Troms hosts this festival of Sami artists; www.riddu.no

AUGUST
Mandal Shrimp Festival
www.skalldyrfestivalen.no

Risør wood boat festival
Old and new wooden craft present themselves.
www.trebatfestivalen.no

Vinstra (Gudbrandsdal) Peer Gynt Festival
www.peergynt.no.

Oslo Jazz Festival
Next to the festivals in Molde, Kongsberg and Voss, the most important jazz festival is held in Oslo
www.oslojazz.no.

Haugesund Film Festival
Norway's most important film festival, during which the annual Armanda Prize – the Norwegian Oscar – is awarded
www.filmweb.no/filmfestivalen.

Ålesund Food and Drink Festival
www.matfestivalen.no

SEPTEMBER
Oslo Marathon
www.oslomaraton.no

DECEMBER
Nobel Prize Awards
10 December in Oslo.

An event on board during the Haugesund Film Festival

Food and Drink

Fish and Home Cooking

Travellers to Norway are not usually there for the local culinary delicacies. Quite the reverse, guide books often warn of strange dishes and rarely praise Norwegian cuisine, but there really isn't anything to worry about and it certainly is not necessary to bring all your own provisions! A small store of beer, wine and sweets is recommended, however, as these items are especially expensive in Norway.

Norway was a poor country, right into the 20th century and therefore the food culture was predominantly made up of simple home cooking. With increased economic wealth, a significant change in the food culture has taken place, especially in the larger towns and cities. The number of restaurants has significantly increased and the simple dishes of the past have been adapted by French, Italian or Spanish influences. The local fish dishes are often especially good. These days, bad eating experiences usually mean a failure to spend more money, because restaurants are substantially more expensive here than elsewhere.

Changing food culture

The day begins with »frokost«, which is normally served from a buffet in hotels. »Lunj« is traditionally a small snack and locals often go to a self-service restaurant (see below), for a »dagens rett«. The main meal of the day is in the early evening, which Norwegians call »middag«.

Breakfast, lunch and supper

For quick snacks between mealtimes there are plenty of food kiosks (gatekjökken) that serve all kinds of sausages (pølse), as well as kebabs and burgers. Good value for money and filling, though rarely memorable, are the daily special dishes (dagens rett) offered everywhere. Normally, you can expect a piece of meat or meat balls (kjøttkaker), potatoes, vegetables and a heavy brown sauce. A very typical local dish is the fårikål: cauliflower and mutton stew.

Snacks

The Scandinavian buffet (koldtbord) is excellent and offers a sumptuous cross section of Norwegian food, ranging from the much-praised fish specialties, to salads, cold cuts and meat, bread, and a variety of desserts. Everyone is allowed to eat as much as they like and seconds are encouraged. This is a treat all visitors should give themselves at least once and a good place for it can be on the ferries.

Scandinavian buffet

Scandinavian buffets, such as on this Hurtigruten ferry, are outstanding

Fish   When studying the menu, fish is always a good choice as it is so fundamental to the local food culture. Thanks to the short distances travelled, the daily catch is guaranteed to be fresh. Standard fillers for hunger pangs are made of shredded fish bound in mashed potato to make items such as fiskeboller, fiskepudding or fiskekaker. The tastiest dish is steamed or fried wild salmon with fresh herbs (parsely, chives, chervil, dill, thyme, basil and fennel), usually served with boiled potatoes. The **farmed salmon** that is cultivated in great aqua farms along the coast is substantially cheaper, but also has less flavour. Farmed salmon is predominantly destined for the fish counters of supermarkets. In recent years, **cod** has become quite rare due to overfishing, and is therefore often more expensive than salmon. Cod was once everyday food for Norwegians. **Herring** is another Norwegian fish speciality that has become rarer in recent times – served in many variations and with a variety of marinades. Boiled monkfish fillets and fried halibut slices are another Norwegian delicacy. Of the freshwater fish, **trout** is highly prized in Norwegian cuisine, and fillets smoked over pine cones are exquisite. Between the end of July and the beginning of September, boiled **crabs**, served with a dill sauce, are on the menu.

Meat   For a low-fat meat option, why not try elk (»elg«) or reindeer (»reinsdyr«), which has a pleasant game flavour. The meat is commonly cooked in cranberry sauce, but it is also delicious smoked.

Specialities   Adventurous visitors will want to try traditional Norwegian foods, but it is getting harder and harder to find local delicacies in the supermarkets or on restaurant menus. Blood sausage served with butter and sugar is not to everyone's taste, nor is blood pudding! Shredded lung is another food that requires some courage, while **lutefisk** and **rakörret** are the exclusive preserve of Norway enthusiasts or serious food tourists. The former is dried cod that has spent several days being reconstituted in water and, though it is a traditional Norwegian Christmas dish, there are plenty of locals who have their doubts about it too. The latter, is salted trout that has spent several months curing. Finally, **gammelost** is an old cheese that not only looks its age, but also smells it! Finding pumpernickel style or wholewheat bread in any supermarket is a challenge and something visitors often find surprising, is that a lot of bread is made with added sugar. Flatbröd is a kind of dried bread cracker that used to be baked just once a year, to be stored for times of need. Now it is popular all year round. A common alternative to bread are lefser and lumper, which are soft patties made from potato flour. Goat's cheese (**geitost**) is very common in Norway, as is »**mysost**«, a brown, sweet cheese that is eaten in very thin slices on bread. Preserved fruit covered in sweetened liquid cream is very often served as dessert. The Norwegian national favourite is »**rømmegrøt**«: a porridge type dish drenched in hot butter with cinnamon and sugar.

Beer, wine and spirits

Norway has very restrictive alcohol laws which have, however, been somewhat loosened in recent years. The high prices remain unchanged. Private distilleries are prohibited and the sale and service of alcoholic drinks is strictly regulated. Beer is the only alcohol that can be bought at supermarkets. On the other hand, wine and spirits can only be bought at state-run outlets (»Vinmonopolet «, meaning »the wine monopoly«) which are limited to larger towns and cities. Most restaurants have a permit to serve beer and wine. Hard liquor (»brennevin«) can be purchased in the bars of larger hotels, but there is a complete ban on serving spirits on Sundays and bank holidays.
Understandably, Norway is no place for wine drinkers, though the selection available has improved in recent years. Good wine can be purchased, but the pleasure of consuming a bottle that cost roughly £25 is slightly dampened by the fact that it is sold for a fiver at home.

Coffee, milk and water

The Norwegians' national drink is coffee, which they happily consume morning, noon and nights, even at midnight. Apart from coffee, they also enjoy all varieties of milk. »H-melk« is full fat milk, »lett melk« is skimmed milk, and »kulturmelk« is buttermilk. »Skummet kulturmelk« is skimmed buttermilk. In addition, there are several varieties of sour milk, such as »cultura« and »kefir«. Mineral water is rare in Norway and the only local source (Farris) is extremely expensive due to a lack of competition.

Typical Dishes

Traditional Norwegian dishes are filling and unpretentious, reflecting the simple home-cooking of a country that was impoverished right up to the 20th century. Yet spekemat (pickled or dried smoked meat) or rømmegrøt (creamed porridge) are certainly tasty, while Norwegian salmon has long since established itself as the world's best.

Gravlax (gravet lax): Of course visitors must try salmon in Norway, which is without a doubt first-class, whether it is fried, steamed, grilled or smoked. A typical Norwegian variant is gravlax salmon, whereby raw filleted salmon is marinated in salt, pepper and dill for 24 hours, before being served cold – a real delicacy.

Geitost: This sweet food should be tried at least once, and either you will discover a taste for the caramelized flavour of this cheese and take some home with you, or you will leave it as a one-off experience. It is made of goat and cow's milk, despite the name indicating it might be a pure goat's cheese. Strictly speaking, it is not even a cheese, because the curd is slowly boiled until it becomes caramelized. Thin slices are normally cut onto crackers and served with a teaspoon of jam.

Rømmegrøt (above middle): A porridge type dish made of sour cream mixed with semolina or flour and drenched in hot butter with cinnamon and sugar. Rømmegrøt is virtually the Norwegian national dish and every region, and virtually every family, prepares this heavy meal to their very own recipe. You will almost always find it on the menu at the country's mountain lodges.

Spekemat (upper right): Salted and dried meat has a long tradition, since it was difficult to preserve fresh meat in the days before refrigeration. Whole hams, mutton legs and sausages were normally hung in the barn after the autumn slaughter. Today, spekemat is the ideal snack for anyone hiking in the mountains. Served with bread, sour cream and scrambled eggs, it also makes for a satisfying main meal.

Moltebeeren: Cloud berries are a popular dessert, especially in northern Norway. These yellow, blackberry-type fruit are delicious served with cream and sugar and they are also made into jam.

Wild or Farmed?

Norwegian salmon (Atlantic Salmon/salmon salar) is an export hit. Most of it is farmed, however, which continues to be controversial, so a variety of approved seals covering quality, environmental protection and sustainable production have been introduced to ensure consumer confidence. The huge increase in production since the 1990s has resulted in a significant drop in the price of salmon and it is now an affordable food item for most consumers

▶ **Mariculture: fish farming in the open ocean**
Farmed salmon are bred in open water net enclosures that are designed to be floating cages in which the fish mature

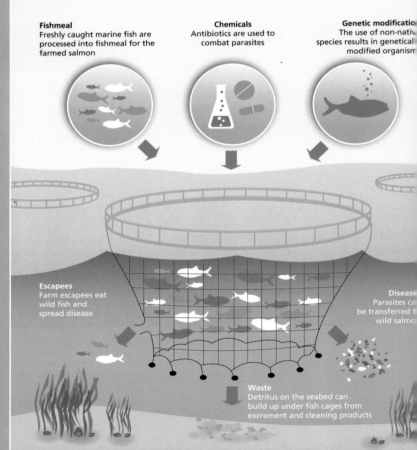

Fishmeal
Freshly caught marine fish are processed into fishmeal for the farmed salmon

Chemicals
Antibiotics are used to combat parasites

Genetic modificatio
The use of non-nativ species results in geneticall modified organism

Escapees
Farm escapees eat wild fish and spread disease

Disease
Parasites ca be transferred t wild salmo

Waste
Detritus on the seabed can build up under fish cages from excrement and cleaning products

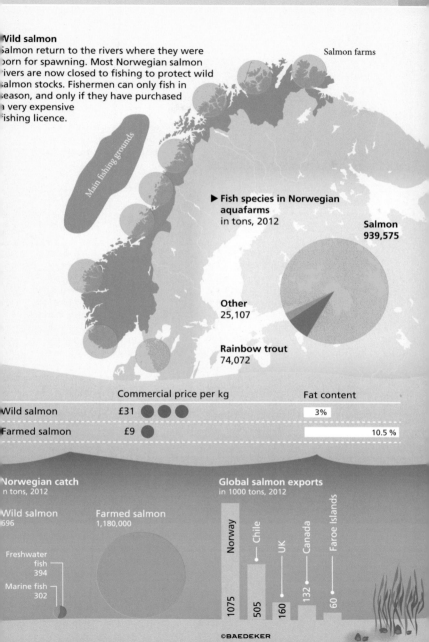

Wild salmon

Salmon return to the rivers where they were born for spawning. Most Norwegian salmon rivers are now closed to fishing to protect wild salmon stocks. Fishermen can only fish in season, and only if they have purchased a very expensive fishing licence.

Salmon farms

Main fishing grounds

▶ **Fish species in Norwegian aquafarms**
in tons, 2012

Salmon
939,575

Other
25,107

Rainbow trout
74,072

	Commercial price per kg	Fat content
Wild salmon	£31	3%
Farmed salmon	£9	10.5 %

Norwegian catch
in tons, 2012

Wild salmon
696

Farmed salmon
1,180,000

Freshwater fish
394

Marine fish
302

Global salmon exports
in 1000 tons, 2012

Norway — 1075
Chile — 505
UK — 160
Canada — 132
Faroe Islands — 60

©BAEDEKER

From the Lofoten to the Table

Atlantic cod was the foundation of life for up to 30,000 Lofoten fishermen, right up to the early 20th century. Even today, a small part of the catch is still dried on large wooden racks, but most of it goes straight to buyers all over Europe as fresh cod filets.

Atlantic cod is known as skrei to Norwegians, which means as much as »wanderer«. It is an apt name, because millions emerge from the ice floes of the North Sea to commence their migration along the Norwegian coast in search of suitable spawning grounds, which they find off the Lofoten Islands, especially around Vestfjord.

They are traditionally welcomed by the Lofoten fishermen, who numbered up to 30,000 men in the later 19th and early 20th century, when catches were very generous. By the 1980s, the fishing crisis finally arrived, when decades of over-fishing meant quotas had to be dramatically reduced and the picturesque little fishing villages became much quieter places.

The heyday of a busy and tough way of life is retold in the novel »The Lofoten Fishermen« by Johan Bojer – a story of fisherman at the turn of the 19th century fighting the wind and the sea in search of riches and happiness.

Cod Stocks Today

The levels of Norwegian cod stocks have recovered due to good management, the successful combat of Russian pirate fishing, and favourable climactic conditions. As a result, both fishermen and consumers can now benefit from seasonal catches of over 300,000 tons of cod each year. Furthermore, the entire Norwegian catch is entitled to the accredited sustainability seal issued by the Marine Stewardship Council (MSC).

Life in the Rorbuer Cottages

The colourful painted fishermen's houses, known as rorbuer, are integral to the image of the Lofoten Islands. Set right by the water, or on stilts directly over the water, many of them have been turned into luxurious holiday cottages that are rented to tourists during summer. Originally, however, they were built for the Lofoten fishermen. The first were probably built by King Öystein, as early as the 12th century, who had a special relationship with the fishermen. Nevertheless, many of them still slept under their upturned fishing boats for the entire months of the hard winters. The owners of the rorbuer rented them to fishermen for whole seasons, and in return they sold their fish for them. The original living conditions in these homes must have been terrible. The standard design was of two rooms: a front room for storing the gear and provisions, and a back room for the crew of up to ten fishermen to share as the sleeping quarter. But this is also where they cooked, eat, smoked and drank and hygiene was a luxury that had no place during a Lofoten winter. No doubt the rorbuer cottages always stank of wet clothing, sweat, fish and oil and the humidity inside must have been dreadful. By the time the wood-fired stove had burnt down in the mornings, everything was covered in a fine layer of frost. Today, fishermen still live in cramped conditions on their fishing trawlers, but in relative comfort, compared to their ancestors.

Dried Cod, Tongues and Fillets

In the old days, the catch was immediately gutted and hung by the tail in pairs on the wood drying racks. There the fish dried over a period of several months; the heads were also dried and turned into fishmeal. The tongues – a delicacy – were traditionally cut out by child labour. The liver was boiled down for oil, and the roe was salted and filled into wood barrels. The best of the saltfish has always been exported to Italy, where it is a popular food during lent. The lower quality fish and the dried heads go to Africa. A proportion of the fish used to be turned into klippfisk, whereby the gutted and salted fish were dried on the rocks by the seashore. These days, fish is no longer dried on the rocks and only a small proportion is dried on the racks, because most is delivered to wholesaler's cold stores throughout Europe as fresh cod fillets. Anyone travelling to Norway should definitely try freshly caught cod, grilled saltfish, or pan-fried breaded cod tongues. Around Christmas, many menus will also offer lutefisk (Beadeker INSIGHT, p. 292), which is dried cod that has been reconstituted in water over a period of several days.

Especially popular in Italy: dried cod

Shopping

High Quality Craftwork

Although Norway is expensive, the outstanding quality of its craftwork is worth serious consideration. The high prices are also somewhat ameliorated by the tax-free shopping system.

Norway has long had a reputation as one of the most expensive holiday destinations, so no one comes here for the shopping. Visitors have traditionally filled their trunks with provisions, especially taking a store of wine and beer, since alcohol is substantially more expensive than anywhere else. But the high prices should not deter you from having a look at the art and craft shops every now an then.

Pricey destination

Norwegian craftwork makes for popular souvenirs, especially domestic items made of wood such as spoons and forks, as well as glass, tin, enamel and pewter goods. Handmade dolls in national costume also make pretty souvenirs, as do woven wall-hangings and embroidered tapestries. **Norwegian jumpers** with their beautiful patterns are world famous and the colourful knitted hats and even socks and stockings made of pure wool go down well with the folks back home. The region of Setesdalen is famous for its knitwear. A good selection of traditional crafts can be found in the Husfliden shops in most towns and cities. Stylish design Modern Norwegian design is characterised by simple clear lines. This does not just apply to the pine furniture, but also to household goods and craftwork products.

Arts and crafts and handmade items

Norwegian glassmakers have been bringing their beautiful works to market since the 18th century, and there is great demand for the various crystal figures (especially animals). Norwegian pottery, especially porcelain, is very popular. Norwegian porcelain is exported all around the world and is worth the money.

Glass and porcelain

Semi-precious stones, such as thulite, mylonite, peridotite and amazonite, are popular souvenirs, as are valuable items made of gold and silver, especially the silverwork from Telemark. Gold and silver jewellery made in the Norse style copied from original Viking jewellery is an absolute hit with many.

Jewellery and semi-precious stones

Many motorized visitors to Norway take advantage of the opportunity to purchase reindeer hides or antlers, including carved horn to bring back as souvenirs. Goods made by Norwegian tanners and **furriers** are considered the best of their kind in the world, and the prices are fair given the high quality.

Skins and fur

Comforting souvenir: fur slippers at a Sami market in Kautokeino

A »Real« Norwegian Jumper?

One of the most useful and popular souvenirs from the high north of Europe is a Norwegian jumper. Unmistakable because of its typical patterning, this warming item is bound to be used on cold winter days, even back home.

The Norwegian jumper is available to buy in souvenir shops, department stores and even on the internet, where the choice is huge and these days the designs are no longer limited to the traditional ones with rounded collars. Now there is a wide variety of styles, ranging from roll neck, to cardigan, and hoodies in a huge range of colours and pattern combinations. All kinds of raw materials are used, including natural wool, cotton, mohair, and even synthetic yarns, which make it hard to establish what exactly a »real« Norwegian jumper should be like.

Historic designs

In the old days, fishermen's wives knitted their men folk thick chunky jumpers made of sheep's wool to keep them warm in the cold and wet weather. As they generally used natural wool, the jumpers were brown, with white patterning and traditional family emblems were just as popular as diamond shapes, snowflakes, stars, ice crystals, elks or reindeer. Patterns were normally knitted for the sections between the collar and the chest; sometimes the wristbands and upper arm were also decorated. Characteristic of this knitwear was the traditional T-shape, whereby the main body was a smooth section front and back, with sleeves added on. This distinguishes the tradition-al Norwegian jumper from the Icelandic one that was normally knitted of a piece using a pair of circular knitting needles. The sleeve join reached right up to the neckline, as with a raglan jumper, but was not added on separately.

Icelandic roots

Strictly speaking, the Norwegian jumper does not even originate in Norway, but in Iceland and the Faroe and Shetland Islands. In Iceland, it is called a Lorapeysa, and has always been knitted from rough natural sheep's wool, creating a warm, water-repellent, breathable item that is surprisingly windproof, which makes it ideal for being outside, even during horrible weather. That makes it the predecessor of modern outdoor clothing. The Icelandic jumper is only genuine if it is made of Icelandic sheep's wool (Lopi), because the key distinction is that it is spun from both the longer and thicker outer fleece, as well as the fluffy thick inner layers of fleece on the animal's skin. In this way it combines the best qualities of new wool and Mohair, and the high grease content in traditional Lopi wool also makes it water repellent.

Many cringe at the thought of a jumper made of rough sheep's wool and it is indeed the only reason not to buy one, because if you can't get used to the scratchy feeling, you will never get to enjoy your beautiful jumper.

No matter whether you travel in Finland, Sweden, Denmark, Norway, Greenland or Iceland, the designs on the jumpers are very similar. Some claim this is thanks to the Vikings, who spread the patterns all over Scandinavia, Iceland and the Shetland Islands on their fast ships, from the 8th century onwards.

Breakthrough

The breakthrough from practical fishermen's attire to fashionable item for society in general came in 1922, when the Prince of Wales stepped out in one during a prestigious golf tournament. In 1960, when aerodynamic clothing had not yet been invented, Willy Bogner wore a Norwegian jumper for the Olympic Games in Squaw Val-ley California. By the 1970s, the alternative and green movements had established the Norwegian jumper as an integral part of many people's wardrobe throughout Europe, especially among hippies.

Differences in quality

A real Norwegian jumper is not cheap, but with the right care, it will last a lifetime. If the price is low, you can be sure the item was made with manmade fibres. If you want to be really traditional, stick to black jumpers with white patterns, rather than the ones that use blue, red or green as the main colour. Of course they need to be made of genuine natural wool too.

The genuine Icelandic jumper is also only made of natural, uncoloured wool, which is traditionally brown with white patterning, and knitted as a single piece.

Originally from Iceland: the Norwegian jumper

Norwegian household goods made of wood make fine souvenirs

Toys Beautifully carved wooden toys and lovingly made stuffed dolls are not just a pleasure for children. The carved troll figures based on Norwegian mythology are offered as anything from attractive wood carvings to cheap plastic kitsch. Decorative vernacular painting Norwegian vernacular painting is particularly typical of the Telemark and Hallingdal region. Furniture and other items made of wood have traditionally been decorated for many centuries, particularly using rose motifs. Food and drink souvenirs Norwegian hard liquor, such as genuine Aquavit, makes a good present. Other typically Norwegian products also include cloudberry jam and the brown goat's cheese known as geitost.

Tax free The high prices are off-set by the tax free shopping system. Show your
shopping passport proving residency outside Scandinavia prior to purchase in

any of the over 3000 stores displaying the tax-free logo, and you will be given a tax-free form, which should ideally be filled out in the shop. Given that not all shops display the logo, it is also always worth asking if the benefit is available. The general shopping tax in Norway lies at 25% and is included in the price, of which 20% accounts for the valued added tax (VAT), which can be refunded to non-residents. VAT on foodstuffs is charged at 14%. The minimum purchase price set by the government for which VAT can be reclaimed lies at NOK 315 for ordinary goods and 285 NOK for food products. Goods purchased under the tax-free system are packed and sealed and are only allowed to be unpacked outside Scandinavia. On leaving Norway, the sealed goods along with passport must be presented to the Norway tax-free shopping representative (not the customs officials), along with the tax-free shopping form issued by the relevant shop. In this way, the value added tax (VAT) will be refunded (minus a fee). For more information see www.global-blue.com.

There are **no standard official opening hours** for commercial businesses in Norway. Usually, though, **shops** are open Mon–Fri, 9am/10am–4pm/5pm; Thu 9am/10am–6pm/8pm; Sat 9am–1pm/3pm. Many **supermarkets** are open in the evenings until 8pm; on Saturdays they remain open till 6pm. Wine and spirits can be bought at the **Vinmonopolet** shops Mon–Wed 10am–4pm; Thu 10am–5pm; Fri 9am–4pm, Sat 9am–1pm (15 May–31 Aug 8.15am–3pm).

Opening hours

Sport and Outdoors

Unlimited Sport Options

Norway provides a spectacular natural setting to follow your sport, be it fishing or hiking, water sports or skiing, every season offers different possibilities to get active.

The Norwegians really love their outdoor sports and connecting with nature. In fact, there are statistics that claim more than half the population actively practices a sport. Norwegians call this essential part of their lives » friluftsliv«, which can mean many things: it could be a relaxing cabin holiday on a lake and some quiet fishing, strenuous hiking over a fjell, cycle touring on the Rallarvegen over the Hardangervidda, or exploring new routes for cross country skiing. It is no wonder Norwegians love the great outdoors. No other European country has so much nature for their population to enjoy and they take full advantage: hiking and any kind of water sport are very popular during the summer, while skiing comes first during winter, and the fishing rod is an option all year round.

Friluftsliv

FISHING

One of the most popular leisure activities for locals and tourists alike is fishing . The many fjords and bays along the Atlantic coast, as well as the many thousands of inland waters offer more or less ideal conditions for passionate anglers. Furthermore, Norwegian waters are some of the least crowded you will find. Fishing card and fishing licence Fishermen need a **fishing card** (fiskekort), available for purchase at local tourist offices, at hotel receptions, at campsites, in sports shops and at post offices. The price depends on the period of validity required, as well as on the dimensions of the fishing territory. As a rule, there are waiting lists for the salmon rivers known to insiders. All fishermen over the age of 16 also have to acquire a **state fishing licence** (fiskeravsgiftskort), available at post offices with the special payment card.

Paradise for fishermen

Those who want to fish for salmon (laks), trout (brown trout; sjøørret) and char (sjørøye) must pay an increased fee for their fishing card and fishing licence. There are also varying limits set on the minimum and maximum weight permitted for salmon catches. Be aware that in many places there are waiting lists for salmon fishing, so timely en-

Salmon fishing, brown trout and char

Norway has the most glaciers of any country in Europe and is ideal for guided glacier tours

quiries are very worthwhile. Sea fishing for salmon is only allowed during the months of June and July; in rivers only from the beginning of June to mid-August. There is good salmon fishing in all the fjords, including in the northern regions. These days, travel agents also offer all-inclusive salmon fishing tours. The best salmon rivers are the Alta, Drammenselva, Gaula, Målselva, Namsen, Neiden, Numedalslågen, Orkla, Størdalselva and Tana.

Fjord fishing and fishing at sea

Fishing **without a licence** is permitted at sea and along the fjords as long as the intended catch is not salmon or trout. Fishing huts and boats can be hired all along the coast. Tours to the high seas on fishing boats are also organized locally and it is possible to catch mackerel (makrell), shellfish (hyse), cod (torsk), halibut (kveite), coley (sei) and herring (sild) all year round.

Fishing on the ice

Good catches can be expected by fishing at holes (about 25cm/10inches in diameter) cut into the ice. Good hunting grounds are Glomma (Hedmark), Kongsvinger, Sørland (pike, carp, whitefish and eel), Mandalselva, Audneselva, Aust-Agder, Finnmark and east Norway (pike, char, grayling, trout), the Kristiansand area, the region north of Røros, Østerdal, Gudbrandsdal, Hallingdal, Valdres, and the rivers of the Hardangervidda (especially trout).

Fishing seasons

Spawning time is the closed season. This varies according to region and fish species, and is regulated by the relevant municipalities or counties. The ideal fishing seasons also vary from region to region. May and June can be successful months in low-lying areas, whereas late summer is best for fishing in the highland regions.

Information

The Norwegian tourist board publishes a free brochure entitled The Official Fishing Brochure that contains detailed information. Additional information is also supplied by the Norwegian hunting and fishing association (Practical Information, p.452).

CYCLING

Good fitness and preparation needed

Cycling in Norway is a challenge due to the segmented and mountainous landscape, yet it offers some very fine touring opportunities for those with plenty of gears and stamina. A close study of the map is required in order to avoid the worst gradients and the many tunnels that are closed to cyclists. There are only a few dedicated cycle paths and cyclists must compete on the roads with cars and mobile homes, especially during high summer (avoid main arteries like the E6). Transporting bicycles on public transport has not yet been developed particularly well, so that a great deal of initiative is needed. Rewarding cycle tours The natural surroundings of Norway can be fully appreciated on minor roads. A worthwhile route is the Rallarvegen following the Bergen railway line over the Hardangervidda, while the Lofoten Islands offer pleasant touring and views of mountains without significant differences in elevation en route. Route 17 along the coast, from Steinkjer to Bodø, is ideal for cyclists because it offers plenty to see while tracing the outlines of every fjord, mostly at sea level. Another advantage is that cars prefer the faster E6 that avoids all the ferry crossings. Terrific cycle touring is possible in the national parks and the many hiking regions, where only a few routes permit vehicle transport. Cyclists are allowed to use the many forestry and national park roads closed to traffic and have a free pass on all toll roads.

Mountain biking is very popular. Enthusiasts should remember, though, that the use of footpaths, as well as cross-country cycling in protected areas, is strictly prohibited. The thin and very delicate lay-

Mountain biking

Mountain biking in Norway requires awareness of fragile environments

Norway offers ideal conditions for mountain climbers and hikers

er of vegetation only recovers very slowly when damaged and it often takes many years for gashes through moorland and moss to grow together again.

Information sources
Information on carrying cycles on public transport and bicycles hire, as well as other touring tips, is provided by local tourist offices and by Sykkelturisme i Norge, who also offer excellent suggestions for tours along with all the necessary background information at www. bike-norway.com.

HIKING AND CLIMBING

Hiking season
The Norwegian mountains offer ample opportunity for mountaineering and hill walking, as well as mountain and glacier touring. Appropriate equipment is needed, however, as well as careful planning before you go. As far as the weather in Norway goes, the best months for a »fjelltur« (mountain tour) are June, July and August. The country's landscapes are covered by an extensive network of

footpaths, all signposted with the generally recognizable red »T«. Information and suggested tours can be supplied by local tourist offices and by the Den Norske Turistforening or DNT (Norwegian Trekking Association). Easy day trips can be made to the ice tongues of the Jostedalsbreen. Norway's highest mountain, the 2468m/8097ft-Galdhøppingen is a relatively moderate hike if approached from Spiterstulen and the Juvass hut. There will be plenty of company if walking the two or three hours it takes to reach the Prekestolen, or the five to seven hours it takes to reach the Beseggen-Grat in the Jotunheimen Mountains – both considered absolute classics of Norwegian trekking tours. Impressive tours can also be made over the Dovrefjell and around Rondane and Hardangervidda. Relatively easy walks can be enjoyed in the Rondane National Park, despite several summits over 2000m/6562ft. The 1526m/5006ft-high Steinbuhøi can be reached in five hours, and the 2140m/7021ft-high summit of Storronden is also easy. Ideal bases for tours in the national park are Høvringen, Mysuseter, or Rondvassbu.

Numerous hiking cabins are dotted throughout the land. The distance between two huts is, on average, the equivalent of a day's walking (between four and nine hours). The comfort levels of these accommodations ranges from simple block houses with a grassed roof, where personal provisions and a sleeping bag must be brought, to catered rustic mountain cabins and luxurious mountain lodges.

Hiking cabins

Climbing fans have ample opportunity to pursue their passion in Norway, at all levels of difficulty, especially in Romsdal, Hurrungane and on the Lofoten Islands. The current mecca for adventurous climbers is the almost 1000m/3281ft high, virtually vertical rock face of Trollveggen in Romsdal (▶Sights from A to Z). Information is available from the DNT.

Mountainee-ring

Guided glacier tours are offered by a number of mountain huts during the main hiking season. For example, setting off from Spiterstulen and Juvasshytta, it is possible to climb onto the »eternal ice« of Galdhøpiggen (2468m/8097ft), Norway's highest mountain. Other impressive glaciers can be found in Sognefjell, the Jotunheimen region, Jostedalsbreen, Hardangerjøkulen and Svartisen. Information on guided glacier tours and glacier lectures are provided by the DNT.

Glacier touring

Those travelling or trekking through the tundra would do well to keep in mind that they are coming into contact with an extremely sensitive ecosystem, where it takes years for damaged vegetation to recover; it may take decades for a discarded tin to rust away. Take extreme **care with open fires** during the dry summer period. Hiking in the tundra necessitates the relevant equipment and clothing. In

Trekking in fragile nature

Den Norske Turistforening

Thanks to its 430 cabins and 20,000km/12,427mi of marked trails maintained by the Norwegian Hiking Association, this country, with its frequently pristine nature, is easy to explore on foot.

Given enough time, it is possible to traverse Norway on foot, from east to west or north to south, and always end up in a cabin run by the Norwegian Hiking Association (DNT) at the end of each day. Located between four and nine hours' walk from each other, you will find anything from a simple hut with just a few mattresses on the floor, to luxurious mountain lodges with hotel-style comforts. No wonder mountain trekking continues to be one of the most popular leisure activities among Norwegians.

Pristine Nature

Few Norwegians would wish every summit to be accessible via a cable car or for roads to connect each and every location. Rather, they want to enjoy pristine nature and reach their destinations through their own physical efforts, even if that requires some stamina. Therefore this is a country where it is still possible to stand on a mountain

The red »T« indicates the DNT hiking routes

top and not see a single road, or house, or other sign of human civilization in any direction. Yet a little bit of infrastructure does not go amiss on the fjell and Norwegians appreciate that too, enjoying the services of their national hiking association for the past 140 years: the Norske Turistforening.

Marked Trails

The DNT is dedicated and expert in making sure hikers find cabins and clearly marked trails throughout the country and it is also in charge of over 430 huts. The range of accommodation varies hugely, and can be anything from a tiny hut with two camp beds to a large comfortable mountain lodge that even offers full board. In addition, the DNT maintains a 20,000km/12,424mi network of trails during the summer and around 6500km/4039mi of cross-country skiing tracks in winter. The summer footpaths are marked by small stone pyramids displaying a red letter »T«. The winter tracks are indicated by poles that are positioned in the snow every few meters, around Easter.

Cabin Categories

There are three categories of DNT cabins: the serviced cabins are on a par with hotels and are also available to non-members; you even get meals. The self-service huts are stocked with provisions and have heating and cooking facilities,

The Norwegian hiking association takes care of 430 huts and 20,000km/12,400mi of hiking trails

though comfort is limited as the water usually comes from the nearest stream. These huts are locked and the DNT lends keys to its members that fit all their cabins. Accommodation fees are left in the huts – a system that relies on trust and works extraordinarily well in Norway. The relatively expensive overnight and provision prices are the result of difficult and expensive transport for goods that can often only be deposited by helicopter. The unserviced huts have similar facilities to the self-service huts, except without the provision store. All huts, however, are reached by clearly marked trails and are often located in superb landscapes. The many large rivers are crossed by swinging bridges, while the many streams have strategic stepping stones across them, all built by the DNT.

Timing and Information

The season in the mountains is short, so most hikers are out on the trails during the school holidays, from the end of June to end of August. August is the ideal month, from the point of view of the weather, but of course the Norwegians know that best, which is why the most popular cabins in the Rondane, Jotunheimen and Hardangervidda get pretty full at that time and the last stragglers can only hope for a mattress on the floor, though no one is ever turned away. During the winter, high season is around Easter. Additional information is available at www.turistforeningen.no

addition to good footwear, all-weather clothing, sufficient provisions, a map and a compass are essential requirements. No one should ever set off alone. Unexpected weather changes are the rule rather than the exception, and biting insects thrive here (remember the insect repellent). Encounters with reindeer, elk, lynx and brown bears are also possible.

WATER SPORTS

Bathing   During high summer, long sandy beaches , remote protected coves and thousands of little islands and ice-smoothed cliffs (holms and skerries) await, and not only for the hardy. Swimming is possible in

Norway, especially along the southern coast where the water reaches temperatures of at least 18ºC/64ºF, and in protected bays and coves after sustained periods of sunny weather up to 20ºC/68ºF. It is also possible to take a cool dip at one of the country's many inland lakes. When there is hot and sunny weather for some time, the shallower of the inland lakes reach quite pleasant temperatures. At the same time, though, the plague of mosquitoes can become unbearable. The absolute dream beaches are on the Lofoten Islands, beyond the Arctic Circle, if only the water was not so cold….

Nude bathing is not generally prohibited, but should be avoided at popular bathing spots and near private property. More information is available from the Norwegian Nudist Association.

Popular beaches for bathing are along the south coast

Canoe and kayak trips   A special natural experience is gliding peacefully across one of Norway's many lakes in a **canoe or kajak**. There are beautiful tours possible in the Sørlandet. The waters east of Lake Femund are also among southern Norway's most popular paddling regions. Good paddling is also possible on the lakes and canals of Østfold and the Telemark region. White water paddlers can find all grades of rapids throughout the country. Guided white water rafting tours are available at Voss and Dagali, both sides of Hardangervidda, or on the Sjoa river in the Heidal valley. A famous paddling tour runs along the **Telemark Canal**, during which 18 locks are traversed to reach an elevation of 72m/236ft above sea level. A great variation on paddling that does require some experience is **sea kajaking**. Popular spots are the fjords between Stavanger and Bergen. Experts also enjoy heading further north, such as to the varied coastline between Mo i Rana and the Lofoten Islands, via Svartisen and across the Arctic Circle. Serious adrenalin junkies get their money's worth with rafting. Guides take large inflatable boats down several rivers, such as the stretch between Voss and Dagali, both sides of the Hardangervidda, and also the Sjoa river in the Heidal.

Few countries possess a coast that is better suited to the sport of sailing than Norway – a fact that was known at the latest in 1928, when the Norwegian Crown Prince Olaf V won Olympic Gold. Around 120 very well-equipped marinas await their visiting yachts in the summer months. The waters of the Oslofjord are especially popular with sailors, as is the region of the Norwegian south coast as well as the west, south and central Norwegian coastline (including the fjords). Experienced sailors head all the way up to the Lofoten Islands and even further north.

Sailing

Surfing is gaining popularity in Norway and **Surfboards** can be hired at numerous beaches.

Surfing

There are excellent opportunities for diving among the coastal skerries. The water is very clear but cold. Waterskiing Waterskiing is especially good in the temperate bays of southern Norway.

Diving

WINTER SPORTS

Guaranteed snow, low temperatures from December to the end of April and ideal natural terrain have allowed Norway to become the cradle of modern winter sports. Skiing was first practiced as a sport in the regions of Telemark, Gudbrandsdal, Oslo and the Holmenkollen hill, and around Lillehammer. The same goes for sports on the ice and Norwegian sportsmen and women have played a major role in championships for skiing and ski jumping, as well as in speed skating, figure skating and ice hockey. Among the many world class sportsmen and women that have put Norway on the map, are the outstanding figure skater Sonja Henie (Famous People), the legendary ski jumpers Birger Ruud (Famous People) and Bjørn Wirkola, and the cross-country skiers Björn Dählie, Vegard Ulvang and Petter Horthug.

Cradle of winter sports

Norway has the makings of becoming Europe's skiing El Dorado since climate change has caused many other destinations in the European Alps to loose the required snow cover. It is now necessary to seek out ever higher locations to find guaranteed snow for both downhill and cross country skiing. Norway, on the other hand, offers guaranteed snow from November to well into May, and provides certainty that winter will come, even in these changing weather years.

Guaranteed snow

Skiing and competitions Numerous sporting competitions are organized each winter throughout the land, from the Oslofjord all the way to Nordkapp. Every year, thousands of fit Norwegian skiing fans meet for the traditional Birkebeiner race (a Nordic ski marathon between Rena and Lillehammer). Additionally, countless spectators are always drawn to the world famous ski jumping at the **Holmenkollen** hill near Oslo, as well as to the World Cup downhill and slalom races in Hamar and Lillehammer. Recently back in vogue are also the Nordic ski combinations of cross-country skiing and jumping, as well as the traditional Telemark style. Summer skiing Even during summer, Norwegians don't like to miss their skiing, which is why there are several snow fields and even glaciers that are used for skiing, even during the height of summer.

Ice skating Ice skating has at least as long a tradition as skiing in Norway. In Viking times, skating blades were made from reindeer horn, and by the 15th century they were made from metal. Competitive skating championships began at the latest in the 19th century, and in 1823 several thousand people participated in an ice skating race on the frozen Oslofjord. Norway quickly rose to become a leading ice skating nation and has produced a continuous stream of champions ever since. There are skating rinks in all the larger towns and at the winter sports resorts. A historic venue for championships of Norwegian skating is the Bislett Stadium in Oslo.

Sled riding The number of husky racing fans, both actively involved and passive, are on the increase. Setting off with a dog sled with snow-heavy clouds hovering above the track is a very special adventure. Information is available from the DNT (▶Hiking) and the tourist office at ▶Karasjok. Riding snowmobiles is another way to explore the Norwegian winter landscape during the cold season).

OTHER SPORTS

Flying The regional operators of the Norsk Aero Klubb offer all imaginable flying sports, including gliding, parachute jumping, hang-gliding, parapenting and ballon trips.

Gold panning Gold panning is possible in various places. This is hardly a chance to get rich, mind you, but it is quite good fun. More precise information on gold safaris or gold panning camps and tours is supplied by the local tourist office at ▶Karasjok.

Golf There are 80 golf courses in Norway, of which 20 are 18-hole courses, such as those at Oslo, Stavanger, Tønsberg and Drammen. The world's northernmost 18-hole golf course is in Tromsø. Further north, there is the smaller North Cape Golf Club at Lakselv. The so-called Midnight Sun Tournament takes place at the golf course in Trondheim at the end of June, beginning of July. The **golfing season** lasts from May to the end of September/beginning of October.

In the southern regions of Norway, the animals available for hunting are the same as those known in the UK and other parts of Europe: deer and small game, as well as wild fowl. The hunting season for **elk** is usually limited to a few weeks of the year and the services of a local hunter with elk hounds must be used. The **kill fees** are substantial. More information is supplied by the local tourist offices.

Hunting

Orienteering is quite popular in Norway . They take place on around 200 routes, from spring to autumn, all over Norway. The tourist information offices have details.

Orienteering runs

In Norway's rural farming areas, horse riding has a long tradition. The Norwegian fjord horses are known for their comfortable riding and are very popular. Many country estates and farms rent out horses and offer riding lessons. So-called trail riding is becoming ever more fashionable too.

Horse riding

The Birkebeinerrennet, which takes place in March, is a real classic: the ski race from Rena to the Birkebeiner Skistadium, Lillehammer has been taking place for over 70 years. In 2008 over 12,000 skiers entered; 10,426 crossed the finish line. The fastest athletes cover the 54km/33.5mi stretch in only 2–3hrs (www. birkebeiner.no).

Ski race

Summer skiing is a typical Norwegian experience and it is possible to enjoy skiing on many névés and glaciers during high summer. See also winter sports.

Summer skiing

Sport

FISHING
Norges Jeger- og Fiskerforbund
Hvalstadåsen 5 ,
N-1378 Nesbru
tel. 66 79 22 00
www.njff.no

CLIMBING
Norsk Tindeklubb (NTK)
www.ntk.no

CYCLING
Stiftelsen Sykkelturisme
Strandgaten 59
5004 Bergen
www.cyclingnorway.com

FLYING
Norges Luftsportsforbund
Radhusgaten 5B
N-0102 Oslo
tel. 23 01 04 50, www.nlf.no

GOLF
Norges Golfforbund
0840 Oslo,
tel.21 02 91 50
www.golfforbundet.no

HIKING
**Den Norske
Turistforening (DNT)**
Youngstorget 1,
N-0181 Oslo
tel. 40 00 18 68
www.turistforeningen.no

Water Sports

NATURISM
**Norsk Naturistforbund
(NNF)**
Postboks 189 Sentrum
N-0102 Oslo
tel. 95 96 46 89
www.naturistnet.org

CANOE, KAJAK
Norges Padleforbund
Serviceboks 1,
Ullevål stadion,
N-0840 Oslo
tel. 21 02 98 35, www.padling.no

RAFTING
Sjoa Raftingsenter NWR
Gudbrandsdalsvegen 430
2670 Otta ,
tel. 47 66 06 80
www.sjoaraftingsenter.no

HORSE RIDING
Norges Rytterforbund (NRYF)
Ullevål Stadion,
N-0840 Oslo
tel. 21 02 69 50,,
www.rytter.no

TENNIS
Norges Tennisforbund
Postboks 287,
N-0511 Økern
tel. 22 72 70 00,
www.tennis.no

SAILING
**Kongelig Norsk Seilforening
(KNS)**
Huk Aveny 1,
N-0287 Oslo
tel. 23 27 56 00,
www.kns.no

DIVING
Norges Dykkeforbund
Postboks 1,
Ullevål stadion
N-0840 Oslo
tel. 21 02 97 42,
www.ndf.no

WATERSKIING
**Norges Vannski og Wake-
board Forbund**
Sognsveien 75L,
N-0855 Oslo
tel. 21 02 98 70, www.vannski.no

Winter Sports Centres

Beitostølen Region
Beitostølen and surroundings

Dovrefjell
Bjorli, Dombås, Hjerkinn

Hallingdal and Bergen
Dagli-Skurdalen, Geilo (family-
friendly resort with 32 runs,
18 lifts and 200km/125mi of
maintained cross-country routes).

Ustaoset, Gol, Golsfjell; Hemsedal (30 runs, major snowboarding centre)

Kongsberg and Numedal
Kongsberg, Flesberg and eastern Blefjell, Numedal to Dagali, Uvdal

Lillehammer and around
Excellent terrain for cross-country skiing tours with over 500km/313mi of tracks, Nordseter, Sjusjøen, Øyerfjell, Tretten; Hamar Hafjell alpine centre 15km/9mi north of Lillehammer: 9 lifts, 23km/14mi easy to medium level runs; greatest difference in elevation 850m/280ft; 20km/12mi alpine touring routes

Central Gudbrandsdal
Espedal, Kvam, Gausdal, Vinstra Kvitfjell: Olympic run 50km/31mi north of Lillehammer, near Ringebu

Northern Gudbrandsdal and Jotunheimen
Bøverdalen, Sjodalen, Vågå

Oslo and surroundings
Oslo, Eggedal, Hurdal, Norefjell, Ringerike, Vikersund-Modum (ski jump)

Østerdal
Atna, Engerdal, Elverum, Folldal, Os, Rendalen, Tynset

Rondane
Høvringen, Mysuseter, Otta

Setesdalen
Byglandsfjord, Hovden, Vråliosen, Vrådal-Kviteseid, Åserdal

Skeikampen
A traditional destination in the Gausdal valley with snow park, 17 pistes, 12 lifts, a 200km/125mi cross-country ski run, evening skiing and spa.

Telemark
Bolkesjø and Blefjell, Gautefall, Haukelifjell, Lifjell, Morgedal, Rauland, Vinje, Rjukan

Trysilfjell
Norway's largest interconnected ski region, with 70km/44mi of downhill pistes and 24 lifts, lies to the northwest of Lillehammer. Early risers can take part in »tidlig-ski« on Wed and Sat. Breakfast on the summit between 7am and 9am is part of the fun.

Valdres and Fagernes area
Aurdal-Tonsåsen, Fagernes, Fjellstølen, Hovda – Sanderstølen, Vaset – Nøsen

Vang and Filefjell area
Tyin, Eidsbugarden – Tyinholmen – Jotunheimen

Vestoppland – Gjøvik
Gjøvik, Toten, Lygnaseter, Synnfjell

Western Norway
Finse, Mjølfjell, Vatnahalsen, Voss, Oppheim, Seljestad, Stranda, Sykkylven, Ørsta, Utvikfjell

The Great Endurance Test

Of course it is a crazy idea to want to cycle non-stop for 540km/335mi, from Trondheim to Oslo: a route that takes riders over the Dovrefjell and several other mountains, and involves negotiating a total of 3400m/11155ft in elevation.

Yet, for Norwegians, the »Store Styrkeprøven« (Endurance Test) is a cycle race with a great tradition that has been held annually, for almost fifty years. Each year, during Midsummer, the country's major highway (E6) is taken over by cyclists, who have no more than 36 hours to cover the 540km/335mi route. It is undoubtedly a unique cycling race in Europe and the distance between Trondheim and Oslo is the equivalent of about two long Tour de France stages.

The largest obstacle on the way to the Norwegian capital is presented by the Dovrefjell that rises a good 1000m/3281ft. But the weather can also throw in a few surprises, as even in summer, it can produce icy wind, rain, and even a short hailstorm in mountainous areas. Nevertheless, the race is extremely popular, with several thousand contestants coming from all over Europe. The winning times are quite amazing too, and are normally a good deal less than fifteen hours from start to finish.

Pushing the Limits

The contestants set off from the start like a never-ending tapeworm wending its way from village to village along the asphalt line of the E6, and very soon the route confronts riders with its brutal challenge by rising to a steep incline. Yet, for many, these are the most satisfying miles they will cycle all year, when their physical and mental capacity is challenged to the full and they attack every stretch along the way, the distances just melting away behind them. The first check-point is reached after 70km/43mi, where riders are served mountains of sandwiches and lots of rehydrating drinks. These pit stops quickly become the most important goals during the entire race, where the body can recharge with vital calories and the mind can refocus. They also divide the entire route into manageable sections that are much easier to contemplate. The endless hours become more bearable when it is just a little further to the next rest stop, and afterwards everything feels possible again.

Recovery time on the Dovrefjell

Before reaching the Dovrefjell, the road heads up hill for an endless 100km/62mi, but despite the extreme effort required, this is one of the most impressive sections of the route. Every push of the peddle takes the rider into a more desolate landscape before reaching the sweeping views over the high plateau at last and the next care station at Hjerkinn. Time seems to be up faster here than anywhere else, with everyone lying on the soft

Huge numbers of participants despite the challenge: the Norwegian »Store Styrkeprøven«

moorland, enjoying the sunshine, drinking hot soup, eating sandwiches and downing huge amounts of coffee, juice and mineral water to revive their tired bodies. The next stretch is pleasant and almost relaxing, as riders sweep over the Dovrefjell plateau, through one of Norway's most beautiful landscapes; and the reward is the heart-stopping descent into the Gudbrandsdal valley.

Heading for the Finishing Line

The 300km/186mi mark is reached at Ringebu, where many riders take an extended break. The amateur cyclists have, after all, been in the saddle for ten to twelve hours by now, to get here from Trondheim. In the meantime, the line of participants has spread out so much that many find themselves cruising along the E6 alone after Ringebu, with nothing but their own thoughts for company. Yet the race is by no means over and there are still some pretty challenging elevations to overcome in this section. Eventually, however, it is done, and riders enter Oslo alone or in small packs, each and every one visibly marked by their exhaustion. Hands, shoulders and neck ache, not to mention backsides and legs. Mind and body are a blank and each and every push is unbelievably hard, despite the deeply satisfying knowledge of having achieved something extraordinary.

The Little Challenge

Those who can't face the entire »Store Styrkeprøven« can also register for one of the four shorter stretches that are covered under the »Lille Styrkeprøven«.
Information at
www.styrkeproven.no

TOURS

The sun-drenched beaches on the south coast, or the icy world of shimmering blue glaciers? Up to Nordkapp, through fjord country, or a trip to see the most famous stave churches? We'll show you Norway at its most beautiful.

Tours through Norway

These tours reflect the many faces of Norway. Whether you would like to explore interesting towns and cities to enjoy their art and culture, explore fjord landscapes, or set off on the lonely journey beyond the Arctic Circle – we will take you there.

Tour 1   **From the South Coast to Telemark**
This round trip begins with some of Norway's most beautiful beaches and coastal towns before heading into the hinterland, where extensive forests, small villages and farms characterize the Setesdal valley (Norwegian: Setesdalen) and the county of Telemark.
►page 133

Tour 2   **Into the Wild Heartland**
A spectacular tour around southern Norway to the highest Jotunheimen mountains, the icy world of the Jostedal Glacier or Jostedalsbreen, the narrow Geirangerfjord and on to the king of fjords: the Sognefjord.
►page 135

Tour 3   **Always in Sight of the Sea**
Keeping to the coast, heading north from Norway's southernmost point, this is no tour for those in a hurry. The jagged coast with its many fjords only allows for narrow, winding roads, and the numerous ferries further ensure sedate progress on this route.
►page 138

Tour 4   **Off to Nordkapp**
It is a long way to Nordkapp (North Cape), but the majestic cliffs in the middle of a bare arctic landscape exert a magical fascination. Consequently there is no shortage of hubbub here.
►page 140

Travelling in Norway

Norway is a large and particularly long country. The many valleys, fjords, mountains and glaciers have been mighty obstacles since time immemorial. In addition, the extremely disciplined driving habits of

the Norwegians and the hefty fines for speeding also guarantee an unusually sedate travelling tempo. For these reasons it is a good idea to choose your route carefully prior to the journey and to plan enough time and resources for detours, hikes, and the occasional day of bad weather. Those heading for Nordkapp should allow at least four weeks, otherwise there will hardly be time for sights beyond the E 6. Petrol is extremely expensive and the cost of road tolls and ferry tickets is an additional expense.

Tourists 18 sign-posted tours (www.nasjonaleturistveger.no) through magnificent landscapes cover Norway's jewels via a network of National Tourist Routes. Catering infrastructure is also being integrated and the first completed route is the »Matroute« over the Sognefjell that leads to regional food producers. Similar infrastructure is planned for the National Tourist Routes from the northern Gudbrandsdal towards the west of Norway (the »Gamle Strynefjellsvegen« and the »Trollstigen-Geiranger« Route), and for the one in Rondane. This network of national tourist routes is being augmented by thematic routes, such as the »Stave Churches along the Sognefjord« that was inaugurated in 2009. This 160km/99mi tour takes in nine cultural monuments, including the typically Norwegian stave churches of Borgund, Kaupanger, Undredal, Urnes and Hopperstad.

Modes of Transport Of course Norway can also be explored by public transport. However, the car does offer considerably more options for detours to the more remote sights. Hiking boots are important, as there are many opportunities to undertake short or indeed longer tours during which the magnificent natural environment can be fully experienced. Cycle tours should be planned carefully due to the heavily segmented landscape. A paradise for cyclists is provided by the Lofoten and Vesterålen islands, where the imposing mountain panorama can be enjoyed in the light of the midnight sun on routes almost completely free of inclines..

The South Rather optimistically known as the »Norwegian Riviera«, the south coast nevertheless offers the most beautiful sandy beaches, small bays and the sheer cliffs of skerries. This is a serpentine water world where a boat grants untold opportunities. Places like Risør, Tvedestrand, Arendal or Mandal fill up with holidaymakers at the drop of a hat during the Norwegian summer vacations. Yet the hurly-burly never gets out of hand and it is almost always possible to find a quiet spot by the sea. The country's interior awaits with a dream holiday for travellers seeking solitude, for this is where it truly exists: a cabin right on a lake, with nothing but nature as far as the eye can see. The water in these small lakes is often warmer than the sea and the swimming is wonderful!

Mountain ranges lie across southern Norway like a pearl necklace: Setesdalsheiene, then Hardangervidda, Jotunheimen, Dovrefjell and Rondane. Scandinavia's highest mountains can be found here, as well as wild jagged peaks and glaciers, and barren and treeless high plateaus. The Norwegian fjells (mountains) begin to impress even when still approaching in the car. A crossing of the Hardangervidda plateau on the RV 7 between Eidfjord and Geilo, or a drive through the Jotunheimen mountains via the Valdresflya (RV 51), or touring on the RV 55 between Skjolden and Lom and over Sognefjell count among the most beautiful panoramic routes through Norway. There comes a point, though, when the visitor should leave the car behind and set off on foot.

The west of the country is cut by countless fjords and driving becomes a trial of patience, because the roads are often narrow and interspersed by tunnels. Caravan trailers and mobile homes can expect painfully slow progress. One of the most attractive times of year for holidays in western Norway is the spring, for this is when the fruit trees are already blossoming along the fjords, while the mountains are still covered by snow. A warning: swimming in the fjords at that time of year is only for the hardy!   **The West**

During summer, the north is illuminated by the light of the midnight sun. The countryside glows in warm colours and the visitor is often alone in a mighty primeval landscape in these sparsely populated northern lands, able to stroll along wild coasts, try their luck in the salmon-rich rivers, or explore the desolate highland plateaus of Finnmarksvidda.   **The North**

From the South Coast to Telemark Tour 1

Length: 876km/544mi   **Duration:** 6 days

During summer, the south coast is among the most popular holiday regions in Norway because of its beautiful beaches. Even those who don't particularly want to swim can experience the country from its sunniest side here. The starting point is Oslo, and visits to interesting museums are followed by opportunities for rafting, collecting minerals, and calling in at Heddal's famous stave church.

After the exploration of Norway's capital ❶****Oslo**, for which two to three days should be planned, the tour heads off on the E 18 (developed into a motorway) to Drammen – which can happily be left by the wayside – before reaching small and quiet ❷***Åsgårdstrand**, which does merit a stop because of its location on the Oslofjord and   Oslo for Starters for its decorative white wooden houses and the many mementos of the painter Edvard Munch. For those with a little more time, the former whaling town of ❸**Sandefjord** has an interesting whaling and seafaring museum. The ferries for Denmark depart several times a day from ❹**Larvik**, while the seaside resort of Stavern to the south is worth a small detour to see the fortress of Fredriksvern with its mighty ramparts. After Larvik the E 18 traverses inland for a time and passes the industrial town of Porsgrunn, famous for its traditional porcelain manufactory.

Beautiful Beaches
The next destination, ❺**Kragerø**, lies somewhat off the main road and marks the beginning of the sun-drenched southern coast that is one of Norway's most popular holiday destinations thanks to its beautiful beaches, jutting skerries and immaculate settlements with their numerous white wooden houses. It is therefore worth making repeated detours off the E 18 to small coastal towns, such as Risør,

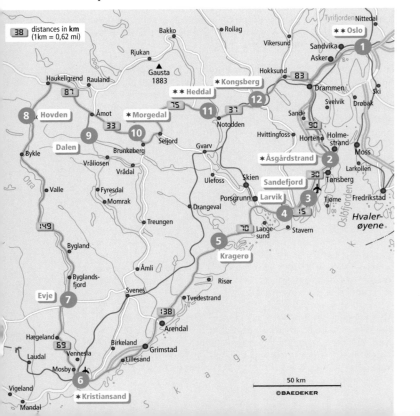

Tvedestrand, Lyngør, Arendal or Grimstad, before reaching ❻*Kristiansand**, which is one of the country's most important ferry ports
and offers a quick connection to northern Denmark. A visit to the
cathedral and the historic wooden houses of the Posebyen quarter
should definitely be on the Kristiansand itinerary.

The RV 9 leads north from Kristiansand through the Setesdal valley   Up into the
and along the Otra river, which forms several lakes. Isolated for many   Mountains
centuries, the richly forested valley surrounded by high mountains
has now become a popular holiday destination. ❼**Evje** is of particular interest to mineral hunters and rafting fans. ❽**Hovden**, one of
Norway's best-known winter sports destinations, is reached along a
steadily ascending road heading north along the length of the Byglandsfjord, a long lake with several attractive bathing spots. Several
miles north of Hovden, the road reaches Sessvatn (917m/3009ft), this
highest point offering a panoramic view of the barren, high alpine
landscape here. Soon afterwards the descent to Haukeligrend and the
E 134 is marked by tight serpentine bends. From there a widened
road leads to the little town of Åmot before turning into the RV 38 in
the direction of ❾**Dalen**.

A visit to Dalen, on the banks of the long, narrow Lake Bandak, is the   Visit Heddal
endpoint of the Telemark Canal. The Dalen Hotel – a historic wood
construction in the dragon style – and the nearby stave church of
Eidsborg are worth taking a look at here. The main road is reached
again via the RV 45, which soon leads on to ❿*Morgedal**. Another
highlight awaits shortly before the small town of Notodden, in
⓫**Heddal**, where Norway's largest stave church can be viewed.
The old mining town of ⓬*Kongsberg**, which owes its foundation
to the surrounding silver mines, is today known as a centre for jazz
and also for the marvellous interior of its Baroque church. Finally,
Oslo and this round tour's starting point are reached once more via
Hokksund and Drammen.

Into the Wild Heartland   Tour 2

Length: 1545 km/960mi   **Duration:** 9 – 10 days

This panoramic tour on adventurous serpentine roads leads
to the craggy Jotunheimen mountains and through the narrow Romsdal valley, introducing the Geirangerfjord and the
Sognefjord, as well as the icy world of the Jostedal Glacier
(Jostedalsbreen) and the austere Hardangervidda highland
plateau.

Crossing the Jotunheimen Range

Hønefoss is reached from ❶**✳✳Oslo** via the E 16, where a worthwhile detour can be made to the **✳Hadeland Glassverk**, Norway's most renowned glassworks at the southern end of the Randsfjord. After Hønefoss, the E 16 follows the river Begna (which soon widens into Lake Sperillen) all the way to ❷**✳Fagernes**, the most important town in the Valdres region. Fagernes is a significant tourist centre at the southern edge of the Jotunheimen range and has an open-air museum worth visiting. Steadily climbing, the RV 51 now leads in the direction of the Jotunheimen mountains, reaching the tree line at the winter sports resort of Beitostølen. A beautiful view of Lake Bygdin surrounded by imposing mountains can be enjoyed at the town of the same name. The road reaches its highest point at the Valdresflya mountain pass, and then leads on to ❸**Gjendesheim**, which lies on the long, narrow Lake Gjende and is one of the most important bases for hikes into the Jotunheimen mountains. The crossing of the Jotunheimen ends shortly before ❹**Vågåmo**, which boasts a stave church that is worth taking a look at.

To Trollwand and Dombås

The highlights of the journey via ❺**Dombås** include the 1000m/3280ft-high, vertical **✳Trollveggen** (»troll wall«), reached shortly before ❻**Åndalsnes,** and the no less imposing Romsdalshorn. Shortly afterwards, the serpentine road leads up to the **✳✳Trollstigen** (»troll ladder«), which is one of Norway's most impressive roads. The viewing point at the pass is not to be missed. The spectacular road continues through the Meirdal valley down to the fjord, which is crossed by a ferry, before turning back into the mountains on the winding **✳Eagle Road** followed by the descent into ❼**Geiranger** on the **✳✳Geirangerfjord.** The road from Geiranger past Dalsnibba mountain to ❽**Stryn** is also a worthy fjell-and-fjord panorama tour. From Stryn, the road follows the banks of the fjord to Olden, where it turns off for ❾**✳✳Briksdalsbreen glacier**, which numbers among the most beautiful arms of Jostedalsbreen and is roughly an hour's walk from the car park..

From the Sognefjord to Hardangervidda

It is well worth paying a visit to the Norwegian Glacier Museum in ❿**Fjærland**, located at the southern end of Jostedalsbreen and reached via Olden, Byrkjelo and Skei. From there the route follows the E 5 to Sogndal and continues on the RV 55 to Hella and the ferry, from whichh ⓫**✳Balestrand** is reached via Dragsvik. Take a look at the Swiss-style wooden villas on the sunny Sognefjord here as well as the magnificent Kvikne Hotel. From Balestrand return to the ferry at Dragsvik and take the boat to Vangsnes before heading for ⓬**✳Voss** on the RV 13 via Viksöyri. Voss boasts an impressive location on Lake Vangsvatn, but the townscape is modern. During summer a cable car takes hikers directly

into the mountains, and during winter it is the ski slopes that attract people to Voss. A detour to ⑬**Bergen**, the capital of the
fjord region, is possible at this point, for which at least an extra
day should be planned. The drive to ⑮**Geilo** via ⑭**Granvin** leads
through Mabødal, where it is worth stopping at one of Norway's
best-known waterfalls, Vøringfoss. Afterwards the RV 7 traverses
the austere Hardangervidda before finally reaching Geilo, a popular winter sports resort because of its excellent alpine sports facilities. ⑯**Gol** is reached via Hol, Ål and Torpo, after which the
RV 7 leads through the Hallingdal valley to Noresund via Nesbyen. Oslo and the starting point of this tour is then reached once
more via Hønefoss.

Tour 3 # Always in Sight of the Sea

Length: 1268 km/792mi   **Duration:** 10 days

Plenty of time is a real boon for this route, as at many fjords the only way forward is to take the ferry. Some of the country's most important towns are on the itinerary: oil-boom town Stavanger, atmospheric Bergen, Ålesund with its art nouveau buildings, and Trondheim, once the glittering capital of the kingdom.

The starting point of ❶ *****Kristiansand** is one of Norway's most important ferry ports and maintains regular routes to northern Denmark. After visiting the district of wooden houses in Posebyen and the imposing cathedral, leave town in a westerly direction on the well maintained E 39. The route soon reaches ❷ *****Mandal**, the southernmost town of the »Norwegian Riviera«. A draw here is the long sandy beach of Sjøsanden, right by the centre, and the nearby recreational area of Furulunden, which also boasts attractive beaches. From Mandal, the southernmost point of the Norwegian mainland is reached at ❸*****Lindesnes**. A sweeping view of the austere skerry landscape can be enjoyed from the small lighthouse.

Stavanger and Bergen

On the way to ❹*****Stavanger**, it is worth making stops at the nearby Flekkefjord – the »Dutch town« – with its narrow lanes and restored white wood houses, and also at Orresanden, a long, sandy beach to the south of the oil town. Stavanger itself is Norway's modern boom town: expensive, lively and open to the world. The ferry can take you to the island of Karmøy, to the north, and to the small fishing village of ❺*****Skudeneshavn**, which feels a lot like an open-air museum. In ❻**Haugesund**, the largest town between Stavanger and Bergen, there is an opportunity to stroll along the water on the promenade and visit the pink town hall. The E 39 then continues in a northerly direction, very often along the water's edge and, after several breaks for ferry trips, eventually reaches ❼******Bergen**, capital of fjord country. It is easy to spend several days here: strolling around the fish market, enjoying the view from Fløyen, and exploring the Hanseatic Museum.

To Trondheim

Several ferries, including those that cross the broad ❽*****Sognefjord**, ensure there are repeated breaks along the way to the art nouveau town ❾*****Ålesund**. The jazz town of ❿**Molde** can also only be reached after a wait for the ferry at the Romsdalsfjord. ⓫*****Kristiansund**, on the other hand, has been connected to the mainland since the elaborate bridge and tunnel construction of 1992. From here

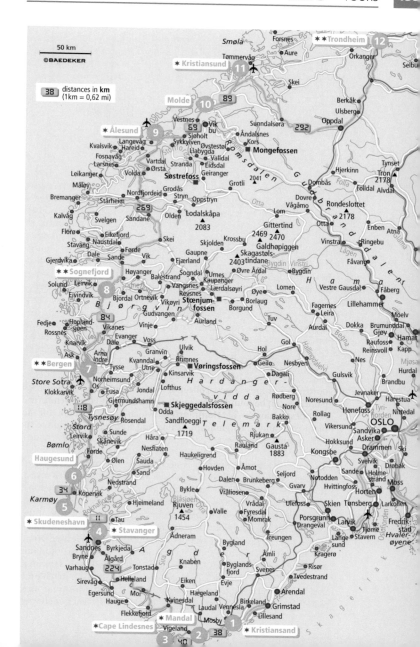

50 km

©BAEDEKER

38 distances in **km**
(1km = 0,62 mi)

there are two routes to ⑫ ****Trondheim**: Trondheim: the shortest in terms of distance, but a considerably slower option due to the numerous ferries, is the route via small serpentine roads along the coast; alternatively there is the inland route via Sunndalsøra and Oppdal.

Tour 4 # Off to Nordkapp

Length: 1017 km/636mi   **Duration:** 4 days

At the latest from Narvik onwards, there is no alternative but the E 6 for those who are heading north. Many at this point are in a hurry to reach Nordkapp (North Cape) at last, but travellers who leave themselves a little more time and who are lucky with the weather will fall in love with the solitude of these northern lands bathed in the midnight sun. It is an overwhelming wilderness that has no equal in Europe.

Towns beyond the Arctic Circle

The route follows the E 6 north from the iron ore mining town of ❶ **Narvik** on the Ofotfjord, through the sparsely populated county of Troms and passing the small town of Andselv, until it reaches a junction at Nordkjosbotn. This is where the E 8 turns off and runs 73km/46mi to the port of ❷ ***Tromsø**. The city lies on a small island connected to the mainland by a daringly arched bridge. Tromsø likes to refer to itself as the »Paris of the North« and its emblem is the modern Arctic Cathedral. Returning to the E 6 after this detour, the route continues on its way to Nordkapp. Next stop is ❸ ***Alta**, where northern Europe's largest collection of Stone and Bronze Age rock paintings can be found to the south of the town, at Hjemmeluft. The next destination is ❹ ***Hammerfest**, which lies 57km/36mi off the main road and is a significant fishing and trading centre due to its year-round ice-free port.

Hubbub at the cape

To reach ❺ **Honningsvåg**, it is necessary to return to the E 6 and follow it to the turn-off for the E 69, where the route leads to Kåfjord. A toll tunnel and bridge has connected Kåfjord with the island of Magerøya since 1999, where ❻ ****Nordkapp** is located. The most expensive part of the road is made up by the roughly 7km/4mi of the North Cape Tunnel (Nordkapptunnelen) between Kåfjord and Honningsvåg. In good weather, there is a beautiful view of the neighbouring disjointed peninsulas and the Polar Sea from the flattened summit of the Nordkapp cliffs, which are a good 300m/984ft high. However, you will never be alone at Nordkapp: indeed the tourist hubbub here reaches unsuspected extremes. Those enraptured by the north can now set off for the 544km/340mi two-day journey to Kirkenes, following

the E 69 along the Porsangerfjord back to the E 6 and then driving almost to the Russian border, through the barren and almost uninhabited landscape of the Finnmark.

SIGHTS FROM
A TO Z

From the streets of Oslo up to the high fjells; onwards to the fjords and north to the Lofoten Islands and Nordkapp – there is much to discover in Norway.

* Ålesund

✦ a E 3 ●

Region: West Norway
Population: 44,500

Ålesund is one of Norway's most beautiful towns: the location alone makesit worth a visit, situated on several islands in the midst of fjords and skerries,but the art nouveau buildings turn it into a veritable jewel.

Islands and klippfisk

Looking down onto Ålesund's seaof houses from the local hill of Aksla, this lively market town and port appears to spread itself over numerous islands. The largest part of town reaches across the islands of Heissa (4 sq km/2 sq mi), Nørvøya (7 sq km/3 sq mi) and Aspøya (0.5 sq km/0.2 sq mi). Several of these islands are connected by road, though 12km/8mi isvia underwater tunnels. Home to Norway's largest and most up-to-date fishing fleet, Ålesund has become one of the country's most important fishing portsand, globally, one of the largest export bases for dried salt cod or »klippfisk«. 80% of the world's requirement for this product is met from Ålesund, with the largest customer being Portugal.

Waterways run through Ålesund's town centre

Ålesund

INFORMATION
Destination Ålesund and Sunnmøre
Skateflukaia
6002 Ålesund
Tel. 70 15 76 00
www.visitalesund-geiranger.com

FESTIVALS
Mid-June: Dragon Boat Festival
(www.dragebat.no)
Around the 10th July: boat festival.
End of August: Norwegian gourmet festival (www.matfestivalen.no)

EXCURSIONS
Motor boats and high-speed ferries connect to the outer islands and into the smaller fjords to the south of the city. There are also sightseeing helicopter flights departing from the airport.

WHERE TO EAT
XL Diner £ £ £
Skaregata 1
Tel. 70 12 42 53
This elegant restaurant offers a wonderful view over the harbour along with a world tour of cod dishes, using one of Norway's top exports: bacalao from Portugal, Spanish bacalau, or Italian stoccafisso.

Sjøbua Restaurant £ £ £
Brunholmgata 1a
Tel. 70 12 71 00
www.sjoebua.no
A popular fish restaurant located in a former warehouse where the raw materials are delivered directly from the fishing boat. The interior décor is maritime, the view over Brosund very beautiful. Closed at weekends.

Café Brosundet £ £
Rasmus Rønnebergsgate 4
Tel. 70 12 91 00
Ålesund's best pastries from their in-house bakery are served at the café in the First Hotel Atlantica. They also do lunch and evening meals.

Apoteker'n Café £
Apoteker gata 16
Tel. 70 10 49 70
Charming café in the art nouveau town centre and an ideal place for a snack and an espresso. The specialty is »Queen Maud's cake«.

WHERE TO STAY
Clarion Collection Hotel Bryggen £ £ £ £
Apotekergata 1-3
Tel. 70 12 64 00
www.nordicchoicehotels.com
85 rooms.
Very elegant and comfortable hotel in a converted warehouse with wonderful views of the Brosundet.

Hotel Brosundet £ £ £
Apotekergata 5
Tel. 70 11 45 00
www.brosundet.no, 47 rooms.
Another art nouveau hotel is right next door, whose excellent combination of historic and modern gained it a Traveller's Choice Award in 2012. By the way, room 47 is outside the main building, in the Molja fyr lighthouse.

Ålesund Vandrerhjem £ £
Parkgata 14
Tel. 70 11 58 30
www.hihostels.no
This youth hostel offers simple accom-

modation two to 12-bed dormitories in a beautiful art nouveau building; open all year round.

Goksøyr Camping £
Runde
Tel. 70 08 59 05
www.insel-runde.de
Meeting place for ornithologists and nature photographers at the foot of the cliffs that are home to hundreds of thousands of nesting birds. Knut Asle Goksøyr ensures well-informed service, and there are also cabins and rooms.

Tipp for solitude seekers: since 2004, it has been possible to stay in the restored pilot house on the island of Runde. The facilities in this tiny place are simple, but the exposed location on a spit of land really does make you feel like Robinson Crusoe, especially out of season when the wind howls around the building.

WHAT TO SEE IN ÅLESUND

Art nouveau town

Ålesund is famous for its art nouveau architecture, which is a style that hardly exists elsewhere in Norway. Numerous houses in the town centre were rebuilt in this style with the help of international aid after a massive fire in 1904, during which 10,000 people were made homeless. Among the donors was German Emperor Wilhelm II, who was an enthusiastic Norway fan. A tour of the town centre reveals colourful embellishments on the façades and countless turrets and towers.

Aspøya, Nørvøya

The centre of Ålesund is on the two main islands. Ålesund's church (1909), with its remarkable frescoes and wonderful painted glass, stands on Aspøya. A patrician house on Nørvøya contains the **municipal museum**, with an extensive section devoted to art nouveau architecture and historic craftsmanship, aswell as an interesting section on fishing, complete with old ships. Ålesund's most magnificent *****Art nouveau houses** with colourful façades line Hellesundet, the inner harbour between the two islands. Thehouses on Kongensgata on Nørvøya and Apotekergata on Aspøya are especially worthseeing. The **Art Nouveau Centre** is housed in one of the most beautiful buildings in the city, at Apotekergata 16, right on the sound (Norwegian: sund). The museum in the former Svane pharmacy was opened by Queen Sonjain 2003, and provides information on the fire in the town as well as telling thestory of art nouveau. The changing exhibitions of the KUBE art museum can be found right next door and form part of the Møre og Romsdal district's regional art museum. Together with the Art Nouveau Centre, it is known as the Kulturkvartalet Foundation.

Jugendstilsenteret/Kunstmuseet KUBE: June–Aug daily 10am–5pm; otherwise Tues–Sun 11am–4pm; 70 NOK (valid for both museums); www.jugendstilsenteret.no, www.kunstmuseetkube.no

The quays lie to the south and north of the islandsof Aspøya and Nørvøya. Fresh fish and shellfish are sold at the harbour on Skansegata.

Harbour

East of the city centre, lies the municipal park(Norwegian: bypark) with its 7m/23ft Bauta stone with a relief portrait of Emperor Wilhelm II, recalling German assistance after the great city fire of 1904. There isalso a statue of the Viking chief Rollo (Gange-Rolv), who allegedly came from Ålesund and who founded the Duchy of Normandy in 911.

Park

East of the park, 418 steps lead up to the 189m/620ft-high hill ofAksla, from which there is a wonderful view of the city, the sea and the islands around, as well as of the Sunnmøre mountains to the southeast. The view from the cafeteria »Fjellstua«, which can also be reached by car, is especially breath-taking at sunset.

*View from Aksla

On a spit of land known as Tueneset, about3km/2mi west of the city centre, lies one of Norway's largest aquariums. It is discretely incorporated into the otherwise untouched coastal landscape. The gian-

Atlantic aquarium

Experience the wonders of the ocean in one of Norway's largest aquariums

tacrylic tanks of the Atlantic Ocean Park contain fish and marine-animals from the North Sea. Special attractions at Norway's best museum for children (2009 vote), are feeding time for the sea lions and penguins, and the opportunity for young and old to try their hand at crab fishing.

❶ June–Aug Sun–Fri 10am–7pm, Sat till 4pm; Sep–May Mon–Sat 11am–4pm, Sun 11am–6pm; 140 NOK; www.atlanterhavsparken.no

AROUND ÅLESUND

Borgund   Not to be confused with the home of the famous stave church (▶p. 177), Borgund is located around 4km/2mieast of the city centre. The oldest part of the churchhere was built in 1130. It burnt down in 1904, but it was then reconstructed true to the original. The interior contains beautiful wood carvings in the old style.

> **MARCO POLO TIP**
>
> *Travel in a Viking ship*   Insider Tip
>
> During summer, the Borgund-Knarren replica Viking ship departs from the Sunnmøre Museum for a one-hour tour every Wednesday. Various boats are also for hire between June and August.

Right next to the church, the **Sunnmøre Museum** attracts visitors to its open air exhibition of around 50 historic houses. There is also an interesting fishing exhibition with 30 old boats and theBorgund-Knarren, a historic merchant ship from the year1000.

Sunnmøre Museum: Mid-June–Mid-Aug, Mon–Sat 11am–5pm, Sun from noon; May–Sep till 4pm, closed Sat; otherwise till 3pm and closed Sat and Mon; 80 NOK; www.sunnmore.museum.no

Runde   Norway's southernmost **nesting cliffs**, the »Rundebranden«, (▶ MARCO POLO Insight, p.150) are on the island of Runde, southwest of Ålesund. So far, over 200 different species of birds and around 170,000 breeding pairs have been observed here,especially puffins, guillemots and gannets. Hundreds of ornithologists and nature photographers come to the island's only settlement of **Goksøyr** every year. However, it is also possible toview the lower sections of the cliffs' guano speckled rocks from on board asmall fishing boat that makes several daily **sightseeing trips** (Information at Runde Camping by the port).In 1725, the Dutch merchant ship »Akerendam« sank off the coast here. Divers found over 60,000 gold and silver coins in the old wreck in 1972, and divers can still go treasure hunting in the area.

Ishavsmuseet   At Brandal on the island of Hareidlandet, 4km/2.5mi north of Ha-
(Arctic Sea   reid, the Arctic Sea Museum has displays on seal hunting, which was
Museum)   of great economic significance in the early 20th century, as well as

many stuffed polar bears and arctic wolves. The highlight is the ice breaker »Aarvak«, built in 1912, which was used for sealing for almost 70 years.

❶ Jun–Aug daily 11am–5pm; May, Sep noon–4pm; 50 NOK; www.ishavsmuseet.no

The Ivar Aasen Museum is located near the E 39 road, between Ørsta and Volda. Aasen formulated the basis for Nynorsk, which isone of the two Norwegian official languages. The museum was designed by one of the country's foremost architects, Sverre Fehn, and provides exhaustive informationon language and literature.

Ivar Aasen Museum

❶ Jun–Aug Mon–Fri 10am–5pm, Sat–Sun Noon–5pm; rest of the year: Mon–Fri 10am–4pm, Sun Noon–5pm; 75 NOK; www.aasentunet.no

Stordal is around 50km/31mi east of Ålesund, and its church really isworth a visit. The entire interior of this Rosekyrkja (rose church) rebuilt in 1789to replace an earlier one is covered in paintings. Large parts of the interior furnishings still originate from the first medieval church.

*Stordal church

❶ 20 June–20 Aug, daily 11am–4pm

Magnificent: the interior of the Stordal rose church near Ålesund

Cliffside Life

A unique spectacle is watching hundreds of thousands of marine birds find their mate for nesting in the windswept cliffs of the North Atlantic and of the North Sea during breeding season. Each species occupies its own regular level in the sheer rock face, which is often several hundred feet above sea level: shags and black guillemots nest on the ground floor, puffins get the penthouse, and the rest find their spot in between. Moving home is not encouraged!

▶ **Norways bird cliffs**
It is no mean feat getting to see the nesting sites of Norway's cliff bird colonies, but regular tour boats make the trip. The most comfortable journey is undoubtedly possible on the island of Runde, which is Scandinavia's most southerly nesting colony for marine birds and home to about 170,000 pairs. The region's largest colony is on the island of Røst, but getting there involves a 100km/62mi-journey by boat.

Great
Skua
50

Gjesvaerstappan
Syltefjordstauran
Vardø/Hornøya
Store Ekkerøy

Bleiksøya

Lofoten
Røst

Runde

The breeding colonies for marine birds are in the rock faces on the western side of the island of Runde, 250m/820ft above sea level.

Bird cliff   RUNDE

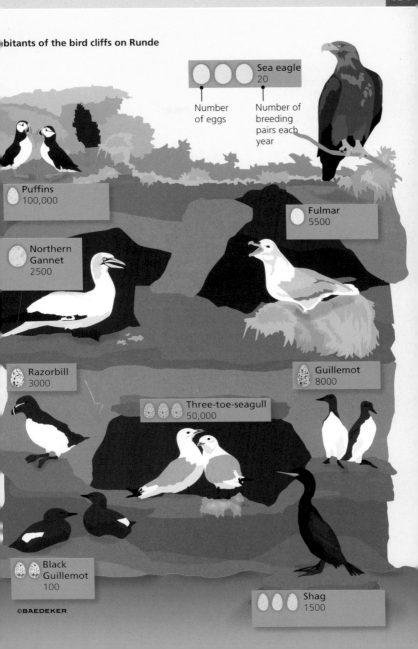

bitants of the bird cliffs on Runde

Sea eagle
20

Number of eggs

Number of breeding pairs each year

Puffins
100,000

Fulmar
5500

Northern Gannet
2500

Razorbill
3000

Guillemot
8000

Three-toe-seagull
50,000

Black Guillemot
100

Shag
1500

©BAEDEKER

* Alta

✦ M 20

Region: North Norway
Population: 19,300

People lived in the region around the Altafjord as early as the Stone Age, leaving thousands of rock paintings. Today the Sami settlement of Alta in the far north is an ideal base for tours in the direction of Nordkapp and Finnmark.

Mild climate in the far north

The largest town in the sparsely populated county of ►Finnmark lies at the point where theAlta river – Norway's best known river for salmon – flows into the Altafjord.The excellent tourist infrastructure of the town make it very suitable as a base fortours to ►Nordkapp, ►Hammerfest, and the Samitowns of ►Karasjok and ►Kautokeino. Even though the town is on the 70th northern latitude, the mild climate softened by the Gulf Stream creates ideal conditions for agriculture and forestry.

The roughly 3000 rock paintings at Alta are part of our global heritage

Humans inhabited the area around Alta more than 10,000 years ago. This fact is proven by the rock paintings of Hjemmeluft and by excavations on the Komsa mountain (Komsa culture). The Sami settlement of Alta developed into an administrative centre early on, after increasing numbers of Norwegians moved here inthe 17th century to trade in reindeer meat and other goods. Immigrants from southern-Norway and Finland also arrived with the beginning of copper mining in Kåfjord. Altawas totally destroyed by German occupying troops towards the end of the Second WorldWar. With the exception of the churches of Alta and Kåfjord, therefore, the entire townscape dates from the post-war era.

WHAT TO SEE IN ALTA

The area around the Altafjord is one of the most ancient population-centres in the county of Finnmark, as proved by the giant fields with close to 3000 rock paintings discovered in 1973, immediately south of Alta, on the E 6. It is the largest collection of its kind in northern Europe and listed among the UNESCO World Heritage Sites. The oldest of the paintings, which have been coloured in by archaeologists, go back to the Stone Age and are 6200 years old; the most recent are 2500 years old. The question of how humans survived the Ice Age here remains unanswered to this day. Hunting scenes, dancers, circles and fertility symbols can be discovered by following a 5km/3mi educational route.

*Rock paintings Helleristninger

Access to the rock paintings is via the prize-winning **Alta Museum** next door, which has been designed on the latest pedagogic principles for museums. The museum gives an interesting overview on slateextraction, river and fjord fishing, the craftsmanship of the Finnmark Sami, and theStone Age culture of Sørøya Island. A special exhibition also recalls the Sami's bitter campaign (1978/82) against the development of a hydro-electric dam on the Alta river. The Sami lost the battle, though they won politically: as aresult of this conflict, a Sami parliament was set up by the Norwe-

MARCO POLO TIP

Insider Tip

A thousand barking dogs

Visiting Alta is especially worthwhile at the beginning of March, when the whole town is gripped by the thrill of the forthcoming Finnmarksløpet. There is tremendous excitement surrounding the event. 70 mushers competing in Europe's longest and most northerly dog sled race arrive with around one thousand huski dogs. After 12 stages, racing 1000km/625mi across the deeply snowed-in north, they cross the finishing line at Alta. Until 2012, the race was always won by Norwegians (and one Swede), but the record was broken by the German Katy Meier, when she became the first non-Scandinavian to gain first place (information at www.finnmarkslopet.no).

Alta

INFORMATION
Destinasjon Alta
Parksenteret
9504 Alta
Tel. 78 44 95 55
www.destinasjonalta.no

GETTING THERE
There are direct flights from Oslo.

MIDNIGHT SUN
The midnight sun can be seen in Alta between 16th May and 26th July; from 24th Nov to 18th January the sun does not appear at all.

WHERE TO EAT
Gargia Fjellstue £ £
Gargia (near Alta Canyon)
Tel. 78 43 33 51
A cosy restaurant offers traditional Finnmark and Sami dishes in this wilderness. Accommodation is available and outdoor activities can also be arranged, including horse-riding, boat and fishing tours, as well as dogsled tours and snowshoeing.

WHERE TO STAY
Sorrisniva Igloo Hotel £ £ £ £
Sorrisniva 20
Tel. 78 43 33 78
www.sorrisniva.no, 30 rooms
A 2000sq m/ 21,528 sq ft world of ice and snow: 30 rooms, an ice bar, a chapel and several lounges. Warm sleeping bags and reindeer pelts protect from the freezing conditions (-4°C--7°C) on the ice beds. The ice hotel is open from around mid-January to mid-April.

Rica Hotel Alta £ £ £
Løkkeveien 61
Tel. 78 48 27 00
www.rica.no, 241 rooms.
The largest hotel in town is ultra modern, with two restaurants, a bar and nightclub. Wake up to the Northern Lights.

Thon Hotel Vica £ £ £
Fogdebakken 6
Tel. 78 48 22 22
www.thonhotels.com/vica, 23 rooms.
Good restaurant with regional cuisine and a stylish bar.

gian governmentand Sami culture was incorporated into the national constitution, officially recognized as worthy of preservation (▶Finnmark and ▶MARCO POLO Insight p.34).

Alta Museum: end of Aug–April Mon–Fri 8am–3pm, Sat–Sun 11am–4pm; May–mid-June daily 8am–5pm; mid-June–end of Aug, daily 8am–8pm; 90 NOK; www.alta.museum.no

Tirpitz
Museum

An extensive exhibition and photo collection on the role of the German war ships »Tirpitz« and »Scharnhorst« can be viewed at the Tirpitz Museum off Route E 6.

❶ June-Sep daily 10am–5pm; 60 NOK; www.tirpitz-museum.no

Sautso
Canyon

Alta's main attraction, next to the rock art, is the excellent choice of leisure activities andexcursion options on the Alta river. With a length of 6km/4mi and a depth of 300–400m/980–1300ft, the **Sautso Canyon** (or Alta Canyon) is the largest in Europe and provides a fascinating insight into the power of nature. Just under 30km/19mi from Alta, the canyon is reached via the old road passing Gargia on the way to the Baskades highlands. From there a sign-posted path leads to the gorge, a two-hourwalk from the Gargia hut. This natural wonder can also be reached via the Altariver, though every boat should have a guide.

Beginning each 22 June, salmon fishing is the most popular leisure activity on the Altariver. At this time anglers come to Alta from all over the world and, with their highly-prized fishing card in their pockets and their fly fishing rod in hand, they go after the salmon.

Salmon fishing

AROUND ALTA

Kåfjord, the largest community in the Finnmarkduring the mid-19th century, is reached by driving west along the coast from Alta.Travelling further to Isnestoften (also known as Toften) via Talvik, it is possible to find both old German fortifications and the remains of four Stone Agesettlements. The Langfjord cuts deep into the countryside here.

Kåfjord

From Langfjordbotn it is possible to make a beautiful excursion onminor roads to the large **Øksfjordjøkul** glacier – the only glacier on the European mainland that empties into the sea (▶Troms).

* # Arendal

✴ A 5

Region: South Norway
Population: 42,800

Arendal is the largest town on the country's southern coast, a stretch known as the »Norwegian Riviera«. The busy town once had numerous canals. Today it enchants the visitor with its attractive wooden houses. Pleasant holidays can also be enjoyed in nearby Gimstad, where the 15-year-old Henrik Ibsen once embarked on his pharmacy apprenticeship.

The picturesque port of Arendal is spreadover seven islands and was originally cut through by many canals, a fact that earned it the name »Venice of the North«. After repeated fires, however, most recently in the 1960s, the canals were filled in. The last relic of the canal system is the lively Pollen marina, were numerous yachts and motorboats bob in the water. Arendal is the largest town of those known as the »white pearls« (named for their whitewooden houses) on the Norwegian Riviera, stretching between Kragerø to the north and Lillesand to the south. Arendal was one of Scandinavia's most important seafaring towns up to the end of the 19th century. In addition to wood exports to the Netherlands (particularly during the heyday of the East India Company), shipbuilding and the port, the economic life oft he town was defined by the mining of iron ore for 400 years.

WHAT TO SEE IN AND AROUND ARENDAL

Town centre To the west of the harbour basin of Pollen, in the crooked lanes of the Tyholmen district, well preserved wooden houses in the styles of Baroque, Rococo, Empire and Biedermeier recall the age of sailing, before steam shipping was invented. The four storeys of the mighty town hall building stand right by the harbour basin. It was built as a private home for the Kallevig shipping family in1815, and is the country's second largest wooden building after the Stiftsgården in ▶Trondheim. The Aust Agder Museum is locatedin several buildings on the northern edge of town, and displays furniture, costumes,dolls, minerals and ship utensils. The **Bomuldfactory** (Oddenveien 5) is also worth a visit, with its permanent exhibition of contemporary art in an area of 2500 sq m/26,910 sq ft featuring works by 40 orwegian artists; there are also temporary exhibitions.

> ! **MARCO POLO TIP**
>
> *Sun, sea and car-free* Insider Tip
>
> For the locals, the most popular destination during the summer is the car-free island of Merdø. The ferry from Arendal takes 25mins. There are several old Sørlands houses, the Merdøgaard Museum and, of course, the beaches – partly sandy and partly rocky – that all make a visit worthwhile. Those little hunger pangs can be satisfied with a light lunch at the island café.

Kulturhistoriske Senter: Parkveien 16; end of June–Mid-Aug; Mon–Fri 9am–5pm, Sun Noon–5pm, otherwise Mon–Fri 9am–3pm; Sun Noon–3pm; www.aaks.no
Bomuldsfabrik: Tue–Sun noon–4pm.

Lyngør A tiny settlement without streets or cars, Lyngør is spread over four islands off the eastern coast of Sørlandets. Very little has changed here in the past 130 years and, in 1991, this well-kept town of wood frame houses was voted Europe's best preserved town. You can explore while staying at Norway's first book hotel, the Lyngørporten Resort, on the nearby mainland.
🌐 www.lyngorporten.com.

Arendal

INFORMATION
Arendal Turistkontor
Sam Eydes plass 1
4809 Arendal
Tel. 37 00 55 44
www.arendal.com

FESTIVALS
June: International Market, craftwork, music, dance and theatre from all over the world (www.internasjonaltmarked. no).
July: Summer market, shopping and street art (www.arendal-sentrum.no).
End of July/early August: Canal Street, major jazz and blues festival with international artists (www.canalstreet.no).
End of July/early August: APL Race Week, renowned regatta with various classes for boats; be sure not to miss the After-Sail-Party in the yacht harbour (www.asf.no).

EXCURSIONS
The nearby islands of Hisøy and Tromøy can be reached by ferry or bridges. The latter island has very attractive sandy beaches and a viewing point on the Vardåsen hill.

WHERE TO EAT
Stangholmen fyr
£££ – ££££
Stangholmen, 4950 Risør
Tel. 37 15 24 50
www.stangholmen.no
This unique restaurant in the old lighthouse offers fantastic views along with excellent fish dishes, such as its famous bouillabaisse. Open May–end of August; boat ferry between town and the lighthouse every half hour.

Fiskebrygga £ £
Nedre Tyholmsvei 1
Tel. 37 02 31 13
www.fiskebrygga.no
Buy fresh fish and seafood here or treat yourself to fish soup or the typically Norwegian »Fiskekaker«.

WHERE TO STAY
Arendal Herregaard £ £ £ £
Tromøy, 4818 Færvik
Tel. 37 06 08 30,
www.arendalherregaard.no
This upscale hotel on the island of Tromøy offers refurbished rooms, suites and family apartments, as well as ten cabins. The Spa is one of the most beautiful in Norway.

Clarion Hotel Tyholmen £ £ £ £
Teaterplassen 2
Tel. 37 07 68 00
www.clariontyholmen.no, 96 rooms.
Hotel built in the style of the 19th century, complete with the »Tre Seil« (Three Sails) terrace restaurant.

Arendal Gjestehus £ £
Batteriveien 17
Tel. 99 36 86 09, 3 rooms.
Small guest house with three rooms, communal kitchen, and a fine view out to sea from the garden.

Hove Camping £
Hove, Tromøy
Tel. 37 08 54 79
www.hove-camping.no
A generously laid out campsite in a forested area and with a nice beach, about 15mins from Arendal on Tromøy. There are also 21 huts for 4–5 people.

Risør Around 50km/31 mi north lies Risør, the »Pearl of the Riviera«, which is also a popular holiday spot for members of the Norwegian royal family. The elegant promenade and fine villas indicate the wealth of this art and craft haven with its great Windjammer past, and it also boasts the beautiful Baroque church of Hellige Ånds. There are many tempting beaches for swimming on the off-shore skerries, and kayaking is also a popular activity.
ⓘ www.lyngorporten.com

*Grimstad The holiday resort of Grimstad (pop. 18,000) lies around 20km/12mi away on the E 18 in the direction of ▶Kristiansand. It is especially popular for the wonderful sandy beaches located to the east of the town. The skerries just off-shore make for an idyllic backdrop. The town itself is also an excellent place to relax, enhanced not least by the picturesque old wooden houses by the harbour. Near the landing-quay, on Østregate, the former pharmacy of **Ibsenhuset** can be found, where the dramatist began his apprenticeship in 1843, aged 15. He wrote his first play, Catilina, during that time, publishing it under a pseudonym in 1850. The authentically decorated rooms containing manuscripts and pictures painted by Ibsen can be viewed. The literary Nobel Prize winner Knut Hamsun also lived near Grimstad for some time, on the Nørholm estate about 6km/4mi away.
Ibsenhuset: May–Sep Mon–Sat 11am–4pm, Sun from noon; 80 NOK; www.gbm.no

Charming wooden houses provide the backdrop for a visit to Grimstad

** Bergen

C 2

Region: West Norway
Population: 267,800

27 kinds of precipitation drizzle, fall and drive down on Bergen where, on 248 days of the year, they give Europe's rainiest town a mystical, fairylike and even dramatic aspect, which it celebrates with an exuberant rain festival. Bergen's babies are born already wearing little raincoats, according to folklore, yet Norway's former capital exhibits a positively Mediterranean flair whenever the sun comes out.

Nestling in a crown of partly forested hills (up to 643m/2110ft), the city is surrounded by slopes amphitheatre style, making it one of Norway's most beautiful places. A breathtaking view of the city, the coastal landscape with the islands of Askøy and Sotra, and all the way outto the open sea is offered from 319m/1047ft-high Fløyen – especially in the mornings and at sunset – which can either be reached in 8mins (every half hour) by the Fløibanen cable car or via a 3km/2mi footpath. | **Jewel of the north**

Until the building of the Bergen railway line from Oslo in 1908 (►MARCO POLO Insight p.444), it was very hard to reach the city overland. Countless tunnels were blasted into the rockin order to connect the city to the road network that for the longest time was focused exclusively on the sea. Norway's second city is the most important port along the west coast, with an impressive merchant fleet and several large dockyards, aswell as being home to the country's second-largest university with 12,000 students. Thanks to the moist and unusually mild climate, almost all centralEuropean deciduous trees and a richly varied flora survive here, despite the location at 60° northern latitude. The flipside of this, however, is that Bergen is renowned for its persistent heavy rain (2000mm annually, compared with approx. 750mm inOslo). The city is the starting point for the ►Hurtigrutenshipping route (MARCO POLO Insight p.247). | **Renowned for constant rain**

The oldest quarters of the cityform a semicircle around Vågen harbour, busy with shipping traffic, and also stretch along the northeastern slopes of Fløyen. Bergen was repeatedly destroyed by devastating fires, so that few of the original buildings survived. Stone buildings and wide roads characterize the city centre today. Nordnes quarter and those on Fløyen hill, where wooden houses and narrow lanes (called »smug« by the locals) predominate, are popular destinations for city walks. ***Gamle Bergen** In the northern quarter of Sandviken (Nyhavnsveien 4) in a park directly on the fjord, more than 50 17th– | **Historic buildings a rarity**

Bergen

INFORMATION
Bergen Turistinformasjon
Vågsallmenningen 1
Tel. 55 55 20 00
www.visitbergen.com

BERGEN CARD
Parking is only permitted in Bergen for a fee, and then only in marked spaces. The Bergen Card, valid for 24hrs or 48hrs (adults 200/260 NOK, children 75/100 NOK), allows free travel on local public transport, reduced admission into the town's attractions, discounts on theatre and cinema tickets as well as a 30% reduction at the Byggarasjen car park.

SHOPPING
There are numerous shops to the southwest of the market square, including the Galleriet shopping centre. Attractive little shops and arts and crafts places can also be found in Lille Øvegate.

Oleana
Strandkaien 2a
The impulse-buy by Michelle Obama made this Norwegian knitwear firm world famous.

Fish market
❶ Market square: June–Aug daily from 7am–5pm, Sat till 4pm, otherwise Mon–Sat 7am–4pm.

FESTIVALS
May/June: Bergen International Festival, Northern Europe's largest music festival (www.fib.no).
Mid-May–early June: Night Jazz Festival (nattjazz.no).
Mid-July–mid-Sep: medieval plays by Hanseatic Theatre (www.bergenbyspill.no).
Beginning of Sep: Bergen Food Festival (www.matfest.no).
Oct: International Film Festival (www.biff.no).
Nov/Dec: Holberg Days Baroque Music (www.holbergdagene.uib.no).

EXCURSIONS
The »Coast Bergen« offers waterbourne sightseeing tours of the inner harbour and skerrie landscape off Bergen. Around 80 passengers can be accommodated on the 23m/75ft boat that sets sail on the hour every hour. Special dinner cruises for up to 60 passengers include fish and seafood dishes (www.visitbergen.com).
Bergen is also the starting point for a whole variety of short tours into the surrounding fjord landscape. One that combines the railway and a ferry is called »Norway in a Nutshell«; a trip on the Bergen Railway Line (►MARCO POLO Insight, p.444) is just as much a must as a cruise on the Aurlandfjord and the Nærøyfjord (www.fjord-tours.com).

WHERE TO EAT
❷ *Lucullus Restaurant* £ £ £ £
Valkendorfsgt. 8
Tel. 55 30 68 00
French-inspired cuisine and a large selection of wines is presented by Fredrik Hald, voted Chef of the Year in 2001, in this gourmet restaurant at the Neptun Hotel. The artworks in the restaurant make for an elegant atmosphere. Closed Sundays.

**❹ Enhjørningen
Fiskerestaurant £ £ £ £**
Bryggen
Tel. 55 32 79 19
Those wishing to dine in this historic and
excellent fish restaurant should be sure
to book ahead. During the summer, they
also offer a somewhat expensive cold
fish and seafood buffet.

❸ Holbergstuen £ £ £
Torgallmenningen 6
Tel. 55 55 20 55
www.holbergstuen.no
Norwegian specialties and small dishes
at acceptable prices can be found at this
traditional tavern dating from 1929,
decorated with richly coloured rose
painting and quotes from Ludvig Holberg on the walls.

**❺ Bryggen Tracteurstend
£ £ £**
Bryggestredet 2
Tel. 55 33 69 99
www.bellevue-restauranter.no
Norway's oldest restaurant serves typical
national and Hanseatic dishes. From
11am between May and September, the
small beer garden opens. Hanseatic culinary evenings are also organised for
groups of 30 people and up.

❼ Bølgen & Moi £ £ £
Rasmus Meyer allé 9
Tel. 55 59 77 00
Exquisite cuisine in the Bergen Art Mu-
seum; closed Sun and Mon.

**❶ Café Opera £ £
Engen 18
Tel. 55 23 03 15
www.cafeopera.org**
The old wooden house painted white

opposite the theatre is a popular haunt
for both young and old, for journalists
and students, and for local residents.
Good coffee and unpretentious small
dishes, live music and readings.

❻ Fløien Folkerestaurant £ – £ £
Fløyfjellet 2
Tel. 55 33 69 99   Insider
www.bellevuerestauranter.no   Tip
Don't miss the sunset from the restaurant and café with the best view of Bergen and its surroundings. The café
serves delicious snacks such as waffles,
cake and soups.

WHERE TO STAY
**❹ Grand Hotel
Terminus £ £ £ £**
Zander Kaaesgt. 6
Tel. 55 21 25 00
www.grandterminus.no, 131 rooms.
The Grand Hotel was built near to the
train station in 1928 and has won prizes
for its architecture. The interior décor of
its rooms and salons is stylish and the
café is one of the best on the Norwegian fjord coast.

**❶ Clarion Collection Hotel
Havnekontoret £ £ £ £**
Slottsgaten 1
Tel. 55 60 11 00
www.choicehotels.no, 116 rooms.
Lilac opulence complete with chandeliers
and velvet meets cool Nordic design: a
stylish mix that has been housed in a
1920s mansion near Bryggen since
2006. Free for resident guests: waffles
and dinner snack.

❸ Det Hanseatiske Hotel £ £ £ £
Finnegården 2a
Tel. 55 30 48 00

www.dethanseaiskehotell.no, 16 rooms. Where once Hanseatic merchants stored their goods, guests sleep in fine cotton and dine under rustic beams.

❺ Sandviken Brygge £ £
Sandviksveien 94
Tel. 55 39 61 00
www.sbhotel.no, 45 rooms.
New hotel with a highly modern interior of pleasant, light colours, situated on the fjord, just 2km/1.2mi from the city centre. The hotel also has a good spa.

❷ Citybox £ £
Nygårdsgaten 31
Tel. 55 31 25 00
www.citybox.no

Centrally located, clean and stylish, with five types of rooms: single or family, you will get value for money and a good night's sleep.

❻ Lone Camping £ £
Hardangerveien 697
Haukeland
Tel. 55 39 29 60
www.lonecamping.no
The largest and most attractive camp site in the area around Bergen, on route 580, 19km/12mi from the city centre. Direct access to a lake, with the Liafjell as a backdrop. Facilities include tents, mobile homes, 18 cabins of varying sizes, motel with 18 apartments, restaurant and canoe rental.

19th-century wooden houses have been grouped together to form the open-air Old Bergen Museum.

Old Bergen Museum: May–Sep Mon–Sat 11am–3pm; Sun 10am–4pm; park open all year; 70 NOK; www.gamlebergen.no

History
Olav Kyrre elevated the already important harbour settlement of Bjørgvin (»hillside meadow«) to town status in around 1070, after which the **occasional royal residence** developed quickly. In 1233, Håkon Håkonsson's right to the throne was recognized during a national assembly here. Germans had already settled in Bergen by 1236, and the town's real heyday was thanks to the **Hanseatic Bureau** first mentioned in 1343. A codicilissued by the Danish kings had ensured that no trade in fish was permitted north of Bergen. Thus all northern fishermen had to transport their catches down to Bergen on dangerous sea journeys and the German merchants were able to dominate the entire Norwegian trade. Cereals, salt and beer were traded against stockfish (dried fishwith no salt) from the Lofoten Islands and dried salt cod from Kristiansund. The Hanseatic Germans lived in a separate district near theGerman bridge, where 16 long and narrow »courtyards« stretched out to serve as both homes and warehouses. Each courtyard was run by a »byggherre« and had several quarters (»stuer«) that each belonged to a different individual. The might of the Hanseatic League was broken in 1559, though the accounting bureau continued for around another 200 years, until the last »stuer« was sold to a Norwegian

Bergen

N

Nordnes-
parken

Aquarium

Skolegrunnskaien

250 m
825 ft
©BAEDEKER

Skuteviken

Gamle Bergen

Nordnesbakken

Nordnesveien

Nordnesgaten

Haugeveien

NORDNES

Tolbu-
almenning

C Sundtsgaten

Strandt.

Long
distance
ferries

Fishing
Museum

Bergenhus

Vågen

Håkons-
halle

Rosenkrantz
Tower

Sandviksveien

Jerlhskaten

Nykirken

Nyk. alm.

gaten

C Sundtsgaten

Slottsgaten

Sandbrugaten

St Mary's
Church

Bryggen-
Museum

Schøt-
stuene

Puddefjorden

almenning

Vågen

Holbergs.

Klostergaten

Skottegaten

Nostegaten

Ø. Muralm.

Strandgaten

Valkendorfsvg.

Bryggen

Øvregaten

Catamarans

Cruise and
tour boats

Fish
Market

Hanseatic
Museum

Vetrlidsalm.

Fløi-
banen

Nostegaten

Sjøgaten

Professor Hansteens Gate

Teatergaten

Rosenbergsgaten

Engen

Vaskerelven

Håkons Gate

Neumanns Gate

Theatre

Chr. Michelsens-
gaten

Ole Bulls Plass

Torgalmenningen

Strandgaten

torget

Stock
market

Kors-
kirken

Town Hall

Cathedral

Oscars Gate

Kong

Steinkjeller

Fløyen

Marken

Nygaten

Kaigaten

Johannes-
kirken

University

Hurtigruten
quay

Dokkeveien

Vestre Torg Gate

Olav Kyrres Gate

Chr. Gate

Pauls-
kirken

Fosswinckelsgaten

Arts and
Crafts Museum

Municipal
Art Museum

Meyers
Collection

Nygårdsgaten

Festplassen

Fest-
plassen

Lille Lunge-
gårds vann

Kaigaten

Jørgens-
kirken

Leprosy
Museum

University
Collections

Grieg
Hall

Seafaring
Museum

Nygårdsgaten

Parkveien

Rasmus Meyers vei

H. Holmboes gate

Strömgaten

Gate

Railway
Station
Library

Bus
Station

Chr. Kaae gate

Where to eat
1 Café Opera
2 Lucullus Restaurant
3 Holbergstuen
4 Enhjørningen

Fiskerestaurant
5 Bryggen Tracteursted
6 Fløien Folkerestaurant
7 Bølgen & Moi

Where to stay
1 Clarion Collection Hotel
  Havnekontoret
2 Citybox
3 Det Hanseatiske Hotel

4 Grand Hotel Terminus
5 Sandviken Brygge
6 Lone Camping

in 1764. Bergen also suffered considerable losses during the **Second World War**, including the old theatre on Sverres gate – Norway's first stage – which had been inaugurated by the famous violinist Ole Bull in 1851. Ibsen was thedirector there from 1851–57, and his successor was Bjørnson, in the position from 1858–60 (▶Famous People).

WHAT TO SEE AROUND VÅGEN HARBOUR

Fish! Bergen's wealth has always been founded on seafaring and the trade in fish. Even in the 17th century, Bergen was significantly more important as a trading location than Copenhagen and by the beginning of the 19th century the city still had more inhabitants than Kristiania (now Oslo). Bergen was to remain Norway's most important fish trading centre until modern times, even if today the large fishing multinationals and canning factories nearer the fishing grounds have allowed other fish trading centres to flourish.

*Fish market The heart of the city is the **market square** (Torget) in the middle of the main Vågen harbour area, at whose landing stages the fishing boats land their catches each morning. The large selection of various types of seafood, freshly cooked shrimps, red lobsters, salmon and caviar is a joy for the eyes and palate – though the prices charged at the picturesque fish market are impressive too. A statue by John Börjeson of the local Bergen poet **Ludvig Holberg** (1684–1754),cre-

The Bergen Hanseatic Museum also shows how people used to sleep

ator of Danish-Norwegian comedy theatre, stands at the south-eastern side of the marketsquare. The former **stock market** lies behind the statue, today home to the tourist information office. At the upper end of the Vetrlidsallmenning, which leads off the market in a northeasterly direction, the **base station of the Fløibahn cable car service** canbe found.

At the northern side of Vågen harbour, beginning at the market, stands the Bryggen (formerly also known as the Tyskebryggen = »German Bridge«). It got its name because the wooden houses used for loading and unloading ships stood directly at the harbour basin. This is where the »courts« of the German merchants once stood, later to be replaced by the stone warehouses whose architecture recalls the era of the Hanseatic League. The merchant houses and warehouses were rebuilt after the great fire of 1702. Today these colourfully painted wooden houses are on the **UNESCO World Heritage List** of cultural sites worthy of preservation (▶photo p.142).

**Bryggen

Only the first trading hall (the Finnegården) at the front on the square or »torg« survives in its original form, and this building has housed the Hanseatic Museum since 1872. Even though it was rebuilt after the fire of 1708, the Finnegården is an outstanding example of the traditional architecture of the early Hanseatic era. The squat, dark rooms with their small windows recall a ship's hull. The museum gives a good idea of the Hanseatic court interiors. The exhibits include weapons, household goods and pieces of equipment, mostly from the 18th century. The ground floor was once the warehouse and the first floor contained the manager's office, as well as the dining room and bedroom. The second floor contains the »klever«, the dormitories for the apprentices and market helpers. Take a look at the collection of the Hanseatic city seals, whose independence was confirmed by these official markings. Many seals contain images of ships that reflect the art of shipbuilding at that time.

*Hanseatic Museum

?	Rune inscriptions

MARCO ⊕ POLO INSIGHT

The Bryggens Museum owns the world's largest collection of rune inscriptions in wood. They appear to have been in use until the 14th century. Around 500 examples were unearthed during excavations in the city between 1955 and 1972.

❶ mid-May–mid-Sep daily 9am–5pm, otherwise Tues–Sat 11am–2pm, Sun till 4pm; 60 NOK; www.museumvest.no).

The Bryggens Museum displays archaeological finds from medieval Bergen. The basement floor contains the oldest fragments of urban settlement from the 12th century. The **Bryggen Ship**, originally a 30m/33yd-long and 10m/11yd-wide merchant ship,can be seen in

Bryggens Museum

the cultural historical exhibition entitled »The Medieval City – Bergen around the year 1300«. Furthermore, traditional trades are illustrated, including those of cobblers, comb makers, coopers and goldsmiths.

❶ mid-May–Aug daily 10am–4pm, otherwise Mon–Fri 11am–3pm, Sat noon–3pm, Sun till 4pm; 60 NOK; www.bymuseet.no

*St Mary's Church

Close to the Bryggens Museum stands the twin-spired Romanesque-Gothic St Mary's Church (Mariakirken), which dates from the 12th and 13th centuries and is the city's oldest building. It is very well preserved and has been incontinuous service since the early Middle Ages. The church belonged to the Hanseatic League between 1408 and 1766 and sermons were held in German until 1868. Tombs in the choir recall the German merchants, seamen and priests laid to rest here between the 15th and 17th centuries. Much about this parish church resembles a cathedral,and the architectural style is that of a basilica.

The impressive, colourful **interior** dates predominantly from the 17th century. The winged altar in the choir is the oldest piece in the church and was built by north German masters in the 15th century, and repainted in the 17th century. The magnificent ***pulpit** is unique in Norway and was probably a gift from German merchants at the end of the 17th century. The canopy with its twelve astrological signs is topped by a Christ figure. The pulpit itself displays eight female statues with a variety of adjuncts that illustrate **fundamental Christian virtues**: repentance (with pelican), wisdom (with snake), the bare truth, chastity (with two doves), patience (with lamb), hope (with dove and parts of an anchor), faith (with the book and cross) and love (with two children).

Schøtstuene

Opposite the church, at Øvregate 50, are the Schøtstuene. These were the Bryggen's only heated rooms during the winter and therefore meeting rooms of the German merchants, for no fire or candlelight was permitted in the merchant houses due to the risk of fire.

❶ daily 9am–5pm

Bergenhus fortress

The northwestern continuation of theBryggen is the Festnings quay with the old **Bergenhus fortress**. King Øystein Magnusson moved his royal court (built of wood) onto »Holmen« (»island«) as early as the 12th century. King Håkon Håkonsson then had the wood structures gradually replaced by solid stone buildings and had the entire royal residence encircled by a protective wall from the 13th century onwards. Military equipment is still on show today.

*Rosenkrantz Tower

At the southern end of the fortress, directly by the quay, stands the Rosenkrantz Tower named after the castle captain Erik Rosenkrantz,

Highlights Bergen

who combined twoolder installations into one and gave it a Renaissance façade between 1562 and 1567.The most historic core of the
building was King Magnus's square residential fortified tower (1273)
known as the »Fortress by the Sea«. The king's bedroom and the
chapel with a soapstone altar date from that time. The tower was restored around 1520 by the castle captain Jørgen Hanssøn, who added
a barbican. The Rosenkrantz Tower was extensively damaged during
the explosion of a German munitionsship in 1944, and later rebuilt.
The tower exhibition rooms display a model of the fortress Bergenhus, swords and uniforms, and there is also a nice view of the entire
city from here.

❶ May–Aug daily 10am–4pm, otherwise Sun noon–3pm

Behind the Rosenkrantz Tower stands Håkon Hall,which was built
by King Håkon Håkonsson between 1247 and 1261 to commemorate
the wedding and coronation of his son Magnus Lagabøte. It was
modelled on English Gothicstone halls. It is **Norway's largest medieval secular building**. After the royal court moved away from
Bergen in thelate Middle Ages, the hall increasingly fell into ruin and
was used as a warehouse.It was restored at the end of the 19th century, but during the explosion of theGerman munitions ship in the
harbour in 1944, the hall burnt down to its foundations. It was
opened to the public in 1961, the seven hundredth jubilee of King
Magnus' coronation. Concerts, state receptions and other official fes-

Håkon Hall

tive events take place in the large festival hall whose beautiful wood vaulting recalls a Viking ship.

Fishing Museum

A good overview of the Norwegian fishing industry can be obtained at the Fishery Museum (Fiskerimuseet) at the Bontelabo, near the landing quay for ferries from Iceland and the Faroe Islands.

● May–Sep daily 11am–4pm; 50 NOK; www.museumvest.no

*Aquarium

Nordnes Park (good views) lies in the northwest of the city, at the tip of the Nordnes spit between Vågen and Puddefjord. In the park is Bergen Aquarium, one of **northern Europe's largest aquariums** and definitely worth a visit. A particular attraction is the feeding of the seals and penguins that swim in the giant pool in the museum courtyard.

● May–Aug daily 9am–7pm, otherwise 10am–6pm; Summer entrance fee: 200 NOK; www.akvariet.no

Pretty as a piture: Bergen in the sun as seen from Fløyen

SOUTH OF THE MARKET

Many day trippers restrict themselves to the sights along Vågen har- City centre
bour, but a stroll around the streets to the southwest of the market,
where most shops, including the attractive **Galleriet shopping centre** are located, is also worthwhile. Beyond lies the municipal park
with a statue by Ingebrigt Vik of the composer **Edvard Grieg** (1843–
1907), who was born in Bergen. Another **memorial** for a famous
citizen of Bergen can befound on the long Ole Bulls Plass, namely the
statue of the »violin king« Ole Bull (▶Around Bergen) created by
Stephan Sinding in 1901. Norway's oldest theatre stands on the western side of the square. It is called Nasjonale Scene, and was built in
the art nouveau style between 1906 and 1909.

Kong Oscars gate leads southeast from the northern end of the mar- Cathedral
ket, past the Korskirke, originally dating from the 12th century and
rebuilt in the Renaissance style in 1593, to the cathedral, which was
originally built in 1248 as a monastery church in Romanesque style.
It was given a60m/66yd-long Gothic choir in 1537. The beautiful
Gothic windows and the altar that recall a medieval reliquary shrine
are considered the cathedral's most noteworthy features.

Following Kong Oscars gate further out of the city, one of Bergen's Leprosy
most beautiful wooden buildings is reached, the Danckert Krohns Museum
Stiftelse, built in the style of an 18th century Danish mansion. Op-
posites tands the small Leprosy Museum, which gives an insight into
Norway's contribution to the international leprosy research programme.

❶ mid-May–mid-Aug, daily 11am–3pm, July till 4pm; www.bymuseet.no

The architecturally interesting **Grieg Hall**, in which concerts, operas Bergen art
and ballets are performed, stands to the south of the Lille Lungegårds- collections
vann lake, on Strømgate.Nearby, at Rasmus Meyers Allé 7, is the **art
collection** donated by the businessman **Rasmus Meyer** with paintings by Norwegian artists from between 1814 and 1914, such as J. C.
Dahl, H. Gude, E. Munch, and G. Munthe. The collection is managed
by the Bergen Art Museum.
Next door, at Rasmus Meyers Allé 3, the **City Art Museum** exhibits
Norwegian painting (J. C. Dahl, E. Munch) and European art. The
building also houses the Bergen Art Society which presents temporary exhibitions of contemporary art and the **Stenersen Collection**,
with works by Munch, Picasso and Klee.

❶ daily 11am–5pm, mid-Sep–Mid-May closed Mon

Arts and
Crafts
Museum

Rare ceramics, Bergen gold jewellery and modern Norwegian arts
and crafts are shown at the Vestlandske Kunstindustrimuseum (»Per-

manenten«), located around 200m/220yd further on, at the southern edge of the municipal park.

University collections

University collections on the subject of natural history can be reached by following Christies gate south, past the Catholic Church of St Paul and up Sydneshaugen hill, where the university buildings can be found by the Botanical Garden. Right next door is the **Seafaring Museum** with curiosities and illustrations of life on the ocean wave.

AROUND BERGEN

Hiking on Fløyen

A road (30mins on foot) leads from the basestation for the Fløyen cable cars via the increasingly barren mountain plateau to the foot of Blåmann (551m/1808ft) to the northeast. From there a footpath can be followed to the peak, which offers an attractive panoramic view, especially with evening lights. The ascent of the somewhat higher peak behind is frankly not worth the effort. The road also continues on to the radio station on Rundemann (556m/1824ft). There are nice

The composer Edvard Grieg lived and worked in Troldhaugen

views along Fjellvei half way up the side of Fløyen, and a rest stop can be made at the Bellevue restaurant at the southeastern end of the footpath, about 25mins from the Fløyen cable car station.

En route to Troldhaugen, 6km/4mi south of the city centre in a small-forest, stands the Fantoft stave church, which can be reached by buses 19, 20 and 21from the terminal. Originally constructed in Fortun on the Sognefjord in 1150, the church was moved to Fantoft in 1883. It was rebuilt after being totally destroyed byfire in 1992.

Fantoft stave church

❶ daily 10.30am–6pm.

Follow the sign for Troldhaugen, Edvard Grieg's home (▶Famous People) after another 2km/1.2mi. In the house, the foundation of Bergen's claim to being Norway's cultural capital, the life and work of the world famous composer canbe explored. Edvard and Nina Grieg only managed to realize their dream of having their own home after eighteen years of marriage. They moved into the villa in 1885,which was built in the style of a Victorian mansion, though its bare interior woodwalls recall Norwegian farmhouses. Troldhaugen (Troll's Hill) was named after asmall ravine not far from the house that is known to locals as »Troll'sValley«. The original interior can still be found in the dining room and the livingroom. Among the numerous presents that

*Troldhaugen

? MARCO ⊕ POLO INSIGHT

Self-taught success

Though the world famous violin virtuoso and composer Ole Bornemann Bull never received systematic violin tuition, he gave his debut performance at the age of nine. A life changing event occurred when he went to Paris in 1930 and met Paganini, on whose style he based his own playing. He achieved international success and his fellow Norwegians celebrated him as a national hero.

Grieg received is the Steinway grand piano, given to the couple on the occasion of their silver wedding anniversary by Bergen fans of his music. Grieg practiced undisturbed in the »**composer's cabin**« down the slope. The 1.52m/5ft tall composer's final resting place is in a rock face at the lake. Grieg concertsare presented in the new Troldsalen concert hall during the summer.

❶ For opening times and concert programme see www.kunstmuseene.no; tickets at www.billettservice.no (lunch and evening concerts, as well as private concerts and song events are possible)

On a clear day, a wide panoramic view can be enjoyed from the highest of Bergen's seven hills, the Ulriken (643m/2110ft), which stands to the southeast of the outskirts of the city. The base station of the Ulriksbanen cablecar can be reached in a few minutes via the double decker buses departing from the city centre every half an hour. The ascent to the summit takes two hours on foot.

Ulriken

Lysøen   Another famous Norwegian lived just under 30km/19mi south of Bergen, on the little island of Lysøen :namely the **eccentric violinist and composer Ole Bornemann Bull**. He was born in Bergen in 1810 and died here in 1880. He had his villabuilt between 1872 and 1873 which, with its onion domes and Moorish style elements,evokes a »fairy tale castle«. The eccentric style of the owner is also reflected in the castle's unusual interior. The villa can only be reached by boat: from Sørstraumen every hour on the hour

Villa Bull: May–Aug Mon–Sat noon–4pm, Sun 11am–5pm, Sep Sun noon–4pm

Lyse monastery   The ruins of Norway's first Cistercian monastery, founded by monks from Yorkin 1146, can be found nearby. Lyse monastery was Norway's largest until the Reformation. The ruins were excavated between 1822 and1838, and today they provide an insight into monastic life during the Middle Ages.

Hardanger-fjord   ▶Hardangerfjord

Bodø

──────────────────────────────── ✳ K 11

Region: North Norway
Population: 48,400

────────────────────────────────

Bodø makes a good base for visits to the Lofoten Islands, though due to the devastation wreaked during the Second World War, the city itself is hardly idyllic. Nearby, the historic market town of Kjerringøy is worth a detour – and not only forfans of Knut Hamsun – while the tidal river of Saltstraumen is an impressive naturalphenomenon.

Military base   Most tourists only make the 60km/37mi detour from the main E 6 in the direction of Nordkapp to the port of Bodø if they want to catch a ferry to the Lofoten Islands. The city is home to northern Norway's most important military air force base. Bodø is also an important traffic hub and the final destination for the Nordland rail route from Trondheim. The town gained its municipal charter in 1816, but it wasonly herring fishing during the second half of the 19th century that accelerated development. Today Bodø is a lively trading town with a busy harbour. Ferries to the ▶Lofoten Islands and the ▶Hurtigruten boats land here, and anairport offers connections to the Scandinavian airline network. Thanks to numerousmusic festivals, Bodøis not short on culture, and is considered to be the »**music capital of northern Norway**« thanks to the contemporary Nordland Music

Festival (www.nmfu.no) and the Parken Rock Festival (www.parken-festivalen.no) that both take place in August.

WHAT TO SEE IN AND AROUND BODØ

The town hall was completed in 1959, and there is a fine view from its tower. It stands on the town hall square (Rådhusplassen).The nearby **cathedral** (1956) is impressive, particularly its interior of beautiful painted glass by Aage Storstein. Finds from prehistoric and medieval times, as well as exhibitions on agriculture, fishing and arts and crafts are shown at the **Nordland County Museum** (Nordland fylkesmuseum), to the south of the cathedral. Of particular interest are the displays on the hard life of the so-called »fish farmers«, who were forced to work both the land and the sea to make ends meet; also the »Bodø silver hoard« that was hidden near today's city centre, about 1000 years ago, and rediscovered in 1919. Next to coins and Arabian jewellery, it also contains the largest Viking or Iron Age brooch ever found. The city's most interesting sight is the Norwegian FlightCentre, opened in 1996, **Norwegian Flight Centre** which offers an overview of the history of Norwegian and international airborne transport. Among the attractions are the only JU 52 water aeroplane in the world, and an American U 2 spy plane. The museum also has a **flight simulator.**

Town centre

Nordland County Museum: June–Sep Mon–Fri 11am–6pm, Sat–Sun till 4pm, otherwise Mon–Fri 9am–3pm; 40 NOK; www.saltenmuseum.no
Norwegian Flight Centre: June–Aug daily 10am–6pm; otherwise Mon–Fri 10am–4pm, Sat–Sun 11am–5pm; 110 NOK; www.luftfart.museum.no

Idyllic port at Bodø with an impressive mountain backdrop

Bodø

INFORMATION
Destinasjon Bodø
Tollbugata 13
8001 Bodø
Tel. 75 54 80 00
www.visitbodo.com

FESTIVAL
One of northern Norway's largest annual cultural festivals is during the first half of August: the Nordland Music Festival offers every kind of music, from classical to pop and jazz (www.nmfu.no).

WHERE TO EAT
Blix Restaurant £ £ £
Sjøgata 25, Tel. 75 54 70 99
www,blixrestaurant.no
A restaurant in 1960s style housed in the Hotel Rica. The seafood dishes are recommended. Closed Sunday.

Kafé Kafka £
Sadgata 5b
Tel. 93 40 60 03
An institution in Bodø since 1998. An original cultural and literary café with a cosy interior. The kitchen offers a good cross section of the world's delicacies, as well as tasty homemade cakes. Closed Sunday.

WHERE TO STAY
Radisson Blu £ £ £ £
Storgata 2
Tel. 75 51 90 00
www.radissonblue.com, 190 rooms.
Hotel tower with panoramic views, especially from the top floor bar, in the town centre. The rooms are comfortable and pleasingly decorated in various styles.

Kjerringøy Rorbusenter £ £
Tårnvik
(20km/13mi north of Kjerringøy)
Tel. 75 58 50 07
www.kjerringoy.info
These fishermen's cabins in a wonderful off-the-beaten-track location are very comfortable and right on the water. Large sauna and open-air swimming, good fishing and hiking opportunities too.

Kjerringøy Parish House £
Amtmann Worsøes gt. 28a
Tel. 75 50 77 10
www.kjerringoy.info, 8 rooms.
The listed old parish building in Kjerringøy, dating from 1889, has been a simple hostel for the past 25 years.

Rønvikfjell A broad panoramic view can be enjoyed from Rønvikfjell (155m/508ft; tourist cabin), around 4km/3mi north of Bodø. From there, it is about another two hours by marked footpath to the summit of **Løpsfjell** (603m/1978ft), from which there is a good view towards the 100km/62mi distant mountain chain of the Lofoten Islands; to the east, glacier-covered **Sulitjelma** (1913m/6276ft) is visible, which is 90km/56mi away near the Swedish border. To the left is **Blåmannsis**, with its néve fields (expanses of compacted snow) reaching a height of 1571m/5154ft.

The coastal road north leads to Geitvågen, the most beautiful sandy beach north of the Arctic Circle. The midnight sun in Geitvågen is one of the annual highlights formany inhabitants of Bodø.

Geitvågen

The old trading centre of Kjerringøy and one of northern Norway's most important commercial centres in the 19thcentury, is 40km/25mi north of Bodø. An interesting overview of life and tradinghabits along the Norwegian coast is offered by the **open-air museum**. There are 15 buildings, including a domestic house inEmpire style, a general store, a post office and a pub. The beautiful filmDina – My Story by Ole Bornedal was partly filmed here atthe open-air museum of Kjerringøy. Based on a novel by Herbjørg Wassmo, the filmtells the dramatic story of Dina, a young woman in the Norway of 1860. The shopkeeper K. Zahl had his shop in Kjerringøy, where a certain Knud Pedersen from the island of Hamarøy began his apprenticeship. The apprentice later called himself Knut Hamsun (▶Famous People), after hisparents' farm on the Hamsund farming estate. Born in Gudbrandsdal, he came to Nordland when he was three years old. The impressions he gathered here during hischildhood and youth are recorded in his novel

Kjerringøy

> ? | *City of sea eagles*
>
> **MARCO ⬤ POLO INSIGHT**
>
> Bodø boasts the largest population of sea eagles in Europe and the majestic birds, which nest near local waters,can often be seen gliding over the town. There is even a monument to the sea eagle in the pedestrian precinct.

entitled *Benoni and Rosa* (1908). Kjerringøy is called »Sirilund« in Knut Hamsun's writings, and K. Zahl the shopkeeper is portrayed in the main character of Mack in his novel entitled *Pan* (1894). Several of his novels have been filmed on location here. The house in which Hamsun grew up is now a museum containing a small exhibition on his life story. Near the open-air museum is the Zahlfjøsen **cultural centre**, where visitors can view a weaving workshop, a boat-building workshop, a gallery and various arts and crafts. Excerpts from around 20 films inspired by Hamsun's work can be seen on the first floor.

Open-Air Museum: End of May–end of Aug daily 10am–5pm; 90 NOK; www.nordlandsmuseet.no

Hamsun House: mid-June–Mid-Aug daily 11am–6pm; fast boat service between Bodø and Skutvik, followed by a short bus journey.

It is worthwhile taking an excursion 35km/22mi east to the Saltstraumen **tidal waters**. 2km/1mi long, about 150m/164yd wide and up to50m/164ft deep, the Saltstraumen connects the Saltfjord with the Skjerstadfjord between the islands of Straumen and Straumøy. Each time the tide turns, around 370million cubic metres of water is squeezed through the narrow gap, creating **rapids and whirlpools** (tide tables are available from the tourist information office). Numer-

Saltstrau-men

ous fishermen try their luck here. In 1998, a leisure park was opened complete with restaurants, a camp site, a hotel and souvenir shops, so it gets pretty busy. The Saltstraumen Experience Centre illustrates the region's 10,000-year old cultural history and includes a multimedia show. The largest fish ever caught here was a 32.7kg/72.1lb cod.

Fauske Renowned for its marble, Fauske lies about 65km/41mi from Bodø on the E 6. The red marble from here was used for the buildings of the UN in New York, as well as for Oslo city hall. The bus to ▶Nordkapp (2 days) and ▶Kirkenes (3–4 days) departs from Fauske. Those travelling by train will have to change onto buses here, as Bodø is the end of the line.

RAGO NATIONAL PARK

Small, but special Located north of Bodø between the E 6 and the Swedish border, the Rago National Park covers an area of only 171 sq km/66 sqmi. To the east, the Swedish parks of Padjelanta and Sarek adjoin. By car the park is reached by leaving the E 6 at Nordfjord to the north of Fauske and parking at Lakshola village. Rago is among the wildest and most remote regions of northern Norway and many rare plants thrive on the nutrient-poor granite surfaces of the mountains there. With luck, you might spot a wolverine around Mount Rago (1312m/4304ft), whose southern flank is lined by the Rágujiekna Glacier. Elk and beavers live in the Laksåga Valley filled by tall pine forest. Accommodation can be found in two unserviced mountain cabins: the Storskogvasshytta on the lake of the same name, and the Ragohytta, about 1km/0.6mi from the Swedish border; and there is also the Øvereng campsite at the end of the branch road to Lakshola (tel. 75 69 65 40).

Storskog valley The main artery through the park is the Storskog valley, with the Trolldals river and the impressive Trollfoss. Waterfalls tumble through moist, green pine forests that climb several hundered metres up the slopes of the mountains. Snow and ice fields begin at elevations as low as 1000m/3281ft.

Hiking in the national park The hiking tour from Laksholaleads east, initially through the valley and then slowly upwards into the mountains. Past the park's only cabin (accommodation free), the path follows the old route to Sweden that was once used by the Sami to herd reindeer from their summer pastures to their winter ones. To the right rises the barren Rago mountain (1300m/4265ft). Silver and lead were discovered here before the First World War, but the seam was too small and extraction too expensive to make mining worthwhile.

** **Borgund Stave Church**

✦ D 4 ●

Region: Central Norway

Borgund stave church at the entrance to the Lærdal valley is one of the most interesting and beautiful in the country. The dragon heads of the upper gables arespecially noteworthy, as are the two doorways elaborately decorated with carvingsand the almost windowless interior.

This rather small stave church, blackened with tar, was probably constructed as early as 1150. It has been sensitively restored and still exhibits its original design today, baring one window that was cut in at a later date. The roof rises insix levels covered in wooden shingles. Roaring dragon heads reach up into the airfrom the upper gables, recalling ancient heathen traditions. The two doorways are embellished with beautiful ornamentation. The **woodcarvings** of the west doorway is especially magnificent, displaying fighting dragon-like creatures along with leaf motifs.

Stave church

Only the 16th-century pulpit and the altar from the early 17th century survive from the original interior, which appears very dark and sombre. Mighty wooden pillars support the artful roof construction and separate the nave from the lower aisles. The pillars are supported by connecting crossbeams that display carved masks of humans and imaginary animals at their ends. To the south of the stave church between the new and old church stands the **bell tower**; it was rebuilt in the original style around 1660. By the way, this church is among Norway's main tourist attractions and **long waiting periods for permission to enter are sometimes necessary** due to overcrowding. A visitor centre provides information on everything there is to know about Norway's stave churches.

❶ May–Sep daily 10am–5pm, mid-June–Mid-Aug daily 8am–8pm; 75 NOK; www.stavechurch.com

Always popular with visitors: the stave church of Borgund

Masterpieces in Wood

The wooden stave churches (»stavkirker« in Norwegian) are the most famous and original testaments of medieval architectural art in Norway. Of an original number of around 600 of these wooden churches, only 31 have survived the ravages of time to the present day. These architectural treasures are now jealously guarded.

Stave churches are wooden churches with either a single nave or a nave and two aisles, and steep roofs over several levels. They owe their name to the stave building method which, in contrast to a block building with horizontal pillars, utilizes posts anchored into the ground or fixed to

The stave church of Gol today stands in Oslo's open-air museum

an open fixed frame that supports the saddleback roof. Similar to ship construction methods from Viking times, the succession of frames, cleats, and diagonal crosses strengthen the building to such a degree that it can well resist the Nordic storms. Massive round corner posts stabilize the outer wall, which is separate from the church interior. In between the pillars and posts of the interior, built without the use of a single iron nail or iron component, rounded arches ensure the necessary elasticity. The stave church was documented as early as the 9th century, but its heyday was between the 12th and 13th centuries – a period when the emergence of Christianity had also already resulted in the building of stone churches in Scandinavia.

Viking Heritage

Romanesque forms combined with the ancient techniques of building with wood, though ornamentation initially remained entirely bound to the traditions of the Vikings. Artful stylized animal and vine carvings date from this era, whose decorative compositions with motifs from the pre-Christian Edda sagas create a fantastical, almost spooky impression. However, with the emergence of Christianity, this figural sculpture art, considered heathen, was replaced by the more sombre ornamentation of the Norman-style epoch which took contemporary stone buildings as its models. At the same time, the older single-nave design of the main body of churches was supplanted by the basilica style which had an excessively high central nave separated from the aisles by mast-style pillars. While the Roman basilica established itself as the pre-eminent architectural style, the first bishoprics were also established in Norway, where once there had only been missionizing itinerant bishops. Gradually, the wealth of

forms of figural sculpture decoration revived, and the Viking tradition experienced a Renaissance. The heathen ornamentation of the past was exchanged for symbols influenced by European Christianity. Thus the famous »Dragon style« emerged, named after the fear-inspiring dragon heads mounted at the crowns of buildings. Large wall paintings were relatively rare, due to the inadequate lighting conditions.

Stave Churches Today

Around 1300, there are believed to have been over 600 stave churches

A love of detail also shows itself in the carvings of the stave church at Lom

Borgund Stave Church

©BAEDEKER

in Norway. After the plague decimated the Norwegian population by more than half, most of these sacred buildings fell into disrepair and, from the 17th to the 19th century, many churches had become too small for their communities and were demolished, so that only 31 stave churches survive (more or less unchanged) to this day. Most of these wooden churches still stand in their original locations, though some have been moved to other places and rebuilt as museum pieces (see map p.57).

A renewed interest in these sacred buildings developed in the mid-19th century, largely because of the Norwegian painter Johann Christian Dahl, who was a professor at the art academy in Dresden from 1824 onwards and who, after many journeys to his Norwegian homeland, initiated the battle to preserve these unique cultural monuments. He persuaded the Prussian King Friedrich Wilhelm IV to buy the stave church of Vang in Valdres that was first rebuilt on Peacock Island near Berlin, and later in the Karkonosze mountains (also known as the Giant Mountains, bordering Poland and Czech Republic). He thus brought the Norwegian stave church into the limelight.From then on, work began to preserve the remaining sacred buildings, although some restoration efforts resulted in a loss of authenticity: for example, windows were installed where once there would only have been dim lighting provided by small openings high up.Todays surviving stave churches are found in the southern region of Norway, an area that extends from Oslo to Bergen and Trondheim to the north.

Stave Churches in Norway

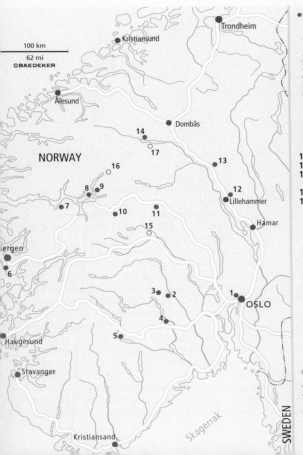

● **Stave churches**
(entirely or partially preserved)

1 Gol (c 1200; Norsk Folkemuseum, Oslo)
2 Nore (late 12th cent., altered)
3 Uvdal (c 1200, altered)
4 Heddal (started in 1147)
5 Eidsborg (c 1150)
6 Fortun (c 1150, Fantoft near Bergen; completely rebuilt after arson)
7 Hopperstad (c 1130)
8 Kaupanger (c 1185)
9 Urnes (from 1100 an; present-day building, 12th/13th cent.)
10 Borgund (c 1150)
11 Lomen (12th cent.)
12 Garmo (Maihaugen near Lillehammer c 1200)
13 Ringebu (from 1220 on)
14 Lom (12th cent.)

○ **Original locations**

15 Gol (dismantled 1884, see no.)
16 Fortun (dismantled 1883, see no. 6)
17 Garmo (dismantled 1885, see no. 12)

Borgund

INFORMATION

Lærdal Touristinformation

Lærdalsøry, town centre

Tel. 57 64 12 07

www.alr.no

GETTING THERE

The famous Borgund stave church is reached via the E 16 coming from Valdres. The idea base for exploring the region around Borgund, especially the Lærdal Valley, is the main settlement of Lærdalsøry. Since 2000, the world's longest road tunnel (24km/15mi) connects Lærdal with Aurland (in a southerly direction), which cuts the journey time along the E 16 to Bergen by several hours.

WHERE TO EAT/STAY

Lindstrøm Hotel £ £

Lærdal, Tel. 57 66 69 00

www.lindstroemhotel.no, 86 rooms. Hotel with an interesting mixture of traditional romance and modern elements. It is also possible to eat well here – albeit expensively. Open early May–end of Sep.

Lærdal Ferie- og Fritidspark £ £

Lærdal, Grandavegen 5

Tel. 57 66 66 95

www.laerdalferiepark.com

Five-star campsite with comfortable cabins, a café and restaurant at the end of the Lærdalfjord.

Lærdal Leaving Borgund, the road leads through the picturesque Svartegjelgorge, which the Lærdalselv, **one of Norway's best-known salmonrivers**, has cut through the rockface of the Vindhella. Another imposing gorge is traversed beyond Husum (316m/1037ft), before finally reaching the sleepy little town of **Lærdalsøyri**. The place was an important fjord port for centuries and British aristocrats came here to fish for salmon from the middle ofthe 19th century. The historic 17th-century town centre with its countless wooden houses is on Norway's national heritage preservation list.

*Villaks- A few years ago, the largest and most impressive of the many **salmon**
senter **aquariums** opened on the banks of the Lærdalselv. Visitors here discover all they ever wanted to know about salmon: their habitats, migration patterns, and the history of salmon fishing (in films and exhibitions). Large display windows in the observatory also offer views of wild salmon and sea trout, while a workshop runs exhibitions on the practicalities of the art of fly fishing.
Villakssenter: mid-May–mid-Sep 10am–5pm, July–mid-Aug till 7pm; 75 NOK; www.norsk-villakssenter.no

To Aurland or To enjoy the breathtaking passage through the Nærøyfjord, those with
Sognefjord time should avoid the tunnel in the direction ofAurland and instead take the ferry operating between Kaupanger (▶Sognefjord) and Gudvangen.

Dovrefjell

E 6

Region: East Norway
Height: 982m–2286m/3222ft–7500ft

The highest mountain of the Dovrefjell range, the imposing Snøhetta, is already easily recongizable from the E 6, which cuts through the Dovrefjell-Sunndalsfjella National Park. Around 300 musk oxen have made themselves at home in this barren mountain landscape carved out during the Ice Age. Rivers, such as the Driva, are suitable for rafting as well as swimming.

Mountains of fur on the fjell: around 300 musk oxen now live in the national park once more

Dovrefjell

INFORMATION
Oppdal Turistkontor
Olaf Skasliensvei 24
(in the centre by the E 6)
7340 Oppdal
Tel. 72 40 04 70
www.oppdal.com

Dombås Turistkontor
2660 Dombås, Postboks 172
Tel. 61 24 14 44
www.dovrenett.no

WATERSPORT AND LEISURE
The Driva River offers many opportunities for kayak trips, from family-friendly tours to white water adventures. Trainded guides also conduct rafting tours; for information contact the tourist office. There are also many leisure activities away from the water: there are five different tours for cyclists; cycle rental costs around 125 NOK per day. Airborne activities include expensive, but spectacular parachute jumps; tandem jumps, including for beginners, and parachuting courses are available; information from the tourist office and at www.fallskjermhopp.no.

Insider Tip

A special experience is a boat tour on the »Trolleimen II« through the Trollheim mountain world via the Gjevilvatn; book via the tourist information.

WHERE TO EAT/STAY
Dombås Hotell £ £ £
Dombås
Tel. 61 24 10 01
http://rica.no/dombas, 78 rooms.
The best and most expensive hotel locally is housed in a large imposing wooden house with modern extensions. Tip: the simple holiday houses behind the hotel are cheaper.

Quality Hotel Oppdal
£ £ £
Oppdal
Olaf Skasliensvei 8
Tel. 72 40 07 00
www.choicehotels.no, 75 rooms.
This traditional hotel primarily attracts mountain walkers. The »Perrongen« restaurant's house specialty: steaks cooked on the wood-fired grill. Round off the meal with a visit to the hotel's English-style pub.

Vangslia Hytter £ £ £
Oppdal
(3 km/2 mi west of the centre)
Tel. 72 40 08 00
Large comfortable wood cabins with fireplaces, a sauna for up to 12 people, and wonderful views.

Kongsvold Fjellstue
£ £ £
Dovrefjell
(south of Oppdal by the E 6/Kongsvold railway station)
Tel. 72 40 43 40
www.kongsvold.no, 32 rooms.
A former stagecoach post dating back to 1720, the Kongsvold Fjellstue is a cosy tavern in the middle of the national park offering simple dishes during the day, including waffles and »smørbrød«. In the evenings, diners can spoil themselves with outstanding elk dishes and an imaginative menu, while the rooms all have their own unmistakable charm.

The change in vegetation on the way to the fjell is remarkable. An   King's road
initially homogenous pine forest becomes ever lighter as it transforms into a birch forest before giving way to the barren highlands.
One of the country's main transport routes was established here during the time of theVikings. Pilgrims and kings alike – the former visiting the tomb of St Olaf in Nidaros (later ▶Trondheim), the latter on
their way to coronations there – had to brave the challenges of crossing the Dovrefjell mountains, which is why this route is also known
as the Kongevegen (king's road).

Fokstua (982m/3221ft) can be reached after 10km/6mi on the E 6   Fokstumyra
from Dombås, crossing Dovrefjell. To the left of the road spreads the
bird-rich moorland of Fokstumyra, a nature reserve. To the right,
there is a view of the Fokstuhø mountain(1716m/5630ft), which can
be climbed in just under three hours. The E 6 follows Lake Vålåsjø, at
the end of which a minor track leads to Dovregubbens Hall (pub and
accommodation).

Then Avsjøen follows to the right, before Hjerkinn (956m/3137ft),   Hjerkinn
10km/6mi further on. Located in a broad highland valley of Dovrefjell, this is the driest place in Norway, with an average rainfall of just
217mm per annum. A restricted military area extends to the west. A
memorial plaque marks the **Kongevegen** (king'sroad), along which
41 ruling monarchs travelled; the road's highest point(1026m/3366ft)
is less than a mile further north. A »culture route« leads from the car
park at Hjerkinn up to an elevation of 1200m/3937ft, where the panoramic viewpoint of the Tverfjellhytta stands: an equally impressive
construction of steel, wood and glass, built in 2011, by the world-famous architectural office of Snøhetta. It was awarded the Best Nordic
Building Award that same year. Those who head northeast on foot,
climbing Hjerkinnhø (1282m/4206ft), which takes about 1.5hrs, are
rewarded withwonderful views of Snøhetta and the mountain chains
of the ▶Rondane and ▶Jotunheimen ranges.

After the E 6 has reached its highest point to the north of Hjerkinn,the   *Dovrefjell-
route descends through the Driva valley to the national park and its   Sunndalsfjel-
alpine plants, musk oxen and wild reindeer. The **Kongsvold Fjell-**   la National
stue (887m/2910ft) is reached after 12km/7mi,by the railway station   Park
of the same name. The University of Trondheim maintains a **bio-**
logical research station here, and th euniversity also established the
small botanical garden with alpine plants, which issituated
700m/770yd behind the mountain hotel. Kongsvold is the starting
point for the ascent of Søndre Knutshø (1690m/5545ft; 3–5hrs) towering upwards to the east, and for hiking paths (4–5hrs) to the Reinheim hut (key kept in Kongsvold), from which it is possible to ascend
Snøhetta (2286m/7500ft) in about four hours.

*Vårstigen   Further down the Driva valley, the road is partly blasted from the rock. 9km/6mi further on, a section of the old Kongsvegen begins to the east of Vårstigen. Today a footpath, this route was firstmentioned in 1182 and offers wonderful views. About 5km/3mi further on, to the right, the Drivstua hut, a former mountain cabin (accommodation option), lies at 680m/2231ft; further on to the left, Åmotsdal valley can be glimpsed.

> **!** *Musk ox safari* **Insider Tip**
>
> **MARCO ⊕ POLO TIP**
>
> Those who don't want to leave encounters with musk oxen to chance can join a guided walking tour. During the high season, there are daily departures from Kongsvold Fjellstue (Tel. 72 40 43 41), which can also be booked via Moschus-Safari Dovrefjell (Tel. 46 42 01 02, www.moskus-safari.no) or at the Dombås tourist information (price per person: 350 NOK).

The sparse birch stands give way to pine forest once more and, around 10km/6mi behind Drivstua,the Driva foams through the Magalaupet flume for 100m/109yd. Shortly afterwards, Iron Age burial mounds are reached at Rise. Smedgarden camp site and Driva railwaystation are within close reach. To the right, a toll-road leads into the beautiful Loseter (1100m/3609ft) mountain landscape. To the northeast stands the1621m/5318ft-high Sissihø mountain, which can be climbed from Oppdal in about five-hours.

Oppdal   The valley broadens out again and to the right, thesteep Ålmenberg (1340m/4396ft) can be ascended from Oppdal in three hours. Skiers are attracted to the Oppdalarea: along with Trysil, this is Norway's largest interconnected ski area, with55km/34mi of downhill pistes. Appropriately, the winter sports resort of Dombås is the birthplace of one of Norway's top biathletes, Tora Berger. The E 6 continues northeast to ▶Trondheim (122km/76mi).

HIKING IN THE FOOTSTEPS OF KINGS

Getting there   The ideal starting point for hiking trips is Kongsvoll stasjon on the rail route between Oslo and Trondheim, reached by car onthe E 6 coming from Dombøs and travelling in the direction of Oppdal. Hjerkinnstation is less suitable, because of the necessity to negotiate a military shootingrange.

Three-day hike   Arrangements for accommodation and getting the key for the Reinheim hut (provisions supplied) should be made in Kongsvoll prior to setting off on this walking tour. The sign-posted track goes directly

The waters of the Driva tempt visitors to genuine laps of courage

from the railway station, and heads west through **Stroplsjødalen**. This section of the national park features the typical fjell vegetation. After around two hours, the track passes Hestgjeterhytta, where horses are grazed during summer. After a further three hours, the day's final destination is reached at Reinheim.

The second day begins with an ascent of **Snøhetta**, the highest mountain of Dovrefjell. This day tour ends at the Reinheim hut once more, so only a light pack is required. The marked route follows the eastern flank of the mountain to its southern peak. The view of Dovrefjell in its entirety is impressive, though somewhat spoilt by the military helicopter landing pad. During the descent across the northern flank, snowfields can be expected, even during summer. The route heads in a northwesterly direction, directly to the main hiking path, marked by a red »T«, that connectsReinheim with Åmotdalshytta. At the junction, a right turn should be taken forthe return to Reinheim and the night's accommodation. The return leg fromReinheim to Kongsvoll is the same as the first day in reverse. Experienced and fithikers can also do this tour of 42km/26mi in two days, or extend it by heading northeast in the direction of Driva from Åmotdalshytta. Camping is possible along the entire route.

Primeval inhabitants of the arctic tundra

Encounters withthe archaic looking musk ox that sometimes cross the hiker's path are unforgettable, though you should always keep at a safe distance. One of the world's largest herds of musk oxen, native to the area since prehistoric times, lives in the 200 sq km/77 sq mi once covered by theDovrefjell National Park (now part of the much larger Dovrefjell-Sunndalsfjella National Park), though the species was only reintroduced to the area with animals from Greenland in 1932, and boosted by more in the 1950s. The original herd of 15 has now expanded to around 300 animals.

✳ **Femundsmarka**

 E 8/9

Region: East Norway

The Femundsmarka region is a thinly populated wilderness near the Swedish border. It is very beautiful here, though lonely – precisely the conditions valuedby certain hikers and canoeists.

Wilderness without roads

Norway's third largest lake, Lake Femund, is 60km/37mi long north–south. It is 150m/492ft deep, and the water temperature is a chilly 12°C/54°F. Most of the region between the eastern banks of the lake and the Swedish border was declared a national park in

Femundsmarka

GETTING THERE
There is no road leading into the national park, but the »Fæmund II« ferry offers a convenient way in. Alternatively, a tour can start off from Elgå or Vardalen on the Norwegian side or from Sylen/Grøvelsjøen on the Swedish side. The »Fæmund II« travels daily during summer (timetable available at Tel. 96 39 20 17 or at www.femund.no).

BOAT HIRE
Femund Canoe Camp
Drevsjø, Sorken
Tel. 62 45 90 19
www.femund-canoe-camp.com
Boats and equipment can be hired at the southern end of the lake, in Fermundsenden. The camp also offers four small cabins for accommodation.

WHERE TO EAT
Bryggeloftet Villmarksrestaurant
£ £
Elgå
Tel. 62 45 95 43
www.bryggeloftet.net
There is a nice view of the lake from this Worden house with a grassed roof. The menu includes elk, reindeer, trout and whitefish, with delicious berries for dessert. The shop also sells freshly caught fish. The guest house offers accommodation; open June–Sep.

WHERE TO STAY
Femund Fjellstue £ – £ £
Elgå
Tel. 62 45 95 41
www.femundfjellstue.no, 12 rooms.
Hotel and camp site is centrally located on the eastern banks of Lake Femund. The Eriksen family ensures a comfortable stay and provides excellent food in the restaurant, where a great deal of game, fish, poultry and berry dishes are served. In addition to hotel rooms, there are also cabins for 4–5 people.

1971. The Femundsmarka National Park (573 sq km/221 sqmi) is a wilderness of mighty spruce trees, boulders, rivers and lakes – and not a single road.

The Femundsmarka region is the southernmost settlement area of the Sami people. The Blokkodden Wilderness Museum near Drevsjø explores their lifestyle as nomads and hunters.

Blokkodden open-air museum

Three-day mountain tour	The starting point for a walking tour that offers insight into the primal environment of the Norwegian fjells is the small settlement of Elgå. Initially, a path marked with the familiar red »T« is followed from the local bus stop, turning off to the right onto a narrow path at the signpost for Revlingkletten. This route soon breaks through the tree line, crossing several little streams, and ascends to the highland plateau where superb views await. Towards the end of the long fjell the path disappears and from this point it is advisable to follow a dried-out river bed in a strictly easterly direction. The route then leads left past a smallish lake. From the lake, the route descends to a transverse valley in which two electrical pylons can be spotted from afar. Here, rejoin the main hiking path that comes from the Svukuriset DNT hut belonging to theNorwegian hiking association. Marked with the red »T«, the main path bears right and there are beautiful camping opportunities all along here.

The route continues east past Mount Storslåga (1344m/4410ft) in the direction of **Valdalen**, where it is possible to stay the night in simple cabins or get a meal. The path from Valdalen leads onwards to Småsjøvollen. The road is crossed here before the path leads along a wire fence and directly into a marshy area that should only be crossed on the tracks marked by red sticks. After about 1.5hrs there is a low-lying lake to the left of the path, at the foot of the Sorkvola Mountain (1011m/3317ft), which offers ideal camping opportunities. After a steep incline up Sorkvola, the route then continues in the direction of Tolgevollenseter, where a barrier is passed (stop on the left). A gravel road then leads to the main tarmac road that runs between Sorken and Røstvollen. Turn right here and follow the road for around 300m/330yd before turning left onto the sign-posted hiking path into the forest. The path now passes several smaller lakesand crosses a reindeer enclosure – used only in September – before finally reaching the banks of Lake Femund. There is affordable accommodation in cosy cabins as well as on a well-maintained camp site at **Femundsvika**. From here there are also buses that connect with the tour's starting point back at Elgå.

*Lake Femund	The wealth of lakes in the Femundsmarka region make an almost unlimited number of different **canoe tours** possible. Lake Femund itself is especially attractive for its numerous small islands, especially in the central portion south of Elgå. Sudden winds causing high waves can often crop up, so extreme caution is necessary here. It is especially inadvisable to enter the lake when there is a **north wind**. **Lakelsteren** to the west of Lake Femund is much safer. Isteren is only 18km/11mi long, but experience with the use of compasses and maps isnecessary because its many beautiful islands turn the lake into a **labyrinth**.

Another recommended area is the lake district to the east of the southern end of Lake Femund. Fishermen's huts can be found by driving from Sorken in the direction of Storknallen and turning off right after 7km/4mi onto an unpaved track, which ends at the huts around 6km/4mi away. From here, the entire region around the Gunnarsjøen and the Storgyltingen lakes can be toured by boat. Most of the small lakes here are connected by rivers, so that when water levels are high enough, portage can be avoided. **Very rare animals and plant species** can still be found in this highly remote part of Femundsmarka.

*Gunnars-jøen, Storgyltingen

South of Femundsmarka, right by the Swedish border, lies the **Gutulia National Park**, a veritable paradise for all tree lovers. The Norwegian spruce trees here are up to 300 years old, and many pine trees have been standing for 500 years. The forest in the national park is allowed to evolve without the interference of mankind so that scientists can study its development over several generations of trees. A car park can be found at the end of a signposted track leading off road number 654. A cabin offering coffee and waffles during July is half an hour's walk away along the banks of Gutulisjøen.

Paradise for tree lovers

Magical colours enliven the autumnal Femundsmarka

* Finnmark

$\dotplus$ M/N 19-27

Region: North Norway
Population: 73,800

Finnmark, the land of the Sami people, is the largest and most sparsely populated province of Norway: a giant wilderness area, the like of which can rarely be found in Europe today. The coast is characterized by broad, open fjords, and the interior by a flat highland plateau that is typical of the Finnmarksvidda region.

Lakes, fjords and tundra
Although it is characterized by Arctic tundra vegetation, the several thousand lakes of Finnmark recall the Finnish lake district. Broad, open fjords that are up to 120km/75mi long characterize the Finnmark coastline. The interior consists of a flat highland plateau that lies at anelevation of 300m/984ft–600m/1968ft above sea level, known as Finnmarksvidda. It encompasses 36% of the region, yet it is only inhabited by 7% of the provincial population, mostly Sami people.

Rough climate
Even though extensions of the Gulf Stream keep the ports free of ice, a cold and stormy climate prevails. Summer temperaturesnormally struggle to reach 10°C/50°F in sheltered areas, such as valleys and fjords, while a record-breaking -52°C/-62°F was once reached during winter in Karasjok.

Land of the Sami
This is »Sápmi« – the land of the Sami (►MARCO POLO Insight p.34, 264). The county of ►Troms, whose coast is also deeply fissured by fjords, is part of Norwegian Lapland (Norwegian: Sameland). But, while agriculture is still possible in Troms, and fertile pastures do exist, the region becomes ever more barren and hostile to the northeast. The high mountain groups to the west give way to low plateaus to the east, where just occasional bare hills stand out. Centres of Norwegian Sami populations are at ►Karasjok (administrative centre) and ►Kautokeino (cultural centre).

Reindeer herding
Reindeer are the Sami's most important possession (►MARCO POLO Insight, p. 264). In this cold-loving game animal, both males and females grow a set of antlers. An individual Sami must have at least 100–200 animals to maintain him or herself, though a person rarely owns more than 500. Since a region grazed out by reindeer takes many years to recover, the herds need extensive territories. The former nomads have become modern reindeer breeders, who herd their animals with motorized snowmobiles and even on occasion do their counting from a helicopter. In addition to reindeer breeding,

The Formula One of the high north? Reindeer races are very popular among the Sami people

the Sami also often carry out other animal husbandry and a small amount of arable farming.

The present day borders of Finnmark date from 1751and 1826. Prior to that, the countryside was the communal region of Norwegian, Swedish and Russian Sami people. Between 1920 and 1944, the area of the former Soviet Union that now borders Finnmark was Finnish territory. The border near Tromshas existed since 1866. For centuries, the **Russian Pomor people** were welcome traders in Finnmark. They exchanged flour, cereals, rope, tar and wood beams for coffee, sugar, herring, cod and halibut. Not least because of the long Russian winters and the high demand for fish, the so-called Pomor trade achieved great significance. When the occupying German forces attempted to cut off Allied supplyroutes to Murmansk at the end of the **Second World War**, they eliminated northern Norway's entire infrastructure. The scorched earth policy of the retreating troops in November 1944 resulted in the destruction of most houses and only a few places, such as Hamningberg and Bugøynes, survived the devastation. For a long time after 1945, northern Norway was considered a **developing country**. Thousands of fishing families were close to ruin because their incomes had become too small. Nowadays, fishing stocks have recovered and tourist numbers have been growing for years. The exploitation of gas and oil reserves in the Baring Sea is also destined

History

Finnmark

INFORMATION
For addresses for tourist information, hotels and restaurants, see the sections on Alta, Hammerfest, Katasjok, Kautokeino, Kirkenes, Nordkapp and Vardø.

GETTING THERE
All larger settlements have their own airstrip. Ferries and speed boats, as well as numerous bus routes, connect the northern Norwegian settlements, as well as heading into Sweden and Finland.

The most important ports are also serviced by the Hurtigruten shipping line.

FISHING
A good time is during the ocean fishing festival at Sørvær, on the island of Sørøya, to the west of Hammerfest. Worthwhile fishing grounds can be found at Straumen under the Langfjord bridge (15km/9mi off Kirkenes), and the salmon catch is especially good along the Alta river and the Tanaelva.

to improve standards of living here. ►Kirkenes, final destination of the ►Hurtigruten shipping line, has evolved into the gateway to the east. Day trips to the Russian town of Murmansk, the world's largest city north of the Arctic Circle, are organized from here.

*Øvre Pasvik Nasjonalpark

The Øvre Pasvik National Park at the end of the 120km/75mi-long forested Pasvik valley between Finland and Russia is, as it were, the westernmost extension of the Siberian taiga. The primeval pine forests here are very impressive. The highest point is Steinfjell, which barely reaches 202m/663ft above sea level. A quarter of the national park is covered by water. A single cohesive water labyrinth is formed by the lakes of Ellenvatnet, Parvatnet, Skinnposevatnet, Grenseparvatnet and Dagvatnet. **Lynx, bears and wolverines** still survive in the national park and it is also possible to spot birds that are normally residents of Siberia, such as the great grey owl. **Wood grouse, fish eagle and whooper swan** are also seen here. This pristine national park is best explored by canoe. There is only one hiking cabin at the Ellenvatnet, which can be reached by a path leaving from the car park. In the meantime, however, organized canoe and husky tours have also been made available within the Øvre Pasvik National Park.

> **!** MARCO ⊕ POLO TIP
>
> *Arctic wilderness*   Insider Tip
>
> Untouched Arctic wilderness can be experienced on the Nordkyn peninsula 40km/25mi east of Nordkapp. Thiis huge tundra region, set with lakes and moors, is one of Scandinavia's most important bird breeding colonies. Among many other types of bird there are nesting snow grouse and numerous duck and seagull species, including Arctic tern.

* Fredrikstad

✦ B 7

Region: South Norway
Population: 75,600

The former fortress town on the Oslofjord has survived completely intact. Lovingly restored 17th-century houses line the streets, and the lanes of the charming Old Town are wonderful for strolls along ramparts, past bastions and over drawbridges.

Scandinavia's best preserved fortress town is located where Norway's longest river, the Glomma, flows into the ▶Oslofjord. It was founded on the orders of the Danish King Fredrik II in 1567, and redeveloped into **Norway's most impenetrable fortress** in 1660. The town was only released from military control in 1903, and 60 of the original 130 cannons are still to be seen on the bastions of the fortified walls. A statue on the main square recalls Fredrik II, after whom the town was named. This now modern industrial town and port extends along the western bank of the Glomma river and can be reached by boat, or via the 40m/131ft-high Fredrikstadbrua. The neo-Gothic **cathedral** here dates from 1880, and contains one of the largest church organs in Norway, with 4000 pipes, as well as glass paintings by Emanuel Vigeland, the brother of Gustav Vigeland (▶Oslo).

Founded by Sweden

First he gave the town his name, now he stands on the market square: Danish King Fredrik II

Fredrikstad

INFORMATION
Fredrikstad Touristinformation
Tøihusgaten 4
1632 Gamle Fredrikstad
Tel. 69 30 46 00
www.visitoslofjord.com

BOAT TOUR
The eight-hour boat tour on the Halde canal is a real pleasure. The historic steamboats of »M/S Turisten« and »M/S Strømsfoss« set off from Strømsfoss to Tistedal from June–Aug on Wed, Fri, Sat and Sun at 10am and 11am.

CYCLING
A nice way to explore the town and its environs is by bicycle tour along one of the five sign-posted cycle routes, such as along the Oldtidsvei or on the Glommastien along the Glomma river. Infor-mation and bike hire from the tourist office.

WHERE TO EAT
Engelsviken Brygge £ £
Engelsvikenveien 6
Tel. 69 35 18 40
www.engelsvikenbrygge.no
This hidden gourmet inn on the bay of Engelsviken (15km/9mi north) makes such wonderful fish and seafood dishes that people even come from Oslo.

WHERE TO STAY
Quality Hotel Fredrikstad £ £ £
Nygata 2–6
Tel. 69 39 30 00
www.qualityinn.com
Modern hotel and restaurant with con-ference rooms in the town centre.

WHAT TO SEE IN AND AROUND FREDRIKSTAD

*Old Town   A walking tour around the Old Town leads along narrow streets paved with rough cobble stones. Several of the old buildings now house the workshops of craftsmen. It is worth looking in at the **Fredrikstad Museum**, whose office is in the Tøihuset that also houses the local history museum. The provisions store dating from 1687 and the old »slaveriet« (slave house) dating from 1731, are part of the museum. The **Minemagasinet** is dedicated to an exhibition on Norway's maritime history and local boat builder Bjarne Aas, entitled »White Sails and Salty Sea«. Aas built his renowned regatta boats at the »Isegran« shipyard. The rebellious Count von Borgarsyssel, Arv Erlingsson, also used Isegran as his base for carrying out raids on ships sailing between Norway and Denmark, towards the end of the 13th century. The small **Whaling Museum** in the basement of the Bullgården (Toldbodgate) has a detailed display on the history of whaling in Arctic waters, while Norway's tiniest museum, opened in 2008, is the **Konglelig Norsk Museum** featuring work by the Norwegian cartoonist Morten M. The history of football is covered in the **National Football Museum** at the new stadium. Kongsten fort, which was built on the occasion of a visit by King Christian V in 1685, is one of the exterior constructions of the fortified town and lies 500m/550yd beyond the Old Town. Underground rooms and passages in the fort give insight into the military thinking of the period. Another satellite of the town lies on the island of Isegran. Norway's last »jarl« (a royal governor) had his castle there around the end of the 12th century.

Fredrikstad Museum: Tue–Fri noon–3pm, Sat–Sun noon–4pm; 50 NOK (incl. the Football Museum); www.ostfoldmuseene.no

Minemagasinet: no fixed opening times, check: www.isegran.no

Konglelig Museum of Norwegian Humour: Sat–Sun 11am–3pm; www.humormuseum.no

Football Museum: 21st June–30th Aug Tue–Fri and Sun 11am–4pm; 50 NOK (incl. FrederikStad Museum); www.fotballmuseet.no

A drive along the Oldtidsvei (ancient history route) between Fredrikstad and Skjeberg on the RV 110is a journey through several thousand years of European history. At **Begby**, there is a sign for »Helleristninger«, the **3000-year-old rock paintings** with images

*Oldtidsvei

Maritime expedition of 3000 years ago? The riddles of the rock paintings of Begby

from agriculture and seafaring dating from the Bronze Age (1800–600 BC). Representations of ships, fishing nets, the sun (a fertility symbol), a dancer, cultitems and footprints can be seen. The Horn-nesrock paintings, with numerous magnificent images of ships decorated with animal heads at the bow, can be viewed shortly before Skjeberg. Also along the Oldtidsvei is the church of Borge dating from 1861, though the foundations indicate there was an older church here dating from the early Middle Ages. The famous polar-explorer **Roald Amundsen** (▶FamousPeople) was born in Borge in 1872. He spent his childhood in the »Tomta« house that contains numerous mementos of his life.

Tomta House: Wed–Sun 11am–5pm

*Halden

Halden, which was known as Fredrikshald from 1665 to 1927, enjoys an attractive location on the Iddefjord and is surroundedby numerous idyllic lakes. High above the town towers the **Fredriksten fortress**, which Fredrik III had built as protection against the Swedes in 1661–71 and 1682–1701. There is a wonderful view of the town and the skerry coastal landscape from up here. The fortress was constructed on the ridges of two hills and today accommodates a restaurant and a camp site. The Queen's Bastion stands at the western end of the walls and the Prince Christian Bastion at the eastern end. The Prince Georg Bastion stands to the south, while the main bastion of Overkongen is located at the highest point.The citadel stands between the two elevations, with fortifications on the western slope facing the town. A museum devoted to war and cultural history documents the history of the fortress, which is a popular venue for cultural events of all kinds these days.

Fortress: guided tours mid-June–Mid-Aug daily: noon, 1.30pm and 3pm

*Halden canal

One of the country's most beautiful technical cultural monuments is the 70 km/43 mi long Halden canal, which winds through the region and connects five lakes and rivers. It is also popular with **canoeists**. There are several locks along the canal. The Brekke lock has four compartments that cover a water height difference of 39m/128ft, which is a record in Europe.

Svinesund Bridge

Svinesund Bridge was opened on 10 June 2005in a ceremony with Norway's King Harald and Sweden's King CarlGustaf. Spanning 247m/270yd, this filigree construction is the **largest single-arched bridge in the world**, connecting Norway with Sweden via the road that goes between Oslo and Göteborg. Four lanes on the new bridge are intended to ease the long and frequent traffic jams on this stretch. The border crossing is especially popular with the Norwegians themselves, who stock up on meat, cigarettes and alcohol in the cheaper supermarkets across the border.

★★ Geirangerfjord

——— ✦ E 3/4 ●

Region: West Norway

Tourists have been streaming to the Geirangerfjord since the middle of the19th century. An area of great natural beauty, it is among the most beautiful places in Norway. The mountains rise almost vertically out of the water, waterfalls thunder into the depths, cruise ships sparkle brilliant white on thedeep waters and breathtaking serpentine roads wind up the slopes.

The famous Geirangerfjord forms the eastern end of the Sunnylvsfjord that itself branches off the Storfjord. The car ferrysails the 16km/10mi across the fjord travelling between Hellesylt and Geiranger,passing imposing waterfalls: »The Seven Sisters«, »The Suitor« and the »Bride'sVeil«. Several abandoned farms cling precariously on rock promontories. Impressive, too, are the views from

Seven Sisters

Norway's most famous postcard motif is the narrow Geirangerfjord

Geirangerfjord

INFORMATION
Geiranger Turistkontor
Gamle Fergekai
6216 Geiranger
Tel. 70 26 30 99
www.geiranger.no

FERRIES
Sightseeing
A cruise on the Geirangerfjord is one of the highlights of any visit to Norway. The MS Geirangerfjord set off daily from the old ferry quay near the tourist office for the 90-minute fjord tour between June and August. Departures at 8am, 9.30am, 11.30am, 2pm, and 5pm. Demand is often high so expect queues.

Transport
The car ferry between Geiranger and Hellesylt operates between May and September, during high season, up to eight times daily; but queues must still be expected. From 15th June to 15th August, the ferry travels between Geiranger and Valldal, with departures from Valldal at 10.30am and 3.30pm. and from Geiranger at 1pm and 6pm.

LEISURE AND SPORT
Sea kayaks are rented out for excursions from near the camp site at the end of the fjord (tel. 91 11 80 62). The rafting centre in Valldal offers two four-hour tours daily during summer (tel. 90 01 40 35; 11am and 3pm, Sun 1pm). The meeting point is the tourist office. Downhill bikers can book a spectacular 17km/10.5mi tour: a car takes you up to the Djupvas cabin and then a guide leads a speedy way down to Geiranger (Geiranger Adventure, Stefånaustet, tel. 47 37 97 71).

WHERE TO EAT
Union Hotel £ £ £
(On the RV 63, above the centre of Geiranger)
Tel. 70 26 83 00
Diners here have the choice between spoiling themselves with the à la carte menu at the excellent restaurant or enjoying the hotel buffet. Either way, make sure to enjoy an aperitif with a breath-taking view on the Nina Grieg Terrace. **Insider Tip**

Westeras Hytteutleige £ £
4km/2.5mi before Geiranger
Tel. 70 26 32 14
www.geiranger.no/westeras
This rustic inn run by Iris and Arnfinn Westerås is als popular with the locals. Accommodation is available in cabins and holiday apartments. Children love the Shetland ponies and the goats.

WHERE TO STAY
Union Hotel £ £ £ £
On the RV 63, ca. above the centre of Geiranger
Tel. 70 26 83 00
www.union-hotel.no,197 rooms.
This hotel is equipped with every comfort and also boasts an indoor swimming pool with attached outdoor pool, a spa, and an stunning view over the Geirangerfjord. Most rooms have views over the fjord. It is worth studying the family packages available here.

Villa Utsikten £ £ – £ £ £
Tel. 70 26 96 60
www.villautsikten.no, 31 rooms.
Traditional establishment that goes back over a century. The name of »Utsikten«

(view)is entirely appropriate, since the Geirangerfjord is nearly always in sight, whether from the Aida restaurant, the lobby, or from many of the rooms.

Grotli £ £ – £ £ £
Tel. 61 21 74 74
www.grotli.no, 53 rooms.
Several national ski teams have used this hotel as a base to train at the Stryn summer ski centre. Guests enjoy the cosy evening atmosphere of a Scandinavian wooden house and the generous portions of Norwegian food.

Fossen Camping £
Tel. 70 26 32 00
www.fossencamping.no
The site offers several huts with shower, bath and kitchen for 2–6 people, as well as a beautiful location with views of the Geirangerfjord.

the eleven hairpin bends of the Eagle Road (Ørneveien), and from the viewing point of the 1495m/4905ft Dalsnibba mountain, both accessible from Geiranger. Over 100 cruise ships weigh anchor in Geiranger annually and even the Hurtigruten line does not pass up the chance to make a detour to this picturesque fjord during the summer months.

WHAT TO SEE AROUND THE GEIRANGERFJORD

The narrow, winding RV 63 road to Geiranger branches off to the north from the E15, to the west of Grotli. Initially it runs along Lake Breidalsvatnet, at whose western end stands the Djupvasshytta hotel. A worthwhile detour here is to the Dalsnibba: the so-called Nibbevei road, open from June to September, which branches off to the right near the Djupvasshytta hotel, leads up to the summit of the 1495m/4905ft-high Dalsnibba, climbing the 5km/3mi upto the top via many hairpin bends (toll payable; up to 12.5% incline). The summit offers a magnificent view over the mountains and down to the Geirangerfjord lying far below.

Narrow access road

An impressive alpine road to Geiranger begins shortly after Djupvasshytta – a distance of just 7km/4mi as the crow flies, but 17km/11mi on the ground. The road was completed in 1885 and surmounts a difference in elevation of 1000m/3281ft in 20 occasionally very sharp bends, with gradients of up to 8%. There are also several bridges. During the journey, the sudden transformation from rough alpine climate to the gentler mild climate of the protected valley can beexperienced. 2km/1.2mi along the road, **Blåfjell** can be seen rising up to the left with an ice field known as the »Jettegryte« (giant pot), an glaciated area about 2m/2yd wide and 10m/33ft deep at the top of the mountain.

*Road to Geiranger

Flydal	Beyond the **Øvre Blåfjellbro** bridge, there is a wonderful view of the »**Eagle Road**« winding its way up from Geiranger to Eidsdal: to the left stands the Flydalshorn, to the right the Vindåshorn, and beyond the 1779m/5837ft high Såthorn. Further on, the route leads over the Nedre Blåfjellbro and past the Kvandalselv waterfalls before descending initially to the first ledge of the valley and then down to the second, the Flydal. Flydalsjuvet (300m/984ft; car park) can be found beyond Ørjeseter, from where there are good views to be had. Shortly afterwards by Hole, it is worth making a detour to **Vesterås**. A signposted footpath leads to the Storseterfoss, a 30m/98ft high waterfall. Back on the main road, the Hotel Utsikten Bellevue appears beyond Hole, and to the left of a bridge after that a stone memorial records the establishment of the Norwegian Constitution in 1814.
Geiranger	Finally, Geiranger is reached, the little port and often overcrowded tourist resort with a lovely location at the eastern end of the Geirangerfjord. The Geiranger's Fjord Centre gives a good idea of living conditions along the fjords: visitors are guided through a historic fjord settlement as well as seeing typical fjord landscapes. The RV 63 follows the northern bank of the Geirangerfjord, reaching **Møllgårdene** after 3km/2mi, where there are several houses over 200 years old. This is also where the Eagle Road begins. The Skageflå goat farm has been abandoned since 1916, but was the most significant goat breeding centre in Geiranger during its heyday. A steep footpath covers the elevation of 250m/820ft to reach the farm, where panoramic views onto the cliffs make the hike well worthwhile. It is a view loved by the Norwegian royals as well, who celebrated their silver wedding anniversary here. **Fjord Centre:** May–Aug daily 10am–6pm, otherwise Mon–Sat 10am–3pm, Sun on request; 110 NOK; www.verdsarvfjord.no
*Sunnylvsfjord	To the west, the Geirangerfjord flows into the Sunnylvsfjord which has two settlements: Hellesylt to the south and Stranda to the north. There is a ferry connection between Hellesylt and Geiranger between May and September.
*Ørnevegen	The Eagle Road connects the Geirangerfjord with the Norddalsfjord. Initially the road winds its way to Korsmyra (624m/2047ft) – the route's highest point – in eleven loops offering beautiful views onto the Geirangerfjord and the waterfalls. Afterwards it leads past Lake Eidsvatnet before descending all the way to **Eidsdal** on the Norddalsfjord. The octagonal church there, which dates from 1782, is worth taking a look at. A ferry travels to Linge on the north bank of the fjord. Åndalsnes (►Romsdal) is east of Linge, while heading west the route leads to ►Ålesund.

** **Gudbrandsdal**

✦ D 6/7

Region: South Norway
Population: 70,000

Gudbrandsdal is one of the most popular tourist destinations in Norway. Andnot without reason: the climate is mild and the valley full of charm, with forested hillsides and blossoming meadows. The mountains nearby are ideal for every kind of sporting holiday.

The central Gudbrandsdal valley (Norwegian: Gudbrandsdalen, meaning »the valley/dale of Gudbrand«) is 200km/125mi long, with the small side valleys of Gausdal, Espedalen, Vinstradalen, Heidal and Ottadalen branching off. The main valley extends from Lillehammer in the south to Lesja and Romsdal in the north, and is washed by the mighty Gudbrandsdalslågen River that rises in the northern Lesjaskogsvannet and flows into the Mjøsa Lake. Its inhabitants, the Gudbrandsdøler, are known to be very fond of their traditions and live predominantly from farming and woodworking.

Central and side valleys

WHAT TO SEE IN GUDBRANDSDAL

Leaving ▶Lillehammer(180m/590ft), the E 6 follows the Lågen up-river through the Gudbrandsdal valley.North of Lillehammer lies the **Hunderfossen powerstation**, which is fed by a 7km/4mi-longreservoir. There is a fish ladder and a trout farm producing 20,000 fish annually. A camp site with cabins can be reached via the dam. On the same side, about3km/2mi further on, a 37m/121ft-high troll indicates the location of the **Hunderfossen Family Leisure Park** that celebrated its 25th anniversary with the installation of a new attraction in 2010: visitors can now rescue the princess from the jaws of the trolls. Additional attractions, aimed particularly at young children, include a go-cart rink, rafting, swing boat, children's farm, and waterpark. Not far from the Hunderfossen leisure park is the **world's most northern ski bob and toboggan rink**, where all the races for the 1994 Winter Olym-

Hunder-fossen

> ! **Marco Polo Tip**
>
> *Marvels of technology* **Insider Tip**
>
> Those interested in tunnel and road construction from medieval pilgrim routes to contemporary high-tech projects would do well to visit the Norwegian Road Museum (Norske Vegmuseum) near the Hunderfossen Family Leisure Park (opening times: June–Aug daily 10am–6pm, otherwise Tue–Sun 10am–3pm; www.vegmuseum.no).

Fun for kids: the miniature houses at the Lilleputthammer

pics took place. Now anyone can race down the track on wheels during summer.

Hunderfossen Family Leisure Park: June, Aug 10am–3pm/5pm; July 10am–6pm; from 250 NOK; www.hunderfossen.no

Øyer Around 6km/4mi beyond Hunderfossen, the Øyer church(1725) stands to the right, whose interior is in the rustic Baroque style of the region. In Øyer itself there are several ski lifts and 20 pistes of the **Hafjell Olympic Grounds**. An attraction for children awaits at the **Lilleputhammer** by the »Øyer Gjestegård« (inn): a reconstruction of the Storgata district of Lillehammer in miniature and all kinds of entertainments for children.

Lilleputhammer: end of May–mid-Aug daily 10am–6pm, July sometimes till 9pm; 225 NOK; www.lilleputthammer.no

Stave churches The E 6 continues along the eastern bank of the Lake Losna. 4km/2mi before reaching Fåvang, the **Fåvang church** stands at the Kirkestuen crossroads. Originally a stavechurch, it was converted into a cross-shaped church in the 17th century and restored in 1951. After 7km/4mi a short road turns off right at Elstad and leads to the Ringebu

Gudbrandsdal

INFORMATION
Otta Turistkontor
Ola Dahlsgt. 1
2670 Otta
Tel. 61 23 66 50
www.rondane-dovre-fjell.com

WHERE TO EAT
Kornhaug Gjestegård £ £
Follebu
(17km/11mi north of Lillehammer)
Tel. 61 22 92 50
This imposing 100-year-old wooden
building in the Dragon style is the perfect setting for an excellent five-course
game menu. The à-la-carte meals are
perfectly affordable, while the »Lunsme-
ny« offers value for money (daily except
Sunday noon–6pm).

Sinclair Vertshuset £
Kvam
Tel. 61 29 54 50
www.vertshuset-sinclair.no
Simple motel with cafeteria, buffet and
shop between Vinstra and Otta, along
the E6.

WHERE TO STAY
*Spidsbergseter Gudbrandsdal
Hotell £ £ £ £*
Ringebu
Tel. 61 28 40 00
www.sgh.no
A top class hotel in the midst of the
mountain landscape of Ringebufjell. Ex-
clusive spa and numerous sproting op-

portunities, such as ice-hole fishing and
hiking.

Rondablikk Høyfjellshotell £ £ £
Kvam
Tel. 61 29 49 40
www.rondablikk.no, 82 rooms.
A wonderful mountain lodge right by
the Rondane National Park, including a
swimming pool, saunas, a fitness centre
and nightclub. All-inclusive deals are
worth booking here, as the price difference for bed and breakfast only is relatively small.

Sygard Grytting £ £
Sør-Fron
Tel. 61 29 85 88
www.grytting.com, 7 rooms.
The estate by Harpefoss (70km/44mi
north of Lillehammer) was a pilgrim hotel 700 years ago. Today it is an excel-
lently restored historic hotel and the
three-course evening meal is served in a
wonderful atmosphere harking back to
bygone days.

Rondvassbu Turisthytta £
Mysuseter, Sel
Tel. 61 23 18 66
www.rondvassbu.com
Basic hut belonging to the Norwegian
hiking association (DNT) in the Rondane
National Park, for those with simple
needs. Travel by car or bus (from Otta)
as far as Mysuseter, after which another
1.5hrs' walk is necessary.

stave church (approx. 1200). The old main road through the valley
(the »king's road« to Trondheim; ▶Dovrefjell) used to run past here.
The church was extended around its choir, transept and aisles in
around 1630, and then restored in 1921. Th ecolourful interior orig-

inated from the 17th–18th century, including the altar painting from 1688 and the pulpit from 1703.

Ringebu Stavkirke: end of May–end of Aug daily 9am–5pm, July 8am–6pm; 40 NOK; www.stavechurch.no

Hundorp

The Gudbrandsdal high school was once located in the village of Hundorp (193m/633ft), in an old house dating from 1850. In its courtyard there are **burial mounds** and Bauta stones (memorial or tomb stones) from **the Viking era**, as well as beautiful arts andcrafts to be seen. The octagonal **stone church of Sør Fron** (1787) is also known as »Gudbrandsdal Cathedral«. It was built in the style predominant in the reign of the French King Louis XVI, although the interior vaulting and altar displays Baroque characteristics. The church also has an electronic glockenspiel.

Vinstra

The Sødorp **wooden church** (1752) and the **Peer Gynt gården** with its 18 old houses (private) are worth seeing inVinstra (241m/791ft). Peder Olsen Hågå, who lived on Nordgardhågå farm from 1732 to1785, was the inspiration for Henrik Ibsen's play *Peer Gynt*. The Peer Gynt Stugu dating from 1743 documents various versions of Ibsen's drama with photos, dolls, costumes and posters. The play is also performed annually on the open-air stage by the lake.

Peer Gynt Stugu: mid-June–Mid-Aug 10am–5pm; open-air theatre info: www.peergynt.no

Kvam

The valley becomes narrower behyond Vinstra. A decisive battle for the Gudbrandsdal occurred in Kvam in 1940, and a military war museum recalls the events. The 1027m/3369ft Teigkamp mountain rises south of Kvam and, on the continuing drive to Sjoa (285m/935ft), the Torgeirkamp (1186m/3891ft) can be seen.

Heidal

A road branches off left into the Heidal valley.15km/9mi beyond Heidal itself – complete with many listed houses and farms – the village church is reached, a reproduction from 1938 of the original church dating from 1752, which was burnt down in 1933. Adjacent, on the attractive Bjølstad farm, stands a chapel (approx. 1600) with 11th-century portalsections from a stave church. The crucifix dates from around 1200.

Kringen is reached via the E 6. A monument recalls the farmers' victory over Scottish troops

---

! MARCO POLO TIP

Wonderful white water rafting Insider Tip

An inflatable boat ride on the wild Sjoa river near Heidal is a unique way to experience the wilderness, as well as a great sporting thrill. The best introductory choice for a white water rafting trip would be the three-hour tour on grade two and three rapids. Reservations can be made through Sjoa Rafting (Heidal, tel. 90 07 10 00; www.sjoarafting.com).

which were on their way to Sweden in 1612. To the northwest stands the 849m/2785ft-high Pillarguritoppen from which, legend has it, a man of this name is said to have warned the farmers of the advancing Scots.

Otta is an important traffic junction at the mouth of the Otta into the Lågen, as well as the most important base for hikes in the ▶Rondane mountains. It is possible to get just short of the summit of Pillarguri-toppen by car, from where there is a panoramic view. To the north-east, the Rondanevegen offers the easiest access to the Rondane National Park.

Otta

Those who enjoy geological phenomena or bizarre photo opportuni-ties should make a short detour and take the road to Mysuseter at Sel/Selsverket. After 3km/2mi, a short, relatively steep footpath leads to the extraordinary »Kvitskriuprestinn«: 6m/20ft-high gravelstone **pyramids**, also known as »priests« because of their shape. From Mysuseter, it is another 10km/6mi on foot to the Rondvassbu tourist hut on the edge of the 570 sq km/ 220 sq mi ▶Rondane National Park, a veritable hiking paradise.

Side trip to Mysuseter

The three farms of **Romundgård,** Laurgård and Jørundgård in northern Sel play a significant rolein the literary trilogy *Kristin Lavransdatter* by **Sigrid Undset** (▶Famous People). The14th-cen-tury Jørundgård farm was recon-structed on the occasion of **film-ing** for the Kristin Lavransdatter movie. Today it is possible to expe-rience the everyday life of a medi-eval farm here.

The valley becomes narrower and the landscape wilder during the next 14km/9mistretch. In Rosten, a narrow road (10km/6mi) leads off to the right for the popular **hol-iday cabin region of Høvringen** (960m/3150ft). It is possible to take a hiking tour from Høvringen to Peer Gynthytta (see below).

The bizarre »Priests« at Mysuseter testify to the power of erosion

Brennhaug The E 6 continues as far as Brennhaug (449m/1473ft). To the north-east, there is a view onto the Storkuven (1452m/4764ft), and to the south, the Jetta mountain chain with Mount Blåhø (1618m/5308ft) can beseen, from which there are good views. From here there is a road that cuts through to Vågåmo.

Dombås Dombås is the central settlement of the ▶Dovrefjell region. The E 136 road now follows the Lågenvalley to the northwest, to Åndalsnes (▶Romsdal).

PEER GYNT TRAIL

Trolls and mountain spirits Traces of the legendary figure of Peer Gynt, who is supposed to have lived in this region, are regularly encountered on the highland tracks and hiking routes to the west and east of Gudbrandsdal. The ambitious young man set off into the world fullof vigour, survived the wildest adventures with mountain spirits and trolls, only to discover peace and happiness when he returned home, a broken and old man. Henrik Ibsen (▶Famous People) was inspired to write his drama *Peer Gynt*, for which Edvard Grieg (▶FamousPeople) wrote the music, by P. Ch. Asbjørnsen's story *Rondane Reindeer Hunt*, whose main character was the farmer and hunter Peder Olsen Hågå (1732–85). The visitor can get an idea of what inspired the two different artists by following the Peer Gynt Trail, which is also possible by car.

Setting off on the Peer Gynt Trail The 91km/57mi long, narrow and very winding Peer Gynt Trail (tolls payable along some stretches) forms an alternative route to the E 6 through the Gudbrandsdal, between ▶Lillehammer and Vinstra. This scenic route is around 7km/4mi longer, but worth it for the forests and deep blue lakes, as well as the marvellous views onto the Rondane Mountains. Setting off from Lillehammer, take the E 6 as faras Fåberg (6km/4mi) and turn left onto the RV 255, following the Gausdal valley with the river of the same name as far as **Follebu**. The large farm of **Aulestad** is located here, where the poet Bjørnstjerne Bjørnson(▶Famous People) lived from 1875 onwards. Today the estate is a Museum.

Aulestad: mid-May–Aug daily 11am–5pm, Sep weekends only; 110 NOK; www.maihaugen.no/no/Aulestad

Highest point at Rauhagen The route that now leads further west to Vestre Gausdal and on to the ▶Espedal Road is left behind at Segalstad. Instead follow the signs for the Peer Gynt Trail, which winds ever higher. Skeikampen is passed at the foot of the bizarrely shaped mountain of Skeikampen (1123m/3684m; 11 ski lifts and great views), as well as Frøysehøgda (views over the Gausdal) and Fagerhøy. At Rauhagen, the highest point of the road is reached, an altitude of 1053m/ 3454ft, and there is a magnificent view: to the north lie the mountain chains of ▶Rondane and ▶Dovrefjell with Snøhetta; to the northwest, the ▶Jotunheimen range can be seen. Skjærvangen is reached after another 8km/5mi, where a private road turns off right to Hundorp on the E 6. It is then another 5km/3mi to the tourist resort of **Gålå** and to Wadahl, which lies 930m/3051ft above Lake Gålåvann and has a very attractive viewing platform. Henrik Ibsen's *Peer Gynt* is performed with the help of 130 actors on the lakeside each year.

In Vollsdammen it is worth making a detour west as far as **Dalseter** (21km/13mi). At Fefor lies the lake of thes ame name and those who dare to attempt the 45-minute walk to the summit of Feforkampen (1175m/3855ft) are rewarded with a panoramic view onto the peaks of the Rondane and the Jotunheimen mountains. At Vinstra, the road rejoins the E 6.

> **!** MARCO ⊕ POLO TIP
>
> *Delicious cheese!*   Insider Tip
>
> Those who wish to visit the home of the famous Gudbrandsdal caramelized goat's cheese (Norwegian: geitosts or brunost) that the farmer Anne Hov created by chance in 1863 should turn off towards »Solbråseter« farm shortly after Gålå. This sweet, brown cheese is an essential part of any breakfast buffet. The traditional dairy is still in operation and open to the public in July and August, Wed and Sat, 11am–3pm.

ESPEDAL ROAD

This worthwhile alternative route to the E 6 through the Gudrandsdal leadsthrough a wild mountain landscape with numerous lakes and rivers. A well developed area for tourism, and a good hiking and cross-country skiing region is found around Lake Espedal. From Lillehammer to **Segelstad**, the Espedal Road (R255) follows the same route as the Peer Gynt Trail, before turning west to Vestre Gausdal. The Espedal Road now follows the Svatsumdal valley for the 22km/14mi to **Svatsum** (octagonal wooden church dating from 1860). It is then another 3km/2mi to the **Fjellstue Strand**, from where there is a beautiful view onto the long, idyllic Lake Espedal. Thereare good fishing opportunities at Espedalen Fjellstue. Beyond is **Dalseter**, where the Peer Gynt Trail is rejoined. During winter, Espedal counts as one of Norway's best regions for guaranteed snow and there is an extensive network ofcross-country routes.

Lakes and rivers

»Helvete« (hell) can be found at the southern end of Lake Espedal, around 13km/8mi beyond Svatsum, in the form of two giant cracks in the landscape that were created by glacial erosion during the Ice Age. With depths of up to 100m/328ft and a width of up to 50m/164ft,

Go to »hell«

they are the largest examples of this geological phenomenon in Norway. The largest cavern measures around 100m/109yd by 40m/44yd.

Ormtjern-
kampen
National Park

A mountain landscape with numerous rivers and lakes extends to the west of the Espedal Road, which is also suitable as a hiking region for families with children. Only those who wish to explore the summit area of Ormtjernkampen (1127m/3697ft) need mountaineering experience. At 19 sq km/7 sq mi, the Ormtjernkampen National Park is Norway's smallest national park, famous for its pristine landscape. To reach the northwestern sector of the hiking region, a road heading southwest off the main route through **Vestre Gausdal** should be followed to **Fagernes**. The road is only open during summer, has many bends and beautiful viewing points (up to 1000m/3281ft), and is 84km/52mi long. There are plenty of huts providing food in Fagernes that also offer accommodation. The hiking region can be reached via the RV 51 from Fagernes, heading in a northwesterly direction.

✳ RONDANE NATIONAL PARK

Wonderful
hiking region

The Rondane mountain range stretches between Gudbrandsdal to the west and Atnedalen to the east. 572 sq km/223 sq mi of this area was turned into a national park in 1962 and, even though there are **ten summits over 2000m/6562ft**, the range is a popular and relatively easy hikingregion. A high alpine dry climate with sparse vegetation is typical for the Rondane mountains: grey-yellow lichen covers the chalky sandstone that predominates here. During the Middle

Heaven and earth touch in a very special way in the Rondane National Park

Ages, the Rondane range formed a natural obstacle for farmers and merchants who wanted to reach the important markets of the copper town of ▶Røros. Derelict stone huts recall that ancient journey route and also the Rondane region's significance as a **hunting ground** for English aristocrats in the 19th century. Despite their limited numbers here, reindeer were hunted in the area from ancient times and walkers can find numerous **Viking trapping pits** built of stone.

At the heart of the national park stands the Rondvassbu tourist hut, where all walking paths through the mountains converge. The hut is at the western border of the park and can be reached on foot in about 1.5hrs from Mysuseter. The long, narrow Lake Rondevatn, at an altitude of 1100m/3609ft, extends north, squeezing itself through the high mountains. To the left and right lie the highest mountain summits. Hikers of average fitness will manage the ascent of **Rondslott** (»Ronde Castle«), whose summit is at 2178m/7146ft, in less than five hours. The walk through the Rondane mountains that continues into the adjacent ▶Dovrefjellto the north is very popular with Norwegians. The entire region is dotted with a network of huts belonging to the Norwegian hiking association (DNT ▶Enjoy Norway/Hiking), so comfortable day walks on well signposted paths are possible.

The heart of the national park

The Rondane massif boasts numerous rivers and lakes that are ideal for paddling tours. A river tour on the **Atna** is a very special experience. The river flows through impressive natural landscapes and is also suitable for inexperienced paddlers, with only class one and two rapids. During a 2–3-day river tour, several sandbanks are passed that make for excellent camping. Embedded in the mountains of the Rondane range, the river winds its way between primary forests and a wild, completely isolated meadow landscape. A little excitement is provided by the rapids near Staumbu bridge. On the other hand, crossing the 9km/6mi-long **Atnasjø** requires strong paddling muscles, and beware the high waves in windy conditions! At its southern end the lake flows back into a river that runs alongside the road. Progress should be made carefully along the right bank from here and early preparations made forlanding, as there is a life-threatening stretch full of boulders in the river afterthe bridge that **must be avoided by portage**. Once back in the water, it is not far to the **Skogli Camp**, where making land is made easier by means of a wooden jetty on the right river bank. Beyond this point, only **experienced paddlers** should continue along the Atna, as the rapids ahead are difficult to judge. An alternative means to exploring the enchanting landscape at a comfortable pace is provided by guided horse-riding tours. Options range from one day to several, and are organised by a variety of companies, including Brekkeseter Fjellridning (tel. 61 23 37 11, www.brekkeseter.no).

Exploring by canoe

Hiking in Peer Gynt's world
It is also possible tofollow in Peer Gynt's footsteps through the Rondane National Park on well signposted paths, for example during a one-day hike from Høvringen to Peer Gynthytta. **Hiking maps** are available from the tourist information office at **Otta**. Høvringen is reached by continuing to follow the E 6 in the direction of Dombås. A steep secondary road to **Høvringen** turns off to the right shortly after Laurgård, from where the very pleasant three-hour walk to the **Peer Gynt hut** begins.

Laurgårdseter Fjellstue
The famous Laurgårdseter Fjellstuelies on the way to the Peer Gynt hut. This alpine cabin is where writer and winner of the Nobel Prize in Literature Sigrid Undset gathered material for her novel *Kristin Lavransdatter* (▶Jørundgård, p.207; guided walking tours from Otta). The waterfalls, lakes and moraine landscape combine to make this walk a first-rate experience of Norwegian nature. A hanging bridge leads over the Imbertglupen ravine. The high path to Høvringen between theeast and west summits of the Skorutberget requires sure-footedness for the section from the southern slope of Baksidevassberget as far as the Rondane Haukeliseter Fjellhotell and is definitely not recommended for vertigo-sufferers.

Take the bus
It is also possible to do the route in the **opposite direction** by catching a **morning bus** at 9am from Otta to ▶Haukeliseter, and walking to the Peer Gynt hut from there. The route onwards to the Smukksjøseter Fjellstue takes around one hour, and a bus returns to Otta via Høvringen. Those who want to extend the experience canspend the night at the Smukksjøter Fjellstue and hike to Høvringen the next day.

In the Rondane National Park, the Sjoa, Lågen and Otta rivers are especially suitable for adventurous rafting tours

✳ Hallingdal

Region: South Norway   ✦ C 5/6

The valley of Hallingdal is lined with tourist resorts like pearls
on astring. During summer it is possible to do first-class walking tours here, as wellas climbing and cycling, and to get re-
freshment at the many alpine huts. During winter, Geilo and
Hemsedal are considered to be world-class ski resorts.

The richly forested, broad Hallingdal valley spreads from the northern endof Lake Krøderen in a northwesterly direction to ►Hardan-
gervidda, along the gently flowing waters of the Hallingdalselv. Only
the adjacent heights are barren, with smoothly weathered, lone boulders. The valley is an ancient settlement area, but in recent centuries
many left the area. Only with the completion of the mountain railway
at the beginning of the 20th century and the subsequent emergence
of tourism did people return to Hallingdal.

ADVENTURE TOUR THROUGH HALLINGDAL

In Gulsvik, the »Gateway to Hallingdal« at the northern tip of Lake   Gulsvik
Krøderen, the R 7 passes through the Hallingporten tunnel, the ac-
tual entrance into the valley. To the right is the Hallingdalselv river.
Continuing on, there are several camp sites and accommodation op-
tions (at Stavn, at an island in the river at Kolsrud, at Bromma and at
Roløkken).

In Nesbyen, you can visit the **Hallingdal Folkemuseum**. Most of the   Nesbyen
25 farmhouses are adorned by rose painting, an art with a long tradition in this valley. Traditional arts and crafts are demonstrated on
Wednesdays. Excursions to beautifully located alpine dairies (be
aware of the charges for accommodation and road tolls) can be made
from Nesbyen, as well as trips onto the ►Hardangervidda mountain
plateau. 650 million years ago a meteorite hit an area close to Nesbyn.
Gardnos Meteorite Park arranges tours of the 5 sq km/2sq mi cra-
ter created by the impact.

Hallingdal Folkemuseum: June–Aug daily 11am–4pm; 50 NOK;
www.hallingdal-museum.no
Meteorite Park: guided tours June–9th Sep daily 10am–5pm; 75 NOK;
www.gardnos.no

With more than 200km/125mi of maintained tracks and seven ski   Gol
lifts, including the chairlift at an altitude of 1600m/5249ft that climbs

Hallingdal

INFORMATION
Tourism Geilo
Vesleslåttvn. 13, 3580 Geilo
Tel. 32 09 59 00
www.geilo.no

Gol Turistkontor
Garnlevegen 4,3550 Gol
Tel. 32 02 97 00
www.golinfo.no

Hemsedal Turistkontor
Information at the Hemsedal Centre,
3561 Hemsedal
Tel. 32 05 50 30
www.hemsedal.com

SPORT
Hiking, fishing and outdoor activities
A great deal of outdoor action is on offer in the Hallingdal alongside the traditional classics of hiking and fishing; canoeing and elk tours are two examples. Tour companies can be contacted through the tourist information office.

Ski hang-gliding
Ski hang-gliding enthusiasts consider Hardangervidda to be the best place in the world for this new sport. The constant wind ensures that even tours from hut to hut are possible. Courses costing around 100 euros can be booked through the tourist information office in Geilo (www.geilo.no).

WHERE TO EAT/STAY
Dr. Holms Hotel £ £ £ £
Geilo, Timrehaugvegen 2
Tel. 32 09 57 00
www.drholms.com

This is one of the best Hotels in all of Scandinavia. Tastefully decorated dining rooms, wine from the house cellar, a delicious cold buffet in the summer, a dance floor and numerous fishing and sporting options ensure that stays here are an absolute pleasure.

WHERE TO STAY
Skarsnuten Hotel £ £ £ £
Hemsedal
Tel. 32 06 17 00
www.dvgl.no, 37 rooms.
Inaugurated in 2008, this designer hotel at an elevation of 1000m/3280ft, offers contemporary stylish rooms with lots of wood and glass. The cuisine and wine cellar are divine. Even better, the ski slopes begin right in front of the door. Early reservations are absolutely essential.

Oen Turistsenter AS & Geilo Vandrerhjem £ – £ £
Geilo, Lienvegen 137
Tel. 32 08 70 60
www.oenturist.no
Large leisure centre with a youth hostel, as well as several apartments and cabins for up to 9 people.

450m/1476ft, Gol is especially popular as a winter sports resort. The view from the mountain top is beautiful.

About 2km/1mi beyond Gol, the Heslabru leads from the Hallingdal valley past the Hemsila waterfall, which flows into the Hallingdalselv river. The RV 52turns off right towards Hemsedal. Initially, this road passes the new church at Gol (the old stave church was moved to the Ethnological Museum in Oslo) and then the valley of Hemsedal gradually opens up at **Robru**. The journey continues to Ulsåk, passing the **Hjelmen bru** power station to the left. There are views of Veslehorn (1300m/4265ft high) on whose eastern flank the Hydnefoss waterfall cascades down from a height of 140m/459ft. Behind Veslehorn rises the 1478m/4849ft-high Storhorn. From **Ulsåk**, a high alpine road turns off to the right to **Lykkja** (toll payable). It passes Skogshorn (1728m/5669ft) whose summit can be reached in two to three hours on foot. From Lykkja, it is either possible to continue on to Røn (48km/30mi) and Fagernes, or to head south to Fjellheim and Gol. From

*Side trip into Hemsedal

MARCO POLO TIP

! *Howling with wolves* Insider Tip

Langedrag Nature Park is located along the elongated Runhovdfjord between Hallingdal and Uvdal. Wolves, lynx, Arctic foxes and reindeer run wild in these extensive grounds, which attract many visitors during summer. There are numerous activities laid on for children and nourishment is provided in the restaurant (tel. 32 74 25 50; daily 10am–4pm; 190 NOK; www.langedrag.no).

Wolves still range in the Langedrag Nature Park, though in enclosures

Ulsåk it is another 3km/2mi to the winter sports resort of **Hemsedal** (609m/1998ft), one of Scandinavia's largest alpine centres that can certainly compete with the European Alps. The stable winter climate guarantees snow from November to the beginning of May and the large choice of runs – including 13 green, 8 blue, 10 red and 8 black – enchants good skiers. During the summer visitors can don wetsuits, diving masks, and snorkel and, from June to mid-October, embark on a trout safari in the Hemsil river. The section of road from Hemsedal down to Borlaug, where the road rejoins the E 16, **is among Norway's most beautiful high mountain routes**. There are hardly any people in this barren and wildly romantic landscape dotted with several small lakes.

Torpo

From Gol onwards, the journey continues through the Hallingdal valley in a southwesterly direction, the R 7 road mostly following the wild Hallingdalsev and its many waterfalls. At Torpo, after 13km/8mi, stands the **stave church**, with beautiful dragon ornamentation on the doorways and a well preserved painted ceiling from the 13th century. The church looks more like a tower than anything, because only the central nave with its high pillars and boxed capitals and painted masks survives.

Ål

The tourist resort of Ål also has a small **village museum** with rose paintings. Art lovers should not pass up the opportunity to visit the Rolf Nesch Museum. Fleeing the Nazis, **Rolf Nesch** (1893–1975) came from Germany to Norway in 1933 and lived in Ål until 1951. The museum displays drawings, oil paintings and sculptures by the internationally acclaimed artist Beyond Ål the Hallingsdalselv opens into the Satrandefjord and the road follows the northern bank. A power station is located at the end of the fjord at Kleivi.

Rolf Nesch Museum: Mon–Fri 8am–4pm; 45 NOK; www.aal.kulturhus.no

Aurland Road

From Hagafoss, it is possible to take in the impressive landscape along the **Aurlandsvei** (RV 50) to the Aurlandsfjord, 97km/61mi away. Thanks to numerous tunnels, this road is also passable during winter. After a short distance, the **13th century stave church of Hol** is reached, which however has been extensively modernized.

Geilo

Lillehammer excepted, Geilo (pronounced »Yeilo«) is entitled to call itself Norway's most famous winter sports resort. It sits at around 800m/2624ft in a broad valley and also offers excellent conditions for hikers, cyclists and horse-riders during summer, with many signposted footpaths and hiking huts. Fishing, canoeing and white water rafting are also possible. Those who want a magnificent view without the exertion can take the chairlift up to the 1056m/3465ft-high **Geilohøgda**. From there, it is also possible to follow a footpath to

Geilo's »local« mountain, **Hallingskarv** (1933m/6342ft), which even in summer is partly covered in snow. The chairlift can also carry bicycles and mountain bikers can enjoy 50km/31mi of mountain tracks to their heart's content. Note: the descent into the valley is for experienced riders only.

∗ Hamar

✦ C 8

Region: South Norway
Population: 29,050

Hamar is beautifully located on the eastern shore of Lake Mjøsa, which flows into the Furnesfjord here. The most interesting sights are the »Vikingskipet« events hall, built on the occasion of the 1994 Olympic Games, as well as the open-air Hedmark Museum and Norway's largest railway museum.

The town, originally founded as a bishopric in 1152, was an important trading centre during the Middle Ages. The cathedral was destroyed during the Danish-Swedish War in 1567 and only steam-   Important industrial town

The ruins of Hamar cathedral are protected by a modern glass construction

Hamar

INFORMATION
Hamar Turistkontor
Grønnegata 52, 2317 Hamar
Tel. 40 03 60 36
www.hamarregionen.no

WHERE TO EAT
Elgstua £
Elverum, Trondheimsveien 9
(junction of the RV 3 and RV 25)
Tel. 62 43 10 10
Norwegians travelling in the region are
willing to make a detour to savour the
delicious elk dishes in this small tavern.
Accommodation available.

WHERE TO STAY
*Radisson Blu Resort
Trysil £ £ – £ £ £*
Trysil, Hotellvegen 1

Tel. 62 44 90 00
www.radissonblu.com/resort-trysil
This hotel at the foot of the Trysilfjellet is
set in the middle of the country's most
popular ski destination, complete with
66 runs and 31 ski lifts (and three children's areas). Named Best Winter Sports
Hotel during the World Travel Awards in
2011, it has a spa and leisure pool, as
well as a bowling alley.

Eidet Gård £ – £ £
A farm dating from 1699, located
27km/17mi north of Trysil. Margit and
Ingjald Eidet make sure guests feel at
home in their two comfortable apartments that contain a total of 15 beds.
Ideal for fishing holidays.

shipping on Lake Mjøsa in the 19th century, as well as the opening
of the railway line in 1880, brought new impetus. The skyline of this
important industrial andcommercial town is not very attractive,
however. Hamar was chosen, along with ▶Lillehammer and Gjøvik,
to host competitions in figure skating and speed skating during the
1994 Winter Olympics.

WHAT TO SEE IN HAMAR

*Hedmark
open-air
museum
The impressive ruins of the 12th century cathedral that lie next to the
remains of a Romanesque episcopal castle can be viewed on the
grounds of the Hedmark Museum on the southwestern edge of town,
which also includes 50 buildings from theHedmark region, the oldest
dating from 1583. The renowned Norwegian architect Sverre Fehn
designed a museum for the castle restored in 1979. Clever wood constructions, protective glass roofs, ramps, walkways and steps combine to create an atmospheric setting for the museum displays. One
section of the building contains the folklore museum.

❶ Mid-May–mid-Sep daily 10am–4pm, mid-June–Mid-Aug till 5pm;
100 NOK; www.hedmarksmuseet.no

The Olymic Hall at Hamar has the world's largest free-floating ceiling

A modern sporting city, Hamar's emblem is the Olympic Hall that is also known as the »Vikingskipet« (Viking Ship) due to its striking roof construction (96m/315ft x 110m/361ft), designed by the architectural firm of Biong &Biong/Niels Torp A.S. The roof was designed to look as if it was light and floating, so the roof area was sectioned with glass slits. Among the city's other sporting venues, the Northern Light Hall on Knut Alysons gate is notable for being one of the largest wooden buildings in the world.

*Olympic Hall

Hamar deals only in superlatives when it comes to railways: the town is home to Norway's oldest railway station, Scandinavia's largest and oldest railway museum (Jernbanemuseet), as well as Norway's largest steam engine, the Dovregubben. With 2200 horsepower, it once managed the ascent onto Dovrefjell at aspeed of 70kmh/44mph. The museum collection includes numerous engines, sumptuous saloon coaches and historic railway fittings. During summer, the Tertitten narrow gauge museum train travels the 2km/1mi distance to Killingmo.

*Railway Museum

❶ July–Aug daily 10am–5pm, otherwise Tue–Sun 11am–3pm; 75 NOK; www.norsk-jernbanemuseum.no

The history of Norwegian emigration to America is documented in the Utvandrermuseet at Ottestad, located by the pier for the »Skibladner« steamboat that crosses Lake Mjøsa.

Emigration Museum

Emigration Museum: summer, Tue–Sat 10am–4pm, Sun noon–4pm; 50 NOK; www.emigrantmuseum.no

Kirsten
Flagstad
Museum

The Kirsten Flagstad Museum at Kirkegata 11 is dedicated to one of the greatest voices of the last century, where you can find original costumes worn during the Wagner soprano's era at the New York Metropolitan Opera. She died in 1962.

❶ April–May, Sep–Oct, Tue–Fri noon–3pm, June–Aug Tue–Sun noon–6pm; 60 NOK; www.kirsten-flagstad.no

AROUND HAMAR

Elverum

Elverum (pop. 20,200) lies around 28km/18mi to the east of Hamar and is known as Norway's »forest capital«thanks to its 972 sq km/375 sq mi of forested area, and is also the birth place of cross-country skiing legend Bjørn Dæhlie, the most successful athlete ever in this sport. An important road and railway junction, Elverum forms the southern gateway to Østerdalen. The Glomma riverflows right through the middle of the town and is popular with fishermen for its abundance of fish; it is also surrounded by wonderful wilderness that offers goodhunting opportunities. The open-air **Glomdalsmuseum** is especially interesting and worth visiting for its 91 old farmhouses from Østerdalen and Solør. The forest, hunting and fishing life is well represented in the **Norwegian Forest Museum**, one of the country's most visited museums. Among other things, it contains a collection of hunting weapons, as well as Norway's only fresh water aquarium, which contains around 40 species of freshwater fish from the highlands, lakes, and estuaries.

> **! Insider Tip**
>
> MARCO POLO TIP
>
> *Music all around town*
>
> The Elverum Music Festival at the beginning of August is popular, with concerts at the large estates, in churches and in the open-air (www.fie.no; tickets at tel. 62 43 33 33, www.billettluka.no).

Glomdalsmuseum: mid-June–Mid-Aug daily 10am–5pm, other months till 4pm; 100 NOK; www.glomsdalsmuseet.no
Norwegian Forest Museum: July–Aug daily 10am–5pm, other months till 4pm; 100 NOK; www.skogmus.no

Trysilfjell

During winter, sporting legends and jet setters alike are drawn to their private cabins by the Trysilfjell to enjoy Norway's most extensive skiing area, including 70km/43mi of downhill runs, 93km/58mi of cross country routes, 24 ski lifts and several snowboarding half pipes. Night skiing is ensured by illuminated runs. During summer and autumn, it is also possible to go rafting, riverboat fishing and even panning for gold. Unique in Europe is the option of drift boat fishing on the Trysilelva, whereby even the most inaccessible spots on the river can be reached using swivelling chairs capable of 360 degree turns and standing supports fixed to especially high flatbed boats.

Drift boat fishing: www.callofthewild.no

* Hammerfest

✦ N 20

Region: North Norway
Population: 9933

The skyline of Hammerfest is characterized by bijou houses, its port is icefree all year round and in the immediate vicinity is the world's northernmost forest. Yet for many tourists this is just astop-over on the way to Nordkapp.

Located on the west side of the island of Kvaløy, Hammerfest has always been a **significant commercial and fishing settlement** due to its protected ice-free port. It received its municipal charter in 1789 and Hammerfest continues to be the base for fishing in the North Polar Sea. Its status as the world's most northerly town has been challenged lately, however, as Honningsvåg, further to the north, has recently been granted its municipal charter. Hammerfest was bombed by the British in1809, destroyed by fire in 1890, and razed to the ground after a forced evacuationby the Germans in 1944. Only the cemetery chapel remained standing. The inhabitants rebuilt their town from the ashes on the narrow strip of land between Salen, a ridgeof hills on the south side of the town, and the sea, and the **colourful façades of the houses** really catch the eye. In recent times, thetown has profited from the oil boom and with approx. 200,000 visitors to Nordkapppassing through each year, **tourism traffic** struggles to move during the summer months.

Home of the polar fishermen

Stop-over on the way to Nordkapp: Hammerfest

Hammerfest

INFORMATION
Hammerfest Turist AS
Havnegate 3
9615 Hammerfest
Tel. 78 41 31 00
www.hammerfest-turist.no

GETTING THERE
Hammerfest can easily be reached by air via Tromsø and Oslo, as well as by bus from Oslo via Sweden. The ships of the Hurtigruten line weigh anchor here daily, and faster boats also connect the town with Tromsø, as well as Honningsvåg on Magerøya island, a stop-off on the route for Nordkapp.

EXCURSIONS TO NORDKAPP
The postal ships of the Hurtigurte line depart from Hammerfest daily at 7.45am and reach Honningsvåg at around 12.45pm. From there the journey to Nordkapp is by bus (one hour). After a short stay, the return journey is to Honningsvåg, where the evening bus for Hammerfest awaits. The Hurtigruten ship heading south does not set off from Honningsvåg before 6.45am in the morning, but when the light conditions are good an opportunity to experience the midnight sun is an excellent reason to stay awake all night.

MIDNIGHT SUN
The midnight sun shines from 17th May to 28th July.

WHERE TO EAT/STAY
❶ Turiststua Panoramarestaurant£ £
Am Salen
Tel. 78 41 46 11, 6 rooms.
The meals are simple and basic, but people come here for the view onto town and the surrounding countryside.

WHERE TO STAY
❶ Rica Hotel Hammerfest £ £ £
Sørøygata 15,
Tel. 78 42 57 00
www.rica.no, 86 rooms.
Modern, friendly, yellow-brick hotel with an atrium that reaches over two floors. There is a nice view from the hotel and in the new restaurant it is possible to enjoy the midnight sun through the large panoramic windows.

❷ Thon Hotel Hammerfest £ £ £
Strandgata 2 – 4
Tel. 78 42 96 00
www.thonhotels.com, 63 rooms.
Modern hotel in the town centre, next to the town hall, with friendly service.

❸ Hotel Skytterhuset £ £
Skytterveien 24
Tel. 78 41 15 11
www.skytterhuset.no, 66 rooms.
Friendly medium-range hotel near the Salen viewpoint, with sauna and solarium.

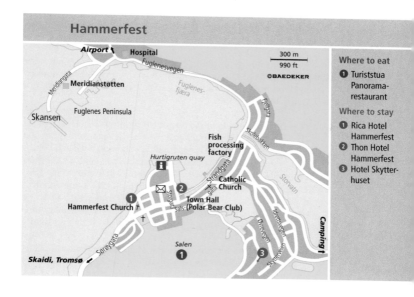

WHAT TO SEE IN HAMMERFEST

The Arctic Cultural Centre with its glass frontage bathed in blue lighting was built in 2009, and has since become the icon of modern Hammerfest.

Directly next to the jetty used by the ferries it is possible to become a member of the »**Royal and Ancient Society of Polar Bears**«. A small museum shows Arctic exhibits, including a 3m/10ft-long polar bear pelt, which recall the time when the town was the metropolis of the North Polar Sea and a centre of whaling.

A statue of the composer **Ole Olsen** (1850–1927), who was born here, can be seen on the market square. To the north, the pier for the Hurtigruten ships isreached via the Storgata quarter. A footpath leads up onto the Varden hill behind the town hall, a vantage point from which the entire town can be viewed.

Royal and Ancient Society of Polar Bears: summer Mon–Fri 6am–6pm, Sat–Sun till 4pm; winter Mon–Fri 9am–4pm, Sat–Sun till 2pm; Havnegata 3; www.isbjornklubben.no

Port metropolis

To the west of the market, Lutheran Hammerfest church, built in 1961, is reminiscent of the Arctic Cathedral of Tromsø. The missing altar was replaced by a large section of painted glass by Jardar Lunde (1962), inserted into the gable. There are church concerts here every

Hammerfest church

night during summer. Next door stands the wooden chapel that survived the last war.

Catholic Church
Following Strandgata to the northeast from the market square, the **Catholic church** (1958) appears, which was almost entirely built by German volunteers. The cross was carved by the former prisoner of war Georg Wimmer, after 1945.

Museum of Reconstruction
After the German attack on the Soviet Union in June 1941, the Finnmark became strategic for troops gathering on the Lappland Front. No other province had so many German soldiers stationed in it and bombing raids by the Allies and Russians began as early as 1942. 25,000 people became refugees in their own country, forced to live in caves. These events and the recovery of the Finnmark up until 1960 is illustrated at the Museum of Reconstruction (Gjenreisnings Museum).
Museum of Reconstruction: mid-June–Aug 9am–4pm, other months 11am–2pm; www.kystmuseene.no

Meridianstøtten
The road follows the bay around to the Fuglenes spit and the »Meridianstøtten«: a bronze atlas on a granite pillar. The monument is intended to recall the joint survey of the earth's shape and form undertaken by Norwegians, Swedes and Russians between 1816 and 1852. Its southern counterpart was a point near Ismail at the mouth of the Danube, 2872km/1795mi away. The concrete lump next to the monument dates from 1929, and indicates a subsequent measurement, which was at variance to the first but only slightly. At the end of the Fuglenes peninsular stand the fortifications known as the **Skansen**, which were built in 1810 during the Napoleonic Wars.

? Avant garde

MARCO POLO INSIGHT

Hammerfest was the first town in Europe to get street lighting. That was way back in 1890, and it has been a blessing for over a century, especially during the long polar night from 21st November to 23rd January.

AROUND HAMMERFEST

Salen
A footpath (20mins) runs from the market square up Salen (»Saddle«; 86m/282ft), a ridge of hills at the southern end of the town. Salen can also be reached via a road that passes the small lake of Storvatn to the east of town. An extensive view over the open sea is offered from the western slopes (stone indicator). At the southern edge of town to the left lies the Jansvatn open-air swimming pool, and the **world's northernmost forest** is a little further on. Early risers who have watched the Hurtigruten ship come in can often see **reindeer** heading towards town at the foot of Salen.

The road leads onwards to Skaidi. Take a look at Tyven (419m/1374ft) towering up to the left. From its summit, the island and many small lakes to the east can be seen, while to the south and west the partly snow and ice-bound mountains can be seen. To the north the view is onto the endless Polar Sea.

Skaidi

✱✱ Hardangerfjord

✦ B 2 - C 2/3

Region: West Norway

There is still snow on the mountain peaks in May when 500,000 fruit trees begin to blossom and the banks of the Hardangerfjord are smothered in a sea of delicate colours and scents. Norway's second largest fjord penetrates into the interior via dozens of inlets and twists and turns, a wealth of spectacular landscapes along its banks.

Due to the mild climate influenced by the warm Gulf Stream along the west coast, sweet plums, juicy apples and morello cherries ripen in the wind-protected valleys during the short summer season with its long and lightnights. The fruit is sold all along the road. **Over one fifth of the country's fruit trees** thrive here. It was probably Cister-

Norway's garden paradise

Thanks to Knud Knudsen, thousands of fruit trees blossom by the Hardangerfjord

cian monks who first introduced fruit farming to Hardangerfjord at thebeginning of the 13th century, but it was the photographer **Knud-Knudsen** (▶Famous People), born in Odda in 1832, who really made decisive progress in fruit growing. Even the German Emperor Wilhelm II regularly stopped by with samples from the imperial frui torchards for Knudsen's trees on the Hardangerfjord. Several attractive villages are located on the banks of the main fjord and along its side arms, but there is also a hydro-electric power station and sig-

Hardangerfjord

INFORMATION
Destination Hardanger Fjord
Sandvenvegen 40, 5600 Norheimsund
Tel. 56 55 38 70
www.hardangerfjord.com

Odda Turistkontor
Postboks 114 (office in the centre)
5751 Odda
Tel. 53 65 40 05
www.hardangerfjord.com/odda

Eidfjord Turistkontor
Ostangvegen 1, 5783 Eidfjord
Tel. 53 67 34 00
www.hardangerfjord.com/eidfjord

WHERE TO EAT
Tjødnadalen Gard £ £
Hildal, Odda
Tel. 90 52 81 70
www.tjodnadalen-gard.no
Around 10km from Odda, the historic farmhouse of Tjødnadalen enjoys superb views. Good Norwegian home cooking at moderate prices; children enjoy the garden complete with animals to pet.

WHERE TO STAY
Utne Hotel £ £ £ £
Utne, Tel. 53 66 10 88
www.utnehotel.no
There was already an inn here in 1722 and the old furniture and antiques in the guest room alone make a visit worthwhile. The good home-cooking is lovingly prepared and meals are served at one long table. There are no radios or TVs in the rooms, which completes the sensation of stepping into the past.

Rica Brakanes Hotel £ £ £ £
Ulvik i Hardanger, Tel. 56 52 61 05
www.brakanes-hotel.no, 143 rooms.
This outstanding hotel has been popular with tourists for decades. The hotel also has boat jetties and a bathing beach.

Sauda Fjord Hotel £ £ £
Saudasjøen, Tel. 52 78 12 11
www.saudafjordhotel.no, 35 rooms.
This hotel in a former mansion has been restored with a loving eye for detail and lies in the wildly romantic Saudafjord region (Ryfylke, Røldal). The fjord's good fish stocks have long made it popular with passionate and wealthy salmon fishing enthusiasts.

Vik Pensjonat £ £
Eidfjord, Centre, Tel. 53 66 51 62
www.vikpensjonat.com
Comfortable cabins and rooms in the centre of Eidfjord for 4–6 people. The café serves breakfast, lunch and dinner, and there is pleasant seating outside in good weather.

nificant industrial settlements,too. East of Eidfjord in the interior of the fjord, ►Hardangervidda, Europe's largest mountain plateau begins, which offers an unforgettable experience in good weather and clear visibility.

WHAT TO SEE AROUND THE HARDANGERFJORD

The starting point is the attractive tourist resort of ►Voss, which is on the Bergen railway route (►MARCO POLO Insight p.444). Just a few miles from Voss the RV 13starts to wind its way through a varied landscape, looping around breathtaking mountain scenery and traversing narrow valleys with wild waterfalls hemmed in byhigh cliffs. Once past the highest point of the route at 262m/860ft, the **Skjerve-foss** waterfall can be seen crashing down from the heights.

From Voss to Bergen

Shortly before Granvin church (1720), which contains what are probably Norway's oldest bells, the RV 572 turns off towards the Osafjord, an arm of the Hardangerfjord where the idyllic tourist resortof Ulvikis located. The impressive panoramic road – whose several narrow sections will present a challenge to drivers of mobile homes – winds past green meadows, small farms and orchards before reaching Ulvik. The views of the resort and the upto 1600m/5250ft-high mountains surrounding the fjord are superb. Ulvik is also home to Norway's oldest state school for fruit-growing, founded in 1765 by **Kristofer Sjursen Hjeltnes** who was also the first to cultivate potatoes in Norway. The small, white, wooden church (1858) contains a pretty altar panel dating from 1630 and beautiful leaf motifs painted by localartist Lars Osa (1860–1958). A real experience is a tour over the fjord and the Hardangerjøkulen glacier by waterplane.

**Ulvik

The RV 7 turns off into the 7511m/24643ft longVallavik tunnel heading for the **Bruravik** ferry port at Granvin, at the northern tip of the Granvinfjord. The port can also be reached from Ulvik and the idyllic Osafjord. The ferry to **Brimnes** (10mins) leads to the other side ofthe fjord heading east. Before the tunnel was built, it was often necessary to wait several hours in **Kvanndal** (14km/9mi south of Granvin), for the 50-minute ferryjourney to Kinsarvik. In fact, this ferry trip is still worth a detour, especially for those who want to visit Utne (20mins, ►p.234).

Ferry ports

A **smelting works** for ferrosilicium and ferrochrome can be seen on the western side of the Hardangerfjordat in Ålvik. Above the works, its system of pipes using the 880m/2888ft-high Bjølvefoss waterfall is visible. The warmed water is then also used in the fjord for **salmon farming**, which is an important economic sector in the Hardanger region.

Ålvik

Hardanger Akvasenter

At Fykesund it is possible to have a peek behind the scenes at a typical Norwegian fish farm – from the rearing of the young fish to the production of the seafood speciality ready for the table. An expert takes visitors out on the fjord to the salmon farm, and an underwater camera provides live pictures of the life of the salmon.

After 12km/8mi, the **Fyksesund bru** comes into view, a narrow suspension bridge, built in 1939, crossing the mouth of Fyksesund. Passing strawberry fields and fruit plantations, the RV 7 reaches the village of **Øystese**. Opposite the church, there is a **museum** containing the 150 works by the sculptor **Ingebrigt Vik** (1867–1927), whose most famous piece is a statue of Edvard Grieg in Bergen.

Salmon farming: summer only, daily 11am–5pm; www.akvasenter.no
Ingebrigt Vik Museum: June–Aug Tue–Sun 10am–5pm;
www.hardangerogvossmuseum.no

*Norheimsund

An ideal place for an interim stop is Norheimsund (pop.1500), a picturesque holiday resort with a little harbour and the renowned Sandven Hotel, a Swiss style white painted wooden palais dating from 1857. In clear weather, it is possible to spot the icefields of the Folge-

Neither ocean nor lake, but the Hardangerfjord that widens substantially at Strandebarm

fonna glacier on the other side of the fjord. A tunnel over 11km/7mi long was built underneath the glacier in 2001, and connects Odda on the Sørfjord with Rosendal (▶ p.230). In Norheimsund it is possible to watch tradesmen at their traditional work at the **museum dockyard**. A short tour on the fjord is also heartily recommended.

The RV 7 now leaves the fjord, heading west towards Bergen (85km/ 53mi). After 2km/1mi, the wild Steinsdalsfossen waterfall formed by the Fosselva river comes into view to the right, in the midst of lovely countryside. During the summer months tourists virtually step on each other's toes on their way to the waterfall. A curious fact: it is possible to walk behind the thundering 30m/98ft wall of water without getting wet.

*Steinsdalsfoss

The road now inclines upwards, winding along an astounding 3km/ 2mi stretch through the impressive Tokagjelet gorge. While drivers must enter four cleverly hewn tunnels cut into the rock, cyclists and pedestrians have to brave the old path on the outside of the tunnels, directly above the abyss. The road then leads onwards to the Veafjord where it joins the E 16 to Bergen, passing the lively recreational region of **Kvamskogen** and its numerous holiday cabins, going along the Samnangerfjord, and crossing the ski and hiking region of Gullbotn.

Tokagjelet

It is possible to follow theHardangerfjord from Norheimsund to Mundheim on the RV 49 and then drive to Bergen via Eikelandsosen and Tysse (detour of 56km/35mi). Alternatively, there is a route from Eikelandsosen to Fusa, on to Hattvik by ferry (20mins) and via Osøyro and Søfteland to Bergen – a detour of 20km/13mi.

Alternative routes to Bergen

The RV 49 winds its way along the west bank of the fjord from Norheimsund to the little church village of Vikøy, where Norway's well-known painter Adolph Tidemand (1814–76) painted many of his pictures. Several miles beyond Vikøy, at the foot of the Salthammaren cliff in the village of Vangdal, there is 3500-year old rock art to be found, largely with images of ships. High up the hill there are also 5000-year old images of herds of animals, especially elk and deer. These, however, are hard to reach.

Vikøy

13km/8mi south of Norheimsund, in the village of Tørvikbygd, the **car ferry to Jondal** sets out on its 20-minute journey. From there, skiers can reach the popular **Folgefonn summer ski resort** (1200m/ 3937ft) located at the northern end of the Folgefonn glacier which, at 34km/21mi long and up to16km/10mi wide, is Norway's third largest. Skis can be used here from June toOctober, either to head downhill alongside **Norway's longest glacier lift** (1100m/1203yd) or to

Summer skiing

go cross country skiing and glacier hiking on routes of varying degrees of difficulty (glacier guides: www.folgefonni-breforarlag.no). The 36km/22mi-long stretch between Jondal and Utne is extremely narrow but a very rewarding way to experience nature in all its glory.

From Strandebarm to Holdhus

Once there was a flourishing boat-building industry in the church village of Strandebarm (on the RV 49 south of Nordheimsund) on the Strandebarm bay. Few now build the traditional wooden boats known as the »Strandebarmer«, though the beautiful bathing beach remains. Mundheim is reached 15km/9mi after Oma, where aluminium catamarans are built for customers from around the world. From there the RV 48 can be followed north in the direction of Holdhusand Eiklandsosen (17km/11mi). The interior of the **wooden church at Holdhus** is decorated with wonderful vines and friezes. The pulpit dates from 1570 and is possibly the oldest west Norwegian ulpit from the time of the Reformation. Shortly outside **Eikelandsosen**, the Koldalsfossen waterfall crashes down into the depths.

**Rosendal Barony

The Hardangerfjord intersects the RV 48 at its southern end and at the southern continuation of the road lies the Rosendal Barony. It can either be reached from the north via the 11km/7mi-long Folgefonn tunnel, or by means of the ferry from Gjermundshavn (25mins,

The Rosendal barony is a popular excursion destination thanks to its rose garden and its fine interious

13km/8mi south of Mundheim) to Løfallstrand; or from the south via the E 134 and Skånevik. Karen Mowat, one of Norway's wealthiest heiresses, and the poor Danish aristocrat Ludvig Rosenkrantz were given the Hattenberg estate in Rosendal as a wedding gift in 1658. Rosenkrantz had the estate remodelled into a Nordic Renaissance-style palace by 1665, and King Christian V elevated it to a barony 13 years later. Todayit is one of the region's most visited sights. Since the 19th century, it hasalso been surrounded by a **picturesque, land-scaped park** which provides wonderful views onto the Hardanger-fjord and its mountain backdrop with several waterfalls. The **rose-garden** is especially worth seeing. The palace is now a **museum** offering guided tours and also serves as avenue for concerts played on its Pleyel grand piano dating from 1860, theatrical performances in the courtyard and art exhibitions in the wine cellar.

Not far from here is one of Norway's oldest medieval stone churches, **Kvinnherad church** dating from 1255, which has Romanesque and Gothic style elements. For a long period it was the private property and burialground of the barony.

Rosendal Barony: May–Sep daily 11am–3pm, July–mid-Aug 10am–6pm, tours every hour; 100 NOK; www.baroniet.no

WHAT TO SEE AROUND THE SØRFJORD AND EIDSFJORD

Small fjord villages dot the shores of the northern end of the narrow, 45km/28mi-long Sørfjord – the longest branch of the Hardanger-fjord. Pleasant banks give way to more dramatichigh mountains and the mighty Folgefonn glacier lies above the western shore, whereas the steep slopes of the ▶Hardangervidda mountains on the eastern side make excellent hiking country.

Sørfjord

The industrial town of Odda, a place of great economic significance for Norway inthe past century, lies at the southern end of the fjord surrounded by high mountains. Workers from all over Scandinavia flocked here at the beginning of the20th century, when several smelt-ing works, industrial outfits and the Tyssedalhydro-electric power station opened in the interior of the fjord. Daily life during those times is recalled in three worker's apartments on Folgefonngata that have been turned into a **museum**.Not far from the constructions of the industrial era you can enjoy the unadulterated natural landscape of the millennia-old Buarbreen close-up, an outflow glacier of the Folgefonna Glacier. An easy hike leads through the ancient wood-lands of the green Buardal Valley and out onto the edge of the glacier, though you can only step onto the glacier itself, if on a guided tour.

Odda

Glacier tour: among others, Hardanger Breføring, tel. 90 64 49 75

Tyssedal   The Tyssedal hydro-electric power station stands majestically to the north of Odda, right on the Sørfjord. It is possible to relive the days between 1906 and 1918 when the great turbines here produced energy for the industrial plants in Odda and Tyssedal. The high pillars of the turbine hall, which was one of the first high pressure plants in Europe, are somewhat reminiscent of a cathedral. Meanwhile, the former administrative building in Tyssedal today houses the **Norwegian Hydro-power and Industry Museum**, which recounts the history of the two industrial settlements and the lives of the workers who once lived here. The 33m/108ft-high and 529m/1735ft-long **Ringedal Dam**, a masterpiece built by hand out of granite between 1910 and 1918, lies above Tyssedal, in the barren landscape of the Hardangervidda mountain plateau near Skjeggedal.

Norwegian Hydro-power and Industry Museum: May–Sep daily 10am–5pm, otherwise Tue–Fri 10am–3pm; 90 NOK; www.nvim.no

Side trip to   To the south of Odda, it is worth making a detour to the formerly
Sauda   important industrial town of Sauda. Just a short distance after leaving Odda, the **Låtefoss** waterfall appears to the left, its mass of water tumbles down a 400m/1312ft-long series of steps descending from the Hardangervidda mountains. The final 165m/541ft section is especially spectacular and covers the road in a **haze of spray**. Crossing the barren Røldalsfjell and passing through the Ekkjeskaret ravine (closed in winter), the RV520 finally reaches its highest point at 900m/2952ft. Driving along the Eld ravine, there is then a wonderful view of the imposing mountain landscape before reaching Sauda, where **Europe's largest ferrous alloy works**(Eramet Norway) can be visited by guided tour. From July to mid-August, it is also possible to take a tour of the nearby **zinc mine**. A visit to the settlement built for the miners at Åbøbyen and the industrial workers museum housed in two restored apartments dating from 1920and 1960 provide a fascinating insight into the workers' lives.

Ferrous Alloy Works: tours July–mid-Aug during the week at noon, book at the tourist office, tel. 52 78 39 88
Zinc mine: 2-hr tours July–mid-Aug, daily 2pm

»Agatunet«   Leaving Odda, the narrow RV 550 winds its way along the west bank of the Sørfjord, beginning underneath the snow fields of the Folgefonn and continuing between numerous fruit orchards to Aga (28km/18mi) and »Agatunet«, a really beautiful hamlet of around 30 to 40 buildings among narrow lanes, all listed buildings under a preservation order, and complete with a medieval smoke house, the Lag-

The Låtefoss foams madly as it descends from Hardangervidda and cascades down a 400m/1312ft-long series of steps into the Hardangerfjord

mannstova (»judge's chamber«). The oldest letter held at the University of Bergen's library is from Aga and dated 1293, proving that people were already living here at the end of the 13th century.

Agatunet: mid-May–mid-June, Wed–Sun, mid-June–Mid-Aug daily 10am–5pm; 70 NOK; www.hardangerogvossmuseum.no

*Utne   About 17km/11mi further to the north, on the west side of the mouth of the Sørfjord, lies one of this region's most romantic fjord villages: Utne is especially worth visiting for its **view over the Hardangerfjord**. Those arriving by ferry, either from Kvanndal or Kinsarvik, can spot the small church from 1895 and anEnglish-style little wooden palace painted white (the Utne Hotel) from a good way off. The **Hardanger Folkemuseum**, not far from the pier, is worth seeing. Its oldest building dates back to the 13th century and there are also historic boat houses with boats and fishing equipment, right by the water. Above the main building containing tools and folk arts and crafts, it is also possible to take a stroll inthe orchard where historic fruit varieties are cultivated. On Tuesdays during July, women bake the traditional Krotakaker, which is definitely worth tasting.

Hardanger Folk Museum: May–Sep daily 10am–5pm, otherwise Mon–Fri 9am–3pm; 70 NOK; www.hardangerogvossmuseum.no

Lofthus   After leaving Tyssedal and Odda, the RV 13 winds its way along the eastern bank of the Sørfjord, through orchards and blossoming meadows, until it reaches the pretty tourist resort of Lofthus 30km/19mi away. South of the settlement stands the **stone church of Ullensvang**, which dates from the 13th century and contains a medieval font and bells. New strains of fruit and berries are constantly being cultivated at the national experimental orchards here and, in Ullensvang alone, 80%of the country's sweet cherries are harvested. The largest farm in the Hardanger region is the Opedal estate, where the monks from the Lyse monastery at Bergen maintained a chapel during the Middle Ages. They also cultivated a fertileorchard and built the **monks' steps** that lead up to the 900m/2953ft Hardangervidda highland plateau: a steep ascent that takes around three hours. At the top there is a unique view over the Hardangerfjord. The composer Edvard Grieg's (1843–1907) hut stands in the garden of the deeply traditional Ullensvang Hotel in Lofthus, a place

! MARCO POLO TIP

Four in one   Insider Tip

Four spectacular waterfalls can be passed during a hike through the Kinso valley, walking from Kinsarvik up to Hardangervidda. The valley is one of Norway's loveliest natural landscapes and offers many beautiful views onto the fjord. The spray from the waterfalls encourages an explosion of green vegetation along the path and the rocks are covered in a thick carpet of moss, while many trees sport long beards of moss and lichen.

to which he withdrew, in his early life especially, to compose on the shores of the Hardangerfjord.

Beyond **Kinsarvik**, the centre of the parish of Ullensvang and home to the Brimnes ferry port (ferries to Utne 25mins; Kvanndal 50mins; Bruravik 10mins), sections of the road now follow directly along the bare rock along the steep banks of the Eidsfjord, the eastern branch of the Hardangerfjord, until reaching the small settlement of Eidfjord after around 40km/25mi.

Eidfjord

North of Eidfjord, at the beginning of the Simadal, the Kjeåsen track leads through a 2km/1mi-long tunnel to reach the remote **Kjeåsen farmhouse**, from which there are wonderfully beautiful views onto the Hardangervidda summits as well as down onto the fjord. A more interesting alternative to the route through the tunnel is taking the old climbing track that ascends the almost vertical cliff face to reach Kjeåsen farm. In the old days, this was the only way up to the summer pastures that lie 600m/1967ft above the fjord. The ascent can be made in around 1.5 hrs by those with a good level of fitness.

Simadalen

The Hardangervidda Nature Centre is a major attraction about 6km/4mi south of Eidfjord that presents the history, geology, flora, fauna and wonders of nature of the ▶Hardangervidda mountains and fjord country in an impressive way with the help of dioramas, aquariums and films.

*Hardanger-
vidda
Natursenter

Hardangervidda Nature Centre: April–Oct 10am–6pm, 15th June–20th Aug till 8pm; 120 NOK; www.hardangerviddanatursenter.no

** Hardangervidda

✳ **B/C 3-5**

Region: South Norway
Height: 1200–1600m/3937–5250ft

The Hardangervidda highland plateau is the largest in Europe – an austere, treeless expanse dotted with numerous lakes and broad areas of moorland. For an even more intense experience of the colours and shapes of this light-flooded country, the visitor should strike out on foot rather than touring by car on the RV 7.

3400 sq km/1313 sq mi of Hardangervidda's 9000 sq km/3475 sq mi form Norway's largest national park, while additional areas are also officially protected. It is an impressive landscape characterized by large expanses of moorland, an enormous number of lakes, and rivers

In the land of
wild reindeer

rich in fish, as well as the typical Norwegian fjell vegetation, such as mosses, lichen and dwarf birch. To the southwest, the Hardangervidda mountains present a different character. Here a rough alpine landscape predominates, where the highest peak in the region is **Sandfloeggi** at 1719m/5640ft. Reindeer graze on the bare mountain pastures; these are the largest **reindeer herds living in the wild** anywhere in Europe. This landscape above the tree line is rough and uncomfortable, yet also very impressive, so the Hardangervidda region is renowned for hiking, fishing and hunting and popular among skiers during winter.

Access The best access to the region is offered by the RV 7 from Geilo (►Hallingdal) to Eidfjord, which divides Hardangervidda from the area around Hardangerjøkulen, a snowfield covering 120 sq km/46 sq mi to the north at an elevation of 1862m/6109ft. The RV 7 climbs up from Haugastøl (990m/3248ft) to reach its highest point at the Dyranut turisthytte (1246m/4088ft), before descending into the Bjoreia valley.

Very little distraction, a lot of nature: find yourself in the Hardangervidda

Enjoy Hardangervidda

INFORMATION
Tourist offices in Odda, Eidfjord (►Hardangerfjord) and Geilo (►Hallingdal).

SPORT
Ski Race
The »Skarve Nordic Ski Race« is held in April, a 36km/23mi-long race from Finse to Ustaoset www.skarverennet.no).

Glacier tours
Glacier tours onto Hardangerjøkulen are offered out of Finse (information from the DNT, see p. 124).

WHERE TO EAT
Finsehytta £
Finse, Tel. 56 52 67 32
Close to Finse railway station, value for money meals offered at the comfortable mountain hut. Definitely try the »rømmegrøt«, a delicious porridge (open from beginning of July to mid-Sep and from approx. 20th Feb to approx. 20th May).

WHERE TO STAY
Finse 1222 £ £ £ £
Finse

Tel. 56 52 71 00
www.finse1222.no, 43 rooms.
This alpine hotel is right next to Norway's highest railway station and therefore an ideal base for hiking and ski tours in the Hardangerjøkulen region. The only option is full board which is expensive, though guests do enjoy the excellent cuisine.

Fossli Hotel £ £ £
Vøringfossen, Tel. 53 66 57 77
www.fossli-hotel.com, 21 rooms.
The hotel has seen better days, but the view onto the waterfall and the Måbo valley is still terrific. The list of famous guests is long and includes Edvard Grieg, who found inspiration here.

Halne Fjellstova £ £
Tel. 53 66 57 12
www.halnefjellstova.no
The mountain lodge lies on the RV 7 in the barren Hardangervidda landscape 44km/28mi from Geilo; open from Easter to mid-Oct. Rooms, cabins and holiday apartments.

The famous Rallarvegen constructionand supply route for the Bergen railway line begins in Haugastøl, winding its waythrough the rugged mountain world of Hardangervidda – mostly above the tree line – all the way to Norway's highest railway station at Finse (1222m/4009ft), before descending down to the Flåmtal valley at sea level. The 90km/56mi-long gravel road was built in the most mountainous section of the Bergen line at the endof the 19th century and today makes for one of Europe's most beautiful cycletracks. Accommodation options, such as DNT hiking huts (►MARCO POLO Insight p.118; address: active holidays p.124) can be found at Finse, Hallingskeid and Myrdal. The last20km/13mi stretch of the road from Myrdal down to Flåm (►Voss) isthe most adventurous.

*Rallarvegen

**Måbødal, Vøringfoss   A small toll roadbranches off to the Fossli Hotel about 20km/13mi beyond Dyranut. It lies just ashort distance from the main road above the edge of the Måbødal, at a height of 729m/2392ft, and offers a beautiful view onto the Vøringfoss waterfall. The Bjoreia waterfall cascades182m/597ft in an unbroken vertical drop into the narrow abyss below, from which adense haze of water spray continuously rises to the upper rim, producing wonderfulrainbow effects that are especially beautiful in the afternoon sun. There are alsomagnificent views down into Måbødal and its almost vertical cliff faces from thefalls above, as well as from a viewing point directly on the road. The Vøringfosshas lost much of its drama these days because of the large amount of water siphonedoff for energy production in the nearby power station; the construction of thetunnel didn't help either. But the old railway track has been converted into awonderful footpath that leads downwards after the turning into the wild Måbødalvalley. Passing the almost vertical cliffs in five large loops, the route leads downto Måbø (250m/820ft). Cyclists are fortunate to be directed to the old trackthat has also been turned into a nice footpath and takes one hour to getfrom the lower end of the old road up to the Vøringfoss. The original track hereconsisted of 124 bends and 1300 steps, and some remains of these can still be seenin the rock. To the west, the Hardangervidda uplands descend steeply to the Sørfjord (►Hardangerfjord), the RV 13 following along its east bank. Tothe south, the picturesque ►Haukeli Road gets closest to thisregion.

> ❗ **BAEDEKER TIPP**
>
> *Travelling on the Troll Train*
>
> An attraction for children: from June to August, the Troll Train travels through the Måbødal valley between the Vøringfoss waterfall and the Måbø Gård Museum. Departures from Vøringfoss are every hour on the hour between 10am and 6pm; from Måbø Gård Museum departures are at 30 minutes past the hour from 10.30am onwards; tickets at Eidfjord Turistkontor.

Numedal   A delight, especially with children, is a ride by railroad cart along the closed 23km/14mi stretch of the Numedal railway, in the district of Buskerud, between Veggli and Rødberg. 25 well-preserved railcarts are available to rent from the Veggli Vertshus inn.
   ❶ Tel. 32 74 79 00; www.veggli-vertshus.no

HIKING IN HARDANGERVIDDA

Suitable for families too   Since the footpaths mostly run atan elevation between 1200m/3281ft and 1400m/4593ft and there are almost nodifferences in height levels to overcome, this »moon landscape« is a paradise forfamilies hiking with younger children. Several of the roughly 35 huts (usuallyover-crowded between mid-July and mid-August) are located just a few hours' walk from each other and connected by clearly signposted paths maintained by the Norwegian hiking association (DNT). For experienced hikers, meanwhile, the Hardangerjøkulen glacier (1876m/6155ft) is an absolute highlight. The Fossli Hotel makes a good base for several beautiful-walking tours. A highly recommended route is the path (13–14.5hrs) along the western edge of the Hardangerjøkulen glacier via the Demmevass hut located at 1280m/4100ft, which leads on to Finse (1222m/4009ft). However, the immediate environs of Finse are pretty overrun most of the time.

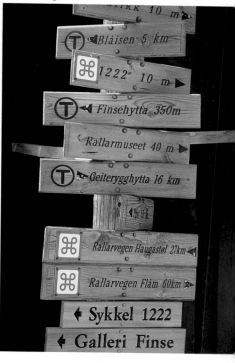

Always pack a map – despite the good sign-posting

From Geilo the route continues in the direction of Bergen, to **Halne Fjellstova** (approx. 42km/26mi; accommodation available), where there is the opportunity to do a one-day walking tour setting off from the **Vegmannsbu Turistsenter**. At first the narrow footpath heads northwest alongside **Halnekollen** (1358m/4455ft), then joining the main hiking route marked with the red »T« coming in from the left. After a short distance a small land-bridge is crossed between the Dragøyfjord in the northwest and the Storekrækkja in the southeast, from which in good weather walkers can enjoy a tremendous view. Next, the route passes the **Krækkja hut** that offers food and also accommodation. At this point walkers have a choice: either to make a large loop east via the **Fagerheim Fjellstue** and return along the southern banks of the Ørteren, or to follow the path that leads **directly to Haugastøl**. The latter goes past several small lakes on the western flank of Flånuten (1248m/4095ft) and then follows the banks of the **Nedre** and the **Øvre Trestiklan**. Care should be taken when crossing the small river on stepping stones. A stony highland plateau is then traversed before descending to the Sløtfjord, where Haugastøl comes into view, which is very close to the Vegmannsbu Turistsenter.

Harstad

✦ L 13

Region: North Norway
Population: 23,700

Harstad is a modern and rather sober town that most travellers use as a stop-off point on the way to the Lofoten or the Vesterålen islands. The medieval Trondenes church is worth a visit.

Located 120km/75mi northwest of Narvik, this industrial town on the northern coast of Hinnøy island has no particular sights to offer, other than its beautiful location on the Vågsfjord. During the 19th century, herring fishing was of great significance for the local economy, and today Harstad is northern Norway's hub for oil and gas exploitation and an important economic and military zone. It does, however, host the annual International Music Festival in North Norway each June, and further lays claim to being a cultural centre with its children's Viking Festival and Hålogaland Country Music Festival in August, and the Illios Festival for New Music in February.

> **MARCO ⊕ POLO TIP**
>
> ! *EA Hurtigruten highlight*   Insider Tip
>
> Among those in the know, the coastal section between Harstad and Tromsø is considered one of the most beautiful on the long Hurtigruten route between Bergen and Kirkenes, so a boat journey along this stretch is a worthwhile taster.

WHAT TO SEE IN AND AROUND HARSTAD

City centre

An impressive set of buildings housing the **Cultural Centre** (»Harstad Kulturhus«), opened in 1992, and stands out at the port. It has a concert hall and a hotel. In front of Harstad's church, which dates from 1958, stands a statue in honour of local man **Hans Egede** (1686–1758), who is also known as »Greenland's Apostle« for his missionary work among the Eskimos there. His name, with its three Es, often features in crossword puzzles.

*Trondenes church

Most of Harstad's sights are to be found on the Trondenes peninsula, about 3km/2mi north of the city centre. Trondenes church, North Norway's best preserved medieval sacred building is here, whose original construction probably dates from around 1250, though the Romanesque stone church was only completed after 1430. Later, the church with its almost 2m/7ft thick walls was used for defensive purposes. The view of the Vågsfjord from here is breathtaking.

Harstad

INFORMATION
Turistkontor Harstad
Sjøsgata 1 b
9486 Harstad
tel. 77 01 89 89
www.destinationharstad.no

FJORD TOURS
The historic sailing boat »Anna Rogde«, built in 1868, and one of the oldest schooners in the world, is moored at the quay in front of the Cultural Centre. Every day at noon it sets off for a tour around the fjord.

FESTIVALS
The 8-day international Festival of North Norway (Festspillene i Nord-Norge) offers a broad cultural programme to appeal to every taste, from classical music and jazz, to literature, musicals, film and art exhibitions. A particular focus is on attractions for children (www.festspillnn. no).
On the other hand, the Ilios Festival of New Music in February is probably not to everyone's taste, but something for specialists and fans (www.ilios.no).

WHERE TO EAT
De 4 Roser £ £ £ £
Torvet 7 a
tel. 77 01 27 50, www.de4roser.no
A mecca for gourmets in the far north. Closed Sundays.

Kaffistova £
Richard Kaarbøsgt. 6
tel. 77 06 12 57
Rich in tradition, this café on the Hurtigruten quay also serves good local dishes.

WHERE TO STAY
Clarion Collection Hotel Arcticus £ £ £ – £ £ £ £
Havnegata 3, tel. 77 04 08 00
www.choicehotels.com, 75 rooms
This luxurious hotel is located right by the water's edge and offers a beautiful view across Harstad and the Vågsfjord. Significantly cheaper prices for holders of a hotel pass.

Røkenes Gård Og Gjestehus £ £
Stornesvn. 127
tel. 77 05 84 44, www.roekenesgaard.no
This country manor dating from 1750 is now a wonderfully nostalgic hotel with ten pretty rooms in which the flair of the past is combined with the modern comforts of today. The wedding suite in the main building is especially beautiful. Famous guests have included King Harald.

Centrum Gjestehus £ – £ £
Magnus gt. 5
tel. 77 06 29 38
post@centrumgjestehus.no, 15 rooms.
Simple but value for money accommodation near the Hurtigruten quay and the Cultural Centre.

To the south of Trondenes church stands the wood building of the Trondenes Historical Centre, where exhibitions on the history of the Vikings and the Christianization of North Norway are held. Located in a historical landscape, the building was especially designed to harmonize with its surroundings. **Historiske Senter**

❶ mid-May–mid-August, daily 10am–7pm

Adolf Cannon The »Adolf Cannon« can be discovered in the German fortifications built by the occupying forces during the Second World War, to the north of Trondenes church. It was intended to guard the access route to Narvik and Troms – and its 42cm/16in calibre makes it the largest land-based cannon in the world.

Bjarkøy Island Leaving Harstad by boat, several islands are passed before reaching Bjarkøy Island about one hour away, famous throughout Norway for the **Viking chieftains** of the Bjarkøy family, who lived here in the 9th century and feature in numerous sagas. Their best-known representative was probably **Tore Hund**, a canny merchant who amassed riches trading with Finns and Russians. In 1026, Tore raided Russian tombs for their gold, and was probably also the killer of King Olav the Holy during the Battle of Stiklestad (▶Steinkjer) in 1030. It seems that after these events his conscience nagged him, as he then set off on a journey to the Holy Land from which he was not to return. The roughly 700 inhabitants of the island have traditionally not only lived from fishing, but also – until recently – from the protected species of **Eider geese**, whose down is considered among the softest in the world. Bjarkøy and its several coastal settlements were autonomous until 2012, but integrated with Harstad on 1st January 2013.

✳ Haukeli Road

✦ B 2-4

Region: South and West Norway

The Haukeli Road is barely 200km/125mi long and is one of southern Norway's most beautiful routes. Full of surprises, it begins in Telemark and winds up the bare Haukelifjell, visits the dramatic Åkrafjord, and ends at the coastal resort of Haugesund.

Road of contrasts The Haukeli Road (Haukelivegen: E 134, 184km/115mi) was opened in 1886, and has since become one of the most important and beautiful connecting roads between east and west Norway. Rich in contrasts, the Haukelivegen initially passes through a naked highland landscape with its deep blue lakes and sheep and goat herds that occasionally stray onto the road, as well as mountain passes that can easily hold their own with the European Alpine passes for sheer magnificence. It then enters a wild fjord landscape along the narrow Åkrafjord, with walls of rock that rise almost vertically out of the water and wild waterfalls. Last but not least, the journey ends with the broad, flat countryside around Haugesund and views onto the open sea.

Haukeli Road

INFORMATION
Haugesund Turistinformasjon
Strandgata 171
5525 Haugesund
tel. 52 01 08 30
www.visithaugesund.no

EXCURSIONS
Recommended only for those who have
found their sea legs, this day trip from
Haugesund goes to the small wild island
of Utsira, home to a great wealth of bird
species. The island is located in the middle of the frequently stormy North Sea
(crossing takes 1.5hrs 2-3 times daily).

CULTURE
Norway's largest film festival is held in
Haugesund annually in September
(www.filmweb.no/filfestivalen).

WHERE TO EAT
Big Horn Steak House £ £ £
Strandgata 130, Haugesund
tel. 52 72 90 00
ww.bighorn.no
Restaurant chain that specializes in
steaks. A modern place with views over
the water.

Lanternen £ £
Torget, Skudeneshavn
tel. 52 82 82 00
Café, restaurant and pub in a central location by the market. The water babbles
under the diners' chairs on »Sjøhus« terrace.

WHERE TO STAY
Clarion Collection Hotel Amanda £ £ £ £
Smedasundet 93

Haugesund
tel. 52 80 82 00
www.choice.no, 102 Z.
Hotel right by the water, in the heart of
Haugesund.

Haukeliseter Fjellstue £ £
Edland
tel. 35 06 27 77
www.haukeliseter.no
Cabin village in the highlands maintained by the Stavanger hiking club, located above the tree line, right on the
lake. The artfully decorated cabins are
over 100 years old and exude an air of
cosiness.

Norneshuset £ £
Nornes 7
Skudeneshavn
tel. 52 82 72 62
www.norneshuset.no, 5 Z.
This venerable, bright white wooden
house built in 1830 is the oldest and
largest of the row of buildings set on the
water. The narrow jetty to the water is
the ideal place for a comfortable breakfast. Per and Berit Nornes have decorated the rooms with a great deal of taste
and provide good service at a decent
price.

Vikholmen Leuchtturm £ – £ £
Skudeneshavn
tel. 52 82 85 97
Built in 1875, the lighthouse is located
at the port entrance of Skudeneshavn.
Included in the price of this unusual holiday apartment is a boat, with which the
lighthouse can be reached in just five
minutes. The three bedrooms offer ample room for six people.

ALONG THE HAUKELI ROAD

Heading west from Haukeligrend

Leaving Haukeligrend, the beginning of the Haukeli Road at the junction of the E 134 and RV 9, the route passes small mountain lakes in which trout can be fished (fishing permits are available at the hotels and mountain cabins). Beyond the Vågslid tunnel at the southeastern end of the deep blue Lake Ståvatnet, the mountain cabin known as **Haukeliseter** (986m/3235ft) comes into view, which has been in service since 1870. **Delicious creamy porridge known as rømmegrøt** can be enjoyed here, and there is also accommodation. This alpine cabin serves as a good base for hiking tours, as well as cross-country skiing tours to the ▶Hardangervidda National Park further to the north.

*Haukeli Pass

A short distance further on, the glowing ice fields of the steep slopes of Store Nupsfonn (1661m/5450ft) can be spotted to the north. The old pass over the **Haukelifjell** that begins right before the eastern end of the 5682m/18643ft long Haukeli tunnel is an absolute must for tourists. This incredibly beautiful highland route following the watershed between the Atlantic and the Skagerrak reaches its highest point at the 1145m/3757ft **Dyrskar**, set in the midst of mighty rock-strewn mountains.

Røldal

Traversing an impressive desert-like expanse of snow and rock and passing through several tunnels, the road leads down to Røldal and the lake of the same name. Here too, it is possible to choose the old road, which was constructed in 1880 as an impressive serpentine route made up of seven large loops, which has memorable views. The 13th-century **stave church** in Røldal contains a beautiful Renaissance altarpiece and a pulpit dating from 1627. The RV 520 branches off to Sauda southwest of Røldal.

? Sweating Crucifix

The stave church of Røldal was once a destination for pilgrims, because, on mid-summer night each year, the crucifix regularly began to sweat. Pilgrims believed this sweat could produce miracles and wiped it onto their wounds, and it was only in 1835 that it was realised the large number of pilgrims themselves were causing the wooden crucifix to »sweat« by increasing the humidity inside the church.

To the west of Røldal, the E 134 gradually winds its way up to the opening of the 4650m/15256ft-long **Røldal tunnel**. To the west, the white snow fields of the up to 1660m/5446ft-high Folgefon (▶Hardangerfjord) appear. Here, too, there are choices to be made: to the southeast of the tunnel, an old road leads up to the **Hordabrekkene**, a masterpiece of road building with a total of 16 hairpin bends and a spectacular view over Lake

Røldalvatn (only passable during summer). An equally impressive road, built in 1896, is the steep route lined by imposing walls of rock that follows the imposing **Seljestad gorge**, where it is still possible to discover remains of the original historic transport path.

The narrow Åkrafjord, surrounded by almost vertical smooth cliffs   ***Åkrafjord**
rising from the water, begins 15km/9mi after the Jøsendal junction (RV 13 to Odda). The old, narrow road running along steep mountain slopes has now been replaced by a modern road with several tunnels, including the 7406m/24298ft Åkrafjord tunnel (toll), at whose southwestern end there is a pretty rest stop with views onto the fjord. A novel way for vertigo-free visitors to experience the fjord is offered by Europe's highest »zip line« that was installed in the Trolljuv Gorge, in 2011. A ride across the gorge by zip line reaches speeds of up to 40km per hour/25 mi per hour, at a height of 105m/344ft. Participants are strapped into a harness attached to the steel cable and end their race across the water on a padded rock, right by the Trolljuv Bridge. The return is either by walking across the bridge or via a steep scramble along a path to the next zip line heading back. The spectacular new Trolljuv Adrenalin Park and Visitor Centre built by the Oslo architectural firm of Reiulf Ramstad took inspiration for its striking design from the surrounding natural landscape with the characteristic pointy elevations of the Trollveggen, and is set at the foot of the sheer cliffs. Visitors enjoy unobstructed views, whether from the glassed-in café, the outdoor terrace, or the large atrium under the open sky. A short documentary film illustrates the history of the rock face since its first ascent.

Trolljuv Gorge Zip line: June–Sep, Sat–Sun, mid-June–mid-Aug also on Tues and Thurs; information from the tourist office
Visitor Centre and Adrenalin Park: June–Aug; tel. 95 89 80 45; www.visit-trollveggen.com

The E 134 now winds its way through gentle countryside with pictur-   **Haugesund**
esque fjords and lakes that contrasts markedly with the dramatic natural landscapes further to the north. The road terminates in Haugesund (pop. 35000). Snorre Sturlasson, author of sagas, mentioned the town as early as 1217, though today the initial impression created by its offshore rigs and the Hydro aluminium giant is not particularly inviting. Down by the **port**, however, the lanes and streets on the Smeda sound lined with pretty white painted houses are inviting for a pleasant stroll.
Around 2km/1mi north of Haugesund, Crown Prince Oscar – later King Oscar II – had the magnificent tomb of **Haraldshaugen** built over the presumed grave of **Harald Fairhair**, who after a naval victory on the Harfrsfjord near Stavanger united Norway into one empire a thousand years ago. The monument consists of a 17m/56ft-

A clear mirror: Skudeneshavn

high obelisk and 29 stones that represent the 29 Norwegian tribes that were united at the time. A stone cross dating from AD 1000 stands to the south of this monument.

Avaldnes, **Norway's oldest royal residence**, lies shortly beyond the Karmsund bridge on the long stretched out island of Karmøy, and was once home to Harald Fairhair in the 9th century. Next to the former royal chapel (around 1250) stands Norway's highest Bauta stone (7m/23ft), known as the Virgin Mary's Needle. West of Avaldnes lie the seven grave mounds of Rehaugene dating from the Bronze Age. The island of Karmøy provided the copper for the New York statue of Liberty and the history of its copper mines is recounted in the local museum at Visnes.

Follow the RV 47 along the hilly western coast, with its occasionally superb views onto the open sea, to reach the small town of *Skudeneshavn in an idyllic setting. Its picturesque, narrow lanes and prettily restored white wooden houses make it a veritable El Dorado for photographers. Those with time should take the ferry to Mekjarvik, north of Stavanger, as an alternative to the main E 39 route that leads to Stavanger via numerous tunnels. The lovingly designed museum in the old Mælandsgården tells all about Skudeneshavn's golden age during the herring fishing era.

Mælandsgården Museum: end of June–mid-Aug, Mon–Fri 11am–5pm, Sun 1pm–6pm).

Vedavågen   The history of fishing since 1950, on the other hand, is covered by the Karmøy Fishing Museum in Vedavågen. The architecturally interesting building also houses a saltwater aquarium.

Karmøy Fishing Museum: mid-June–mid-Aug Mon–Fri 11am–4pm; 30 NOK; www.fiskerimuseum.net

The World's Most Beautiful Voyage

Do you know route 1? You will not find it on any map, although for many Norwegians it is the countrys most important transport route. It is »Hurtigruten«, the shipping route that is plied daily to all ports along the coast between western and northern Norway.

Eleven ships connect 34 ports along the 2300km/1437mi-long route from Bergen to Kirkenes on the Russian border in Norways high north. Until a few decades ago, some of the stops en route were only accessible on the postal ships of the Hurtigruten Line. The coastal express transports locals who have business in neighbouring ports, along with commuters and travellers, and mail, commercial goods and cars. The latter are heaved on board by means of a rather bizarre method using loading nets. The Gulf Stream ensures that all of Norways ports remain ice free throughout the year.

Panoramic View

This northern journey has long since become a tourist attraction, not least because the ships travel within sight of the coast almost the whole time, ensuring grandiose panoramic views. Travellers can feast their eyes on fjords, mountains, glaciers, islands and sub-arctic vegetation during the journey, not to mention such sensational natural phenomena as the midnight sun and the aurora borealis. In short, the Norwegian highlights can be experienced on this comfortable journey, an ideal and restful option for all those who would find a car touring holiday in this great land too strenuous. The journey takes six days. There and back takes eleven

days, and the ports that were visited at night on the way up are visited during the day on the way down, so nothing is missed.

Escaping Isolation

In 1891, the bureaucrat responsible for Norwegian steam shipping, A.K. Gran, authorized the Vesterålens Dampskibsselskap shipping company of Stockmarkens to establish a maritime route between Trondheim and Hammerfest. Sections of the route were already being traversed, but due to the darkness of the northern winter, many bays and islands were only visited as long as ships captains could see the countless skerries and islets. For remote settlements this meant isolation for many months of the

Ships have been plying the imperial Route 1 since 1893

Hurtigruten ships make stops along the route from Bergen to Kirkenes

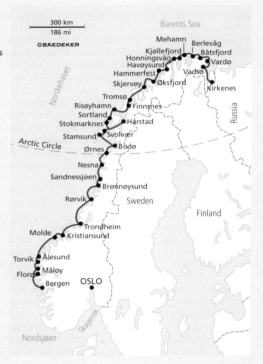

year. The Vesterålen ship owner Richard With was inspired to connect the Norwegian coastal settlements all year round, an idea that contemporaries considered too dangerous. With, however, had precise navigational charts drawn up so that captains could still keep to their course with the help of a watch and compass, even during the darkness of storm-battered polar nights. Withs ship Vesterålen left Trondheim for Hammerfest for the first time on 2 July 1893. Todays ships of between 6000 and 11,000 registered tons (the newest ships weigh up to 15,000 tons) have capacity for 550 to 1000 passengers, of which 312 to 674 can have cabins. Those without cabins can make do with a day trip on deck travelling to the next port.

Luxury and Work

The only accident that has occurred in over a century of service happened in 1964, when a ship went down with 64 people on board. The Hurtigruten ships are modern and safe, the latest models are even equipped with saunas, fitness rooms, gourmet restaurants and bars that give cruise ships a run for their money. The glamour of larger cruise ships is totally missing in the older ships though, and it is very obvious that they are workhorses. There are neither dinner parties nor other luxuries on board. Instead passengers can watch the crew at work and join in the everyday routine of the locals till the next port is reached, just as if travelling by bus. Towards the end of the 1970s, the Oslo government had plans to cut subsidies for the Hurtigruten shipping line, but the howls of protest could be heard along the entire coast and the project was shelved. A compromise has established that the two shipping companies running vessels along the Hurtigruten route will receive around 1.9 billion NOK from the state between 2005 and 2012, in return for continued service all year round to all 34 ports, including the less commercially profitable ones between Tromsø and Kirkenes.

Pure Pleasure

As prosaic as the Hurtigruten route may seem to Norwegian passengers, foreign travellers find it spectacular. The clocks move to a different rhythm during this, »the worlds most beautiful voyage«. The ship glides smoothly between the skerries, occasionally entering the lively open sea. Holidaymakers spend almost every minute on deck to enjoy the changing coastal landscapes: the rock faces of Lofoten rising out of the sea, the entrances into narrow fjords, such as the Trollfjord, and the barren tundra of Finnmark, to name but a few. Several tour operators combine the calls at port with a bus tour to sights inland. Crossing the Arctic Circle at 66.5° northern latitude is just one of the highlights of a Hurtigruten journey, and is usually accompanied by a small celebration. All-inclusive tours with arrival by plane or by railway can be arranged by the Norwegian shipping agent (www.hurtigruten.com).

Since the ships are first and foremost working ships, braver or less wealthy souls can still travel during winter in order to enjoy the icy beauty of the north, the rough seas and the dusky polar light.

Extremely modern ships ply the Hurtigruten route

** **Jostedalsbreen**

✳ D 3/4

Region: West Norway
Height: up to 2038m/6687ft

No matter which side you approach Jostedalsbreen from, the icy mass of the largest glacier on the European mainland is impressive. On no account should an excursion to the ice tongues of Nigardsbreen and Briksdalsbreen be missed, and the same applies to the Glacier Centre in the Jostedal valley.

Europe's largest glacier — The Jostedal Glacier or Jostedalsbreen is located between the Sognefjord and the Nordfjord. It measures almost 100km/62mi in length and encompasses an area of over 1200 sq km/463 sq mi if the adjoining ice fields are included. In geographical terms the glacier, which has been designated a national park, is a kind of »inland ice« or ice sheet, as found in Greenland. Just a few low rocks peek through the body of ice, whose depth is estimated to be around 500m/1640ft. The

The Jostedalsbreen glacier is as high as a house

surrounding valleys are filled with 26 large glacier tongues, of which 15km/9mi-long Tunsbergdalsbreen is only outdone by the Aletsch Glacier in Switzerland for size (in Europe). In the 1990s some glacier arms of the Jostedalsbreen grew again, due to above-average winter precipitation several years in a row – growth rates of 50–80m/165– 260ft per year were observed. However, because of several years with low winter precipitation and hot summers (2002 and 2003), the glacier arms have been significantly shrinking again since 2000.

WHAT TO SEE AROUND JOSTEDALSBREEN

These days tourists can comfortably explore the glacier tongues at several places. A decade ago, the rugged Jostedal valley to the east – a gash in the mighty mountain plateau, running north-south – still lay in a Sleeping Beauty slumber; today the RV 604 leads through the long valley flanked by steep walls of rock, through which the wild Jostedalselv river also flows. The road branches off from the RV 55 at **Gaupne**, on the northern shore of the Lustrafjord. The RV 604 leads on over Høgebru. At **Gjerde**, a small road to the left turns off into the Krundal valley, which can be followed as far as **Bergset**. To the south, the valley is crowned by Høgenipa (1535m/5036ft).
Jostedal

A magnificent, though tough, three-hour guided hike leads from Bergset along Bergsetbreen to the ice field of **Jostedalsbreen**, ascending the glacier to Høgste Breakulen (1953m/6408ft). Continuing in a northwesterly direction, an impressive view of the mountains on the ▶Nordfjord opens up after about an hour. This is followed by the occasionally challenging descent through the Kjenndal valley down to **Nesdal**, which lies at the southern end of Lake Lonvatn.
From the glacier to the Nesdal

At the previously mentioned junction near Gjerde, the RV 604 leads onwards to the north. To the left at Elvekrok (340m/1115ft) spreads Nigardsbreen. The last section (toll payable) of the road leads through a moraine field that has been created by the retreat of the Nigard Glacier over the past 200 years. It is possible to hike right up to the edge of the glacier (good walking shoes needed) along a stony path that starts at the car park at the end of the road.
Nigardsbreen

The very popular Jostedal Glacier Centre (Breheimsenter Jostedalen) at the beginning of the toll-charging road illustrated the 20,000-year-old

MARCO POLO TIP

! *To the glacier by boat* Insider Tip

The glacier tongue of Nigardsbreen can be reached very comfortably and quickly on the small Jostedalsrypa boat that constantly ferries back and forth from the quay at the car park between 10th July and the end of August (10am–6pm).

Jostedalsbreen

INFORMATION
Glacier Centre/Breheimsenteret
6871 Jostedal
tel. 57 68 32 50
www.jostedal.com

GLACIER HIKING TOURS
The Glacier Centre (see tel. above) arranges tours at all levels of difficulty, ranging from 2hrs to 4hrs in duration. Prices include the hire of complete sets of glacier equipment, including glacier boots. No more than average fitness is required for walking tours in the lower part of Nigardsbreen.

WHERE TO EAT
Briksdalsbre Fjellstove £ £
tel. 57 87 68 00
Cafeteria and restaurant at the end of the road into the Briksdal, above the car park. Those looking for peace and quiet should visit in the late afternoons. Accommodation available in 6 rooms and a nice cabin.

Lustrafjorden Kro £ – £ £
Along Str. 55
tel. 57 68 18 80
Restaurant with terrace right on the Lustrafjord with views to the Feigumfoss waterfall on the opposite shore. Home cooking and snacks.

WHERE TO STAY
Walaker Hotell £ £ £ £
Gjesgivargarden, Solvorn
tel. 57 68 20 80
www.walaker.com, 24 rooms.
The setting on the Lustrafjord alone is stunning. One of the most beautiful hotels in Norway, whose rooms with historic atmosphere, quiet garden and excellent restaurant will appeal to lovers of tradition.

Olden Camping £
tel. 57 87 59 34
www.oldencamping.com
Small and friendly campsite for mobile homes and tents, including a few simple and well-priced cabins. Unique location right on the lake, with views of the Jostedalsbreen. Around 13km/8mi from Olden.

Urnes Gard £
Ornes on the Lustrafjord, near Urnes stave church
tel. 91 53 27 84
www.urnes.no, 2 rooms, 3 cabins
Historic farm where the nobility enjoyed a hospitable reception back in the Middle Ages. Britt and Odd John Bugge also cultivate raspberries, blueberries, strawberries, cherries and apples, which they sell in their small farm shop.

natural and cultural history of the Jostedalsbreen area, but was completely destroyed by a fire in 2011. Business continues during reconstruction, however, and tours for the spectacular kayak trips on the glacial lakes of Styggevatnet and Tunsbergdalsvatnet can still be booked, as can rafting tours on the Jostedal river. A café and souvenir shop complete the current services for visitors.

Breheimsenter Jostedalen: May–end of Sep 10am–5pm, mid-June–mid-Aug 9.30am–5.30pm; www.jostedal.com

There are also numerous glacier arms on the northwestern side of Jostedalsbreen, the best-known being Briksdalsbreen. The starting point for a visit is the small settlement of Olden on the Innvikfjord. Here, a road branches off south into the beautiful Olderdal valley. After passing the 11km/7mi-long Lake Oldenvatnet and numerous waterfalls, Briksdal (150m/492ft) is reached. ****Briksdalsbreen** Briksdalsbreen, an arm of Jostedalsbreen, is reached along a footpath after about one hour, where the gigantic blue body of ice can be seen rising above the forest (▶Nordfjord).

*Oldenvatnet

An additional access route to Jostedalsbreen, only opened in 1994, is the toll-charging RV 5 – known as the Fjærlandsveg – which runs through a outstandingly beautiful landscape to **Fjærland**. The interesting Norwegian Glacier Museum there is a good source of information on the secrets of the eternal ice. It is possible to experiment with ice here and answer such questions as why ice is blue and fjords are green. A model hydroelectric power station also shows how meltwater from a glacier produces electricity.

Norwegian Glacier Museum: April–Oct 10am–4pm, June–Aug 9am–7pm; 120 NOK; www.bre.museum.no

> **MARCO ● POLO TIP**
>
> *A village full of books* Insider Tip
>
> Fjærland is worth a detour for its beautiful wooden houses and idyllic setting on the fjord alone. For book lovers, the village is a positive must, as about twelve antiquarian bookshops have roughly 250,000 second-hand books for sale here between May and September. The vast majority are Norwegian paperbacks, but those with time to hunt around a bit will find something in English.

** Jotunheimen

✦ D 4/5

Region: West and East Norway
Height: up to 2468m/8097ft

The Jotunheimen mountains constitute the most alpine landscape in Norway, containing Scandinavia's highest peaks: a range of magnificent summits and glaciers cut into by clear streams and lakes. The Norwegians reverentially call their favourite hiking region the »Home of Giants«, and dig out their walking boots to pay homage every summer.

Inspired by the wild landscape and Nordic mythology, it was the writer Aasmund Olavsson Vinje who christened the region »Jøtunheimen«, meaning land of giants. For him, this was the obvious home of the Jøten, the giant trolls. This predominantly untouched fjell land-

scape is characterized by majestic mountains and glaciers, but also by several extensive lakes, barren valleys and treeless plateaus, and extends between Oppland in the east and Sogn og Fjordane in the west.

IN THE JOTUNHEIMEN NATIONAL PARK

At the heart of the Jotunheimen mountain range lies the national park of the same name. The largest part of the park area is at elevations of 1000m/3281ft and higher, and is therefore above the tree line. Norway's highest mountains lie here: Galdhøppigen (2469m/8100ft) and Glittertind (2452m/8045ft). Galdhøppigen is among the most climbed summits in the country, not only because it is the highest, but also because the ascent is not difficult during summer (p. 257).

Above the tree line

The southwestern part of the national park is formed by the Hurrungane range, which is largely cut off from the rest of the Jotunheimen mountains by the deep Utladal valley. Six of Norway's highest peaks are bunched closely together here, dominated by the most popular climbing summit, the imposing Store Skagastølstind (2405m/7891ft). The Hurrungane mountains may be paradise for rock climbers, but this bizarre mountainous world is also a worthwhile destination for hikers and walkers.

*Hurrungane

Thanks to an extensive network of signposted footpaths and cabins maintained by the Norwegian hiking association (DNT), the shipping routes over the Gjende and Bygdin lakes, and road routes 51 and 55, the Jotunheimen massif is easily explored. For this reason, though, several of the classic routes, such as over **Beseggengrat**, become **unusually crowded** by Norwegian standards during the summer holiday season. The most beautiful time for hiking here begins at the end of June and goes until September – earlier in the year the snow fields, wet ground and total absence of any greenery spoil the pleasure somewhat. During winter, the Jotunheimen mountains are an excellent and popular destination for cross-country ski tours. Easter is peak season, and at this time many Norwegians are drawn to the mountains and almost all cabins are operational.

Walking in the »Home of Giants«

ALONG THE SOGNEFJELLVEGEN

Route 55 winds its way from the Lustrafjord via Skjolden onto Sognefjell. There is a magnificent view onto the valley, fjord and the Hur-

From Skjolden into the Leirdal valley

Norway's most famous and most visited hiking region is the Jotunheimen. Camping wild in the open enhances the experience of nature

Jotunheimen

INFORMATION
Beitostølen
Along Main Road
2953 Beitostølen
tel. 61 35 10 00
www.beitostolen.com

Lom
In the Fjellmuseum
2686 Lom
tel. 61 21 29 90
www.visitjotunheimen.com

GETTING THERE
One of Norway's most beautiful roads leads through the Jotunheimen: route 51 runs from Fagernes via Valdresflya as far as the E 15 near the small settlement of Vågåmo, and ends on the E 15 near Lom. During winter the high mountain sections of the road are closed.

WHERE TO EAT/WHERE TO STAY
Fossheim Turisthotell £ £ £
Bergomsvegen 32, Lom
tel. 61 21 95 00
www.fossheimhotel.no
This former coaching inn was transformed into a luxurious hotel as long ago as 1897. Today, the head chef is Kristoffer Hovland, who was voted Norway's »Chef of the Year« in 2004. The hotel director Svein Garmo complements the service with his passion for the world's best wines, which he imports himself.

WHERE TO STAY
Elveseter Hotel £ £ £
Elveseter, tel. 61 21 99 00
www.elveseter.no
The buildings of the Elveseter Hotel next to the Saga Pillar recall a typical country estate from a bygone era. The entrance hall, tastefully decorated with antiques, creates a special atmosphere. Paintings, by Adolf Tidemandt among others, and antique furniture with rose painting add to the hotel's museum-style character.

Valdresflya Vandrerhjem £ £
Beitostølen, tel. 90 12 23 51
www.valdresflya-vandrerhjem.com
46 beds.
This youth hostel stands at the highest point of the Valdresflya pass, at 1389m/4557ft. It is the ideal base for discovering the Jotunheimen massif. Advance booking recommended. Open during the Easter holidays, and then again from the beginning of June to end of August.

rungane peaks from the **Turtagrø Hotel** (900m/2953ft). The hotel is also a good base for **hiking tours** to Skagastølstind, Dyrhaugstind or Austabotntind. Following the main road, known as the Sogenfjellvegen, the route continues steadily uphill until the highest point is reached at the **Sognefjellhytta** (cabin at 1434m/4705ft). The panorama either side of the road is impressive: a high alpine landscape with jagged peaks, snow fields that survive long into the summer months, and several smaller glaciers. There is a small summer skiing resort on Sognefjell and it is possible to rent cross country skis from the cabins along the road. The signposted footpaths begin from the car parks and make for worthwhile one-day walks as well as longer tours. Beyond the Sognefjellhytta, the road slowly but steadily leads downwards into the **Leirdal**valley. To the right, there now follow three toll-charging secondary roads, one after the other, heading to Leirvassbu, the **Juvasshytta and Spiterstulen** respectively. At the end of each road there is a mountain hut that is ideally suited as a base for hikes into the central Jotunheimen mountains.

If **Spiterstulen** is chosen as a base, which is located in the valley between the Galdhøppigen and Glittertind peaks, Norway's two highest mountains can be climbed from the same place. Note, however, reaching the summit of Galdhøppigen requires an ascent of around 1400m/4593ft on a steep path (there and back takes around 5hrs). The path up Glittertind is equally strenuous and, depending on levels of fitness, at least 7–9hrs should be calculated for the hike. The best point to begin an ascent of Galdhøppigen is the **Juvasshytta** mountain cabin. The ascent to the summit is easy and only takes around 3–4hrs. Nevertheless, it is essential to join one of the daily guided tours, because the path leads across the Svellnos Glacier (Svellnosbreen), which is cut by crevasses. *Galdhøppigen, Glittertind*

To the left of the Elveseter Hotel, shortly before the turn-off to the Juvasshytta, the 33m/108ft Saga Column comes into view. Offering a cross section through Norwegian history, beginning with the first unified empire in 872 and ending with the Council of 1814, the column was designed by W. Rasmussen prior to the Second World War and was originally intended to stand in front of the Storting (national assembly) in Oslo. *Saga Column*

> **!** *Minerals galore* Insider Tip
>
> MARCO POLO TIP
>
> A substantial collection of minerals can be seen at the Fossheim Steinsenter on the edge of Lom, heading out towards Vågå, and afterwards jewellery and minerals are offered for sale in the souvenir shop (tel. 61 21 14 60, http://fossheimsteinsenter.no; during summer daily 10am–6pm).

The Sogenfjellvegen finally ends in **Lom**, the main tourist centre of the northern Jotunheimen mountains. The place compares favourably with many other, more austere, settlements due to its numerous dark wooden houses. The greatest sight is the 800-year-old basilica style **stave church**, whose choir arch and pulpit (1793) are by the wood carver Jakob Sæterdalen. Just a few steps further away stands the **Norwegian Mountain Museum** (Norsk Fjellmuseum), which provides a very useful overview of the Norwegian fjells.

Norwegian Mountain Museum: mid-May–mid-Sep 9am–4pm, Sat 10am–4pm, Sun till 3pm, July–mid-Aug 9am–7pm, Sun till 5pm; 70 NOK; www.fjell.museum.no.

OVER THE VALDRESFLYA PLATEAU

Beitostølen From Fagernes, route 51 climbs slowly but surely northwards until it reaches the tree line and the southern edge of the Jotunheimen mountains near Beitostølen. The large cabin and lodge settlement of Beitostølen makes for a good summer base for walks in the mountains, while in the winter it is known as a winter sports resort with family-friendly pistes. Cross-country skiers will find a unique area here, several of whose well maintained tracks lead deep into the high mountains. Bitihorn (1608m/5276ft) is a striking peak that can already be spotted from the village, and its summit can be reached in 3–4hrs via a footpath that begins right by the road a short drive to the north of Beitostølen.

Trolls and dwarfs belong to Norway as much as fjords, mountains and the midnight sun and visitors can encounter several hundred of these mythical Norwegian beings in the world's largest theme park dedicated to them (Trollenes Kongerike) in Beitostølen, at the foot of the Jotunheimen range, which is the birthplace of all trolls and dwarfs according to Nordic legend. Three floors covering 2000 sq m/21,528 sq ft contain imaginative settings to explore.

Kingdom of the Trolls Theme Park: Sat–Sun noon–6pm, during school holidays daily 11am–6pm; 100 NOK; www.trolleneskongerike.no)

Valdresflya After Beitostølen, the road continues its ascent, passing the Bygdin and Vinstri lakes and reaching its highest point on Valdresflya. Unlike the alpine summits of the surrounding area, Valdresflya is a flat and very barren highland plateau. Before reaching Lake Gjende, there is the option of making a half-day tour up Knutshø, beginning near Vargbakken a short distance south of Maurvangen. Whether or not Knutshø is more exposed than Besseggen is debatable, but its ridge is certainly narrower and the view from the top is simply stupendous. Some even believe that Peer Gynt made his journey on the back of a reindeer not over Besseggen but over the Knutshø ridge.

*Lake Gjende Lake Gjende, which is around 20km/12mi long but only 1km/0.6mi wide, numbers among Norway's most beautiful lakes. Carved out by the glaciers of the last Ice Age, the lake enchants with its intensely blue-green waters and the steep mountainsides that rise up to 1300m/4265ft above it. The three **mountain lodges** on its shore at Gjendesheim, Memurubu and Gjendebu, as well as the campsite at Maurvangen on Route 51 are some of the most visited destinations in the Jotunheimen mountains.

*Besseggen Many Norwegians return year on year to climb the Besseggen ridge, following in the footsteps of the mythical Peer Gynt. Henrik Ibsen took the liberty of turning the Besseggen into a hellish ride, but it is not so daunting. In fact, this panoramic tour requires no more than good fitness, firm shoes, a little surefootedness and a lack of vertigo. The changeable weather, however, should never be underestimated. The starting point for this spectacular **six-hour tour** offering breath-taking views is **Gjendesheim**. The day begins with a 35-minute crossing by **boat** of Lake Gjende to reach the catered cabin at **Memurubu**. The steep ascent then begins immediately next to the jetty. Shortly after the turn-off for **Glitterheim**, the path continues along the southern shore of a small pond before reaching Lake Bjørn-bøltjørna (»Bear's Den Puddle«). A short descent via a narrow path follows, leading to **Lake Bessvatnet**. The just 50m/55yd-wide land bridge between the almost black Lake Bessvatnet and the blue-green Lake Gjende several hundred metres below, at 984m/3228ft, is called Bandet.

The steep ascent of Besseggen then begins over the first ridge (where walkers even occasionally need to use their hands to remain steady) until the highest point is reached, where the giant stone man stands. Before then making the relatively easy descent to Gjendesheim, it is still necessary to walk a good distance across the broad **Veslefjell-**mountainside.

Karasjok · Kárášjohka

—————————————— ✳ **M 22**

Region: North Norway
Population: 2800

For the Sami people, Karasjok – or rather Kárášjohka, which is bi-lingual - is one of the most important cultural centres, where they have their own newspaper, a radio station and their parliament. Tourists can get a good idea of Sami life in the high north in the Sápmi Theme Park.

The »capital« of the Sami people lies along the Kárášjohka river on   **Sami town**
the E 6 east of ▶Alta (around 145km/91mi), 14km/9mi from the Finnish border. In addition to tourism, the economic foundation of the town is based on the traditional Sami activities of reindeer keeping, hunting and fishing.

Due to the inland location, the temperature differentials are extreme   **Temperature**
here, so that during winter the thermometer can sometimes sink to -50°C/-58°F, while on warm summer days, it can rise as high as 30°C/86°F. The bus to Rovaniemi in Finland stops in Karasjok, as does the once daily »Nord-Norge« bus.

WHAT TO SEE IN KARASJOK · KÁRÁŠJOHKA

Sami Centre The Sami Centre at the junction of the E 6 and RV 92 not only houses the tourist information office, but also has a sales centre with outstanding Sami craftwork and a restaurant where Sami dishes can be tried.

Karasjok Church Karasjok church dating from 1807 stands opposite. It is the oldest Protestant church in Finnmark and was the town's only building to survive intact after the retreat of German forces during the Second World War.

Sami collections The Sami collection in Karasjok is the main body of the collections belonging to the RiddoDuottarMuseat Foundation (comprising four Sami museums in western Finnmark) and offers a good insight into the culture and history of Scandinavia's native population. There are displays for costumes, domestic interiors, Sami domestic tools and arts and crafts from the metal and silver workshop.
❶ Mid-June–mid-Aug 9am–6pm, Sep–May Tue–Fri 9am–3pm; www.riddoduottarmuseat.no

Delicate colours and a mild light embrace the land of the Sami near Karasjok

Karasjok

INFORMATION
Karasjok Turistinformasjon
Porsangerveien 1
Postboks 243
9735 Kárášjohka/Karasjok
tel. 78 46 88 02
www.karasjokinfo.no
www.karasjok.kommune.no

EXCURSIONS AND COURSES
The tourist information office can arrange boat trips on the Karasjohka river or excursions to Sami settlements, as well as dog sleigh and ski bob tours during winter, also gold panning courses and fishing tours to the world famous salmon fishing grounds at the confluence of the Karasjohka and the Anarjohka.

WHERE TO EAT/WHERE TO STAY
Storgammen in Rica Hotel Karasjok £ £ £ £
Porsangervn. 3

tel. 78 46 88 60
www.rica-hotels.com/hotels/karasjok
The restaurant is inside an authentic copy of a Sami earth hut complete with open fire. Dishes are prepared according to ancient Sami recipes. Seated on reindeer furs, diners are treated to reindeer casserole (bidos) and smoked hearts. The hotel rooms are also very much inspired by Sami culture.

WHERE TO STAY
Karasjok Camping and Vandrerhjem £ £
Kautokeinoveien
tel. 78 46 61 35
www.karacamp.no
20 huts of varying standard offering a range of accommodation options are available at this youth hostel. The site is a mere 1km/0.6mi from the centre of town.

The Sápmi Theme Park (or »Land of the Sami«) opened in July 2000, is also dedicated to the history and culture of Scandinavia's indigenous people. A Sami family going about their daily chores can be observed in a traditional summer and winter campsite. An entertaining performance in the magical Stálubákti theatre carries spectators off into Sami mythology, while a large earth hut is available for trying Sami food specialities.

Sápmi Theme Park

❶ June–Aug daily 9am–4pm, mid-June–mid-Aug till 7pm, otherwise Mon–Fri 9am–4pm, Jan–Feb till 2pm; www.sapmi.no

It is no surprise that a street in Karajok is named after Mari Boine: the Sami musician was born here and is now known throughout the world. Her many recordings and concerts have not only secured a place for the traditional »joik« song of the Sami in the World Music canon, but with her fusion of joik with other musical forms, such as jazz, rock and folk, she has also created an entirely unique music of her own.

Marie Boine

AROUND KARASJOK · KÁRÁŠJOHKA

Tanaelv The E 6 follows the western shore of the Tanaelv, past several miles of Ailestrykene rapids. The Tana valley was initially exclusively inhabited by Sami, and it was not until between 1730 and 1740, that the first Finnish settlers appeared. Norwegian settlements did not appear until the end of the 18th century. Beyond the Tana bru, the only bridge over the Tanaelv, the E 6 becomes known as the RV 98, should you wish to continue in the direction of Lakselv. An exhibition by the **local museum** of the Tana district can be visited in **Rustefjelbma**, but the main museum on the topic of salmon fishing on the Tanaelv is in Polmak.

Øvre Anarjåkka National Park, on the Finnish border to the southeast of Karasjok, is the largest natural protected area in northern Norway (1290 sq km/498 sq mi). Because of its extensive moorlands, its appeal for hiking is limited, yet there are **superb views** to be had across the endless landscape of the Finnmarksvidda from one of its peaks (none higher than 600m/1969ft).

✶ Kautokeino · Guovdageaidnu

 ✦ M 20

Region: North Norway
Population: 3000

Kautokeino in the county of Finnmark is a traditional Sami stronghold where, with a bit of luck, Sami costume can still be seen worn as everyday clothing. During Easter, it is also possible to take part in the festivities whose highlight is the Sami Grand Prix.

More reindeer than people Norway's largest Sami community lies in Finnmarksvidda, about 120km/75mi south of Alta and 130km/81mi southwest of Karasjok (daily bus connections from both places). Kautokeino is one of the few Norwegian settlements that also has an official Sami name – **Guovdageaidnu**– and an interpreter is indeed occasionally necessary in this bilingual town. One of the cultural centres of the Sami (►MARCO POLO Insight p.34 and ►Finnmark), Kautokeino is the seat of numerous of their institutions. In existence since the 16th century, this Sami community belonged to Swedish Lapland until 1751, after which it came to Norway under the Danish Crown. For centuries, the survival of the indigenous people here was ensured by the hunting of wild reindeer, which were either caught in pits or herded into enclosures. With an area of 9687 sq km/3740 sq mi, Kautokeino is the largest municipality in Norway, although population density is very low. Only **1500 people** live in the place itself – the majority of the population are indigenous Sami – but there are around **100,000 reindeer**, traditional reindeer breeding still being an important source of income in the village today. In the meantime, tourism also plays a key role all year round, since most visitors to Finnmark stop off here.

MARCO ● POLO TIP

! *Jewels at Juhl's* Insider Tip

Probably the best traditional jewellery to be found in Finnmark can be purchased at Juhl's silver workshop 2km/1mi from Kautokeino. Open daily 9am–10pm, otherwise 9am–6pm; tel 78 48 43 30; www.juhls.no.

A Sami herder travels through the endless arctic landscape near Kautokeino with his reindeer

Living with the Seasons of the Reindeer

The homeland of the Sami People – who do not appreciate being called »Lapps« - covers an area that spreads from Norway all the way to the Russian peninsula of Kola. They call it Samiland or Sápmi. Only a minority still keep reindeer for a living but, those that do, live according to the seasons of their semi-wild animals. Increasingly, they use snow mobiles and mobile homes complete with carcass processing equipment as they follow the annual migrations of the reindeer.

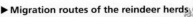

▶ **Migration routes of the reindeer herds**

Late winter/spring: herds move to the calving grounds

Spring:
Setting up fixed camps

Spring/early summer: birthing season; the herds move to the higher summer meadows.

Summer:
calf marking

Late summer/autumn: slaughter; herd sorting

Autumn: herd migrates to rutting grounds

Late autumn/winter: herd moves to the winter feeding grounds in the forest regions

Winter: winter camp – formerly in tented structures (»Gamme«), today in permanent buildings

▶ **Population percentage of Sami People**

Sweden	Norway	Finland	Russia
20,000	40,000	17,000	2000

▶ **Traditional Sami homes**

»Gamme«
Wood poles are covered with peat, wood and birch bark that become naturally insulated with moss and grass over time. A well maintained »gamme« can remain habitable for at least 60 years

»Lavvu«
Birch poles serve to make a tent covered hides or woven wool carpets. These tents are especially suitable for the nomadic life, because they are easy to set up and take down.

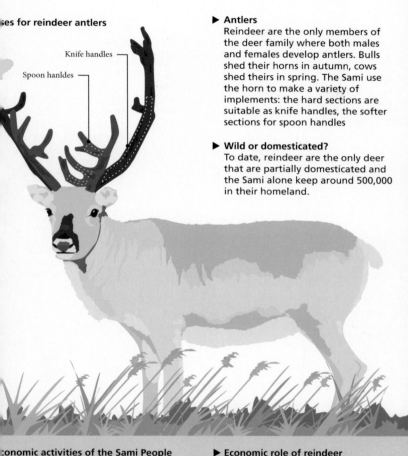

ses for reindeer antlers

Knife handles

Spoon hanldes

▶ **Antlers**
Reindeer are the only members of the deer family where both males and females develop antlers. Bulls shed their horns in autumn, cows shed theirs in spring. The Sami use the horn to make a variety of implements: the hard sections are suitable as knife handles, the softer sections for spoon handles

▶ **Wild or domesticated?**
To date, reindeer are the only deer that are partially domesticated and the Sami alone keep around 500,000 in their homeland.

Economic activities of the Sami People
excluding the Kola peninsula

10 % Agriculture

12 % Tourism

12 % Other

15 % Reindeer keeping as main activity

23 % Forestry

28 % Hunting, fishing, and craftwork, with reindeer husbandry as a sideline

▶ **Economic role of reindeer**
To this day, reindeer products are highly sought after in Scandinavian countries. High prices are achieved, in particular for milk, hides, and the lean meat.

©BAEDEKER

Kautokeino

INFORMATION
Kautokeino
Turistinformasjon
9520 Kautokeino
Bredbuktnesveien 6
tel. 78 48 65 00
www.kautokeino.kommune.no

LEISURE
Kautokeino not only offers a large range of leisure activities for hikers, canoeists and horse-riders in summer, but also attracts visitors during winter, when rides with reindeer, dog sleighs, or on snow mobiles are on offer. Trips in a traditional river boat on the Kautokeino river are also an unforgettable experience (details from the tourist office).

WHERE TO EAT/ Insider
WHERE TO STAY Tip
Madame Bongos Fjellstue
Cunovuoppe

(11km/7mi northwest of Kautokeino)
tel. 78 48 61 60
Madame Bongo alias Karen Anna Bongo is a legend in Kautokeino. She receives visitors in one of her »lavvus«, a traditional Sami tent, where she dishes up »bidos« by the open fireside – once the feasting dish of the Sami for special occasions, consisting of a beef and potato casserole. It is also possible to spend the night in a lavvu for a reasonable sum. To add this to their list of experiences visitors need only a reservation and their own sleeping bag.

WHERE TO STAY
Thon Hotel
Kautokeino £ £ £
Biedjovággeluodda 2
tel. 78 48 70 00
www.thonhotels.no, 65 rooms.
Comfortable rooms in the town centre

WHAT TO SEE IN KAUTOKEINO

Open-air museum
The open-air museum (Guovdageainnu Gilisillju) is especially worth seeing. A traditional Sami settlement with a variety of older buildings conveys an excellent impression of Sami lifestyle a century ago. The numerous exhibits show just how much skill the Sami have traditionally commanded in the creation of their tools and jewellery.
❶ Mid-June–mid-Aug Mon–Fri 9am–7pm, Sat–Sun from noon, other months daily 9am–3pm.

*Sami cultural centre
The Nordic Sami Institute (Nordisk Samisk Institutt), including a library and theatre, is housed in the architecturally interesting cultural centre whose shape is reminiscent of a Sami tent. Information on Sami culture can be found here, and there is also an indigenous teacher training college and a technical school teaching reindeer husbandry.

Kirkenes

✦ M 27

Region: North Norway
Population: 3440

Kirkenes is journey's end. The Hurtigruten ships turn around after a short stop here and even route E 6 goes no further. A trickle of border traffic with Russia has however brought more life into this small town in the far north of Europe.

The Norwegian port and industrial town of Kirkenes lies on the south side of the Varangerfjord, just 150km/90mi from Murmansk, Russia's only harbour not under German control during the Second World War. The Russians retaliated against repeated German attempts to capture Murmansk: more than 1000 air raid warnings and 328 Soviet bombing raids made Kirkenes Norway's most bombed town of the war. What stood up to the bombs was burned down by the Germans as they retreated – in the end, only 20 buildings were left standing.

The Second World War

Originally, Kirkenes served as a port for shipping out the iron ore found at Lake Bjørnevatn, 11km/7mi to the south, and the mining and processing of iron ore were its most significant activity. But streamlining measures in this town on the border with Russia resulted in the loss of over 1000 jobs, and the Bjørnevatn pits were closed in 1996. Yet increased trade with Russia, as well as oil exploitation in the Barent Sea, is set to revive the local economy, and the local Norwegian dockyard is predominantly kept busy servicing Russian ships.

Oil instead of iron ore

The Russian border at Storskog is just a short drive from the town centre and since the opening of the eastern border, the so-called **»Russian market«** has established itself close to the port area. What the local authorities are hoping to achieve in terms of improved economic relationships on a wider scale is already functioning perfectly on a smaller scale: the Russians supply their Norwegian neighbours with cheap cigarettes and vodka and receive Western consumer goods in return.

MARCO POLO INSIGHT **?**

Fantasy in the high north

Kirkenes and the surrounding area provided the backdrop for the movie »The Golden Compass« starring Nicole Kidman and Daniel Craig, in 2007. The Hollywood movie is based on the first part of British author Philip Pullman's trilogy »His Dark Materials«, entitled »Northern Lights« (information at www.goldencompassmovie.com).

Kirkenes

INFORMATION
Kirkenes Turistinformasjon
Sør-Varanger Bibliotek, 1st floor
Dr. Wessels gate 18, 9915 Kirkenes
tel. 78 99 32 51
www.kirkenesinfo.no

MIDNIGHT SUN
Shines from 20th May until 20th July

EXCURSION
A highlight of any Norway trip is the King Crab Tour out of Kirkenes. This giant saltwater crustation has only appeared here in recent decades.

FESTIVAL
The cross-border Barent Spectacle is held each year, at the end of January/beginning of February, when there is music, theatre, readings, live performances, art and seminars over 4–5 days – most with some connection to this northern border district (http://barentsspektakel.no).

WHERE TO EAT
❷ *Vin og Vilt* £ £ £
Kirkegata 5
tel. 78 99 38 11
The name says it all: this gourmet establishment specialises in local game dishes and the best wines from around the world.

❶ *Arctic Restaurant* £ £
Kongensgaten 1–3
tel. 78 99 29 29
The hotel restaurant is good, especially for fish dishes.

WHERE TO STAY
❷ *Kirkenes Snowhotel* £ £ £ £
Gabba Rentier-Safaripark
tel. 78 97 05 40
www.kirkenessnowhotel.com
Every year, between 20th December and 20th April, the Kirkenes Snow Hotel opens its doors. Established in 2006, the 20 suites are entirely of ice and wonderfully decorated with ice sculptures. Guests sleep on reindeer pelts, fortified by a nightcap from the ice bar. This unusual experience comes at a price, which includes transfers from Kirkenes, breakfast, sauna, and a 3-course dinner.

❶ *Thon Hotel Kirkenes*
£ £ £ £
Johan Knudtzens gate 11
tel. 78 97 10 50
www.thonhotel.no
This modern hotel with 143 rooms is situated in the centre of Kirkenes right on the quay with superb views on the Langfjorden.

WHAT TO SEE IN AND AROUND KIRKENES

Barents House In the 18th century, trade in wood, cereals and fish was the foundation of a flourishing trade between Norwegians and Russian Pomors, and today it falls to the Norwegian Barents Secretariat to foster cultural and economic exchange between the two countries. The institution is set to move in 2017, when it will be housed in the new Barents House, built over 17 floors after a design by Reiulf Ramstad Architects, which will make it the highest and most northern wood house in the world. www.barents.no

Andersgrotta

The few tourists that end up in Kirkenes are usually passengers passing through on the Hurtigruten ships. Visitors with more time could visit the former Andersgrotta mine right underneath the town centre. In the dripping wet catacombs, where most of the town's residents survived the Second World War, a film is shown conveying the horrors of the war. Guided tours are available by request from the tourist office.

Fishing and canoeing

The Kirkenes area offers opportunities for white water fishing in the Karpelva, Klokkerelva, Munkelva and Neidenelva rivers, and there is also the possibility to go deep sea fishing and canoeing. Another option is an excursion through the Pasvik valley in the Øvre Pasvik National Park south of Kirkenes (►p.196.

Excursion to Murmansk

Day trips by boat or overland to Murmansk and the Kola Peninsula in Russia can be booked via the tourist information centre. A passport, passport photo and a reservation are needed at least two days ahead of time. During the week, a visa can be requested on the day of travel, though it is cheaper to request it two weeks in advance. Buses to Murmansk depart from Kirkenes Mon–Fri at 2pm and 3pm, Sun at 3pm and 4pm (journey time around 4hrs; Grenseland, tel. 78 99 25 01, www.pasvikturist.no). It is also possible to travel to Russia by car, for which a car stamp is necessary as part of the visa. The border crossing at Storskog is open daily 7am–9pm.

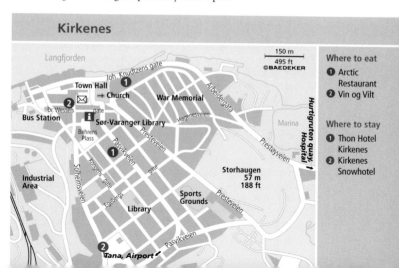

Kirkenes

150 m
495 ft
©BAEDEKER

Langfjorden

Joh. Knudtzens gate

Town Hall ❶
Church
War Memorial
Arbeidergata

Dr. Wessels gate
Bus Station
ℹ
Sør-Varanger Library

Hagenesveien

Marina

Hurtigruten quay; Hospital

Behrens Plass

Pasvikveien
Presteveien
Presteøyveien

Kongens gate
gate

Industrial Area
Solheimsveien

Storhaugen
57 m
188 ft

Egebergs gate

Sports Grounds
Presteveien

Library

Pasvikveien

❷ Tana, Airport

Where to eat
❶ Arctic Restaurant
❷ Vin og Vilt

Where to stay
❶ Thon Hotel Kirkenes
❷ Kirkenes Snowhotel

* Kongsberg

 B 6

Region: South Norway
Height: 170m/558ft
Population: 25,500

Life in Kongsberg is tranquil. Stress is unknown in the old silver town with its magnificent Baroque church. Visits to the Mining Museum and the decommissioned silver mine in Saggrenda should definitely be on the itinerary.

Silver town

The old mining town of Kongsberg, set on either side of the Lågen in the southern part of the Numedal valley, owes its foundation to the silver mines that were established in 1624 a few miles south. Up to 4000 people were employed in the mines during the second half of the 18th century. Today Kongsberg is also known for its jazz festival (www.kongsberg-jazzfestival.no).

WHAT TO SEE IN AND AROUND KONGSBERG

Museums

On the banks of the foaming rapids of the Lågen, the **Mining Museum** is housed in the former works buildings. Among other things, it exhibits the collection of the Royal Norwegian Mint, which traces the production of silver coins since 1686. Furthermore, the small Ski Museum contains the skis of the famous Kongsberg sportsman Birger Ruud. The **silver mine**, shut down in 1957, can be visited on a small pit railway that travels 2.3km/1.4mi through dark passages into the mountain (not suitable for small children). Its destination is the royal pit, which never reaches a temperature of more than 6°C/43°F. Adventurous visitors can also book a 3hr 5km/3mi pit walk (information from the tourist office).

Mining Museum: mid-May–Aug daily 10am–5pm, otherwise Tue–Fri noon–4pm; 80 NOK (museum), 150 NOK (train), 200 NOK (combined ticket); www.norsk-bergverksmuseum.no

*Kongsberg church

The mighty red brick Kongsberg church (1741–61) stands imposingly south of the rapids. A Baroque church, its unusual interior includes 2400 seats distributed across several levels, some at giddy heights. Before they began work in the mines, workers had to assemble here each morning at 5am – those who failed to attend service were not paid.

By Norwegian standards, the unique complex of organ, pulpit and altar are excessively opulent, embellished with gold and Baroque figures. The loges or boxes stand out, especially the royal box concealed behind a beautifully decorated window façade reminiscent of a townhouse in northern Germany. No wonder perhaps: the architects came from Germany.

In **Modum**, about 50km/31mi northeast of Kongsberg in the direction of Gol, it is worth making a detour to the **Pigment Production Works** of Blaafarveværket. The works were established in 1776 for the extraction and processing of cobalt, and produced 80% of the world's requirements for this blue pigment during the 19th century. At one of Norway's most visited exhibitions, beautiful cobalt blue **glass and porcelain products** are shown in the former works buildings below the churning Haugefossen waters. During summer, works by famous Norwegian and foreign artists are shown in changing exhibitions.
Pigment Production Works: mid-May–mid-Sep Tue–Sat 11am–5pm, Sun and holidays till 6pm, mid-June–mid-Aug daily 11am–6pm; 60 NOK (Director's Residence), 90 NOK (Works Art Exhibition); www.blaa.no

Stalls in the Kongsberg Church

Two of southern Norway's most beautiful rock engravings are located around 5km/3mi south of the centre of Drammen: one (at Nordbyveien 49) is of an elk that is estimated to have been created around 6000 years ago; there is also a variety of such figures at Skogerveien 8.   Rock art

Norway's largest stave church (MARCO POLO Insight, p.406), the beautiful 13th-century Heddal church, stands right next to the E 134 to the west of Kongsberg and Notodden.   ****Heddal stave church**

Heading northwest along the RV40 into the Numedal, the visitor will encounter small places like Flesberg, Rollag and Nore, where stave churches can be visited (the Flesberg church was remodelled in the 18th century). The open-air museums of Dåsethof (21 historic buildings), north of Flesberg, and of Rollag (13 historic buildings) are worth a short visit.   Numedal
In fact, this romantic valley is ideal for cyclists, who can travel a 280km/174mi long section of the Numedal Cycle Route that runs

Kongsberg

INFORMATION
Kongsberg Turistservice
Hyttegata 3
3616 Kongsberg
tel. 32 29 90 50
www.visitkongsberg.no

FESTIVAL
The Kongsberg Jazz Festival has established itself as a first-class attraction, offering some of the best from the Skandi-
navian and international Jazz scene on
several of the town's stages (www.
kongsberg-jazzfestival.no).

WHERE TO EAT
Opsahlgården £ £ £ £
Kirkegaten 10
tel. 32 76 45 00
www.opsahlgarden.no
The building is located in the old part of
Kongsberg near the church and its restaurant is considered one of the best in
town. Reindeer filet, duck breast, rack of
lamb or the changing 3-course menus
are all prepared with the freshest high-
quality ingredients – which come at a
price. Beautiful seating in the tranquil
courtyard during summer. Closed Sundays.

Peckels Resept £ £ £
Peckelsgate 12
tel. 32 73 25 25
www.peckels.no
Named after the apothecary Franz
Peckel's recipes, this restaurant is a
great place to eat. Pictures on the walls
tell the story of the town. Closed Sundays.

WHERE TO STAY
*Best Western Gyldenlove
Hotell* £ £ £ £
Hermann Fossgate 1
tel. 32 86 58 00
www.bestwestern.com, 62 rooms.
This hotel with well-appointed rooms
that offer every comfort is centrally located opposite the railway station.

*Kongsberg Vandrerhjem
Bergmannen* £ £
Vinjesgt. 1
tel. 32 73 20 24
www.kongsberg-vandrerhjem.no
Modern youth hostel in the town centre
with 98 beds spread over 26 comfortable rooms.

between Larvik on the coast and Geilo. A specific cycle touring guide
is available (www.numedal.net/numedalsruta). The road winds its
way along the Lågen which rises on the edge of the ▶Hardangervidda
plateau, passing narrow gorges and continuing onwards to **Rødberg**,
where the neo-classical works building of the hydroplant »Nore I« is
a striking sight in the centre of the town. The route first passes the
pretty **stave church at Uvdal** (north of the road, not the one right
next to it), and there are roads branching up onto Immingfjell (heading for Telemark) and the idyllically located mountain lodge of Sol-
heimstulen, on the edge of Hardangervidda – from both there are
good hiking opportunities to the catered mountain cabin of Mårbu.

Eventually the road reaches the 1100m/3609ft-high **mountain hotel of Vasstulan**, from which there is a fantastic view onto the Numedal valley and the Hardangervidda mountain plateau. After traversing two further passes, it is possible to make out the tracks of the Geilo ski lifts on the opposite side of the valley. The jagged **Hallingskarvet** ridge towers high above the popular winter sports resort, where the 1933m/6342ft-high Folarskarnut forms the highest peak of this range.

✳ Kristiansand

✦ A 4/5

Region: South Norway
Population: 82,300

With its numerous stone houses, Kristiansand, Norway's fifth largest town, is not particularly representative of the country. Though for many it is just a place to be passed through on arrival from Denmark, the sandy beaches of the surrounding area are very pretty and there is no shortage of opportunity to indulge in water sports.

Surrounded by large dockyards, off-shore installations and industrial complexes, the town with the country's second largest port does not initially seem inviting to visitors. Nevertheless, as the regional administrative centre for the Vest-Agder region, Kristiansand has quite a bit to offer. Located right by the mouth of the Otra river where it opens into the Byfjord, for example, the pretty quarter of **Posebyen** is a good place to stroll among historic wooden houses, in which galleries and artisan workshops have been set up. To the right and left of the **Christiansholm fortress** (1672), which hosts summer art exhibitions, there are several marinas swarming with fancy yachts and boats during the summer months. It is popular to sail the Skagerrak in the direction of Risør along the »Riviera of the North«.

Second
largest port

WHAT TO SEE IN AND AROUND KRISTIANSAND

The strictly square design of Kristiansand's town centre – known as the Kvadraturen – is thanks to its founder and namesake Christian IV. The Danish-Norwegian king designed the network of streets in a chess board pattern according to strict Renaissance style in 1641. Today, the town's thriving economic and cultural heart pulsates in these right-angled streets, where there is a pretty pedestrian zone (Markensgate) with attractive restored houses.

Kvadraturen

Kristiansand

INFORMATION
Turistinfomasjon
Rådhusgata
64611 Kristiansand
tel. 38 12 13 14
www.visitkrs.no

BOAT TOURS
Tour boats depart from the port in Kristiansand for trips among the skerries to the idyllic island of Ny-Hellesund and its Second World War fortress. Tours to the picturesque little town of Lillesand with its pretty white mansions and harbour are also interesting (tickets from the tourist office).

FESTIVAL
Things really get going during the Odderøya Rock Festival in July, when everyone who is anyone in the Norwegian rock scene descends on Kristiansand, along with divers international rock stars (www.odderoyalive.com).

WHERE TO EAT
❷ *Bakgården Restaurant* £ £ £ £
Tollbugate 5
tel. 38 02 12 11
www.bakgardenbar.no
Excellent restaurant that really lives up to the highest expectations. Once the entrance in the back courtyard of the Bakgården has been found, a rustic interior with dark wood furniture and whitewashed walls is revealed. The delicious marinated dishes are recommended, as well as the tuna.

❸ *Restaurant Sjøhuset* £ £ £ – £ £ £ £
Østre Strandgt. 12a

tel. 38 02 62 60
www.sjohuset.no
Very good though expensive fish dishes in a maritime atmosphere. The Sjøhuset's popularity over the past 20 years has been enhanced by its outdoor seating, where diners listen to the waves and watch the sun go down. The lunchtime fish platter is certainly affordable.

❶ *Café Generalen* £
Ravnedalen
tel. 97 08 66 61
www.ravnedalen.no
The small café surrounded by greenery serves tasty snacks such as hamburgers, waffles and cake. Cultural evenings and live concerts are held on Thursdays and Fridays.

WHERE TO STAY
❶ *Clarion Hotel Ernst*
£ £ £ £
Rådhusgaten 2
tel. 38 12 86 00
www.choicehotels.no, 200 rooms.
The top hotel in town, whose rooms have tasteful interiors and whose atmospheric lobby is huge. Kristiansand locals also appreciate the good restaurant and the bistro.

❷ *Sjøgløtt – Det Lille Hotell*
£ £
Østre Strandgt. 25
tel. 38 70 15 66
www.sjoglott.com, 16 rooms.
This small family hotel lies in the town centre, near the old fortress. No frills, convenient and good value for money.

The neo-Gothic cathedral stands out at the market square in the town centre (Torget), where fresh fruit and vegetables are sold during summer. It was rebuilt between 1882 and 1885 after a fire, and its interior is worth seeing for the altar with its Christ at Emmaus painting and the collection of Baroque wood carvings of the Evangelists. Mon–Sat 11am–2pm Next to the church stands a monument by Vigeland to the poet Henrik Wergeland (1808–45; ▶Art and Culture: Literature), one of the town's famous sons.

Cathedral

To the northwest of the town centre, in the Ravnedalen Nature Park, it is possible to climb the 200 steps to the viewing platform on the Ravneheia boulder, from where there is a wonderful view over the town, its nearby islands, and the sea. Designed around 1875, the park also contains several small bathing lakes, pretty nature walkways and a small café.

Ravnedalen Nature Park

A dead straight street branching off from the »Kvadraturen«, known as the »Bygaden«, comprises around 40 old buildings and various cultural history exhibitions. Complete with furnished houses, work-

Bygaden

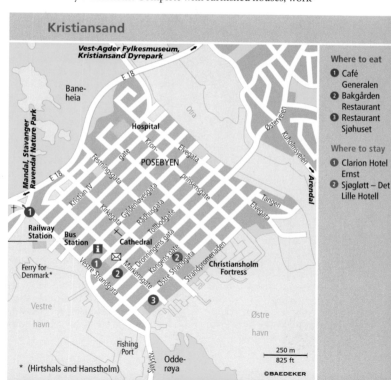

Kristiansand

Vest-Agder Fylkesmuseum, Kristiansand Dyrepark

E 18

Bane-heia

Mandal, Stavanger
Ravendal Nature Park

Hospital

Kron-gate

Festningsgata

POSEBYEN

Elvegata

Prinsensgate

Ora

Østervelen

Kuholmsveien

Arendal

E 18

Kristian IV

Kirkegata

Gyldenløvesgata

Rådhusgata

Tollbodgate

Tangen

Elvegata

Railway Station

Bus Station

Cathedral

Dronningens gate

Kongens gate

Østre Strandgata

Strandpromenaden

Christiansholm Fortress

Ferry for Denmark*

Vestre Strandgata

Markensgate

Vestre havn

Østre havn

Fishing Port

Odde-røya

* (Hirtshals and Hanshtolm)

250 m
825 ft

©BAEDEKER

Where to eat
1. Café Generalen
2. Bakgården Restaurant
3. Restaurant Sjøhuset

Where to stay
1. Clarion Hotel Ernst
2. Sjøgløtt – Det Lille Hotell

shops and junkshops, it has been recreated in the attractive open-air **Vest Agdermuseet Kristiansand**, 4km/2mi east of Kristiansand, near the E 18. The Setesdaltunet farm, with its smoke room dating from the 17th century, is also worth seeing.

❶ Mid-June–Aug Mon–Fri 10am–5pm, Sat–Sun from noon, otherwise Mon–Fri 9am–3pm; 70 NOK; www.vestagdermuseet.no

Every Norwegian has to have been to the Kristiansand Animal and Leisure Park at least once during their childhood. The park is also located on the E 18, 12km/7mi east of town. Unbeatable favourites are the town of the »Thieves of Kardemomme« and Captain Sabretooth's Castle with its secret passages. The large Nordic beast of prey enclosure and the monkey jungle are also impressive. A huge waterpark with many attractions was added in 2010, including a long water slide.
Kristiiansand Animal and Leisure Park: mid-June–mid-Aug 10am–7pm, otherwise till 3pm; 149–319 NOK, depending on the season (day tickets without waterpark); www.dyreparken.no

The best way to experience the coastal skerries of the southern Norwegian Riviera is by paddling a kayak or canoe through the labyrinth of little rocky islands, narrow fjords and silent,

A good atmosphere outside the cathedral

sandy bays. A good base for such activities is offered by the **Skottevig holiday park** (Skottevig = Scottish bay) about 20km/12mi east of Kristiansand.

✳ Kristiansund

✦ F 4

Region: West Norway
Population: 23,800

Kristiansund was only joined to the mainland in 1992, with the construction of a 300-million-Euro bridge. For centuries, the town was oriented towards the sea and its inhabitants lived almost exclusively from cod and herring fishing. Today, the source of most of the town's income is North Sea oil.

Located southwest of Trondheim, Kristiansund's urban area spreads over three islands in the sea, connected to each other by bridges; and, since December 2009, the town has also been connected to the island of Averøy by the 5.7km/3.5mi long Atlantic Tunnel (toll), which replaced the ferry service between Kristiansand and Øksenvåg/Averøy. The protected harbour was already being used over 8000 years ago and is still used by the Hurtigruten ships today. Up to 60% of Kristiansund was destroyed during an air raid in 1940, and the town lost much of its original natural character during the modern reconstruction. Collectively known as the Krifast (Kristiansund og Freis fastlandsforbindelse), the transport connection that links Kristiansund's islands consists of the world's only swimming bridge without side anchors, one of the longest underwater road tunnels, and Norway's longest suspension bridge.

Town on three islands

Kristiansund's history is inextricably linked to cod and herring. Almost all of the town's inhabitants lived from dried salt cod or »klippfisk« between 1750 and 1950, and the »Salt Cod Woman« at the harbour recalls that time. A hint of Portugal can be savoured in the many klippfisk restaurants in town where dried fish is prepared in a very Mediterranean way, with olive oil, olives, peppers and tomatoes. Indeed, cod is still exported to Portugal today, where it is consumed as the traditional dish of »bacalao«.

»Klippfisk«

A warehouse on the Vågen harbour basin where dried salt cod was once stored, today serves as the Klippfisk Museum. A tour and photos illustrate the various processes involved and impress the visitor with just how tough the work to produce this product was. Every fish, usually cod, had to be cleaned, salted and laid out on the cliffs to dry – a process that took from four to six weeks and involved the salt cod women turning the fish several times daily. The dried salt cod produced at the end could last for years. The annual Kristiansund Klippfisk Festival takes place in June. Mid-June–mid-Aug daily noon–5pm; www.nordmore.museum.no

Klippfisk Museum

Kristiansund

INFORMATION
Destination Kristiansund & Nordmøre
Kongens
6501 Kristiansund
tel. 71 58 54 54
www.visitkristiansund.com

EVENT
The annual Nordic Light Festival, at the end of April/beginning of May, is dedicated to international photographic art (www.nle.no).

WHERE TO EAT
Sjøstjerna Fiskerestaurant £ £ £
Skolegata 8
tel. 71 67 87 78
www.sjostjerna.no
To savour typical dried salt cod dishes, head for this restaurant in the middle of Kristiansund. The house speciality is the Portuguese variant cooked with olives, known as »Bacalao«.

Smia £ £ – £ £ £
Fosnagt. 30b
tel. 71 67 11 70
www.smia.no
Award-winning restaurant housed in a former smithy dating from 1787. The bacalao, dried salt cod or mixed platter made from the catch of the day are especially recommended.

Ytterbrygga Restaurant £ £
Håholmen Havstuer
Håholmen island
tel. 71 51 72 50
The crossing from Gjetøy to Håholmen island (during summer hourly between 11am?9pm) is worth making, and not just for the restaurant housed in an 18th century warehouse. Here at the old dried salt cod quay, you naturally also find genuine salt cod on the menu and a delicious lunch buffet is served in the afternoons.

Insider Tip

WHERE TO STAY
Quality Hotel Grand £ £ £
Bernstorffstredet 1
tel. 71 57 13 00
www.choicehotels.no, 158 rooms.
Traditional hotel in the town centre run with flair and to a high standard. The upper rooms offer a nice view of the harbour.

ISLAND HOPPING
The best way to get from island to island is on the boats travelling the sound that commute back and forth every 30 minutes.

What to see in town A substantial part of the town is characterized by parks and green spaces. The oldest buildings can be found on the southern island of Innlandet, such as the first **toll house** (1660–1748). Large sections of the town have been renovated and a walk around the Vågen harbour basin gives a good impression of the architectural style of the old warehouses. Unfortunately, several of the beautiful historic buildings right by the port burnt down in November 2001. The **Mellomvær-ftet dockyard**, founded in 1865 and over on the western shore of the harbour, is of particular interest and still carries out contract work today as part of the Nordmøre Museum. The modern town church (1964) and the late 18th-century Lossiusgården townhouse are more sights worth adding to the itinerary. A fantastic view of the harbour entrance and the Grip Islands on the horizon can be enjoyed from the old **Varden lookout tower** – turn 180 – and you can cast an eye over the mighty Nordmøre mountain range.

AROUND KRISTIANSUND

The Grip Islands, 14km/9mi northwest of Kristiansund, consist of over 80 different islets and skerries. For centuries only up to 400 people lived here, predominantly fishermen and maritime pilots. Today the islands are only inhabited during the summer. Of particular note are the pier and **stave church** (late 15th century) with its altar painting from 1520. A tourist ferry operates during summer.

Grip Islands

The island of Smøla, about 30km/19mi northeast of Kristiansund, is a paradise for anglers, ornithologists, hunters and divers. The island has a wealth of bird and animal species, including deer, mink, grey geese, herons and willow grouse – to name but a few.

*Smøla Island

☀ ATLANTIC ROAD · ATLANTERHAVSVEIEN

Between Kristiansund and ►Molde – or rather, between Vevang and Kårvåg 28km/17mi southwest of Kristiansund – lie countless islands that were only accessible by ferry until just a couple of decades ago. The 8km/5mi-long Atlanterhavsveien runs directly along the sea shore and is a vital lifeline for the rugged skerry landscape, as well as drawing in anglers, divers and visitors who want to experience the sea up close. The islands and islets along this road are connected by an impressive system of a total of **twelve bridges** and several dams. It is probably one of **Europe's most interesting coastal stretches** and offers up a veritable paradise, especially for divers. In calm weather, the views across the open sea are wonderful; when the wild north-westerly wind blows, the elements provide a fascinating spectacle.

Right along the sea

There are several fishing villages (»fiskevær«) along the Atlantic Road whose houses are rented out to visitors these days. At the turn of the last century, 120 people still lived exclusively from fishing on the countless little islands here. Today, water sports enthusiasts and holidaymakers predominate from spring to autumn. There is an hourly ferry connection during the summer from **Gjetøy** on the Atlantic Road out to the fishing village of **Håholmen**. Salt cod was once dried here, too.

Life in a fishing village

Bud   In the Fræna parish south of the Atlantic Road lies the small fishing village of Bud, where Norway's last archbishop convened the Norwegian state council, farmers and burghers in 1553, in an attempt to free the country from its Danish yoke. The attempt failed and four years later the archbishop was forced to flee Norway. The wooden church at Bud dates from 1717.

*Trollkirka (Troll church)   Inland, in the direction of Molde on the RV 64, the Trollkirka is located near Eide, the largest and most imposing of the local **chalkstone grottoes** (70m/230ft long and up to 7m/30ft high), complete with waterfall (good shoes and a torch are required). The 4km/2.5mi-long path leading from the car park through pine forest is sometimes steep and it requires some effort to reach the Troll church.

✷ Lillehammer

✦ D 7

Region: South Norway
Height: 180m/590ft
Population: 26,800

The Olympic town of Lillehammer is beautifully located on the upper reaches of Lake Mjøsa, at the exit of the Gudbrandsdal valley. Its biggest attractions are its charming pedestrian zone, good sporting opportunities and the Maihaugen Open-Air Museum.

A popular holiday destination   A very popular holiday destination among Norwegians themselves, Lillehammer has been internationally famous since the 1994 Winter Olympics. Its beautiful location and mild climate attract thousands of visitors, who annually enliven the picturesque Storgata shopping street and its colourful wooden houses, as well as populating the restaurant terraces along the Mesna river that splits the town in two.

WHAT TO SEE IN LILLEHAMMER

Art Museum and artists   The architecturally interesting **Art Museum** on the Stortorget market place is worth a visit, one of the country's leading art museums. It contains works by the Norwegian painters J. C. Dahl, A. Tidemand, Erik Werenskiold, Christian Krohg and Edvard Munch.

ℹ Tue–Sun 11am–4pm; 100 NOK; www.lillehammerartmuseum.com

A special attraction is the Transport Museum, Norway's first, located on the Lilletorget. The exhibits illustrate the development from sleighs to horse-drawn carriages to the Car.

❶ Mid-June–mid-Aug daily 10am–6pm, otherwise Mon–Fri 11am–3pm, Sat–Sun till 4pm; www.olavsrosa.no

Transport Museum (Norsk Kjøretøyhistorisk Museum)

The Olympic sports facilities and village are located just a few blocks from the pedestrian zone. Standing above the town, the first part is Lund Hangem's **Olympic village** displaying traditional Norwegian architecture, and then the **Håkon Stadium** (Stampesletta) with its light roof and façade construction designed by the architectural office of Østgård AS. Originally the ice-hockey stadium, it is now used for general sporting events, trade fairs, conferences and concerts.

*Olympic Park

Anyone who has ever wondered what it feels like to race in a bobsled can now find out with a realistic experience in the Bob Simulator at the Olympic Park. Even more exciting, however, is a ride on an actual wheelbob down the Olympic bob and luge track. Up to three people with a guide can easily reach speeds of up to 100km/62mi an hour (www.olympiaparken.no).

The ascent to the Lysgårdbakkene (Kantvegen) **ski jump installation**, with its extra high 120m/394ft ramp as well as its standard

Lively city centre: coffe break on the Storgata, Lillehammer's main shopping street

Lillehammer

INFORMATION
Lillehammer
Jernbanetorget 2
2609 Lillehammer
tel. 61 28 98 00
www.lillehammer.com

WHERE TO EAT
❷ *Bryggeriet Bar & Bifhus*
£ £ £
Elvegaten 19
tel. 61 27 06 60
Good and large steaks can be found in this restaurant and bar in a beer cellar. The same house is also home to the Brenneriet nightclub.

❶ *Egon Lillehammer* £ £
Elvegaten 12
tel. 61 05 70 90
A restaurant from the Egon chain set in an old mill that also always has something suitable for children on the menu.

WHERE TO STAY
❸ *Rustad Hotell og Fjellstue* £ £ £
Sjusjøn
tel. 62 33 64 64
www.rustadhotel.com, 46 rooms.

This rustic hotel, especially popular with fishermen, hikers and winter sports enthusiasts, lies in a wonderful mountain landscape, on a lake.

❶ *Mølla Hotell* £ £ £
Elvegaten 12
tel. 61 05 70 80
www.mollahotell.no
Until this mill in the middle of town on the Mesnelva river was converted into an unusual hotel in 1991, it had been grinding corn for 130 years. All the rooms are installed with rustic pine furniture. The best view of town can be enjoyed from the hotel bar on the top floor, in the former grain barn, where the atmosphere and cocktails are also very popular.

❷ *Øvergaard* £
Jernbanegt. 24
tel. 61 25 99 99, 9 rooms.
This 150-year-old building in a quiet and family-friendly location just above the town centre, but still in easy walking distance, offers value for money rooms.

90m/295ft ramp, is a little more strenuous. It is possible to ride up to the top of the ramp's tower by chairlift (daily between 11am and 4pm), from where there is a commanding view across the town and Lake Mjøsa. The more energetic visitor can also climb up the tower's 954 steps instead.
Olympic Park: www.olympiaparken.no

Maihaugen Open-Air Museum   Lillehammer's main attraction, drawing annual visitor numbers of around 175,000, is the Sandvig collection spread over the 40ha of the **Maihaugen Open-Air Museum, on the southeastern edge of town. Founded by the dentist Anders Sandig (1862–1950) in 1887, the museum contains over 175 original buildings from the Gudrandsdal

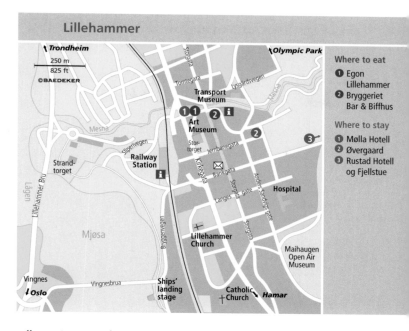

valley set in a natural environment of ponds, streams and tree land-scape. The historic farm houses, complete with barn yards, stables and silos, have been rebuilt here true to their original design, often complete with their original interiors. The oldest building in the museum complex is the **Garmo stave church** dating from around 1200. Of the other buildings, it is worth mentioning the Gynts Stue, originally built around 1700, that was the supposed home of the person Ibsen used as his inspiration for the famous character in his story. In one of the other houses, thin flatbread is baked daily on the open fire: it can be tasted for free. The new museum building houses historic workshops with over 30 different trades represented such as wheel-makers, cobblers, blacksmiths, basket weavers, stone masons and saddlers. The fascinating multimedia exhibition at Maihaugen entitled »How the Land Became Ours« takes the viewer on a journey from the Ice Age to the present and is really worth seeing, especially for children.

The **Olympic Museum** moved from Håkon Stadium in the Olympic Park to Maihaugen. Totally redone it gives on an overview of all the Olympic Games, from 1896 to the present day.

● Mid-May–Sep daily 10am–5pm, Oct–Mid-May 11am–4pm; 150 NOK; www.maihaugen.no

Maihaugen Open Air Museum

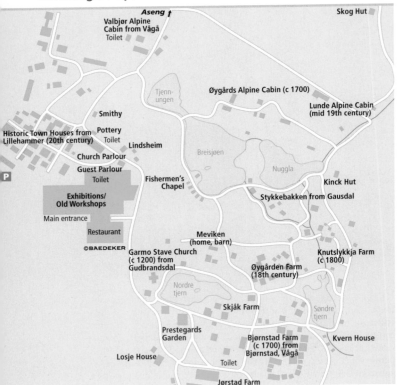

Aseng ↑
Skog Hut
Valbjør Alpine Cabin from Vågå
Toilet
Øygårds Alpine Cabin (c 1700)
Tjenn-ungen
Lunde Alpine Cabin (mid 19th century)
Smithy
Pottery
Historic Town Houses from Lillehammer (20th century)
Toilet
Lindsheim
Breisjøen
Church Parlour
Nuggla
Guest Parlour
Toilet
Fishermen's Chapel
Kinck Hut
Exhibitions/ Old Workshops
Stykkebakken from Gausdal
Main entrance
Restaurant
©BAEDEKER
Meviken (home, barn)
Garmo Stave Church (c 1200) from Gudbrandsdal
Knutslykkja Farm (c 1800)
Øygården Farm (18th century)
Nordre tjern
Skjåk Farm
Søndre tjern
Prestegards Garden
Bjørnstad Farm (c 1700) from Bjørnstad, Vågå
Kvern House
Losje House
Toilet
Jørstad Farm

AROUND LILLEHAMMER

Nordseter, Sjusjøen Around 14km/9mi outside Lillehammer lies the modern holiday resort of Nordseter (786m/2579ft), with 350km/219mi of prepared pistes and tracks and three lifts. A worthwhile ascent to the 1086m/3563ft-high Neverfjell can be made from Nordseter, where a broad panoramic view awaits. A short distance south of Nordseter, a road branches off to the ski lift by Sjusjøen (830m/2723ft), which is located on the pretty Lake Sjusjøen, which is lined by lodges, numerous holiday cabins, ski lifts and a colonial shop. Hunderfossen The Hunderfossen Amusement Park near Lillehammer has invested almost three million Euros in new attractions, in particular, extending the fairytale castle, where young visitors can go on adventurous quests for a princess and save her from the jaws of trolls. The hunt ends with a hair-raising free fall known as the »Trollfallet«. This attraction is unique in Norway and the family fun park offers numerous other entertainments, such as a go-cart range, rafting, waxworks, and a childrens' farm.

❶ www.hunderfossen.no

** Lofoten

✦ **K/L 9-11**

Region: Nordland
Area: 1308 sq km/505 sq mi
Population: 25,000

Mountains up to 1000m/3281ft high with strangely shaped summits rise vertically out of the sea in the Lofoten region, where small fishing villages add colour to the coves and the Nordic light is simply unique. A visit to this group of islands is an unforgettable experience.

Lofoten (Norwegians only refer to the islands in the singular, the Lofot, -en being the article) consists of an island chain almost 150km/94mi long, stretching into the Atlantic from the northeast to the southwest and separated from the mainland by the Vestfjord. From a distance, the four large islands of Austvågøy, Vestvågøy, Moskenesøy and Flakstadøy, along with several medium-sized islands, adjoin each other so closely that they give the impression of being just one long, jagged, mountainous ridge. A swarm of skerries surround the major islands and on some of the more alpine mountains (up to 1266m/4154ft) there is even snow. Many places have rocks with colonies of nesting seabirds. Tree growth is sparse. Near the seashore lie swamps and lakes, meadows and even a few cultivated fields. The coastal climate ensures mild winters and relatively cool summers. The main leisure activities here are fishing – either off piers or out of rowing boats – deep sea fishing, mountaineering and hunting. *Rugged beauty*

The Lofoten population's main source of income is fishing and the season runs from the beginning of February to the middle of April. Significantly less boats come here than they used to, however. Once there were thousands of fishermen, and the Lofoten fishing industry attracted countless fishermen from as early as the 11th century, who would spend several weeks travelling along the coast, mostly in open *Lofoten fishery*

Lofoten

INFORMATION
Destinasjon Lofoten
8301 Svolvær
Torget (between the Hurtigruten quay
and the market place)
tel. 76 06 98 00
www.lofoten.info

GETTING THERE
The Lofoten can be reached on the Hurtigrute ships (from Bodø to Svolvær 6hrs); there are also shipping connections to and from Skutvik (2hrs) and Narvik (9hrs), and daily flight connections from Bodø and Evenes to Svolvær, Røst and Leknes. Since the »Lofast Connection« was established in 2007, it is also possible to reach the island group without using a ferry. The 51km/31mi long E10 traverses four tunnels starting in Fiskebøl, as well as two large and ten small bridges, to reach Gullesfjordbotn.

MIDNIGHT SUN
27TH May to 17TH July on the north and west side of the islands

ACTIVITIES
For many visitors to the Nordland region, a highlight is having a close encounter with a whale and in Andenes on the island of Andøya they have the opportunity of joining a tour on a former whaling ship to see sperm whales; the chances of spotting a whale are virtually 100% (information from the tourist office).
Also exciting is an ocean rafting trip over the Moskenes Mealstrom (tidal waters) arranged via the Moskenes tourist office, or a boat trip to the Stone Age rock paintings in the Refsvikhula Cave.

CHEERS!
The »Akevittloftet« in the Nyvågar Rorbuhotel in Kabelvåg is the first restaurant in northern Norway that has permission to serve the potent Aquavit – 60 Norwegian varieties are on the menu (www.nyvagar.no).

WHERE TO EAT
Fiskekrogen £ £ £
Dreyersgate 29, Henningsvær
tel. 76 07 46 52
How about a portion of dried cod? In this cosy harbour restaurant visitors can be sure that fish dishes have been prepared in an authentically Norwegian way. Former fishermen's cabins for rent (rorbuer).

Børsen Spiseri £ £ – £ £ £
Gunnar Bergsv. 2, Svolvær
tel. 76 06 99 30
The wharf dating from 1828 was once where fish were landed and it is the oldest harbour building still surviving here. Today it offers a unique setting for a good meal. In contrast to the delicate presentation of food dishes, the interior is rustic and characterised by its aged wood. A starter of »En smak av Lofoten« is recommended for trying all kinds of typically local delicacies.

WHERE TO STAY
Henningsvær Bryggehotell £ £ £ £
Henningsvær
tel. 76 07 47 50
www.henningsvaer.no
This hotel in the Lofoten region's largest fishing harbour was built right on the water in 1995 and fits perfectly into its surroundings. 31 comfortable rooms enjoy spectacular views onto the harbour

and the steeply rising mountains in the background.

Nusfjord Rorbuanlegg £ £ £
Ramberg, tel. 76 09 30 20
www.nusfjord.no, 34 cabins
No finer Lofoten setting can be found than that of Nusfjord. Red fishing huts, a tiny harbour, an old merchant shop and, in the background, grandiose mountain scenery. The fishing huts come in various standards, from basic to comfortable, but all are in a beautiful setting. Rowing boats and fishing gear are included.

Northern Lights Base Camp
£ £ – £ £ £
Hov, tel. 76 07 20 02
www.northernlightsbasecamp.com

From mid-October to the beginning of April this campsite offers guests the unique opportunity for up to ten people to stay in a Lapp tent on the beach and watch the Northern Lights. Oil lamps, firewood and reindeer pelts are all part of the service. Typical dishes are served at a camp fire in the Northern Lights Café.

Justad Rorbuer og Vandrerhjem £ – £ £
Stamsund, tel. 76 08 93 34
During the summer this youth hostel is almost always fully booked as it lies close to the Hurtigrute quay and is a favoured destination for backpackers. In addition to dormitory rooms, there are also comfortable huts for rent. There are good fishing opportunities here too.

rowing boats. At night, they sheltered in small wooden huts (rorbuer = rowers' huts) that stood on posts in the water, which today provide the typical holiday accommodation of the Lofoten region.

The bulk of the catch consists of cod or »torsk«, though there is also herring, sea trout, ocean perch, halibut, cusk, ling and shellfish. The predatory cod that usually inhabits the deep waters of the Atlantic Ocean migrates for spawning from the Barents Sea to these coastal waters at the beginning of each January. The depth at which the shoals of cod travel depends on the water temperature, and normally ranges in the region of 100m/328ft–300m/984ft. At one time, 20,000 fishermen took part in cod fishing; since the 1990s only between 2000 and 2500 have remained. While 140 million tons of cod were caught in 1980, today the fishing quotas that have been restricting the industry for years in an effort to replenish stocks allow a maximum of only 22,000 tons a year. In the meantime, some fishing families have moved into hunting minke whales, as well as salmon and trout farming.

Alongside fishing, there are still a few sheep and beef farms in operation and, in recent times, also mink farms. Tourism is extremely relevant all year round, and fishing huts – some in the traditional very spartan style – are rented out; some have even been modernised. Around 220,000 visitors annually have streamed onto these sparsely populated islands in recent years.

Sheep, cattle and tourists

AUSTVÅGØY

Svolvær
The capital and administrative centre of Lofoten is Svolvær, on the southern coast of the island of Austvågøy. The small town has around 4000 inhabitants whose number rises to over 6000 during the cod fishing season (»lofotfiske«). Svolvær is the main port for the fish processing industry, as well as a major transport hub and the islands' most important trading centre.

Art museum
The work of numerous artists who have sought inspiration in Lofoten can be viewed at the **»Nordnorsk Kunstnernesentrum«** on Svinøya. Opposite the landing bridge, the grave of the Nordland painter Gunnar Berg Berg (1864 in Svolvær, † 1894 in Berlin) can be found on the little island of Gunnarholm by crossing the bridge from Svolvær. His most famous painting is the Battle in the Trollfjord (1890), which hangs in the Svolvær town hall. It portrays the bloody battle of 1880 between the traditionalists who used sailing boats and competing fishermen who were using »modern« steamships. North of Svolvær, **Blåtind** (597m/1958ft) rises steeply; experienced hikers with a good level of fitness can get to the summit and back in 5hrs and are rewarded with wonderful views.

Ride to the island of Hinnøy
A brilliant motorboat trip (2hrs) goes from Svolvær through the Raft sound to the southern end of Hinnøy, which is part of the ▶Vesterålen region. A climb up Digermulkollen (1.5hrs) is recommended. Today a bridge also connects Hinnøy with Austvågøy.

**Trollfjord
A narrow entrance through the cliffs leads west from the Raft sound into the slim Trollfjord. The snow-covered mountains of Higravstinder (1161m/3809ft) and jagged Trolltinder (up to 1045m/3429ft) rising out of the usually ice-covered 3km/2mi-long mountain lake of Trollfjordvatnet provide the backdrop beyond. The most popular day tour to the Trollfjord goes from Svolvær to Stokmarknes (via Fiskebøl) by bus, returning by Hurtigruten ship back over the Trollfjord.

*Kabelvåg
About 10km/6mi to the southwest of Svolvær (bus connection) lies Kabelvåg, with its attractively restored wooden houses, originally from the 19th century. Today, most of them are holiday homes. Kabelvåg was the main port for Lofoten before the establishment of steam shipping. A fishing museum and the **Lofot Aquarium** containing fish and sea lions from the Vestfjord are both worth seeing here. **Vågan church** is the largest wooden church north of Trondheim. The well-known Espolin Gallery displays works by the Nordland painter Kåre Espolin Johnson and the entrance ticket is valid for the gallery, the Lofot Aquarium and the Lofot Musuem in the suburb of Storvågan as well.

Lofot Aquarium: May daily 11am–3pm, June–Aug 10am–6pm, Sep–Nov and Feb–April Sun–Fri 11am–3pm, closed Dec–Jan; 110 NOK; www.lofotakvariet.no

Festvåg lies at the southwestern end of Austvågøy island, where the 942m/3090ft Vågakallen can be climbed in 3.5hrs. A bridge there also leads to the typical fishing village of Henningsvær, where a major fishing fleet gathers each winter. The harbour is one of Norway's most popular photographic motifs. Many visitors have a look around the gallery of local artist Karl Erik Harr (Galleri Lofotens Hus), who also owns a gallery near ▶Harstad, in the Røkenes Gård og Gjestehus.

Spiritual contemplation is easy in this little church on the Lofoten island of Austvågøy

Lofotens Hus Gallery: March daily 11am–4pm, April daily 6pm–7pm, May daily 10am–7pm, June–Aug daily 9am–7pm; 85 NOK; www.galleri-lofoten.no

VESTVÅGØY

Stamsund, located on the southeastern coast of the large island of Vestvågøy (pop. 11,000), is one of the most important fishing centres in the Lofoten archipelago and transport hub for western Lofoten. Accommodation is available at the Stamsund Lofoten Hotel, various fishing huts, and the numerous holiday homes. There are several freshwater lakes in Vestvågøy, as well as extensive **wetlands and moorlands**. On the ocean side of the island, there are veritable **dream beaches** on the Vikspollen Bay, with fine, white sand, and an imposing, lush green mountain setting as a backdrop. If only the water were not so cold! This is more than compensated for by the **midnight sun**, however, which can be seen very clearly from here.

Dream beaches for the hardy

The remains of the largest Viking houses known to date were found in Borg, on the E 10 road, 14km/9mi from Leknes. The chieftain's house measures an impressive 83m/90yd x 8m/9yd. Several of the utensils are of Celtic origin, objects looted by the Vikings from France and England. The reconstructed building houses a Viking museum since 1995, where there is weaving, knitting, spinning and dyeing in the main living quarters, while dishes according to original

Borg Viking Museum

recipes are served in the former guild hall where the Vikings once convened their meetings. A new underground cinema presents a dramatic presentation of the history of Borg's Viking chieftain, who was one of around a dozen such leaders in northern Norway.

● May, mid-Aug–mid-Sep daily 10am–4pm, June–mid-Aug daily 10am–7pm, mid-Sep–April Wed, Sun noon–3pm; Viking Festival in Aug; 120 NOK; www.lofotr.no

Ballstad

The fishing port of Ballstad lies at the southwestern end of the island of Vestvågøy, in the shadow of the Ballstadaksla mountain (466m/1529ft). The island is linked to neighbouring Flakstadøy by the 2km/1mi-long Nappstraumen underwater tunnel (toll payable).

Nordland Sculpture Park

In Eggum, on the northwest coast of Vestvågøy, there is interesting art to be discovered in the green meadow landscape. A short footpath leads to the first sculpture: The Head by the Swiss artist Markus Raetz displays different facets depending on the viewer's position, either appearing as a classic portrait looking out to sea, or, if viewed from the mountain side, resembling an upside down head. It is one of 33 sculptures created by international artists for the Nordland Sculpture Landscape Project, of which five are in Lofoten (►MARCO POLO Insight p.320).

Beach near Utakleiv on the island of Vestvågøy: for many, Lofoten is a dream destination – and rightly so

FLAKSTADØY

The small settlement of Ramberg lies on the northwest coast of the   Ramberg
island of Flakstadøy (holiday homes in Nusfjord). Not far to the east
stands Flakstad church (1780), which was originally built from
driftwood. Facing the open sea, Ramberg's 300 inhabitants have a
wonderful view of the **white sandy beach**. There are interesting
artisan and craft workshops in the village and surrounding area.
Flakstadøy is connected to neighbouring Moskenesøy by a suspension bridge. It is worth paying a visit to the blacksmith at Sund,
around 12km/7mi from Ramberg: he makes the handmade »King
Cormorants«.

Around 10km/6mi beyond the Nappstraumen tunnel, a country road   *Nusfjord
turns off for the pretty fishing village of Nusfjord. One of the most
authentic surviving Lofoten villages, it has been added to the **UN-
ESCO** World Heritage List for cultural properties worth preserving.
There are many fishing huts for rent here and professional fishermen
offer fishing trips – for which warm clothing is essential.

MOSKENESØY

The main settlement on the island of Moskenesøy is the fishing   Reinex
village of Reine (holiday homes) on the Kirkefjord – a favourite
location of numerous painters and mountaineers.

Around 10km/6mi to the southwest lies the little village of Å,   Å
which marks the end of the Lofoten road. A misapprehension that
»Å« represents the first letter of the alphabet results in the village
sign regularly being stolen, yet in Norwegian, »Å« signifies Ome-
ga – the last letter! The tidal Moskenstraumen between Cape Lo-
fotodden and Mosken Island can be observed from the hills
around the village. Jules Verne and Edgar Allan Poe described it
as **the original »Maelstrom«**. Å too has its fishing village museum
with a brine boiling room and a dried cod museum worth visiting,
housed in the former packing house by the harbour.

The island of Værøy to the southwest can be reached by boat from   Journey to
Reine (a trip not recommended for those liable to seasickness!).   Værøy
Værøy is home to just 760 people. In the south, the Mostad Mountains rise sharply above the abandoned settlement of **Mostad**. The
hills here are a **paradise for birds**, where over one million of them
breed from May to August each year: most are puffins, but there are
also guillemots, sea eagles and others. The breeding cliffs can be
reached by hired boat in 20mins from Værøy. The last survivors of

From Cod to Stoccafisso

The striking roof-shaped scaffolds used for drying fish stand all along the Lofoten coast, filled with headless and gutted fish bound together two by two. They are part of a centuries-old tradition of conserving fish by drying it in the cold air.

The trade in stockfish – named after the scaffold drying racks – is documented from Viking times, and fish merchants from Milan still come to Lofoten today to inspect the valuable ingredient for their »stoccafisso«. During the Middle Ages, the stockfish was Norways most important export by far. Catholic Europe hungered for fish every Friday as well as during Lent, and due to the wealth of cod along their coast Norwegians were able to supply vast amounts. To ensure that catches did not rot in the Hanseatic boats during their long journeys, they were preserved by drying. Each spring, after the Lofoten fishing season, predominantly cod, but also coley, cusk and ling are cut either lengthways into two pieces (whereby half the spine is removed), or beheaded and gut-

Norwegian stockfish is exported all the way to Portugal

ted. Two fish are then tied together by their tails and hung on the scaffold, known as a »Hjeller«, where they are left to dry in the salty sea air until 12 June at the latest. The fish loses 70% of its original moisture during the drying process, but the nutritional content is preserved. Thus five kilos (11lbs) of fresh fish contain exactly the same amount of vitamin B, protein, iron and calcium as one kilo (2.2lbs) of stockfish, which the Norwegians generally call »tørrfisk«, meaning dried fish. It is even possible to purchase dried fish pieces in small paper bags as a healthy snack for nibbling on.

Strong Odour

Norways most famous dried fish speciality is »lutefisk«. It appears on all fish restaurant menus during the advent period before Christmas (but some claim that more lutefisk is eaten by Norwegian immigrants in North America).This marinated fish dish requires the dried fish to be soaked in a strong solution for two days, followed by one day of soaking in fresh water, after which it is cooked. When its colour turns a faint yellowish grey and the first overpowering odours appear, the dried fish can be sautéed. According to strict tradition at least, the dish should be served with mashed peas, potatoes and bacon cubes.

a strange dog species with six toes live on the island: known as puffin dogs, they were once used to hunt these birds.

Also accessible by boat from Reine (journey time around 5hrs), as well as from Bodø (5hrs) and Værøy (just over 2hrs), is the last outpost of civilization: the **island group of Røst** lies almost 100km/62mi from the mainland. **Scandinavia's largest bird colony** can be found on the high cliffs of Vedøy, Storfjell, Stavøy, Trenyken and Hernyken, where in addition to around three million puffins, there are also rare species of petrel and fulmar. Boat tours to the cliffs set out from Røstland, and there are also helicopter tours from Bodø during the peak season.

*Bird cliffs

✳ Lyngenfjord

✳ **M/N 16/17**

Region: North Norway

The Lyngenfjord is among the most majestic of Norway's fjords. Between it and the Ullsfjord, the Lyngen Peninsula reaches far out to sea. The Lyngen Alps, partly covered in glaciers, provide almost entirely undeveloped hiking and climbing territory.

The Lyngenfjord extends about 80km/50mi south from the foothills of the Lyngstuen (395m/1296ft). While the road winds along the eastern shore, past small villages and occasionally lush, green meadows below the forested hills, the snow and ice covered mountains of the Lyngen Alps (Lyngsalpene) rise directly out of the water on the western shore. From Tromsø, the Lyngenfjord can be reached on the E 8 as far as Nordkjostbotn; from the south the route is via the E 6.

Northern Norway's most beautiful fjord

Lyngenfjord

INFORMATION
See Tromsø

EASTERN SHORE OF THE LYNGENFJORD

The route to **Oteren** at the southern end of the Storfjord (the southern arm of the Lyngenfjord) goes through the valley of the Nordkjoselv, framed by mountains, with its typically north Norwegian birch forests. To the southeast tower the jagged ridge of Mannfjell (1533m/5030ft) and Otertind (1360m/4462ft), whose double pyramid is also known as the »Arctic Matterhorn«. 3km/2mi northeast

Storfjord

of Oteren a road turns off into the **Signaldalen** valley, which is surrounded by mighty mountains, and a sign-posted footpath leads to the Alpine cabin of Gappohytta (4hrs), as well as connecting with the Nordkalotten hiking route in Sweden. A magnificent view onto the Lyngenfjord and the glacier-topped Jiekkevarre (1833m/6014ft) opens up at Falsnes. The peak is the highest summit of the Lyngen Alps on the west side of the fjord.

Skibotn

The small settlement of **Skibotn** was already an important market for Swedish and Norwegian merchants and the Samis in the 17th century. The mountain Sami came with furs, reindeer meat, iron and agricultural goods and traded them for fish, schnapps and tobacco.

Rugged beauty: the Lyngenfjord and the mountainous Lyngen Alps

The E 8 turns off in the direction of Finland (39km/24mi) to the south of Skibotn. The Skibotn Sami's summer camp at the southern end of **Lake Galgojavvre** can be reached via the forested valley of the fish-rich Skibotnelv, past the 25m/82ft-high Rovijokfoss (where a footpath leads to a viewing point). To the south, on the other side of the Norwegian-Finnish border, it is possible to make out the 39km/24mi-long **Lake Kilpisjärvi**. At the northern

To the largest bird island Insider Tip

A really worthwhile trip is taking the ferry for the 20-minute journey from Skjervøy to the island of Arnøy, and then onwards to Årviksand, on the mouth of the Lyngenfjord. There is a wonderful view onto Norway's largest bird nesting island here: Fugløya, which hosts 300,000 puffins and numerous sea eagles.

end of Kilpisjärvi, a round marker stone stands at the tri-border point between Sweden, Norway and Finland. This point can be reached from Norway along a signposted footpath that leads off the E 8 in the direction of the Goldalhytta (around 6hrs) or via the Gappohytta (around 5hrs; see also under Storfjord). All walking tours in this isolated region require good fitness and equipment. Note that it can snow here even during summer.

To the east, the characteristic silhouette of Saanatunturi – the »holy mountain of the Sami people« – catches the eye. The 1024m/3360ft mountain can be climbed in a good two hours from the Kilpisjärvi hiking hostel. The reward is a beautiful panoramic view of snow-capped peaks, mighty highland landscapes, numerous lakes and the endless forests of Finland.

Holy mountain

Passing the viewing point at Odden, the E 6 winds its way along the shore of the Kåfjord – a side arm of the Lyngenfjord. Near the middle of the fjord lies the settlement of Birtavarre (with a small **open-air museum**), which used to be where iron ore from the nearby Birtavarre mine was prepared for transport. Next to fishing and agriculture, an important source of income here is the sale of a type of hand-woven carpet known as the »radno«. The imposing **Goikegorsa Canyon** in the **Kåfjorddal** is witness to the mighty erosive power of the ice-age meltwaters.

Kåfjord

A few miles further on to the north, cast an eye over to the southern shore where the waterfalls from the **Isfjell** fall vertically into the fjord from a height of 800–900m/2625–2950ft. The next significant place is Olderdal, municipal centre for the Kåfjord parish. From here there is a choice: either continue driving in the direction of Rotsund along the scenically beautiful east shore of the Lyngenfjord, where the views are often wonderful; or take a 40-minute ferry ride to Lyngseidet, on the west shore of the fjord.

Olderdal

Langslett In Langslett, 34km/21mi north of Olderdalen, the RV 866 branches off to the idyllic fishing village of Skjervøy, 31km/19mi away. There is a wonderful view of the Kvænangen fjord and the mountains all around the Øksfjordjøkul glacier (1204m/3950ft) from the harbour there, where the Hurtigruten ships stop daily.

WESTERN SHORE OF THE LYNGENFJORD

*Lyngen Alps Lyngseidet, which can be reached either by ferry from Olderdalen (E 6) or from Oteren (Storfjord p.293) on the RV 868 along the western shore of the fjord, is a suitable base for ascending Goalsevárri (1280m/4200ft). Setting off from the hamlet of **Furuflaten**, it is also possible to climb Njallevárri (1525m/5003ft) in about 4–5hrs, from which there is a spectacular view onto the ice fields of Mount Jiekkevarre (1833m/6014ft) to the west, one of northern Norway's highest mountains.

*Store
Jægervasst-
ind
North of Lyngseidet, the imposing Store Jægervasstind towers 1596m/5236ft up into the sky. This mighty mountain is a veritable mountaineering paradise and, even though the Englishman William S. Slingsby climbed it as early as 1898, many mountaineers still enjoy the challenge of finding new routes to the summit. A good starting point for such ventures is the **Jægervasshytta** to the west, on Lake Jægervatnet.

✳ Mandal

✦ A 4

Region: South Norway
Population: 15,200

In good weather, everyone in Mandal heads to Sjøsanden, undoubtedly one of Norway's most beautiful beaches. This pretty south coast town doesn't get really packed, however, until the annual shellfish festival in August, with parties all round.

Norway's
most souther-
ly town
The most southerly town on the Norwegian Riviera is characterized by narrow lanes and the numerous listed buildings in the old town. Once upon a time, wood from the region's great oak forests and salmon from the Mandalselva river formed the basis of the town's economic wealth. During the 17th and 18th centuries, both the wood and the fish were loaded onto ships destined for foreign climes at Mandal's harbour, one of Norway's oldest. Smoked Mandal salmon was even a highly sought-after delicacy at royal courts overseas.

Mandal

INFORMATION
Mandal Turistkontoret
Bryggegata 10
4514 Mandal
tel. 38 27 83 00
www.lindesnesregionen.com

LEISURE
Sjøsanden us Norway's largest beach,
where regular beach volleyball championships are held.

FISH GALORE
During the shellfish festival in August, a
table is set up on the street several hundred metres long and loaded with seafood delicacies. Thousands of people
come to Mandal for the festival alone,
where everyone eats, drinks and has an
altogether good time.

WHERE TO EAT
Art Café £ £ – £ £ £
Birkelandsvannet, Øyslebø
(about 25mins north of Mandal)
tel. 38 28 78 00
www.artcafe.no
Mirrors are an important feature of the
innovative interior of this café, run by an
artist. The adjacent sculpture park is always open.

WHERE TO STAY
Paulsens Hotell £ £ £
Lyngdal, tel. 40 04 40 05
www.paulsenshotell.com
Guests can relive the late 19th century in
this house that has been lovingly restored to its original condition, dating
back to 1894: staff wear the historic
outfits and traditional nightshirts and
bed hats are set out for each visitor in
the rooms. The facilities leave no wish
unfulfilled, yet modernity is discretely
kept in the background.

Kjøbmandsgaarden Hotell £ £ £
Store elvegate 57
tel. 38 26 12 76
www.kjobmandsgaarden.no, 11 rooms.
Cosy little house in the historic centre of
Mandal with an outstanding restaurant.

Lindesnes Camping og Hytteutleie £
Lillehavn, Spangereid
tel. 38 25 88 74
www.lindesnescamping.no
Norway's most southerly campsite lies
right by the sea on the southern tip of
the Lindesnes peninsula. Two cabins in a
wonderful location offer room for up to
8 people.

WHAT TO SEE IN AND AROUND MANDAL

*Old town   One of Mandal's most beautiful buildings is the old merchant's house of Andorsengården (1801), today a museum with a sailing boat gallery, fishing exhibition and an art gallery showing works by Mandal painters, including Adolf Gustav Vigeland (▶Famous People). The former Skrivergården house of a civil servant dating from 1766 was built from Scottish sandstone and is surrounded by an attractive park designed by the German-Danish landscape gardener Ludvig Blumenthal. Mandal's plain church in Empire style (1821), built by Jørgen Gerhard Løser, has seating for 1800, making it one of northern Europe's largest wooden churches. An arts and crafts centre has established itself in a former furniture factory in the Nedre Malmøy neighbourhood. Many artists and artisans work at the Kulturfabrikken (Keiser Nicolausgate 8-12) and there is a varied and lively programme of exhibitions, workshops and themed events in the café, as well as live concerts in the atmospheric courtyard.

❶ www.kulturfabrikken.biz

> **!** MARCO ⦿ POLO TIP
>
> *Fun in the water*   Insider Tip
>
> Those who find the Sjøsanden – Mandal's large beach - too busy, should take the sign-posted foot-path suitable for the disabled and child buggies along the coast to the Sørland cliffs. Along the way, there are many small bathing coves that are usually more or less empty.

*Lindesnes   Precisely 2518km/1574mi from Nordkapp and the most southerly point on the Norwegian mainland, Lindesnes, lies at a northern latitude of 57° 58' 43" around 40km/25mi west of Mandal. Norway's first lighthouse was built here back in 1655 and there is a wonderful view in good weather as far as Mandal to the east and Lista to the west from the new lighthouse, whose flashing light can be seen from up to 19.4 nautical miles away. A special experience is seeing Lindesnes during a storm, when the waves can reach up to 14m/46ft.

Flekkefjord   The narrow lanes and beautifully restored white wooden houses of the quarter known as »Dutch Town« were originally built in the 18th century, when the wood trade with Holland flourished in Flekkefjord (80km/50mi northwest of Mandal). One of the most appealing buildings in the old town is the Grand Hotel, its white-painted wooden façade decorated with bays and turrets. Other attractions include the several beautiful swimming beaches by the skerry landscape on Hidra Island, south of Flekkefjord. A ferry makes the crossing from Kvellandstrand every hour and the journey takes about 10mins.

Coastal road due north   For travellers with plenty of time who want to continue breathing the sea air, the Nordsjøvegen can be taken as an alternative route between Kristiansand and Stavanger. The most varied section of this beautiful coastal road runs from Flekkefjord to Stavanger.

✳ Mjøsa

C/D 7/8

Region: East Norway
Height: 124m/407ft

Lake Mjøsa, Norway's largest lake, lies in a fertile landscape with many large farms. The most comfortable way to enjoy this gentle countryside is by taking a ride on the historic »Skibladner« steamboat.

When the meltwaters from the north flow into the 362 sq km/140 sq mi of Lake Mjøsa in early summer, it takes on a very special greenish colour. The region around Hamar and Stange, »Norway's bread basket«, is characterized by large waving cereal fields and handsome farms painted red. Further to the north the lake, which reaches depths of 443m/1453ft, is only 2km/1mi wide; here it is possible to get a first taste of the Gudbrandsdal valley, fertile land surrounded by steep hillsides. The farms of the area lie in green meadows below steep, forested slopes that soon merge into a barren mountain landscape.

Norway's largest lake

WHAT TO SEE ON AND AROUND LAKE MJØSA

Just a short drive (signposted) to the south of Lake Mjøsa and east of the E 6 stands one of Norway's national shrines: the old Eidsvoll mansion, in whose state hall 112 of the country's representatives met on 17 May 1814 to sign Norway's first constitution (closed for renovations to mark the 200th anniversary).

*Eidsvoll- bygningen

At the southern end of Lake Mjøsa, the RV 33 branches off towards **Gjøvik**, winding its way directly along the lakeshore for the first 40km/25mi, occasionally passing below steep hillsides. North of Skreia stands **Balke church** (1200), an attractive stone church with an altar cupboard and religious sculptures dating from the 13th century. It is worth making a detour to the Stenberg country estate, which dates from 1790 and whose park has an **open-air museum** (Toten Økomuseum) dedicated to the Toten region. Mjøsmuseet There are several small museums in Kapp, Minesund, Gjøvik and other villages around the lake that collectively come under the title of Mjøsmuseet. For example, the historic farmhouse Gjøvik gård, the Eiktunet Open-Air Museum, with its historic buildings dating from 1650 to 1850, and the Mjøssamlingene Shipping Museum at Minnesund that also covers the history of transporting timber by water. www.mjosmuseet.no

Toten Økomuseum

Mjøsa

INFORMATION
Turistkontoret Gjøvik-Land-Toten
Jernbanegt. 2
2821 Gjøvik
tel.61 14 67 10
www.gjovik.com

EXCURSIONS
The most pleasant option is a trip on the oldest steamboat still in operation, the »Skibladner«, that has been providing service on the Mjøsa without interruption (except for 11 years) since 1856. It was somewhat enlarged in 1888, and provided with a larger engine. As a postal boat, it also has its own postmark stamp. Departures are daily except Mondays, from the end of June to mid-August; on board meals and drinks are served (prices: from 180 NOK, children under 12 years old free; www.skibladner.no)..

WHERE TO EAT
Belvedere £ £ £
Hans Mustadsgt. 14, Gjøvik
tel. 61 18 02 58
This high class restaurant is located in a fine villa above town.

WHERE TO STAY
Quality Hotel Grand £ £ £
Jernbanegt. 5, Gjøvik
tel. 61 14 00 00, Fax 61 14 00 01
www.choicehotels.no, 90 rooms.
Traditional hotel that is regularly modernised near the Olympic hall inside the mountain. Its American restaurant is famous far and wide.

*Gjøvik Olympic Cavern Hall
During the 1994 Winter Olympics, the regional centre of **Gjøvik** (pop. 29,200) had the honour of hosting all the ice hockey games in its purpose-built Olympic Cavern Hall, which was blasted out of the mountain right in the centre of town. With a ground plan spanning 5550 sq m/59,740 sq ft and seating for 5830, the venue is the largest **underground spectator hall on earth**. 170 tons of dynamite was used to create the cavern, and the rocks left over were built into the Gjøvik beach promenade. The road rejoins the E 6 17km/11mi north of Gjøvik.

Eastern shore
On the eastern shore, the conveniently widened E 6 initially follows a beautiful route above the lake for about 20km/12mi before leaving Lake Mjøsa and heading through birch and pine forests where elk are frequently spotted, in Norway's most fertile **region around Stange** and ▶Hamar. The **church** (1250) west of Stange is among the most important medieval churches of the Hedmark region. The stained glass windows are outstanding. Near the lakeshore there are numerous country estates (storgårder), often dating from the 18th century, which underline the historic wealth of this fertile region.

*Ringsaker church
Just a short drive beyond the Brummundal on the main road, there is a turn-off to the stone basilica of Ringsaker (1150). The chalk

The »Skibladner« is the world's oldest steamboat still in operation

paintings in the choir portray St Olav (►Trondheim; ►Steinkjer, Stiklestad), who – occasionally by force – brought Christianity to Norway at the beginning of the 11th century. The old Flemish painted wooden altar from 1530 is a real treasure.

❶ summer: Sat 10am–4pm, Sun noon–5pm

The Prøysenhuset, a museum containing an exhibition (of interest for children too) on Alf Prøysen (1914–70), Norway's best known composer and author of folktunes, lies on the E 6, which then continues to Lillehammer via the 1420m/ 4659ft Mjøsa bridge (toll payable) leading over the lake to its western shore. Those who wish to remain on the eastern shore continue through Moelv on the old Europa Route, which winds idyllically above the lake as far as ►Lillehammer.

Prøysenhuset

Mo i Rana

✳ **J 11**

Region: North Norway
Population: 25,600

Mo i Rana itself is not very spectacular and tends to be passed by. However, it is worth taking the time to visit Svartisen – which after all is Norway's second largest glacier – and the grottoes nearby.

Mo (pronounced Mu) i Rana is the largest settlement in the Helge-land region (►Nordland). During the 19th century, the German L. A. Meyer and his descendants ensured that this former trading post de-

Lively port

Mo i Rana

INFORMATION
Mo i Rana Turistinformasjon
O. T. Olsensgt. 2
8602 Mo i Rana
tel. 75 13 92 00
www.visithelgeland.com

EXCURSION
Around 100km/62mi southwest of Mo i Rana, on the tiny island of Seløy (Herøy district), it is possible to observe saltwater eagles, cormorants and sea lions among the countless islands and skerries – a speedy and not exactly cheap thrill on an inflatable boat (reservations via Seløy Kystferie, tel. 47 36 60 87, www.seloykystferie.no).
Other wildlife tours, such as to the world heritage site on the Vega Archipelago can be arranged by the tourist office.

WHERE TO EAT
Meyergården Hotell £ £
Fr. Nansensgt. 2
tel. 75 13 40 80
www.meyergarden.no
This traditional hotel in the centre is well known for its good restaurant. A good deal is the »Dagens Middag« offered between 1pm and 7.30pm.

WHERE TO STAY
Mo Hotell og Gjestegård £ £
Elias Blix gt. 10
tel. 75 15 22 11
www.mo-gjestegaard.no, 15 rooms.
This guest house is in a quiet location in the centre of Mo i Rana surrounded by a well-maintained garden. The 15 rooms (incl. family rooms) are newly renovated with pine-clad walls.

veloped into a lively industrial centre. They installed a mine, shops, and even a wine trading post. After the war, the town also gained an ironworks and a cokeworks that are now both decommissioned. This industrial adventure can be traced in the local **museum**, which in addition provides information on the Sami people (▶MARCO POLO Insight p.34), whose culture and trade also had a strong impact on the town. A local curiosity to the west of the town centre is the 10m/33ft-high statue of the **»Havmannen«** (Man of the Sea), the water reaching up to his stone thighs at each high tide.

AROUND MO I RANA

Mysterious caves

Only two of the 120 caves in this region are open to the public. The most well known is the **Grønli Cave** (Grønligrotta), a maze of winding passages with an underground stream, moulins – and lighting. Indeed it is the only cave in Northern Europe to be illuminated. Access to Grønligrotta, which is signposted, is via a turn-off from the E 6 near Røssvoll (airstrip) 13km/8mi northeast of Mo i Rana, followed by a 10-minute walk to the cave entrance.

❶ 20th June–20th Aug guided tours every hour 10am–6pm, 130 NOK; www.gronligrotta.no

A visit to Setergrotta (Seter Cave) is most suitable for experienced cavers, since the two-hour tour through huge caverns, narrow tunnels and slippery passages requires rubber boots, helmets, waterproof clothing and headlamps (all gear can be hired out). With its 3km/2mi of mapped passages, this limestone cave is one of the largest in the district, and its formations of chalk, ice and white marble certainly make for a spooky atmosphere.

*Setergrotta

Two-hour tours: June, Aug 3pm, in July also at 11.30am; 300 NOK per person; www.setergrotta.no

Beyond the caves, the road continues to Lake Svartisvatn (huts & kiosk), where the great ice fields of Norway's second largest glacier rise up (▶Saltfjell). From 20 June to the end of August it is possible to take a boat over the deep green waters of the lake every other hour between 10am and 4pm, and hike through the magnificent mountain landscape. It takes about 1.5hrs to cover the approximately 3km/2mi to the Østerdalsisen arm of the glacier; the path is often steep and very rocky underfoot (stout hiking boots needed).

*Svartisen

Crossing 20th June–end of August every two hours between 10am and 4pm

The picturesque Sjøgata right on the Vefsnfjord, in the small industrial settlement of Mosjøen (pop. 13,500; 91km/57mi southwest of Mo i Rana), is northern Norway's longest and best preserved historic town road, with around 100 beautifully restored wooden houses dating from the 18th and 19th centuries.

Mosjøen

A very worthwhile excursion from Mosjøen leads towards the sea at **Sandnessjøen**, which is located to the northwest of the mountain range well-known as »The Seven Sisters« (▶Nordland). It is kept lively by the stop of the Hurti-

> **?** *Skiing Pictogram*
>
> MARCO ◉ POLO INSIGHT
>
> In the middle of the fjord landscape west of Mosjøen lies the small island of Tro that can be reached by ferry from Tjøtta. The oldest representation of a skier in Norway can be found here in a rock engraving which inspired the official logo for the Winter Olympics in Lillehammer.

gruten ships and as a transfer point for the oil industry. 20km/12mi further south, on the eastern shore of the Alstfjord, stands the 12th-century Romanesque church in Alstahaug with its magnificently embellished altar.

On *Dønna Island** (25mins by ferry from Sandnessjøen), is worth visiting for the 12th-century stone church with its underground passages and burial chamber. There is a fine view of the bird island of Lovund, where around 25,000 puffins nest, from Dønnesfjell (127m/417ft). Access is by express boat.

Narvik

✦ **L 14**

Region: North Norway
Population: 18 500

Narvik's ice-free harbour has been both a blessing and a curse. On the one hand iron ore from Swedish Kiruna is shipped out from here, but on the other the port was so fought over in the Second World War that the town was almost totally destroyed. The shipping of iron ore today is something to behold for those interested in seeing mighty industry at work.

Distributor of
iron ore from
Sweden

This north Norwegian town was called Victoriahavn right until 1899, but was then renamed as Narvik when the Ofot Line (Swedish Lapland Line) rail connection was built, which comes from the Swedish iron ore mining region near **Kiruna**. Thanks to its ice-free port and its position at the end of the Ofot Line, Narvik enjoys great economic importance. During the Second World War, the German occupation of the town guaranteed their supply of Swedish iron ore. Britain

The Ofot railway line brings iron ore and tourists over the Swedish border

attempted to obstruct this, and the resulting heavy battles caused the destruction of the town. During the reconstruction of Narvik in the 1950s, the old wooden houses were replaced with unappealing stone buildings. Most visitors to Narvik are merely passing through on their way to Nordkapp.

WHAT TO SEE IN NARVIK

The town is sliced in two by the mighty iron ore port, which was extended in 1977. The ore arriving from Sweden by train is moved to various stores and to the Malm quay via long conveyor belts. The expansion of the port ensured that iron ore freighters with a capacity of up to 350,000 tons could be loaded and annual turnover now stands at around 14 million tons. However, since several developing countries, such as Brazil, have been able to offer iron ore at significantly lower prices, the demand for the expensive Swedish ore has declined dramatically, and the significance of Narvik's port with it. Only 300 people still find employment in the port. Tours of the Swedish company LKAB's port installations are organized by the tourist information office.

*Iron ore port

Narvik

INFORMATION
Narvik Turistkontor
Stasjonsveien 1
8515 Narvik
tel. 76 96 56 00
www.destinationnarvik.com

EXCURSION
By good weather, a trip to the Swedish border with the Ofot railway is really worthwhile. The train travels to and from the fjord to the high mountains in three hours, and there are superb views, but only for those sitting on the left-hand side (in the direction the train is heading). Departures are from Narvik railway station.

FESTIVAL
Narvik's annual winter festival founded in 1956, takes place in March, with music, literature, live shows and conferences (www.vinterfestuka.no).

WHERE TO EAT
❶ ***Fiskehallen Restaurant £ £***
Kongensgt. 42
tel. 76 94 36 60
Freshly cooked seafood delights are served in this restaurant in the Narvik fish market, where you can also buy whale meat and other North Sea fish.

WHERE TO STAY
❶ ***Quality Grand Royal £ £ £***
Kongensgt. 64
tel. 76 97 70 00
www.nordicchoice.no, 160 rooms.
Hotel right in the centre with a popular restaurant, a pub and a nightclub.

War Museum

A tank can be seen stationed in front of the entrance to the War Museum opposite the town hall. This is one of Norway's most visited war museums, and documents the events of the war between 1940 and 1945, with collections of uniforms, weapons, medals and pieces of wreckage.

● Mid-April–mid-June and mid-Aug–mid-Sep Mon–Sat 10am–4pm, Sun noon–4pm, mid-June–mid-Aug Mon–Sat 10am–9pm, Sun noon–6pm; 75 NOK; www.warmuseum.no

South of the market

The **Swedish sailors' church**, including a library, is located at the southern end of Kongens gate. Diagonally opposite, a memorial recalls two **tank carriers**, the Norwegian ships Norge and Eidsvold that were sunk during the battles of 1940. Narvik's cultural-historic **Nord-Narvik Museum** provides its visitors with all they need to know on the iron ore port. The **cemetery to the east** of town is the final resting place not only of Allied troops who fell here, but also of 1473 German soldiers.

Nord-Narvik Museum: July 10am–4.30pm, Sat–Sun noon–3pm, otherwise Mon–Fri 10am–3pm; 50 NOK; www.museumnord.no/ofoten

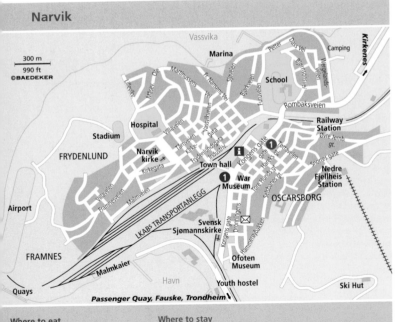

Narvik

300 m
990 ft
©BAEDEKER

Vassvika

Marina

Camping

Kirkenes

School

Petter Dass Vei

Vegglands-veien

Bjørmoveien

Rombaksveien

Hospital

Railway Station

Øvre Jernb. gt.

Stadium

Narvik kirke ×

FRYDENLUND

Kirkegata

Town hall

ℹ

● War Museum

Snorres gate

Nedre Fjellheis Station

OSCARSBORG

Airport

Svensk Sjømannskirke

✉

Ofoten Museum

FRAMNES

Malmkaier

Havn

Youth hostel

Ski Hut

Quays

Passenger Quay, Fauske, Trondheim ↘

Where to eat
● Fiskehallen Restaurant

Where to stay
● Quality Grand Royal

It is worth climbing the 102m/325ft Framme–Sen, twenty minutes west of town, from which there is a panoramic view across the Ofot-fjord and over to Kongsbaktind. To the south, the famous mountain silhouette of »Den sovende Dronning« (Sleeping Queen) is also visible.

Framme–Sen

AROUND NARVIK

East of town, the Narvikfjellet comprises a hiking and winter sports region with mountains up to 1900m/6,234ft high. A cable car travels up to a restaurant with panoramic views and rustic meals at an elevation of 670m/2198ft. Between November and April, five ski lifts carry winter sports enthusiasts up to 1030m/3379ft, where there are nine prepared pistes and four unmaintained runs. The national long-distance hiking route known as the »Nordlandruta« runs through this mountainous landscape cut by streams and rivers that ensure it is also an El Dorado for fishing. Driving south towards Bodø, there is a turning due northeast to Leiknes.

Leiknes, Tømmernes

> **MARCO POLO TIP**
>
> ! *Edvardas charming hotel* Insider Tip
>
> The little Edvardas Hus hotel in Tranøy certainly deserved its cultural prize. The elegant wood house only has nine rooms, all with their own delightful interiors; but what really defines the charm of this place is the service. The hotel feels like home from home and guests are thoroughly spoiled. (tel. 75 77 21 82, www.edvardashus.no).

Here, about 900m/985yd from the RV 814, around 40 animal rock paintings can be found that are between 4000 and 5000 years old. In Tømmernes, around 47km/29mi south of Bognes, the rock paintings found near Sagelva are 5000, perhaps even 8000 years old.

At Ulvsvåg south of Narvik, route 81 turns off to the **Hamarøy** group of islands, whose rugged mountain landscape is well worth a visit. Mount Hamarøyskaftet stands out in particular, jabbing into the sky like a giant green tooth. The architecturally striking international Hamsun Centre in Hamarøy was officially opened in 2009, in time for the 150th anniversary of the birth of Norwegian writer Knut Hamsun (Famous People). The author spent his childhood here and regularly returned.

Hamarøy

Hamsun Museum: June–mid-Aug daily 11am–6pm, otherwise Tues–Fri 10am–3.30pm, Sat–Sun 11am–5pm; 90 NOK; www.hamsunsenteret.no

The photogenic lighthouse of Tranøy Fyr and the art galleries, including the Hamsun gallery (a small shop where Knut Hamsun once worked as a young assistant) near Tranøy, are also worth the trip.

Tranøy

✷ Nordfjord

✦ D 2/3

Region: West Norway

A drive along the many branches of the Nordfjord shows western Norway at its most beautiful. The crowning finale is a trip to the glacier tongues of Jostedalsbreen, of which Briksdalsbreen is the most popular.

Many branches

Glaciers, idyllic fjord and fishing villages, steep, high mountains, lonely beaches, narrow serpentine roads and deep, clear waters – all this is on offer at the Nordfjord which extends over 100km/62mi inland, from Måløy to Olden (at a latitude of 62°). The inner branches of the fjord have the greatest appeal, as here the wild juxtaposition of water, mighty mountains, and glaciers calving far down into the valley below create a truly unique impression.

THE FJORD INTERIOR

✷Strynefjell

The approach from the east is the most impressive, especially via the old unpaved Strynefjell Road that branches off the E 15 at Grotli. This route passes the Stryn summer ski resort with its chairlift up the Tystig Glacier, and makes several hairpin bends on its descent into the Videdal valley and onwards to Stryn on the northern shore of the Innvikfjord, which is an inner arm of the Nordfjord.

✷Lovatn

The little holiday resort of Loen on the Innvikfjord is a good base for climbing the 1848m/6063ft Skåla, as well as for excursions to Kjenndalsbreen, a glacier that can be reached by tour boat from the eastern end of Lovatn, a picturesque lake. In 1905, a **massive stone avalanche** crashed into the lake, causing a 6m/20ft wave that killed 50 people. 74 people also died here in 1936, when large amounts of rock crashed down from the 1789m/5870ft-high Ravnefjell which, like Kjenndalsbreen, is a northern outcrop of ▶Jostedalsbreen.

Briksdalsbreen

Briksdalsbreen is reached via the Innvikfjord and **Olden**, past the pretty Olden church from 1749. The narrow road then winds its way along the deep-green coloured Lake Olden and ends in the heart of the valley surrounded by waterfalls and snow-covered mountains.

The hike up to the glacial lake of Briksdalsbreen, a branch of the mighty ▶Jostedalsbreen, is an absolute must. The occasionally very steep path begins at the Brikdalsbreen mountain cabin, passes a

The Lonvatn near Stryn

Nordfjord

INFORMATION
Stryn
Destination Stryn & Nordfjord
Tinggata 3
6783 Stryn
tel. 57 87 40 40
www.nordfjord.no

EXCURSIONS
»Trollbilar« tours (around 20mins, advance reservations recommended) and glacier hiking trips over the Briksdalbreen can be arranged by Oldedalen Skyss, tel. 57 87 68 05, www.oldedalen-skysslag.com.

WHERE TO EAT
Restaurant Charlotte £££££
Loen, Hotel Alexandra,
tel. 57 87 50 00
Anyone in this region should make sure not to miss the large cold buffet offered between 6pm and 9pm, with its delicious salmon and herring dishes, smoked fish, and divine desserts.

WHERE TO STAY
Gloppen Hotell £££
Gloppen Hotell A A A
Sørstrandsv. 16
6823 Sandane
tel. 57 86 53 33
www.gloppenhotell.no, 40 rooms.
Wealthy salmon fishermen have been enjoying this smart hotel since 1866. Built in Swiss style, the hotel offers sterling comforts.

Hotel Selje £££
6740 Selje
tel. 57 85 88 80, Fax 57 85 88 81
www.seljehotel.no, 49 rooms.
This rustic hotel on the wild West Cape contains Norway's first spa.

Stryn Hotel £££
Visnesvegen 1, 6783 Stryn
tel. 57 87 07 00
www.strynhotel.no, 69 rooms.
A modern and comfortable hotel right on the Nordfjord that makes an ideal base for trips into the Jostedals region.

churning waterfall that produces beautiful rainbows on sunny days, and then leads along the crystal clear glacial stream through sometimes damp terrain up to the glacial lake and the glacier tongue itself, which 80 years ago almost reached all the way down into the valley (there and back takes around 1.5hrs, ►photo p.14). It is also possible to travel two thirds of the route by »Trollbilars« – similar to golf carts - or take part in a guided glacier walk. Finally, another tip: it is quietest here before 10am and in the afternoon, after the cruise ships at Olden have left.

Utvikfjell The RV 60 winds its way alongside the Innvikfjord from Olden to Utvik before travelling up to the 630m/2067ft-high Utvikfjell in broad loops that offer panoramic views across the fjord. The best scenes are near the Pension Karistova. At the top of the route there are wonderful views onto the glaciers of Geitenyken (1621m/5318ft) and Snønipa (1827m/5994ft) to the southeast.

Travelling through the fertile landscape around Byrkjelo (E 39 / RV 5 to the ▶Sognefjord), where agriculture has been practiced since Viking times, it is worth making a detour west to the pretty village of deep in the interior of the Gloppenfjord, yet another side arm of the Nordfjord. Here there is an open-air museum with 35 old buildings, but a special attraction is the magnificent panorama from the **Utsik-ten viewing point** northwest of the settlement. Along the eastern shore of this fjord visitors will also find **western Norway's largest burial mound** at Tinghøgjen. The mound is 50m/164ft wide and 7m/23ft high.

Sandane

FROM STRYN TO MÅLØY

One of the most beautiful stretches along the Nordfjord runs from Stryn out to the mouth of the fjord. The RV 15 heads out past **Europe's deepest lake**, the 514m/1686ft-deep Hornidalsvatn, in the direction of Nordfjordeid. A mecca for fjord horses, Nordfjordeid hosts a state-sponsored stallion show every spring.

Nordfjordeid

From now on the road winds its way directly alongside the fjord, all the way to Måløy on the island of Vågsøy, west of the mouth of the fjord. At Almenningen the eye is drawn to the 860m/2822ft cliff of the Hornelen that rises vertically out of the water. According to legend, **Europe's highest cliff** was once a meeting place for dances between witches and the devil during Christmas Eve and Midsummer's Night.

*Hornelen

During storms, the 42m/138ft bridge to **Måløy**»sings« a high C. Those with delicate noses will quickly realize that the inhabitants of Måløy – one of Norway's most important fishing ports – live predominantly from the fishing industry. Of interest are the **hourglass shaped stone** (a strangely eroded rock right by the sea to the northwest of Måløy) and the old trading square of **Vågsberget** with its seven historic buildings.

> **?** MARCO ◉ POLO INSIGHT
>
> *Fjord horse riding*
>
> They may look like overgrown ponies, but these yellow-brown horses (fjording in Norwegian) with the dark stripe along their backs and their dark legs actually resemble the world's last wild horses, the Przewalski horses of Central Asia. Once upon a time they were hardy working animals, but today they are used for riding out into the idyllic landscape. A good place to try is: Norsk Fjordhestcenter in Nordfjordeid, tel. 57 86 48 00; www.norsk-fjordhest-senter.no.

Detour to Selje	Near Almenningen or Maurstad (8km/5mi or 21km/13mi east of Måløy respectively), it is worth making a detour to the coastal settlement of Selje where a beautiful white sandy beach awaits, perfect for swimming in good weather. The **island of Selja** and its Selje Monastery lies just out to sea: a fascinating place, not only for its 12th-century ruins, but also for the unique play of colours ranging from the blues of the sea to the greens of the meadows. The cave above the ruins was once the hiding place of the legendary Irish **Princess Sunniva**, who fled there from the new heathen king. She is the patron saint of West Norway.
Vestkapp	From the mainland's most westerly mountain plateau, the 496m/1627ft-high Vestkapp, 33km/21mi from Selje, there is a fantastic view out onto the North Sea. For ships heading north, this is the beginning of the unprotected open passage across the sea, notoriously exposed to storms and feared down the ages.

** Nordkapp

✶ O 22

Region: North Norway

The view from the Nordkapp cliffs is breathtaking – though only in fair weather. But since Europe's most northerly point is generally cloudy, rainy, foggy and always icy cold, the Nordkapphallen was built. Using the services of this multi-media centre is shockingly expensive, however, as is everything else at Nordkapp.

High-cost access	A 30km/19mi-long tunnel and bridge connection from the mainland to the island of Magerøya, where Nordkapp is located, has been in operation for over ten years. The toll is 145 NOK for cars and camper vans up to 6m/19.6ft long (www.nordkappbompengeselskap.no). The most expensive section of this prestige project, known as »Fatima«, is the world's longest underwater road tunnel, which lies around 200m/656ft beneath the sea and links Kåfjord and Honningsvåg. It is also possible to fly from Hammerfest to Honningsvåg, from where there are buses or taxis to Nordkapp. A good alternative is the six-hour journey on one of the ▶Hurtigruten ships from Hammerfest to Honningsvåg.
Protected Area	Nordkapp has been a protected area since 1929. Those found picking plants, camping wild, driving off the main road or entering bird sanctuaries during breeding season can expect fines of up to £1,200/US$2300!

WHAT TO SEE AT NORDKAPP

Located at a northern latitude of 71° 10' 21" and an eastern longitude   At the norof 25° 47' 40", Nordkapp (North Cape) is the precipitous northern   thern end of
end of the **island of Magerøya**. The grey-green slate cliff riven by   Europe

Nordkapp

INFORMATION
Nordkapp Reiseliv AS
Fiskeriveien 4, 9750 Honningsvåg
tel. 78 47 70 30, www.nordkapp.no

FESTIVAL
The annual North Cape Festival is held in
June in Honningsvåg, which includes a
70km/43mi orienteering race to Nordkapp, along with films, concerts and a
great deal of eating.

EXCURSIONS, SPORT
Fishing enthusiasts and birdwatchers are
well-served here. Sporty types can also
enjoy speedy ocean rafting tours or
guided hikes, and those more interested
in the indigenous culture can book a
homestay with a local Sami family (reservations via the tourist office and North
Cape Adventures, tel. 78 47 22 22,
www.nordkapp.com).

MIDNIGHT SUN
From 16th May to 28th July and reaches
its lowest point at 23.35pm Central European Time (CET). Between 22nd November and 11th January the sun never rises.

WHERE TO EAT
Havstua £ £
Kamøyvær (10km/6mi from Honningsvåg)
tel. 78 47 51 50
The interior of this unprepossessing fishing hut houses a cosy fish restaurant
with delicious dishes.

WHERE TO STAY
Rica Hotel Nordkapp £ £ £ £
Skipsfjorden, 9750 Honningsvåg
tel. 78 47 72 60
www.rica.no, 290 rooms.
The nearest hotel to Nordkapp reflects
the surrounding mountain landscape in
its architecture of a central peak comprising the main building, surrounded by
extended low architecture all around.
The rooms are typically Norwegian, with
a lot of wood, and the restaurant serves
a full and varied buffet.

Kirkeporten Camping £ £
Skarsvåg
tel. 78 47 52 33
http://kirkeporten.no
Norway's most northerly campsite lies
near the Storvann, by the small settlement of Skarsvåg. There are ten cabins
as well as several rooms in the main
building. The footpath to the Kirkeporten begins right here.

Northcape Guesthouse £
Elvebakken 5a, Honningsvåg
tel. 92 82 33 71
www.northcapeguesthouse.com
Visitors to Nordkapp with simple tastes
can find good value for money rooms
here and also enjoy a cosmopolitan atmosphere provided by backpackers from
all over. A unique place to stay, despite
the crowds, where nations unite at the
end of the world!

The globe marks the »end of the world«

deep furrows is visited for being Europe's northernmost tip. Strictly
speaking, this is untrue, since Cape Knivskjelodden lies a little further north still, at a northern latitude of 71° 11′ 8″. Furthermore, the
northernmost point of the European **mainland** is considered to be
Kinnarodden (Cape Nordkinn), 68km/42mi east of Nordkapp between Laksefjord and Tanafjord (also known as Nordkyn ; 234m/768ft
above sea level). Average temperatures in June and July are
9–11°C/48–52°F; in January and February they hover between -2°
and -4°C/28° and 25°F. 308m/1010ft above sea level, the Nordkapp
cliffs were discovered as early as 1553 by the English seafarer Richard
Chancellor, who was searching for the Northeast Passage (Siberia to
China to America). Drivers on the road from Honningsvåg to Nordkapp (closed in winter) should beware of **reindeer**, as there are
around 5000 of them on the island during summer and they are often
hard to spot due to their camouflage colours – even while they are
crossing the road. Drive slowly, especially in foggy conditions.

The island of Magerøya is Scandinavia's most northerly outpost. Its mighty jagged peninsulas push into the Arctic Ocean between deep fjords, and its 300–400m/1000–1300ft-high plateaus often fall steeply into the sea. Only sparse, hardy vegetation survives in these barren surroundings.

Magerøya Island

The port of Honningsvåg on Magerøya's southeast coast is the main settlement in the municipality of Nordkapp. It is worth paying a vis-it to the **Nordkapp Museum** here, which offers insight into the coastal culture of ►Finnmark as well as into the development of tourism at Nordkapp. The first international tour group arrived in 1875. It is also possible to take a cruise to Norway's largest bird cliffs and to abandoned fishing villages. The economic foundation here remains, as before, fishing, fish processing and shipping. Honningsvåg became a centre for dragnet fishing at the beginning of the 20th century, because the ships working along the dangerous north coast need good pilots, and they normally boarded here. The pilot station here is still of great importance. Like Hammerfest, Honningsvåg was also destroyed during the German retreat in November 1944.

Honningsvåg

Nordkapp

©BAEDEKER

5 km
3.1 miles

Knivskjellodden
North Cape

Tufjord

Skarsvåg

Kamøyfjord

Gjesvær

▲ 417 m **Magerøya**
1369 ft

Kamøyvær

Vannfjord

Honningsvåg

Magerøya

Kobbfjord

Tunnel »Fatima«

Porsangen

Kåfjord

▲ 493 m
1618 ft

Skouttanjargga

Olderfjord ↘ Repvåg

Sværholt
Halvøya

Nordkapp Museum: June–mid-Aug Mon–Sat 10am–7pm, Sun noon–7pm, otherwise Mon–Fri noon–4pm; www.kystmuseene.no

If the weather is bad, the **Nordkapphallen** (North Cape Hall) is a good place to shelter: the attractions include a panoramic restaurant, the northernmost Champagne bar in the world, a multimedia show and an exhibition on the history of Nordkapp. The centre is built as a tunnel that ends with a grotto where a window opens onto the Arctic Sea (Nordkapp diploma, special stamps and postmarks available). An arrow indicates the direction of north and there is also a granite pillar commemorating the visit of King Oscar II in around 1873. In fair weather, the view of the Arctic Sea extends to the west, north and east. To the southwest, the islands of Hjelmsøy, Måsøy and Rolvsøy

North Cape Hall

MARCO◉POLO TIP

! *A luxury bed at the Nordkapp*

Not a guarantee for eternal bliss, but at least a happy memory: quite a few have tied the knot at Nordkapp. After the wedding in the chapel and the feast in the restaurant, the happy couple can stay in the North Cape Centre's tower suite. The exclusive accommodation with panorama view is available to all, not just newly weds. Reservations at tel. 78 47 68 60.

can be seen; in the distant east lies Kinnarodden; to the south, Magerøya's highlands with their snow fields, ponds and sparse vegetation. **North Cape Hall:** mid-May–mid-Aug daily 11am–1am, till end of Aug daily 11am–10pm, otherwise daily 11am–3pm; 235 NOK; www.visitnordkapp.net

En route from Honningsvåg to Nordkapp, a country road branches off to the fishing village of Gjesvær, around 20km/12mi away in the northwest of the island. Islands and skerries protect the very attractive settlement with a mere 300 souls from the rough Arctic Sea. A local nature reserve is famous among ornithologists for its bird cliffs, where great numbers of puffins and even sea eagles can be observed.

Special day, special location: people even like to get married at Nordkapp

There is a signposted footpath (approx. 20mins) from the Nordkapp Turistheim to an interesting rock formation known as the Kirkeporten. The cape can be seen through this »church portal«, and provides a unique sight. The peace and memorable views here at midnight are an appealing alternative for those who wish to escape the crowds on the Nordkapp plateau.

Nordland

✦ F-N 7-19

Region: North Norway
Population: 238,300

The landscape of the long, narrow province of Nordland has several highlights. Along its jagged coast tremendous mountain scenery awaits, as does Svartisen, Norway's second largest glacier. Nordland's only significant towns are Bodø and Narvik, both rather plain due to their post-war architecture.

Nordland is the longest and narrowest of Norway's counties: where the Hellemofjord juts inland, it is barely 6km/4mi to the Swedish border. At six inhabitants per square kilometre (13 per sq mi), the population density is really rather low, and increasing numbers are leaving this economically deprived region. While in former times virtually every coastal community had its fishermen, many villages are now dying out. Income is increasingly dependent on tourism and its associated service sectors, though the oil and gas industry also supplies a few jobs. Tourism is still very limited here, so those seeking solitude have come to the right place. The first autumnal storms in September see off the **mild summers** (12°C/54°F), and very quickly the seemingly endless polar night descends, during which the sun never climbs above the horizon. When the sun shows its face again a few weeks after Christmas, it is time for all Nordlanders to celebrate. No wonder that in many municipalities of the Arctic Circle, **Easter** is also an opportunity to celebrate numerous other events, such as weddings and christenings.

Mild summers, few people

Nordland

INFORMATION/ WHERE TO EAT/ WHERE TO STAY
▶ Bodø, Mo i Rana, Narvik

GETTING THERE
At Bodø in Nordland, it is the end of the line for the railway from Oslo. Those with little time should take the E 6 through Nordland, though the best of the countryside can be enjoyed by driving along coastal route 17.

The southern part of Nordland, known as Helgeland, awaits the visitor with many small islands and coastal villages. North of the Arctic Circle, key destinations include Svartisen, at around 370 sq km/143 sq mi Norway's **second-largest glacier** (▶Mo i Rana, surroundings), and the mightiest tidal waters in the world at the **Saltstraumen** (▶Bodø, surroundings). A world unto itself is formed by the wildly jagged peaks of the ▶Lofoten and ▶Vesterålen island chains that lie off the coast between Bodø and Narvik. With a bit of luck, those with a passion for ocean wildlife may even spot whales and dolphins there.

Flora and fauna

South of the Svartisen massif and ▶Saltfjell in Helgeland, the landscape is green and varied, and occasionally **forested**. North of this area, however, an **Arctic climate** predominates and birch and pine trees only survive the short summers and long winters in a few scattered locations. In sheltered spots, flowering plants not associated

with these latitudes can survive. The animal world is naturally adapted to the cold and includes stoat, fox, mink, beaver and lemming, as well as the almost ubiquitous **reindeer** and **elk**; the rivers meanwhile are alive with salmon and trout. Thanks to reduced fishing quotas, **salmon stocks** are now recovering from a period of overfishing. The sea is also (still) home to good stocks of fish, the Gulf Stream ensuring that temperatures never drop below -1°C/30°F during winter. Only catches of the ever popular cod are restricted.

Elks also live in Nordland

ALONG COASTAL ROUTE 17

Mystic mountains

The RV 17 coastal route, also known as the »Kystriksveien«, leads into the most beautiful corners of Nordland's island and skerry world between Steinkjer in the south and Bodø in the north. Where there are no bridges, ferries ensure a relaxed break to the journey. The tens of thousands of islands and skerries are topped by strangely shaped mountains that have always inspired the imagination of the local people. Going from south to north, the most famous are the »Mountain with the Hole« (**Torghatten**) near Brønnøysund; the *»**Seven Sisters**« (Syv Søstre) near Sandnessjøen; the mountains of the bird islands Lovund and Træna; the »Horseman« (Hestmannen) on the island of Hestmona in the Arctic Circle; and the »Lion« on Rødøya. According to local superstition, these are legendary saga figures turned to stone when they failed to hide before sunrise when the Hestmannen was chasing the girl Lekamøya (mountain of the same name on the island of Leka south of Brønnøysund).

Crossing the provincial border in the south on the RV 17, the journey immediately begins with the ferry crossing from Holm to Vennesund. Further north, at **Brønnøysund**, lies the Hildurs Urterarium, where visitors can not only see numerous rare herbs and around 500 species of roses, but also hear stories from Viking times.

From Holm to Alstahaug

After two more ferry journeys, **Alstahaug** is reached, where the poet priest **Petter Dass** (1647–1708) once preached in the local 12th-century church. He lived in Alstahaug from 1689 until his death, and is well known in Norway as a Baroque poet. There is a museum (Petter Dass Museum) devoted to his life in the church courtyard.

> ! **MARCO ❂ POLO TIP**
>
> *Mrs Haugan's Hotel*   *Insider Tip*
>
> This hotel has been under female management for the past 200 years. It is located in the centre of Mosjøen, in the middle of a picturesque quarter and positively exudes cosiness. After extensive renovations, at least half of its 93 rooms were restored to their historic original, as were the bar and living rooms. The affordable summer prices make this hotel a popular option (Strandgt. 39, tel. 75 11 41 00, www.fruhaugans.no).

There is a speedboat connection between Sandnesjøen and the **bird island of Lovund**, with its large puffin colony. The island of Dønna can also be reached from Sandnesjøen. Dønnesfjell, at 127m/417ft high, provides beautiful panoramic views onto the island world as far as the »Seven Sisters«. Additionally, there is a fertility symbol from the time of the Great Migrations (approx. AD 500–600) at **Glein** on Dønna: this **stone phallus** is the largest of its kind in Scandinavia.

From Sandnesjøen to the Arctic Circle

Continuing on, the small island group of **Træna** can be spotted in the distance, out to sea, with its roughly 400 islands and the striking peak of Trænstaven (331m/1086ft).

Træna

The Arctic Circle is crossed during the ferry crossing from Kilboghamn to Jektvik. The road then becomes a long tunnel, travelling underneath the giant **Svartisen** (▶Saltfjell Mountains and ▶Mo i Rana) glacier before reaching **Glomfjord**, where the Norsk Hydro company produces fertilizer for all of Norway. After passing **Ørnes**, the final highlight of the journey to Bodø is reached: the world's mightiest tidal waters, known as the **Saltstraumen** roar below the bridge of the same name (▶Bodø, surroundings). By the way, this is a good spot for **salmon** fishing. Bodø is reached after traversing the wide bay.

From the Arctic Circle to Saltstraumen

Art in the High North

Spread along the entire coast of the county of Nordland, 34 works by artists from 17 countries stand in the open air. The »Nordland Sculpture Landscape« project was begun in 1992. It is incredibly impressive to find these sometimes idiosyncratic, sometimes moving contemporary works of art in an exhibition area of 40,000 sq km/15,500 sq mi complete with the drone of the sea and wind and the unique qualities of the changing light.

The project was initiated with the three-part granite sculpture En Ny Samtale – a new conversation – by Kain Tapper of Finland, which was set up on the island of Vega. The title was very significant, because the project to erect modern artworks in remote places was intended to inspire new impulses for art

»Head« by Markus Raetz

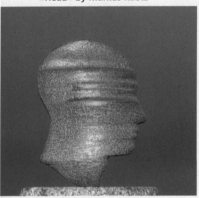

in northern Norway for many years to come. Most exhibits were placed near water, following in the tradition of rock art that Bronze Age people, with a great deal of effort, once scraped onto rocks near the coast. For all the artists the choice of location was a decisive factor in creating a clear symbiosis between

their work and the magnificent landscape of the north.

The Right Perspectives

It is somewhat onerous finding the individual contributions to the sculpture landscape, because they often stand on small islands or in remote sections of the coast. But the effort is worth it. What is on offer is extremely versatile: pierced stones, gold varnished steel flames and entwined ornaments of rusting steel that glow in the light of the midnight sun. There is also a more than 10m/33ft-high granite figure that stands in the water looking out to sea. With every tide it sinks a little lower into the water, only to re-emerge a few hours later. Many artworks offer very different perspectives depending from where they are viewed. Changing weather and seasons also offer continuous variations. A fascinating example is the head by Markus Raetz (see photo left) that changes its shape 16 times during a stroll around it: from the front it is a classic portrait, from behind it turns miraculously upside down..

Choosing Locations

An overview of the entire project can be found at www.skulptur-landskap.no. Here is a selection of locations where works of art are among the attractions:

Ballangen community, Skarstad: *Heaven on Earth* by Inge Mahn, Germany. Turn onto route 741 from the E 6 at Efjord and drive to Skarstad.

Bø: *The Man from the Sea* by Kjell Erik Olsen, Norway. On a spit of land before the settlement of Bø on the island of Langøy.

Evenskjær: *Seven Magic Points* by Martti Aiha, Finland. North of Evenskjaer (E10) turn off onto route 825; after about 2km/1mi, it stands on a peninsula near the road.

Flakstadøy: *Epitaph* by Toshikatsu Endo, Japan. About 2km/1mi from Ramberg on the road to Skjelford.

Hadsel: *Day and Night* by Sarkis, Turkey/France. On the bridge from Stokmarknes to Børøy.

Mosjøen: *Three Flames* by Hulda Hákon, Iceland. Near route 244 off the E 6.

Røst: *The Nest* by Luciano Fabro, Italy. On the bird island of Vedøy.

Sortland: The Eye of the Sea by Sigurdur Gudmundsson, Iceland. In Sortland near the E 10 on Langøya.

Vestvågøy: *The Head* by Markus Raetz, Switzerland. About 2km/1mi outside Eggum.

Vågån: *Untitled* by Dan Graham, USA. By the old quay of Lyngvaer on the E 10.

»Heaven on Earth« by Inge Mahn at Ballangen

✶✶ Oslo

✈ B 7

Region: East Norway
Population: 623,300

Few of the world's capitals are as blessed with beautiful natural surroundings as Oslo: lakes, forests, sand and sea, all on the doorstep. The king lives here, parliament has its seat here, and world-famous museums display their treasures here. Charming taverns, elegant restaurants and the city centre shopping district round off a visit to the Norwegian capital.

City between forest and sea

Oslo, which in 2006 brought an end to Tokyo's 14-year run as the world's most expensive city, is considered Europe's greenest capital, since only a quarter of its 450 sq km/174 sq mi of urban area is built up. More than a third of all Norwegians live around the ▶Oslofjord, which extends around 100km/62mi into the mainland, and at whose northern end the capital stands. The city centre is concentrated around the Pipervika harbour, an area with shops and restaurants in Aker Brygge, the city's cultural heart, as well as the Akershus fortress; along Oslo's most famous street, Karl Johansgate, at whose western end the Royal Palace stands; and, further east, around the Hotel Oslo Plaza, whose 37 floors make it northern Europe's highest building. The Akerselv river flows into the Oslofjord very close to the central railway station and has divided the city into two halves for centuries: Østkanten, to the east, is predominantly inhabited by students, older people and foreigners, while Vestkanten, to the west, is home to richly decorated historic villas. Oslo's population has grown by around 150,000 in the past decade, a trend that is set to continue. Tourism flows have increased at a similar rate, despite the fact that Oslo is one of the most expensive cities in the world, and the reason for this popularity among natives and visitors is undoubtedly the capital's unique location. Set among forests and the sea, a more beautiful setting for a city would hardly be possible. The centre embraces the horse shoe contours of a fjord, while the suburbs melt into the forested hillsides.

Oslo has been investing massively in the Fjordbyen (the city by the fjord) urban regeneration project for some years now. It is the largest urban construction plan being carried out since the early 17th century, when King Christian IV had old Kristiana built behind the Akershus fortress. Since then, the area has been declining ever more into a depressing neighbourhood of port installations, railway tracks and a tangle of motorways, but this is all set to fundamentally change. The seaboard side of the city is once again going to be available for all to enjoy. The revitalization, particularly along the fjord

City development

A striking emblem: the dual towers of Oslo town hall date from the early 20th century

Oslo

INFORMATION
Turistinformasjon
Fridtjof Nansens plass 5
(entrance Roald Amundsen gate)
tel. 81 53 05 55, www.visitoslo.com
The multimedia information centre between the town hall square and Aker Brygge offers free internet access and screens for information on Oslo's cultural programme (www.kulturetaten.oslo.kommune.no). Another office is located at the central railway station and is mostly dedicated to hotel reservation.

OSLO PASS
Money can be saved in expensive Oslo with the Oslo Pass. It is valid for one, two or three days (270–495 NOK, children 120–190 NOK) and entitles the owner to use of public transport and parking spaces, as well as entry to museums. There are also discounts for sightseeing tours by ship and bus.
The pass can be purchased, among other places, at the tourist information office, the train station and the airport, as well as at hotels.

CITY-BIKE
1200 bicycles at 100 stations can be used for three hours at a time. If you need longer, you can exchange yours for another bike immediately.
Visitors can purchase a 24-hour ticket by credit card at the tourist information offices by the town hall and at the central railway station (90 NOK). For extended stays in Oslo it is worth buying a season ticket for 90 NOK at www.oslobysykkel.no.

CITY TOURS
Buses depart from the city hall quay and from Trafikanten at the main railway station (3hrs including museum visit).

HARBOUR TOURS
Departures from the city hall quay every hour from mid-May to mid-Aug 11am–6pm, mid-June–end of July till 8pm; duration around 50mins. Other tours go to the islands in the Oslofjord and include a lunch buffet (2hrs); still others offer a romantic fjord tour at night. Information from Oslo Touristinformasjon.

SHOPPING
Popular shopping streets: Aker Brygge, Karl Johansgate<–sr–>Large department stores: Steen & Strøm (Nedre Slottsgate), Glas Magasinet (Stortorvet). Oslo City with around 100 shops (near the central railway station). Another shopping district is located west of the centre, between the palace gardens and the Frognerpark. Paleét shopping arcade (Karl Johansgate 37–43): over 40 different shops, including Norway's largest bookshop, Tanum, which also stocks foreign language titles. Good value restaurants also found here.

ENTERTAINMENT
The area for going out in Oslo is around the former shipyard at Aker Brygge (Bar 1 at Holmensgate 3 has an unbelievable selection of cognac), as well as the trendy Grünerlokka and Grønland districts and the West End around Bogstadveien.
The **world's largest ice bar,** created in 2010, is redesigned by a different ice artist each year. The warm restaurant area serves Norwegian dishes. In the bar that keeps a constant –5°C/23°F drinks

are served in glasses made of ice (Kristian IVs gate 12; www.icebaroslo.no).

EVENTS
August: Norway Cup, the world's largest youth football championship (www.norwaycup.no); Jazzfestival (www.oslojazz.no).
September: Opera festival (www.operafestival.no); Oslo Marathon (www.oslomaraton.no); ULTIMA, festival for contemporary music (www.ultima.no).
November: Oslo World Music Festival (www.osloworld.no)..

SPORT AND LEISURE
Skiing
There is more or less guaranteed snow around Oslo between January and March. Thanks to the Holmenkoll rail route, the skiing region of Nordmarka is the easiest to reach. There are around 2200km/1375mi of prepared cross country skiing routes around Oslo, of which around 200km/125mi are illuminated at night. For downhill skiing serviced by lifts see: Tryvannskleiva, Rødkleiva, Wyllerløypa, Kirkerudbakken, Ingierkollen, Grefsenkleiva, Fjellstadbakken, Trollvannskleiva, Vardåsen, Varingskollen

Swimming and surfing
The most beautiful beaches are found at Huk (on the Bygdøy peninsula, complete with nudist beach), Hvervenbukta, Katta, and Ingierstrand in the south of the city. The beaches of the islands of Langøyene and Hovedøya can be reached by boat from the Vippetangen quay.
Surfers prefer the waters off Rolfstangen beach. Good swimming possibilities are also offered by the 300 lakes of Oslomarka. Especially popular are Sognsvann, Svartkulp (both can be reached on the Sognsvann railway) and Bogstadvann (near Bogstad campsite).

WHERE TO EAT
❷ *De Fem Stuer* £ £ £ £
Kongeveien 26, tel. 22 92 27 34
www.holmenkollenparkhotel.no
Modern Norwegian cuisine at its best in one of the city's most beautiful wooden houses by the Holmenkollen. Just a few steps away from a unique vista over Oslo and its fjord.

❺ *Statholdergaarden* £ £ £
Rådhusgaten 11, tel. 22 41 88 00
www.statholdergaarden.no
Bent Stiansen and Torbjørn Forste design a new 6-course menu based on Norwegian roots and French flair every day. 8000 bottles of wine in the cellar guarantee the right wine can always be found.

❻ *Det Gamle Raadhus* £ £ £
Nedre Slottgt. 1
tel. 22 42 01 07
www.gamleraadhus.no
Oslo's oldest restaurant is housed in the city's first town hall that was built in 1641. Fish and game dishes are of the highest quality. The garden seating area in the back courtyard offers a haven of peace. Closed Sundays.

❸ *Solsiden* £ £ £
Søndre Åkershus Kai
tel. 22 33 36 30, www.solsiden.no
Possibly the city's best fish dishes are served on the sunny side of Oslo harbour, right underneath the Akershus fortress and with views onto Aker Brygge. The house speciality is the seafood platter. Open in summer only.

**❶ *Bølgen & Moi Briskeby*
££ – £££**
Løvenskioldsgate 26
tel. 24 11 53 53
www.bolgenogmoi.no
Bar, brasserie and restaurant under one
roof. Norway's famous Chef Trond Moi
invites guests for breakfast and lunch at
the bar, complete with bread from the
wood-fired oven at lunchtimes.

❼ *Engebret Café* ££ – £££
Bankplassen 1
tel. 22 82 25 25
www.engebret-cafe.no

Insider Tip

The morning Smørebrød buffet – a typical Norwegian speciality – is recommended. Closed Sundays.

❹ *Theatercaféen* ££
Stortingsgaten 24 – 26
tel. 22 82 40 50
www.hotelcontinental.no
People come to this art nouveau coffee
house dating from 1901 opposite the

Theatercaféen opened already in 1901

National Theatre to see and be seen.
Good Norwegian cuisine at decent prices.

❽ *Fyret* ££
Youngstorget 6
tel. 22 20 51 82
www.fyretmatogdrikke.no
Cosy café and restaurant offering a variety of small dishes and an extraordinary
choice of Norwegian aquavit. Live jazz is
played every Monday from 8pm

***Grand Café* ££**
inside Grand Hotel
tel. 24 12 53 00, www.grand.no
Eat like the Bohemians at the turn of the
19th century in the historic Grand Café.
A large fresco by Per Krohg conveys the
atmosphere of the epoch when Ibsen
and Bjørnson were regulars here. The
menu also offers smaller dishes suitable
for lunchtime snacks. Every first Friday of
the month (4pm–6pm): as many waffles
as you can eat for just 65 NOK.

**WHERE TO STAY
❽ *Grand Hotel* ££££**
Karl Johans gate 31, 289 rooms.
tel. 23 21 20 00, www.grand.no
The city's top hotel opened its doors in
1874 and has continuously adapted to
modern requirements every since. Swimming pool with sauna and solarium; fitness and wellness programme; tasteful
interior in the »Palmen« lunch restaurant.

❻ *Hotel Continental* ££££
Stortingsgaten 24 – 26
tel. 22 82 40 00
www.hotel-continental.no
Don't be fooled by the hotel's unprepossessing façade. The hotel restaurant
»Annen Étage« has earned a star. Com-

pared to other Oslo hotels, the Continental offers very good value for money.

❷ Grims Grenka £ £ £ – £ £ £ £
Kongensgate 5, tel. 23 10 72 00
www.firsthotels.com
In January 2008, Norway's first five-star design hotel opened – with 42 elegant rooms, 24 luxury suites and a spectacular rooftop lounge.

⓫ Anker Hotel Best Western £ £ £
Storgt. 55, tel. 22 99 75 00
www.anker.oslo.no, 161 rooms.
Modern hotel in a quiet location between the city centre and the student district.

❹ Rica Hotel Bygdøy Allé £ £ – £ £ £
Bygdøy Allé 53, tel. 23 08 58 00
www.rica.no, 57 rooms.
Housed in a renovated redbrick building, this is a cosy hotel between the centre and the museum island of Bygdøy. The Magma restaurant with its beautiful interior is highly recommended.

❶ Clarion Collection Hotel Gabelshus £ £ – £ £ £
Gabelshus A A – A A A
Gabelsgate 16, tel. 23 27 65 00
www.clarionhotel.com/hotel-oslo-norway-NO094, 114 rooms.
In a quiet location, just ten minutes from the Color Line quay. Amalgamated with the former Ritz and reopened in 2004, the hotel is an interesting architectural ensemble.

❼ Clarion Collection Hotel Savoy £ £ – £ £ £
Universitetsgaten 11, tel. 23 35 42 00

www.clarionhotel.com/hotel-oslo-norway-NO060, 80 rooms.
This popular and well-run city hotel offers good value summer prices. It is located next to the National Gallery and just a few steps from Karl Johansgate. Good special offers during summer.

❾ Clarion Collection Hotel Bastion £ £ – £ £ £
Skippergt. 7, tel. 22 47 77 00
www.hotelbastion.no, 99 rooms.
Centrally located with very pleasant atmosphere and tasteful antique furniture in all the rooms. If you prefer bright rooms, avoid those looking onto the courtyard.

❺ Cochs Pensjonat £ £
Parkveien 25, tel. 23 33 24 00
www.cochspensjonat.no
One of the few guesthouses established in the capital. Central location behind the palace. Rooms contain kitchenettes.

❿ Oslo Vandrerhjem Haraldsheim £
Haraldsheimvn. 4, tel. 22 22 29 65
www.haraldsheim.no
The youth hostel is not exactly comfortable, but in the expensive city of Oslo it is the best cheap accommodation available and therefore not only used by young people.

❸ Bogstad Camp & Turistsenter £
Ankerveien 117
tel. 22 51 08 00
www.bogstadcamping.no
This large campsite is about 10km/6mi from the city centre (35mins on bus 32); cabins are available, including during winter. The popular swimming lake Bogstadvann is nearby.

Highlights Oslo

waterfront and the rivers Akerselva and Alnelva, will create an attractive urban space that will completely change the city's structural, functional and aesthetic nature.

A good 20 years ago, one of the country's largest port areas was beyond the Pipervika basin, but when the shipyard had to close, an entire new urban district was created and Aker Brygge became a striking mix of old brick buildings and modern architecture of steel and glass. Oslo's inhabitants, especially the young at heart, have taken to this new urban space with enthusiasm. As soon as the sun shows its face, they stroll along the fjord promenade, enjoy the warming rays of sunshine on one of the benches, breathe in the ocean air, listen to jazz on the pontoons, or enjoy a beer in the open air. Meanwhile, they are building at Aker Brygge once more – even out onto the water with artificial islands - to expand the range of apartments and offices. The future looks interesting: 2013 was the year the new Munch/Stenersen Museum near the opera was due to open, in time for the 150th birthday anniversary of Norway's most famous painter. The 57m/187ft-high glass building, known as »Lambda«, was designed by the Spanish architectural office of Herreros. Furthermore, where once the relatively ugly waterside road once was, the new Dronning Eufemias gate will be a low traffic density boulevard, over 40m/131ft wide and lined by greenery. Also, the new Deichmann Library, between the new boulevard and the opera has a completion date planned for 2016. Information on urban developments: www.operakvarteret.no

Oslo is the seat of government, as well as the king's main residence, and also the administrative centre for the municipalities of Oslo and Akershus. With its universities and several technical colleges, Oslo is the capital of Norwegian learning and also enjoys the country's best cultural facilities. Norway's only opera house (in the spectacular new building since 2008) is here, and every year on 10th December, the Nobel Peace Prize is awarded in Oslo's town hall.

Cultural capital and centre of learning

Scandinavia's oldest capital was probably founded by King Harald Hårdråde in 1050, though archaeological evidence proves that a shipping post and settlement must have existed here by AD 900 at the latest. Harald's son Olav Kyrre (1050–93) elevated the place to a bishopric and Håkon V (1277–1319) had a cathedral built, and for a long period after that Oslo remained the **the country's religious centre**, though the kings continued to reside in Bergen. Håkon V was the first to move his residence from Bergen to Oslo **around 1300**, when he also began building the **Akershus fortress**. At the same time the Hanseatic League established a base in Oslo. In 1397 Norway's period under the Danish crown began, and Oslo became less significant.

History

After a fire in 1624, Christian IV, the Danish-Norwegian king at the time, had the city rebuilt around the Akershus fortress. The square network of streets that he designed for the area between Rådhusgata and Karl Johansgate is still recognizable today. He even changed the city's name – to his own – so that between 1624 and 1924 the capital of Norway was called **Christiania** (spelt Kristiania from 1877 onwards). Plagues and the high taxes that were imposed on the city's inhabitants during lengthy wars inhibited 18th-century Christiania's development into a merchant city based on the European model, and the capital only revived economically towards the end of the 18th century as the wood trade flourished.

After 1814, Norway was eventually ceded from Denmark, and Christiania finally became the **new capital and royal residence**. During the reign of Karl XIV Johan the city flourished once more and developed into Norway's most significant centre of transport and trade. The first railway lines were built, new roads were built, and textile and machine workshops were established. At the same time, the mid-19th century saw extensive rural flight. Many tried their luck in Christiania. Residential blocks up to five storeys high and with narrow back courtyards shot up all around Christiania's centre and gradually split the town into two districts. The typical workers and tradesmen's quarters developed in the east, while the middle class lived in spacious, elegant villas in the western districts. The city recovered its old name of Oslo on 1 January 1925 – a name that according to linguists could mean »plain of the gods« or »plain at the foot of a hill«.

Oslo

Holmenkollen

Blindern (University)

MAJORSTUEN

Stens Park

Fagerborg Church

Bislett Stadium

Vigeland Exhibition Area

Frogner Park

Town Museum

Vigeland-Museum

FROGNER

Amaldus Nielsens plass

Uranienborg Church

THOMANS-BYEN

Riddevolds plass

Slottparken

Slottparken Royal Palace

History Museum

Nobel Institute

Carl Johan

Old University

Henie Onstad Art Centre / Trade Fair Centre

SKILLEBEKK

University library

Solli plass

Ibsen Museum

National Theatre

Concert Hall

Nobel Peace Centre

Town Hall

Observatory

Olaf Bulls plass

Aker Brygge

Pipervika

Ferry landing stage (Color Line)

Akershus Festning (fortress)

BYGDØY Seafaring Museum

Oslofjord

Frognerkilen

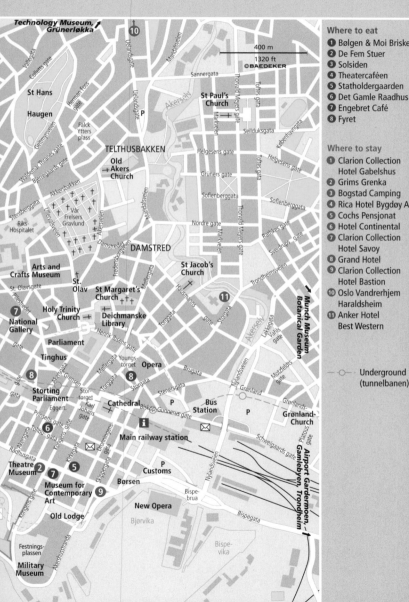

Technology Museum, Grünerløkka

400 m
1320 ft
©BAEDEKER

St Hans

Haugen

Falck
Ytters
plass

St Paul's
Church

TELTHUSBAKKEN

Old
Akers
Church

DAMSTRED

Riks-
Hospitalet

Vår
Frelsers
Gravlund

Arts and
Crafts Museum

St.
Olav

St Margaret's
Church

St Jacob's
Church

❶❶

Holy Trinity
Church

Deichmanske
Library

❼
National
Gallery

Parliament

Tinghus

Opera

❽

❽

Storting
Parliament

Cathedral

Bus
Station

Grønland-
Church

Main railway station

Munch Museum
Botanical Garden

❻

Theatre
Museum ❷ ❼ ❺

Museum for
Contemporary
Art ❾

Customs

Børsen

Old Lodge

New Opera

Bjørvika

Festnings-
plassen

Military
Museum

Bispe-
brua

Bispe-
vika

Airport Gardermoen,
Gamlebyen, Trondheim

Where to eat

❶ Bølgen & Moi Briskeby
❷ De Fem Stuer
❸ Solsiden
❹ Theatercaféen
❺ Statholdergaarden
❻ Det Gamle Raadhus
❼ Engebret Café
❽ Fyret

Where to stay

❶ Clarion Collection
   Hotel Gabelshus
❷ Grims Grenka
❸ Bogstad Camping
❹ Rica Hotel Bygdøy Allé
❺ Cochs Pensjonat
❻ Hotel Continental
❼ Clarion Collection
   Hotel Savoy
❽ Grand Hotel
❾ Clarion Collection
   Hotel Bastion
❿ Oslo Vandrerhjem
   Haraldsheim
⓫ Anker Hotel
   Best Western

—○— Underground
      (tunnelbanen)

KARL JOHANS GATE
AND THE ADJACENT DISTRICT

Railway
station to
Stortorget

A good starting point for a stroll into the city is the **central railway station** (Sentralbanestasjonen), with its two car parks and a tourist information centre. The Oslo City shopping mall is behind the railway station. The city's main shopping street, popular for a stroll, is **Karl Johansgate**, which leads from the railway station to the Royal Palace. This magnificent road is a pedestrian zone as far as the parliament building. The large market square that has existed since the end of the 17th century is known as **Stortorget** and is overseen by a statue of King Christian IV created by C.L. Jacobsen.

*Cathedral

The cathedral (Domkirke), inaugurated in 1697 (and restored 2006–2010), stands on the southeast side of the Stortoget. There are beautiful reliefs (1938) on the bronze doors at the main entrance. The pulpit, altar (both from around 1700) and organ (1725) have survived from the cathedral's early **interior furnishings**.

The windows by Emanuel Vigeland (1910–16) date from more recent times, as does the ceiling fresco by Hugo Lous Mohr (1936–50). The octagonal Chapel of the Redeemer, added in 1950, contains a silver sculpture by Arrigo Minerbi entitled The Last Supper. The cathedral was also the venue for the marriage between Crown Prince Haakon and Crown Princess Mette-Marit in August 2001.

● Sun–Thu 10am–4pm, Fri 4pm–midnight, Sat 10am–4pm and midnight–6am; www.oslodomkirke.no

Bazaar Halls

The Bazaar Halls, built in 1841–42, stand behind the cathedral and now serve as a centre for arts and crafts shops, antique dealers, vegetable stalls, souvenir shops and cafés. The liveliest section of Karl Johansgate begins south of Stortorget. To the west lies **Egertorget**, a major junction for Oslo's rapid transit system, the T-bane.

*Storting

The Storting, the **Norwegian parliament building**, stands to the left of the junction between Karl Johansgate and Akersgata. It was designed in a neo-Gothic style in 1861–66. In the conference hall hangs O. Wergeland's large painting portraying the assembly that established the constitution at Eidsvoll in 1814.

Eidsvollplass Park stretches out in front of the building and contains a statue of the poet Henrik Wergeland designed by Bergslien. Beyond the Storting, the park goes by the name of Studenterlunden and its beer garden, shopping stalls, music pavilion and street musicians make it a popular meeting place during summer.

● During summer (week 26–33) free one-hour tours through the Storting, in English Mon–Fri 10am–1pm; www.storting.no

The Oslo Nye Theatre at Rosenkrantzgate 10, which crosses Karl Johansgate here, is a venue for new work and revues. It opened in 1929 with Knut Hamsun's At the Gate of the Kingdom. Numerous bars can be found in this neighbourhood.

Nye Teater

The classical building of the National Theatre, constructed in 1899, is situated to the northwest of Eidsvollplass. The main entrance is flanked by two bronze sculptures of Ibsen and Bjørnson. The partly art nouveau interior with a beautiful ceiling fresco in the large hall can be visited on request.

National Theatre

ℹ www.nationaltheatret.no, tel. 81 50 08 11

The buildings of the university, founded by Frederick VI of Denmark in 1811, were erected in 1854. They stand to the northeast of the theatre. Today the Faculty of Law is housed in this »old« university, while the new university is in the district of Blindern. In the lecture hall dating from 1911, the pictures by **Edvard Munch** (1926) are noteworthy.

Old university

Oslo's largest theatre, famous for its musicals and performances of Norwegian and foreign new drama, lies east of the university, on Kristian IV's gate.

Norske Teatret

Norway's largest collection of art is housed in the National Gallery on Universitetsgata and run by Nils Ohlsen, the former director of the Emden Kunsthalle. The fine museum building is from 1881 and presents an extensive cross-section of Norwegian painters from the 19th

*National Gallery

It stays light till late during summer on Karl Johans gate

century to the present day. Works by the following artists, among others, can be viewed: J. C. Dahl (1788–1857), T. Fearnley (1802–42), H. F. Gude (1825–1903), H. O. Heyerdahl (1857–1913), C. Krohg (1852–1925), G. P. Munthe (1849–1929), E. Peterssen (1852–1928) and A. Tidemand (1814–76). One exhibition room is entirely dedicated to Edvard Munch. In addition, there are works by Danish and Swedish painters, as well as by El Greco, Rubens and Rembrandt, and a collection of French art including Cézanne, Degas, Gauguin, Manet, Matisse and Renoir. There is also a room with casts of antique figures.

❶ Tue, Wed, Fri 10am–6pm, Thu till 7pm, Sat–Sun 11am–5pm; 50 NOK; www.nationalmuseum.no

History Museum

The History Museum (Historisk Museum; entrance at Frederiksgate 2) is behind the National Gallery and contains the Antiquities Collection of the University of History and Ethnology. Worth mentioning among the Nordic antiquities is the **collection from the Viking era** (around 800–1050), including a treasury, and an exhibition of **stave church portals**. Furthermore, there are exhibitions on the Inuit and indigenous Siberians, and the peoples of Africa, America and East Asia, as well as a coin collection.

❶ Mid-May–mid-Sep, Tue–Sun 10am–5pm, otherwise 11am–4pm; 50 NOK; www.khm.uio.no

*Royal Palace

The long stretched out Empire style building of the Royal Palace, built in 1825–48, is located on a hill in the middle of a large park at the northwest end of Karl Johansgate. The Swedish-Norwegian King Karl Johan, who commissioned this building but did not live to see it completed in 1848, dreamt of a palace where he could see the large parade ground and the entire city from the balcony. He therefore had the palace built outside the city gates at the time, a considerable distance away from the frequently poor housing of the local

The royal palace at Oslo was built in the early 19th century

population. A special attraction is the daily **changing of the guard** at 1.30pm.

❶ Mid-June–mid-Aug; guided tours in English Mon–Thu and Sat noon, 2pm, 5pm; Fri and Sun 2pm, 2.20pm, 4pm; 95 NOK; www.kongehuset.no; advance tickets available via the internet, by phone (tel. 81 53 31 33), or at all post offices; however, sales are from the beginning of April, so with luck, it is possible to purchase unsold tickets directly at the entrance.

Nobel Institute

Along the south side of the palace gardens runs Drammensveien and the Norwegian Nobel Institute stands at the junction with Parkveien. On 10 December every year, the festival hall within the city hall hosts the Nobel Peace Prize award ceremony, during which the individual or organization is named as the prizewinner. Candidates are suggested by parliamentarians from all over the world and chosen by the Norwegian Nobel Committee. Former prize winners include Martin Luther King Jr. (1964), Willy Brandt (1971), Mikhail Gorbatschev (1990), Nelson Mandela and Fredrik Willem de Klerk (1993), and Barack Obama (2009). In 2014 the prize was awarded to Kailash Satyarthi from India and to 17-years-old Pakistani girl Malala Yousafzai for their struggle for the rights of children and their right of education (all prize-winners can be found under www.nobel.no). A wealth of information regarding the Nobel Peace Prize can be found in the Nobel Peace Centre in the former Oslo West railway station (▶p.336).

Ibsen Museum

Henrik Ibsen's apartment, where he lived from 1895 until his death in 1906, can be found complete with its original interior south of the palace gardens at Arbins gate 1.

❶ Guided tours mid-May–mid-Sep on the hour 11am–5pm; other months 11am–3pm, Thu till 5pm; 85 NOK; www.norskfolkemuseum.no/no/Tilknyttede-Enheter/Ibsenmuseet

City hall

Heading south from the National Theatre, the monumental city hall comes into view, built in 1931–50 according to designs by Arnstein Arneberg and Magnus Poulson. This mighty concrete building with its two chunky towers clad in brick has become the city's emblem, despite always being controversial. There is a carillon in the east tower. The rich fresco ornamentation of the interior, the work of 28 artists including Henrik Sørensen, Per Krohg and Edvard Munch, is worth taking a look at.

❶ Mon–Fri 9am–6pm, guided tours 10am, noon, 2pm

> **MARCO ⬤ POLO TIP**
>
> ! *Delicatessen* Insider Tip
>
> The small Fenaknoken delicatessen shop behind the town hall at Tordenskioldsgaten 7 sells all the Norwegian specialities, including hams, sausages, cheese, smoked fish and salt dried cod. Delicious bread to accompany a delicious Norwegian meal is also available (Mon–Fri 10am–5pm, Sat 11am–4pm; www.fenaknoken.no).

Nobel Peace Centre

The Nobel Peace Centre was established in the old Oslo West railway station in July 2005. It contains information about Alfred Nobel and all the winners of the Nobel Peace Prize. Furthermore, there are lectures, seminars and exhibitions on peace campaigns around the world, as well as on current conflict zones.

❶ daily 10am–6pm; 80 NOK; www.nobelpeacecenter.org

**Aker Brygge

It is worth visiting **Aker Brygge** on the western shore of the Pipervika harbour, to the southwest of the city hall quay. The renovated halls of the former Aker shipyard have been transformed into a **modern shopping and cultural centre** with about 35 restaurants, as well as cafés, boutiques and galleries. It is the capital's liveliest and most popular shopping and leisure district, despite being **extremely expensive** by European standards. An additional spectacular building for Oslo's city centre (by Renzo Piano) was completed in 2012, when the Astrup Fearnley Museum of Contemporary art opened on Tjuvholmen.

Aker Brygge: www.akerbrygge.no
Astrup Fearnely Museum: Tue, Wed, Fri noon–5pm, Thu noon–7pm, Sat–Sun 11am–5pm; 100 NOK; www.afmuseet.no

Aker Brygge, Oslo's latest addition to shopping and leisure

SOUTHERN CITY CENTRE

Oslo's old town extends to the south of the Storting and Karl Johansgate. The **stock exchange**, built in 1827 and extended in 1910, is located southwest of the central railway station. In response to a major fire in 1624, King Christian IV commissioned the construction of stone houses on a network of right-angled streets to the west of the stock exchange, known as Kvadraturen. Kongensgate was once the main entrance to the city. The oldest surviving building of the original Kvadraturen stands at Rådhusgaten 19 (1626), and today houses the **Oslo Art Association**. Kongensgate 1 now houses the **state theatre**. The building at Rådhusgate 7, whose oldest sections date from 1625–30, was used as the town hall from 1733 onwards, then as a prison, and also as a police station. Today it is the seat of the Norwegian Author's Association.

Stock Exchange

Further west, on Bankplassen, stands a large granite building (1902) in the Norwegian art nouveau style that was once the main seat of the Norwegian state bank. Since 1990, it has housed **Norway's largest museum for contemporary art**, with works by all of Norway's most important artists from 1945 onwards.

*National Museum of Contemporary Art

❶ Tue–Fri 11am–5pm, Thu till 7pm, Sat–Sun noon–5pm; 50 NOK; www.nasjonalmuseet.no

The history of 20th century Norwegian architecture is illustrated with drawings, photos and models in a building dating from 1830, and now home to the National Museum of Architecture. The remodelled building and new pavilion were designed by Sverre Fehn, who also designed the Nordic Pavillion in Venice and the Glacier Museum in Fjærland.

National Museum of Architecture

❶ Tue–Fri 11am–5pm, Thu till 7pm, Sat–Sun noon–5pm; 50 NOK; www.nasjonalmuseet.no

The Old Lodge dating from 1839 and containing a beautiful concert hall in Empire style is located at Grev Wedelsplaas 2. It is used for concerts and other events.

Old Lodge

Akershus Fortress stands on a spit of land (Akersnes) above the Oslofjord at the western edge of this quarter. Originally commissioned by Håkon V at the end of the 13th century, the medieval castle was turned into a Renaissance palace during the reign of Christian IV. The main area of the fortress is reached via the entrance at Festningsplassen. Christian IV's Hall and the palace church (which contains King Håkon VII's (1872–1957) tomb in the crypt) are open to the public. The other palace rooms are used as setting for various functions by the Norwegian government. A building in the upper

*Akershus Fortress

Akershus fortress

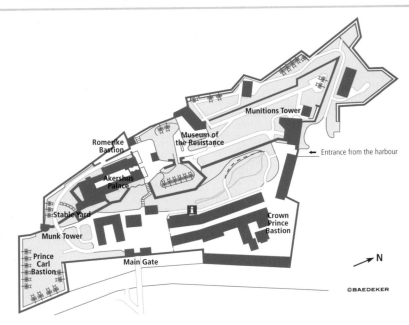

part of the fortress contains the **Museum of the Norwegian Resistance** (Norges Hjemmerfrontmuseum), documenting the resistance
against the German occupation during the Second World War.
The Armed Forces Museum (Forsvarsmuseet) is housed in the old
arsenal. Its weapons and other exhibits illustrate Norwegian military
history from Viking times to the present day. The changing of the
fortress guard takes place daily at 1.30pm. Cruise ships dock below
the Akershus and the Oslo Cruise Terminal has a large but expensive
selection of typically Norwegian **souvenirs**.

Museum of Norwegian Resistance: June–Aug Mon–Sat 10am–5pm, Sun
11am–5pm, other months Mon–Fri 10am–4pm, Sat–Sun 11am–4pm; 50 NOK
Armed Forces Museum: May–Aug Mon–Fri 10am–5pm, Sat–Sun
11am–5pm, other months Tue–Fri 10am–4pm, Sat–Sun 11am–5pm; 50 NOK

****Oslo
Opera House**

Oslo's new opera house, whose artistic director is Bjørn Simensen,
was opened in Bjørvika on 12 April 2008 (picture p. 10). The monumental building was the creation of the Snøhetta company of archi-

tects, who made generous use of marble, granite and glass. It bears a price tag of 500 million euros.

Visitors are able to take a stroll along the impressive roof, which rises directly from the fjord and functions as a vantage point from which to enjoy the spectacular views. The main concert hall, with capacity for an audience of 1370, is decorated with a chandelier made of 17,000 pieces of glass that also function as acoustic reflectors. A smaller hall accommodates 400. The foyer is the work of Olafùr Eliasson from Denmark, while the American Pae White created the large »MetaFoil« stage curtain. All in all, the Oslo Opera House is an architectural masterpiece and has become an emblem of the capital. Not only the opera house plays an important role in the city's vibrant cultural life either. The surrounding district of Bjørvika, which is gradually becoming an attractive neighbourhood of apartments, offices, shops and restaurants, is also becoming very popular. As part of this redevelopment, a new tunnel has been completed, which has released the waterside port area from over 100,000 cars per day.

❶ www.operaen.no; tickets: tel. 21 42 21 21

NORTHERN CITY CENTRE

The Catholic St Olav's Church (1853) is located at the northern end of Akersgata opposite the Museum of Decorative Arts and Design (Kunstindustrimuseet), which offers insight into the development of Nordic arts and crafts. The most important exhibition centres on tapestries, including the Baldishol Tapestry (approx. 1180) taken from the Baldishol Church in the province of Hedmark. The exhibits also include metal and glass works, furniture and royal costumes.

Museum of Decorative Arts and Design

❶ Tue, Wed, Fri 11am–5pm, Thu 11am–7pm, Sat–Sun noon–4pm; 50 NOK; www.nasjonalmuseet.no

Behind St Olav's, Damstredet leads to the junction with Fredensborgveien. The small renovated wooden houses with their tiny gardens originating in the 18th and 19th centuries were once inhabited by poor craftsmen and workers. From 1839 to 1841, the poet Herik Wergeland (1808–1845) lived at Damstredet 1. The two-storeyed panelled wooden house dating from the early 19th-century at Damstredet 5 is also known as the **»Rhubarb Palace«** because large quantities of rhubarb were once cultivated in its garden. The sculpture of Nils Holgerson's Goose designed by Edvin Öhrström (1971) stands at the square a little further on.

Damstredet

The Cemetery of Our Saviour (Vår Frelsers Gravlund) extends between Ullevålsveien and Akersveien to the north. The poets **Bjørn-**

Cemetery of Our Saviour

stjerne Bjørnson and Henrik Ibsen (all famous people), as well as the painters Edvard Munch and **H.F. Gude**, are buried in the »honorary glade« of Æreslunden in the middle of the cemetery.

Old Aker Church Oslo's oldest building stands at the northern end of Akersveien. The Old Aker Church (Norwegian: Gamle Akerskirke) was probably built by Olav Kyrre as a basilica in the Anglo-Norman style in 1150. The church gained its present, somewhat plain interior after the entire inventory was destroyed in a fire in 1703, though that was also when the present baptismal font and the beautiful **pulpit** were created. The building's acoustics are superb.

WHAT TO SEE IN THE EAST AND NORTH

Botanical Garden The Botanisk Have is located at the eastern edge of Oslo, with the entrance on Trondheimsveien. The alpine garden is especially pretty.
❶ Mid-March–Sep Mon–Fri 7am–9pm, Sat–Sun 10am–9pm, otherwise Mon–Fri 7am–5pm, Sat–Sun 10am–5pm; hot houses Tue–Sun 11am–4pm; free; www.nhm.uio.no/english/visiting

Museum of Natural History The Natural History Museum is on the rise above the Botanical Gardens and contains exhibitions in a variety of buildings dedicated to zoology, botany and geology.
❶ Tue–Sun 11am–4pm, 50 NOK; www.nhm.uio.no/english/visiting

Grünerløka To the west of the Botanical Garden, the Akerselv river is quickly reached, where a pleasant walk heading north leads to the fashionable Grünerløka district. It has been the 'in' place to go for a few years now, and the nicest area, with late 19th century architecture and greened courtyards, is around the Olaf Ryes square and reaching north towards the church of Saint Paul. If time is short, the best area to explore is between the parallels formed by the streets of Markveien and Thorvald Meyers gate. Many have fallen in love with this neighbourhood; others rather more pragmatically appreciate the lower rents. Meeting for a beer of an evening, it is also pleasing to know the prices are somewhat lower than on Karl Johan or in Aker Brygge. Comparisons have been made with Greenwich Village in New York or Soho in London. In fact, the architect G. A.

> **!** *Still your »sult«* Insider Tip
>
> MARCO ⊕ POLO TIP
>
> The little restaurant of »Sult« (meaning hunger) offers good meals at sensible prices and is located in the cosmopolitan Grünerløkka quarter, »Oslo's Soho« in the eastern part of the city, where numerous shops and bars can be found (Thorvald Meyers gate 26, tel. 22 87 04 67).

Bull, who was responsible for the architectural designs of the facades in the 19th century, took Berlin as his example. But what also makes Grünerløka so popular, are the bars and restaurants that are often busy till after midnight. Edvard Munch was among those charmed and lived at Thorvald Meyers gate 48 from 1885 to 1889, and also painted several local scenes, such as the »Glimt fra Grünerhaven« from 1887.

The Munch Museum (Munchmuseet) can be found on the southern side of the Botanical Gardens at Tøyengata 53. Its exhibits are the legacy of Edvard Munch (1863–1944; ►Famous People) – Norway's most significant artist – and include paintings, prints, drawings and watercolours, as well as sculptures, from just about all of the artist's major artistic phases. Munch's work is characterized by love and death fantasies, Nordic melancholy and a mystical relationship with nature. The artist imbued his pictures with profound emotional content by using dark, depressing colours and simple shapes. *The Scream* holds the distinction of being the best known picture in art history after the Mona Lisa by Leonardo da Vinci. Munch painted four versions of this picture, one of which can be seen in the National Gallery. The Munch Museum also owns other famous works by the artist, including *The Sick Child* (1886), *Girl on a Bridge* (1899), *The Dance of Life* (1900) and the *Frieze of Life* cycle of paintings.

**Munch Museum

❶ June–mid-Oct daily 10am–5pm, Thu till 7pm, otherwise Mon and Wed–Sat noon–6pm, Sun 11am–6pm, 95 NOK; www.munch.museum.no

The Norwegian Museum for Technology in Oslo's north, at Kjelsåsveien 143, is worth a visit and especially popular with children. The exhibits allow technology to be explored and understood in a playful way. In addition to the development of metal working (from smithies to modern factories) and gas and oil extraction, the history of telecommunications is illustrated from Viking fire signals to the internet.

Technology Museum

❶ Mid-June–mid-Aug daily 10am–6pm, otherwise Tue–Fri 9am–4pm, Sat–Sun 11am–6pm, 100 NOK; www.tekniskmuseum.no

WEST OSLO

Majorstua Walking through the palace gardens adjacent to the western end of Karl Johan quickly leads onto Hegdehaugsveien that soon becomes Bogstadveien. Once in the bourgeois neighbourhood of Majorstua, many handsome buildings line the streets in an area the Oslo locals refer to as »Vestkanten« - as opposed to »Ostkanten« beyond the Akerselva river. Both Hegdehausveienen and Bogstadveien are popular shopping streets, where one shop follows another. A lot of action also continues into the night in the numerous bars and restaurants.

Vigeland Park (Frogner Park) The main entrance of the Frogner Park is reached by turning left onto Kirkeveien, at the end of Bogstadveien. One of the most popular sport and leisure destinations for the city, the summer sees the park full of walkers, joggers and skaters; and in winter there are cross country skiers. The green spaces make for inviting picnic areas, and other sporting activities take place in the Frogner Stadium, the tennis courts and the Frogner swimming pool. The park was the kingdom's first to be designated a protected area and contains 150 different kinds of roses and 3000 trees, of which many are over 250 years old. A great attraction is the famous sculpture park with its 212 works by the Norwegian sculptor Gustav Vigeland (picture p. 61). The Vigeland Bridge alone is surrounded by no less than 58 sculptures, which underneath the bridge, the child sculptures are found. Among the most famous figures in the park is the Little Angry Boy (Sinnataggen) in the middle of the bridge. Adjacent is a bronze figure enclosed in a circle out of which it is desperately trying to escape, which illustrates the recurring theme of the entire installation: namely that there is no escape from **the cycle of life. The **fountain** is the oldest part of the installation and its figures also represent the cycle of life. Walking around the fountain, the first sculpture is of a small child sitting unselfconsciously in its tree of life; then comes the young pubescent person, followed by the meeting of the sexes. Marriage and birth follow and an exhausted mother can be seen in a tree of life. Finally comes old age. The grandfather bids farewell to his grandchild before death catches up with him. The transition from the world of the dead to the world of the as-yet unborn is seamless. The naked giants that stand in the middle of the fountain are condemned to carry the heavy water basin for eternity. Cut from a single piece of stone, the 17m/56ft-high **monolith** is made up of 121 intertwined human bodies. Work on the giant block took from 1928 to 1942 and occupied several people at

Vigeland Exhibition Area

the same time. The sculpture installation is completed by the **Wheel of Life**, which contains seven intertwined bodies and was only completed after Vigeland's death in 1934. The park is open round the clock throughout the year.

The old Frogner HovedGård manor house contains the **Oslo City Museum** (Oslo Bymuseum), which provides an overview of the capital's building and transport history, from the 13th century to the present.

Oslo Bymuseum: Tue–Sun 11am–5pm, free; www.oslomuseum.no

MARCO ⊕ POLO TIP

Children's art   Insider Tip

At the International Museum of Children's Art, the world can be seen through the eyes of children. The museum at Lille Frøens vei 4 shows art by children from 180 countries, including drawings, paintings, sculptures and textiles. Lots of activities are on offer to ensure little ones don't get bored (mid-June–mid-Aug Tue–Thu, Sun 11am–4pm, otherwise Tue–Thu 9.30am–2pm, Sun 11am–4pm; 60 NOK; www.barnekunst.no).

Southwest of the Oslo City Museum, beyond Halvdan Svartesgate, is the former studio of the Norwegian sculptor Gustav Vigeland (1869–1943), now a museum. Vigeland's urn is in the tower.

Vigeland Museum

❶ June–Aug Tue–Sun 10am–5pm, other months noon–4pm; 60 NOK; www.vigeland.museum.no

The Emanuel Vigeland Museum (which also serves a as mausoleum) is dedicated to **Gustav Vigeland's brother Emanuel Vigeland** (1875–1948). It is located at Grimelundsveien 8 in the **Vinderen district** and can be reached via the Holmenkoll railway (alight at Vinderen station, and then walk around 700m/766yd along Holmenveien before turning right into Grimelundsveien). The museum is one of Oslo's curiosities. Vigeland's Vita fresco of naked bodies that are born, love, grow old and die is housed in a church-like, windowless stone building where every sound echoes endlessly.

*Emanuel Vigeland Museum

❶ Mid-May–mid-Sep Sun noon–5pm, otherwise till 4pm; 40 NOK; www.emanuelvigeland.museum.no

BYGDØY PENINSULA

During summer there are boats approximately every half an hour to the Bygdøy Peninsula in west Oslo from the city hall quay. Alternatively, it is a 6km/4mi bus ride. Several genuine highlights of any Oslo visit are gathered together here: namely the Norwegian Museum of Cultural History (Norsk Folkesmuseum), the Fram Museum (Frammuseet), the Kon-Tiki Museum and the Viking Ship Museum. Furthermore, there are several beaches (▶p.325).

**Fram Museum

The Fram Museum is located on the southeastern side of Bygdøy, where the motor boats moor. It contains the polar ship »Fram«, with which **Fridtjof Nansen** completed his drift through the Arctic Ocean in 1893–96 (►Famous People). Using a three-masted schooner fixed with an auxiliary 220 horsepower motor, Nansen wanted to prove that the polar ice drifts from Siberia through the Arctic Ocean past the North Pole and on to Greenland. Nansen and Hjalmar Johansen left the schooner at 84° northern latitude and 102! eastern longitude with 28 huskies, two kayaks, three sledges and equipment weighing 700kg/1543lbs in an attempt to reach the North Pole on skis, but they failed.

❶ June–Aug 9am–6pm, otherwise 10am–4pm, Nov–Feb till 3pm, 80 NOK; www.frammuseum.no

*Norwegian Maritime Museum

The Norwegian Maritime Museum is adjacent to the Fram Museum and is a veritable goldmine for all those interested in shipping. There are models of all kinds of vessels, from small rowing boats to large oil tankers, as well as exhibitions on fishing, deep sea archaeology and meteorology, and multimedia shows. Gjøa, the polar ship used by the Norwegian polar explorer Roald Amundsen to travel the North West Passage between 1903 and 1906 stands on blocks in front of the museum.

❶ Mid-May–end of Aug daily 10am–6pm, otherwise Tue–Fri 10am–3pm, Sat–Sun 10am–4pm, 60 NOK, www.marmuseum.no

*Kon-Tiki Museum

A building opposite the Fram Museum contains the balsa raft Kon-Tiki, with which the Norwegian anthropologist **Thor Heyerdahl** (►Famous People) travelled from Callao in Peru to the East Polynesian islands in 1947. In addition, there are prehistoric boats, an underwater exhibition and a reproduction of a family cave from Easter Island. Visitors can also admire the 14m/46ft papyrus boat Ra II, with which Thor Heyerdahl and a group of men from eight nations crossed the Atlantic from Safi in Morocco to Barbados in the Caribbean, in 1970.

❶ Jan, Feb, Nov, Dec daily 10am–4pm, March, April, Sep, Oct 10am–5pm, June–Aug 9am–6pm, 70 NOK.

**Norwegian Museum of Cultural History

The Norwegian Museum of Cultural History (Norsk Folkemuseum) is spread over several buildings and also encompasses a large open-air museum of around 150 houses from all corners of the country on an area of 14ha/35ac. It is thus **the largest such collection in Norway**. The main building exhibits folk costumes, domestic goods, carpets and old furniture with rose paintings; there is also a **Sami Exhibition** complete with traditional costumes, tents, equipment used in reindeer husbandry, and hunting and fishing tools. Directly behind the main building a street from the former Christiania has

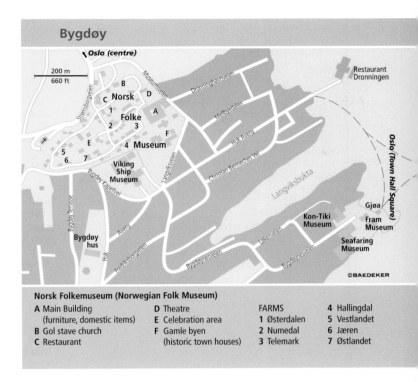

Norsk Folkemuseum (Norwegian Folk Museum)

A Main Building (furniture, domestic items)	D Theatre	FARMS	4 Hallingdal
B Gol stave church	E Celebration area	1 Østerdalen	5 Vestlandet
C Restaurant	F Gamle byen (historic town houses)	2 Numedal	6 Jæren
		3 Telemark	7 Østlandet

been recreated, in which small worker's apartments and little suburban houses, animal sheds, a sweet shop and fine 18th and 19th century houses can be viewed. The old pharmacy with its **Apothecary Museum** is especially appealing and includes mortar and herb vessels from 1867. A small herb garden lies a few steps away. The main attraction of this museum is the open-air section that spreads out over a large park area. Here the visitor can experience fine bourgeois houses, country estates complete with barns (stabbur), stables, and servant housing from every district in the country. The Raulandstue (around 1300) from the Numedal valley is especially worth taking a look at. A further attraction is the **Gol stave church** from Hallingdal, which dates from around 1200, donated to the museum (founded in 1894) by King Oscar II. He bought the church when it was due for demolition. The interior is very well preserved, while the exterior was reconstructed using the stave church in Borgund as a model.

❶ Mid-May–mid-Sep daily 10am–6pm, otherwise Mon–Fri 11am–3pm, Sat–Sun till 4pm, 100 NOK; www.norskfolkemuseum.no

** *Oseberg Ship*

A farmer at Oseberg came upon strange pieces of wood in the ground during agricultural work in the summer of 1903. These turned out to be a Viking ship that had been used for a burial in AD 834, and although the more valuable funerary goods had long since been stolen, the peat enveloping the ship had at least conserved the wood perfectly. Today the Oseberg Ship is the greatest treasure at the Viking Ship Museum in Oslo.

ⓘ ▶p.348

❶ Dragon head
The figurehead, a dragon or snake head with a spiralled throat had been hacked off the Oseberg Ship.

❷ Side rudder
Viking ships always have their side rudder at the steering end, to the right of the direction travelled. The floor of the hull is flat and the ship can be rowed or sailed at up to 10 knots.

❸ Rudder
All 30 oars, each 3.1m/10.4ft long, survive. 30 men used them while seated on boxes.

❹ Oxen as grave goods
The remains of an ox survive, whose last meal consisted of juniper, reeds, Erica and rosehip.

❺ The dead
The ship's bow pointed south and a chamber of 5.5m/18ft x 5.3m/17.3ft was constructed on deck: the tomb for two women. One, about 60-70 years old, suffered from pronounced arthritis; the other was 20-30 years old when she died.

❻ Runes
The front section of the ship contained a 2.42m/7.9ft-long spar that is embellished with Norway's oldest runic script: »Itiluism«. Could it have been the name of the ship?

❼ Planks
The decking planks of the 21.4/70.2ft long and 5.1m/16.7ft wide ship were of pine and were fixed with nails made of ebony.

❽ Mast
The mast was 20cm/7.9in thick and around 13m/43ft high. The roughly 90 sq m/969 sq ft sail was missing.

Oslo's unique location, surrounded by endless forests on the fjord, can only really be appreciated from above and the easiest way to do that is to take the Holmenkollen train from the city centre to the Holmenkollen ski jump, and then onwards to Frognerseteren. Finding a seat is a challenge on weekends – summer or winter – because the locals like nothing more than to head out into nature. The Holmenkollen railway line that was later transformed into the **T-Bane Line** was Oslo's first suburban railway, originally inaugurated in 1898. The service runs out of the city in a northwest direction, from the central railway station at Jernbanetorget, via Storting, the National Theatre, and Majorstuen. The capital's apartment blocks cede to suburban family homes with small gardens and, by the time Holmenkollen is reached, after a 20-min journey, neat terraces of little houses spread up the hill that enjoy stunning views over Oslo and its fjord. Naturally, the rents are commensurate with the privilege! A short walk takes visitors to the foot of the ski jump. The silhouette of the Holmenkollen ski jump has drawn the eye from down below for decades, though the first championship actually took place up there as long ago as 1892, albeit on much smaller ramps. The Winter Olympics were held at the Holmenkollen in 1952 and, since then, there have been regular World Cup competitions in ski jumping, cross country skiing and biathlons here. A major annual event that attracts

**Holmen-kollen

> **?** **MARCO POLO INSIGHT**
>
> *Ski jumping at the Holmenkollen*
>
> As before, the point of no return on the new ski ramp is at the end. In addition to the distance achieved, flight and landing technique also influence the number of marks gained. These days jumpers reach much further than before with their skies spread out in V-form, unlike earlier sportsmen who paddled wildly with their arms. The record on the new ski jump stands at 141m/463ft, achieved by Adreas Kofler (Austria) on 5 March 2011. Statistics for the new ramp:
>
> - Length: 90.1m/295ft
> - Gradient: 36°
> - Table length: 6.6m/21ft
> - Table gradient: 11°
> - Speed: 94.7km/h/58.8mi/h
> - Landing gradient: 33.2°
> - HS (Hillsize): 134
> - K-Point: 120m/393ft
> - Spectator capacity: 30,000

thousands of spectators is the Holmenkollen Games. The 20th century ramp, however, fell under international standards for major competitions, and so the Oslo authorities reluctantly decided to replace their emblem with a new construction, making it the 18th time Oslo's ski jump was remodelled, since 1892. Over a hundred designs were considered in the pursuit of something that would maintain the traditional vision of the emblematic structure and yet be uniquely modern, and the new building was finally completed in 2011, just in time for the Nordic World Ski Championship. A lift takes visitors to the viewing platform, from which panoramic views over Oslo can be

savoured. Below the tower, the new Ski Museum illustrates the history of skiing, from its earliest days to the present. The museum is close to Norwegian hearts as they take pride in their claim to have invented skiing. In fact, according to a local saying, genuine Norwegians are born with skis already strapped to their feet.

Holmenkollen Ski Jump and Ski Museum: June–Aug 9am–8pm, May, Sep 10am–5pm, Oct–April 10am–4pm; www.holmenkollen.com

A worthwhile detour from the Ski Museum is to the imposing wood palace in the Dragon Style that is the Holmenkollen Park Hotel. The oldest sections date from 1894, and the hotel is worth seeing from the inside as well. The honey coloured wood interior exudes elegance and cosiness and is lined by fine furniture, such as trunks and cupboards, and beautifully carved beams and handrails. Don't miss the magnificently decorated back entrance to the hotel. In the evenings, the building and the ski ramp are illuminated, which also makes for a beautiful view. The »De Fem Stuer« is one of Oslo's finest and most expensive restaurants. Ski Resort The 371m/1217ft-high Holmenkollen is the capital's most important ski resort during winter. These forested hills become one single ski arena during the Holmenkollen Ski Festival each March. A good road leads from Oslo to Frognerseteren (13km/8mi) and the viewing point of the Tryvannstårnet tower. A much nicer and more comfortable way to get here, however, is by the train from the National Theatre (▶p. 349).

Holmenkollen Park Hotel

The road continues up past the turning for the Voksenkollen to the popular Frognerseteren restaurant that lies at an elevation of 437m/1434ft. A 20–25mins walk away from there in a northwesterly direction leads to Tryvannshøgda (529m/1736ft) and its 118m/387ft-high Tryvannstårnet television tower (1962). An elevator takes visitors to the top to experience the wonderful panoramic view.

Frognerseteren Tryvannstårnet

In addition to Frognerseteren, Lake Sognsvann (end of the Sognsvann railway line) is also a good departure point for cross-country skiing tours. Among the most popular destinations are the Ullevålsseter (approx. 5km/3mi from Sognsvann) and Tryvannstua (approx. 6km/4mi from Frognerseteren) huts. Accommodation is available at the Skjennungsstua, Kobberhaughytta and Kikutstua huts. During summer, these huts also make popular destinations for hikers and cyclists.

Cross country skiing and cabins

Heading south of Oslo, leave the E 18 that runs along the Bunnefjord and follow the RV 182 until the turning near Lake Gjersjøen to

*Amundsen's house

The new ski ramp at Holmenkollen is captivatingly elegant

Svartskog. The former home of the polar explorer Roald Amundsen (1872–1928; ►Famous People) stands here, in an idyllic location right on the Bunnefjord, an arm of the Oslofjord. »Uranienborg« is a wooden villa in the Swiss style. Amundsen lived here from 1908 until his death, which occurred during an attempt to save the life of the Italian airship captain Nobile. Amundsen Museum The Amundsen Museum in his birthplace of Torp is dedicated to Norway's greatest explorer and his polar expeditions (Framveien 7).

❶ Mid-June–mid-Aug Wed–Sun 11am–5pm; www.visitoslofjord.no

Tusenfryd East Norway's most popular theme park lies directly at the junction of the E 18 and the E 6 and includes **northern Europe's largest wooden rollercoaster**. The »Land of the Vikings« is especially pretty and offers insight into Viking traditions. Children have their own park and also an aquapark.

❶ The park opens beginning of May with varying opening times: July–mid-Aug daily 10.30am–7pm; depending on height, from 280 NOK per day; www.tusenfryd.no

* Oslofjord

―――――――――――――――――― ✦ B 7

Region: East Norway

The Oslofjord is the country's lifeline. About a third of all Norwegians live nearby and the capital city of Oslo lies at the fjord's far end. Nevertheless, there are still some quiet corners along its shores and many opportunities to have a swim.

Already popular in prehistoric times Those arriving in Norway by boat should choose Oslo as their destination, which is where the Oslofjord (roughly 20km/12mi wide and 100km/62mi long) opens into the Skagerrak strait. The loveliest **summer destinations** are found along the western shore in particular.

The 589km/368mi-long Glomma River empties into the fjord at ►Fredrikstad on the eastern shore, to the north of the holiday islands of Hvaler with their strikingly smooth eroded rocks. The **oldest finds** proving human habitation in Norway have been found in this region and to the north as far as Svartskog: up to 9000 years old, they include **rock paintings** and burial sites. The earliest inhabitants followed the receding ice after the end of the last Ice Age. Norway's **most densely populated** area lies around the inner part of the Oslofjord. In addition to agriculture, there has been intense development of industry and important commercial centres and the coastal settlements are also home to a large merchant fleet.

Oslofjord

INFORMATION
Turistkontoret
Tollbugt 1a
3187 Horten
tel. 33 03 17 08
www.visithorten.com
www.visitoslofjord.com

Sandefjord Reiselivsforening
Thor Dahls gate 1
3210 Sandefjord
tel. 33 46 05 90
www.visitsandefjord.com

WHERE TO EAT
Det gamle Bageri Ost & Vinhus £ – £ £
Det gamle Bageri Ost & Vinhus A – A A
Havnebakken 1, Drøbak
tel. 64 93 21 05
www.detgamlebageri.no
This cosy, rustic tavern is a good place to have lunch after visiting the Drøbaker Christmas shop. The locals also like to meet here in the evenings for a glass wine; frequent live music.

Brygga Restaurant £
Nedre Langgate 35
(right on the quay)
Tønsberg
tel. 33 31 12 0
The large seafood plate in this harbour restaurant is not only of mighty proportions but also very reasonably priced. The large terrace right on the water is especially attractive.

WHERE TO STAY
Hotel Refsnes Gods £ £ £ £
Godset 5, Moss
tel. 69 27 83 00
www.refsnesgods.no, 61 rooms.
This luxury hotel on an island in the Oslofjord is set in a grand 18th-century country estate. Despite modern extensions, the hotel is still very quiet and has its own beach and boat jetty. The hotel boasts 400 artworks, including pieces by Munch and Warhol.

Thon Hotel Åsgårdstrand £ £ £
Havnegata 6
Åsgårdstrand
tel. 33 02 07 40
www.thonhotels.com, 78 rooms.
A comfortable hotel with a pleasant atmosphere right on the beach that pays homage to Edvard Munch, the most famous tourist to come to this small settlement.

Hotel Kong Carl £ £ – £ £ £
Torvgt. 9, Sandefjord
tel. 33 46 31 17
www.kongcarl.no, 29 rooms.
This very centrally located historic house was built at the end of the 17th century. It has been an inn since 1721 and its cuisine is famous throughout the country.

HI Hostel Horten £
Borreveien 44 A, Horten
tel. 33 31 06 00
http://hihostels.no/en/hostel/horten-hostel/
This youth hostel is next to the Borre golf course, with good bus connections into the town centre (approx. 2km/1mi) and to the station. The hostel has a bowling ally and there is a fitness centre and thermal baths nearby; bicycle hire available.

Edward Munch painted his *Three Girls on a Bridge*, among others, in his studio at Åsgårdstrand

WHAT TO SEE ON THE WESTERN SHORE OF THE OSLOFJORD

Horten   The first major settlement on the actual Oslofjord is the port of Horte (pop. 26,300, car ferry to Moss 30mins). The old marine buildings of Karljohansvern, north of the town centre, house the **Maritime Museum**. The world's oldest torpedo boat, the Rapp, dates from 1872 and can be seen in front of the museum. The internationally renowned **Preus National Museum of Photography** is in the same building complex and the only one of its kind in Norway. The exhibition halls were designed by the famous architect Sverre Fehn. 4km/2.5mi south of town, near the medieval church of Borre, the new and artfully designed **Midgard Historical Centre** offers memorable documentation on the history of the Vikings. A visit is just as interesting for children as for adults. The small **Borre National Park** contains northern Europe's largest collection of royal burial mounds (six large ones up to 7m/23ft-high and 21 smaller mounds). A beautiful cycle track of about 4km/2.5mi through forest leads from here along the waterside to Åsgårdstrand (coastal route 1).

Preus National Museum of Photography: July daily noon–5pm, otherwise Tue–Fri noon–4pm, Sat–Sun till 5pm; 50 NOK; www.preusmuseum.no

Midgard Historical Centre: 1st May–15th Sep daily 11am–4pm, otherwise Wed–Fri and Sun 11am–4pm; 60 NOK; www.midgardsenteret.no

In the middle of the old village of this idyllic swimming resort and artists' centre there are several galleries, as well as the old Corsmeier Thuen clockmaker's workshop in which historic clocks and watches are restored. The white-painted wooden houses are very picturesque; in »**Munchs lille hus**« beyond the guest quay, Edvard Munch (►Famous People) painted Girls on the Bridge, one of the most famous images of Åsgårdtrand. The studio and old fishermen's cabin are from the 18th century. The pretty beach can also be recognized on several more Munch pictures. The annual Åsgårdstrand Days in June celebrate this small resort's famous guest and include a revival of the scene portraying the three girls, when they can once again be seen posing just as in Munch's day. The **Oseberg ship** (►Oslo, Viking Ship Museum) was found in a 6m/20ft-high burial mound at Oseberg, 6km/4mi south of here, in 1904.

*Åsgård-strand

Munchs lille hus: May Sat–Sun 11am–6pm, June–Aug, Tue–Sun 11am–6pm; 40 NOK

Tønsberg (pop. 40,700) is Norway's oldest town and was founded by Harald Hårfagre in 871. King Magnus Lagabøte resided in his brick fortress (1276) up on the rocky castle hill during the 13th century, when he wrote the country's first constitution. Today only ruins of the fortress remain in the castle grounds on the hill, but the **ruin-park** is one of northern Europe's largest. Håkon Håkonsson's 12th-century fortress of **Castrum Tunisbergis**, with its mighty buttress walls and bastions, was Norway's largest castle in the Middle Ages, but only a few partly reconstructed stone walls survive, as is the case with the St Michael's Church from 1150. A wonderful view onto Tønsberg and over the jagged skerry landscape can be enjoyed from the **lookout tower** (1888). This area is especially popular with Norway's high society during summer when hardly a seat can be found at the restaurant quay to the southeast of the historic Norbyen quarter. The **Vestfold Festival** at the end of June/early July is also popular and offers plays, concerts and exhibitions.

*Tønsberg

Odd Nerdrum (born 1944), one of Norway's best-known contemporary painters, has his own exhibition in the **Haugar Vestfold Art Museum**. The museum is located on Haugar Hill, which was the site of an important Viking »ting« (assembly). Until the mid-20th century, whaling in the southern ice floes was also a source of income for the town (►MARCO POLO Insight p.438). More on whaling and Norway's great seafaring era can be found at the **Vestfold Fylkesmuseum**, at the foot of the castle Hill. A tip for families with children: check out the wonderful long **sandy beaches** at Valløy (campsite) and Skallevoll to the west of Tønsberg.

Haugar Vestfold Art Museum: mid-May–mid-Sep daily 11am–4pm, otherwise Wed–Sun 11am–4pm; 60 NOK; www.vfm.no

*Islands of Nøtterøy and Tjøme

The islands of Nøtterøy and Tjøme to the south of Tønsberg boast several sandy beaches and are popular holiday destinations (reached via the RV 308). A particularly pretty spot is Verdens End, »The End of the World«, in the south of Tjøme. Numerous coves, good for bathing, lie between the smoothly polished cliffs here. In fair weather, the 300-year-old Færder fyr lighthouse is visible in the middle of the mouth of the Oslofjord.

Sandefjord

Those who fly to Oslo with Ryanair land southeast of Tønsberg, in the former whaling town of Sandefjord (pop. 44,200; for more on whaling see ►MARCO POLO Insight p.438). The **Whaling Museum** and the Seafaring Museum offer an insight into the old days; a whalers' memorial by Knut Steen stands at the harbour. Until the 19th century, the town was also a well-known spa. Opened in 1837, Sandefjord Spa played host to many a personality. The former wooden spa building was transformed into a **cultural centre** that has an exhibition on Sandefjord's past. In the south of the Østerøya Peninsula, beginning at the Tallakshamn beach, a narrow path leads to the **Tønsberg Tønne fire tower** (35mins), from where there is a good view towards the Skagerrak Sea. East of Sandefjord, it is possible to climb onto the Gokstad mound from which the Gokstad ship was dug out in 1880 (►Oslo, Viking Ship Museum).

MARCO POLO TIP

Sail like the Vikings Insider Tip

The »Gaia«, a replica of the approximately 1200-year old Gokstad Ship, is anchored at the museum's quay at Sandefjord and makes occasional round trips out to sea (info from the tourist office).

*Viking town of Kaupang

One of the largest and oldest Viking trading posts can be found by following the road past the turning for **Ula pilots' harbour** and taking the road that branches off shortly before Larvik (in the direction of Bjønnes and Gloppe; in Kaupang in the direction of Lamøya). Along with Ribe and Hedeby in Denmark and Birka in Sweden, the Viking town of Kaupang, in an idyllic setting on the Viksfjord, was among the North's most important trading posts. Mentioned in the Yngling saga as **Sikringssal,** it was probably the **capital of the Norwegian Vikings**. Archaeological excavations have unearthed the remains of a royal hall, houses with fireplaces, workshops (smithies, weaving workshops and glass bead manufactories), streets and a port which all indicate a fixed settlement with a permanent market was located here between 770 and 920. Kaupang can therefore perhaps outdo Tønsberg, so far considered Norway's oldest town.

The RV 303 ends at the former county capital of Larvik (pop. 43,000), where the ferry for Denmark departs once or twice a day. The sulphurous saltwater spring Kong Håkon's kilde, Norway's only natural **mineral spring** lies here. In the southeast of the town stands the stately HerreGården estate that was constructed between 1670 and 1680 to serve as a residence for the Larvik counts and today houses the town museum. The interior of the 17th-century **Larvik Church**, to the south of the railway, is pretty. To the left of the altar there is a painting by Lucas Cranach the Elder portraying Martin Luther. **Bøkeskogen**, Norway's largest beech forest, stretches northwest of Larvik and contains around 90 burial mounds from the Iron Age.

Larvik

200 days of sun per year – this bold claim is designed to tempt visitors to the seaside resort of Stavern to the south of Larvik. In the middle of the town stands the impressive maritime fortress of Fredriksvern, encircled by thick walls. It was built as a dockyard by King Frederik V in 1760. Artisans now work and exhibit in the former commandant's house.

*Stavern

WHAT TO SEE ON THE EASTERN SHORE OF THE OSLOFJORD

Oslo's winter port was once located at the small seaside resort of Drøbak, at the narrowest point of the Oslofjord. When the fjord was frozen over, passengers and goods for Oslo had to be transported overland from here. Picturesque wooden houses and an aquarium stand by the small marina. Further north, by the bathing park, stands a pretty wooden church from 1736, while the attraction in the town centre is **Norway's all-year-round Christmas shop**, »Treegaardens julehus« (with its own special postmark).

*Drøbak

One of eastern Norway's most famous galleries, the **F 15 Gallery** is housed in the Alby mansion on the island of Jeløy (bridge), which lies just offshore of Moss and is reached via the bathing resorts of Hvitsten and Son. There is a car ferry from Moss to Horten (duration 30mins, every 45mins). The personal union between Sweden and Norway was signed in the old estate located on the present site of the Moss paper factory on 14 August 1814.

Moss

F 15 Gallery: Tue–Sun 11am–5pm; www.punkto.no

✳ Romsdal

✦ E 4/5

Region: West Norway

The mighty Romsdalshorn, the 1000m/3281ft-high vertical Troll Wall and, to top it all, the serpentine curves of the Trollstigen road. A visit to the Romsdal valley is a spectacular experience.

Magnificent mountain valley
Cutting inland from Åndalsnes on the mighty Romsdalsfjord, the Romsdal valley is one of the most beautiful in western Norway. The Rauma river flows through the approximately 60km/37mi-long valley, which is embraced by magnificent mountains. Romsdal can either be reached from Åndalsnes or from the southeast through the ►Gudbrandsdal valley. The E 136 leads from the end of Gudbrandsdal across the watershed between the Atlantic and the Skagerrak Sea into the lower Romsdal valley.

WHAT TO SEE IN AND AROUND THE ROMSDAL VALLEY

Down the Romsdal to the sea
The Romsdal valley, which can be followed on the E 136, gets narrower and narrower as it descends to the sea. The serpentine road regularly offers beautiful views down onto the churning Rauma river that has cut itself a dramatic chasm through the rock at the Slettafoss waterfall. The railway crosses the river on a 76m/249ft-long and 59m/194ft-high bridge, the Kylling bru at Verma (273m/896ft), from where the Vermafoss Power Station can be seen close to the road. A

You just have to get through it: the Rondslottet in Romsdal

short drive further on, the road reaches the valley floor where it is flanked by rugged mountains on either side. To the left of the road at Flatmark, Døntind (1676m/5499ft) towers up into the sky.

Where the valley widens at Malstein, the mighty 1799m/5902ft-high Kalskråtind catches the eye. Further north, Romsdalshorn towers 1550m/5085ft into the air, dominating the landscape.

*Romsdals-horn

Opposite Romsdalshorn stands the mighty Trollveggen (Troll Wall) crowned by the Trolltindene (Troll Peaks). It is **Europe's highest rock face** and measures 1800m/5906ft from its base to the summit, there being a 1000m/3281ft-high vertical part and an overhang of 50m/164ft. Several extremely difficult climbing routes lead up the Troll Wall, which was scaled for the first time in 1965. The first climbers needed two weeks to complete their mission.

*Trolltindene

At the Sogge bru bridge, the RV 63, the Trollstigen, branches off to the left and leads through the Isterdal valley to Valldal (image p. 361). In a series of eleven breathtaking bends and with a 12% slope, the Trollstigen winds 18km/11mi up the mountain, offering wonderful views of the wildly romantic mountain scenery. Earth slides have made it necessary to rebuild the road (visited by over half a million tourists each year) in several places. The road crosses the Stigfoss at the Stigfoss bru bridge before reaching Trollstigen Fjellstue at the top of the pass, from where there is a viewing point. Afterwards the road leads down into Valldal and the magnificent Tåfjord.

**Trollstigen

The E 136 ends at **Åndalsnes**, a lively holiday resort with the picturesque Romsdalsfjord lying to its west. The town is connected to the railway network via the Rauma route and is suitable as a base for excursions into the fjords (www.raumabanen.net). A tourist train (departures daily 1pm) runs between Åndalsnes and Bjorli (114km/71mi) from the end of June to the end of August, and on several days a steam train is used.

! MARCO POLO TIP

The sweetest fruit Insider Tip

Valldal, at the end of the Trollstigen, has been famous for its aromatic fruit since the importation of strawberries from Denmark about one hundred years ago. The »Syltetøybutikken« sell homemade juices and jams (tel. 70 25 75 11; opening times: Mon–Fri 10am–5pm, Sat till 2pm).

The history of climbing is presented in the Norsk Tinde Museum and includes photos and equipment once used by the climbing pioneer Arne Randers Heen, who loved the Romsdalshorn so much, he climbed it over 200 times.

Norsk Tinde Museum

www.tindemuseet.no

Romsdal

INFORMATION
Åndalsnes og Romsdal Reiselivslag
Jernbanegata 1, 6300 Åndalsnes
tel. 71 22 16 22, www.visitandalsnes.com

Destinasjon Molde & Romsdal AS
Torget 4, 6413 Molde
tel. 71 20 10 00, www.visitmolde.com

SPORT/FESTIVAL
There are opportunities for guided hikes
and kayaking (romsdalaktiv.com), as well
as paragliding (beginners can book a
tandem flight strapped to an expert); information from the tourist offices and at
www.rpk.no. During July, you can join
the fun at the Norsk Fjellfestival that offers a range of attractions for the whole
family (www.norsk-fjellfestival.no).

EXCURSIONS
Thanks to its beautiful beaches, the
small island of Hjertøya in the Romsdalsfjord is ideal for day trips. A boat travels
between Torget and Hjertøya between
mid-June and mid-August, departing at
11am, noon, 2pm and 4pm (last return
trip at 5.45pm)

Driving is sometimes a tight squeeze on the Trollstiegen

WHERE TO EAT
Trollstigen Camping & Gjestegård £ £

Åndalsnes
tel. 71 22 11 12
www.trollstigen.no
Large inn and also a popular tour bus stop on the route from Åndalsnes to Trollstigen. Breakfast, lunch, coffee and cake, supper, and an extensive cold buffet are on the menu. The well-maintained campsite and comfortable cabins make this attractive to those wishing to stay longer.

Rød und Bare Blå £ £

Storgt. 19, Molde, tel. 71 21 58 88
The »Rød« is the town's most modern café and the »Bare Blå« the most popular coffee bar. With interiors are full of art works, they are found next door to each other inside the Hotel Molde. The Rød is a popular meeting place at lunchtime, while the Bare Blå is a good place to find a drink, even after midnight. A visit to the Hot Hat Jazz Club in the hotel basement is also recommended.

WHERE TO STAY
Rica Seilet Hotel £ £ £ £

Gideonvegen 2, Molde, tel. 71 11 40 00
www.scandichotels.com/Hotels/Norway/Molde/Seilet

This hotel must be unique in northern Europe, with its building designed like a large sail partially jutting over the Romsdalsfjord. All rooms have panoramic views and a new wing is connected to the main building by a bridge. The restaurant with views over the fjord is on the second floor, and the Sky Bar is at an elevation of 60m/197ft; another restaurant is located on the shore itself.

Molde Fjordstuer £ £ £

Julsundveien 6, Molde
tel. 71 20 10 60
www.classicnorway.no, 44 rooms.
Newly-built hotel in the modern »Sjøbu style« located right by the water at the Hurtigruten quay. Bright and elegant rooms with lake views. The excellent restaurant is expensive, but the salt cod soup is authentic and affordable.

Mjelva Camping Hütten £ – £ £

Åndalsnes
tel. 71 22 64 50
www.mjelvacamping.no
This campsite was voted the region's best in 2004. Quiet location and beautiful views onto the spectacular Romsdal mountains. Space for mobile homes and tents; simple but comfortable cabins can be rented.

Molde (pop. 25,500) lies on the coast. It was given its nickname of »Rosetown« by Norway's well-known poet Bjørnstjerne Bjørnson (▶Famous People), who went to school in Molde. Though located at 62° northern latitude, the effect of the Gulf Stream means the climate here is so mild that even chestnut trees, lime trees and, most of all, countless roses grow. Molde's panorama of 22 mountain peaks, sometimes covered in snow, on the other side of the fjord is truly beautiful. Jazz musicians from all over the world come to this lively resort every year at the beginning of August to take part in the international **Molde Jazz Festival** (www.moldejazz.no). Bjørnstjerne

Bjørnson was a frequent visitor at the former magistrate's court of **MoldeGården**, built in 1710, and the playwright Henrik Ibsen (▶Famous People) wrote his play Rosmersholm there. The altar painting from the church destroyed in 1940, The Resurrection by Axel Ender (19th century), hangs in the aisle of the modern **cathedral** (1957), which has beautiful stained glass windows. In the west of town lies the Reknesparken forest park and the **Romsdal Museum**, an open-air museum containing around 70 historic Romsdal buildings including the Synnøve Solbakken parlour that recalls Bjørnson's story about the farm girl Synnøve. An entire section is dedicated to the German Dadaist poet and artist Kurt Schwitters, who spent several years exiled on the island of Hertøya, and includes his »Merzpicture«.

Romsdal Museum: mid-June–mid-Aug Mon–Sat, 11am–3pm, Sun noon–3pm, July till 5pm; 70 NOK; www.romsdalsmuseet.no

View of the sea
Beautiful viewing points near Molde are Tusten (696m/2283ft; ascent 3hrs) and Varden (407m/1335ft), which can be climbed from the town centre in about one hour. There is also a road and panorama restaurant. On the RV 64 about 28km/17mi north of the town lies the Trollkirka grotto, which can be reached on foot via a steep path in one and a half hours (▶Kristiansund, Atlantic Route).

✶✶ Røros

✦ E 8

Region: Central Norway
Population: 5500

Røros, the only town in Norway located in the mountains, is often bitterly cold in winter, and yet it is one of the most beautiful places in the country. The historic town centre, whose wooden houses still date from the copper mining era, has been on the UNESCO World Heritage List since 1980.

Fate of a mining town
The last pit near the mining town of Røros was closed in 1977. An era that had lasted over 300 years and produced a total of 110,000 tons of copper was thereby ended. What remains are the large, dark brown **slag heaps** and the damage to the natural environment caused by centuries of **deforestation** around Røros. The town was founded in 1644 after large deposits of copper ore were found in the Arvedal pit; and in 1723, the Royal pit and the Christianus Sextus pit were also established (tours in summer). The »Rørosmartnan« folk festival, held in February every year, recalls the heyday of the mining town with concerts in the old smelting works and the miners' church, horse-drawn sled parades, ski races, dance and »miners' buffets«.

Røros

INFORMATION
Destinasjon Røros
Peder Hiorts gt. 2
7361 Røros
tel. 72 41 00 00, www.roros.no

MARKET
The five-day »Rørosmartnan« is held in mid-February, with a winter market that attracts many traders, musicians and visitors.

ACTIVITIES
The huskies and reindeer are ready to go in the winter; sleigh tours with either (one-day or several days) can be booked via the tourist office. Tours including overnight stays in a Sami tent are offered by Laaratour (www.laaratour.no). Another option is to ride a snow mobile to the winter feeding grounds of the reindeer (information from the tourist office).

WHERE TO EAT
Kaffestuggu Røros £ £ – £ £ £
Bergmannsgata 18
tel. 72 41 10 33
www.kaffestuggu.no
This café is housed in one of the town's oldest buildings. Its pastel coloured walls, old stove, portraits and rustic furniture make it a charming place for a snack.

Vertshuset Røros £ £
Kjerkgata 34
tel. 72 41 24 11

www.vertshusetroros.no/
A small restaurant in the centre with genuine Norwegian »rømmegrøt« sour cream porridge on the menu

Suppestasjonen £
Kjerkgata 7
tel. 95 83 14 80
Small prices but a large selection of soups and home-made bread to stave off hunger, including beer brewed on the premises; during summer, outdoor seating in the courtyard. May–September, closed Sundays.

Thomasgaarden £
Kjerkegata 48
tel. 98 69 06 79
The Thomasgaarden is a historic Røros building. Coffee and cake is served in the very cosy guest room that also hosts exhibitions; art and craftwork for sale.

WHERE TO STAY
Vertshuset Røros £ £ £
Kjerkegata 34
tel. 72 41 93 50
www.vertshusetroros.no
Comfortable inn in the old town. The cellar bar hosts live music every week.

Erzscheidergården £ £ – £ £ £
Spell Olavn 6
tel. 72 41 11 94
www.erzscheidergaarden.no, 24 rooms.
Small guesthouse with charming staff on a hill with views of Røros

WHAT TO SEE IN RØROS

The 75 listed buildings of the Bergstaden (old town) have been restored in a manner true to their original style and give an excellent   ****Bergstaden** insight into the local mining town architecture. The earliest examples of the characteristic dark brown workers' apartments were built at the end of the 17th century near the first smelting works at the Hitter River. A housing block often also included stables, bakeries and storage buildings. A good example is the 18th-century **Per Amundsa Court** at Bergmannsgata 37, where slag from the pits was used for the roofing. The wealthier citizens and pit directors settled in the lower part of the old town. The size and interiors of the houses are evidence of the class barriers that existed.

The oldest testament to the town's history is the AasenGården. The estate stands on an area that was cleared in the 17th century by Hans Olsen Aasen, the first to discover that the region was ore-rich.

Røros Museum   There is a fascinating **Mining Museum on Malmplassen (Ore Square) with several models (1 : 10) showing old mining technologies. The museum's pit room installed in the reconstructed smelting block shows how the ore was extracted in the lower pits using explosives during the 18th century, among other things, and also how a pump was operated via a horse-drawn treadmill. The Nyberget and Olav pit (50m/164ft and 500m/1640ft underground respectively) outside town can also be visited.
Mining Museum: mid-June–mid-Aug daily 10am–6pm, otherwise Mon–Fri 11am–3pm/4pm, Sat–Sun 11am–2pm/3pm; 70 NOK; combined ticket with Olav pit 125 NOK; www.rorosmuseet.no

*Røros Church   Built of stone in 1784, the octagonal Baroque church on Kjerkgata (also known as »Bergstadens Ziir«) is the town's emblem and remained the only stone building in Røros for a long time. The square tower is decorated with the hammer and mallet images of mining. The Baroque interior of this light and pleasant church contains a royal lodge decorated in real gold, the organ, and several portraits.

Falkeberg monument   The artist Sivert Donali created the Falkberget monument in honour of the writer Johann Falkberget (1879–1967), whose novels made a substantial contribution towards putting this, Norway's only high fjell town, on the map. The title of his Røros Trilogy is Christianus Sextus.

AROUND RØROS

Norway's most southern Sami families still keep reindeer on the   Olav Mine
Rørosvidda. The Olav Mine, about 13km/8mi east of town, is a copper mine that was discovered in 1936. There are daily guided tours
of the mine during summer. The mine cavern, at a depth of
500m/547yd inside the mountain, also hosts concerts during summer. Inside, the temperature is a constant 4°C/39!F, so warm clothes
are necessary.
Guided tours: early June–mid-Aug–early Sep, Mon–Sat 1pm–3pm, Sun
noon, mid-June–mid-Aug daily 10.30am, noon, 2pm, 3.30pm, 5pm,
otherwise Sat 3pm; 90 NOK (combination ticket with the mining museum,
▶p. 364); www.rorosmuseet.no

For those searching for even more obscure things, a detour into the   Hessdal
Hessdal valley north of Røros is recommended. This is where **UFO
hunters** study a phenomenon of mysterious appearances of lights
and cigar-shaped objects in the sky. Their studies are frequently published and eye witnesses regularly report their sightings. A summary
of mysterious happenings in Hessdal can be found at http://hess-
dalen.hiof.no/station/alarm.shtml.

✳ Saltfjellet

✦ M 13 – 15

Region: North Norway
Height: 0–1600m/5250ft

**The sheer barrenness of the Saltfjellet plateau cannot fail to
impress. Here, at the Arctic Circle, those who have not yet
spotted a reindeer could be in luck: you may well encounter
one while driving along the E 6. Of course the much larger attraction is the Svartisen glacier.**

The 2250 sq km/869 sq mi of Saltfjellet (meaning »the salt moun-   Primordial
tain«) have consituted northern Norway's largest and most varied   landscape
national park since 1989. Bordered by the North Sea and the Svartisen glacier to the west and the Swedish border to the east, it is also
traversed by the **Arctic Circle**. The **only visible intervention** into
the landscape is the E 6 running parallel to the railway line between Mo
i Rana in the south and Bodø in the north; the most important road
connection across the highland plateau, it becomes impassable during winter due to huge amounts of snow. Typical for Saltfjellet is the
juxtaposition of a glacier landscape in the west with broad valleys and
highlands to the east.

WHAT TO SEE ON THE SALTFJELLET

Saltfjellet is covered by a network of footpaths and self-catering huts that are each one day's walk away from the next. The best route into the area is via the E 6, travelling as far as Rognan and then taking the road that branches off to the west as far as Storjord. **Historic sacrificial sites**, hunting pits and stone walls prove that the indigenous Sami people were already using Saltfjellet as a **hunting and grazing ground** centuries ago.

Arctic Circle
Centre

The Arctic Circle (Polarsirkelen) in Norway is located around 80km/50mi north of Mo i Rana. At the spot where the E 6 cuts the Arctic Circle, the Arctic Circle Centre, designed after the shape of a Sami dwelling, presents exhibitions on the culture and economy of

Engabreen, a side arm of the Svartisen glacier, rolls majestically into the valley

northern Norway. The Arctic Circle Pillar stands in front of this architecturally interesting building and provides a popular photo opportunity.

❶ 20th May–1st Sep daily 8am–10pm; www.polarsirkelsenteret.no

An impressive draw for visitors to this region is the **Svartisen glacier** (»black ice glacier«), the largest of northern Scandinavia's ice massifs, which reaches all the way to the fjords in the west. Individual summits protrude from the 1200m/3937ft–1400m/4593ft-high plateau, including Snøtind (1599m/5246ft), Sniptind (1591m/5220ft) and Istind (1577m/5174ft). Coming from the south, it is advisable to head northwest via ▶Mo i Rana in the direction of Svartisdalshytta or Melfjordbotn. Both roads end at the foot of a Svartisen outcrop. On no account should anyone venture onto the ice. During summer the ice moves several metres each day; fractures and splits can appear that are usually only noticed when it is too late. Coming from the north along the coastal route 17 (▶Nordland) between ▶Bodø and Glomfjord, it is possible to combine a glacier trip with a worthwhile drive along what is probably **northern Norway's most beautiful coastal road**. Furthermore, the narrow Nordfjord, whose western shore falls steeply into the water and features countless waterfalls, numbers among Norway's most beautiful fjords.

Saltfjell

INFORMATION
Saltdal Turistsenter
Storjord
8255 Røkland
tel. 75 68 24 50
www.saltdal-turistsenter.no

MARCO ⊕ POLO TIP

! *Hiking made easy* Insider Tip

Bodø's hiking association (Bodø og Omegns Turistforening) runs 17 simple mountain huts that are ideally suited as accommodation during longer hikes: the Argaladshytta and Trygvebu are in the Junkerdal valley; the Bjellåvasstua, Lønsstua, Midtistua and Krukkistua are on Saltfjellet; the Tåkeheimen is at an elevation of 1100m/3609ft near the Svartisen glacier and the Lurefjellhytta is below Lurefjelltind near Bodø. Information at tel. 75 52 14 13; www.bot.no

Natural Caves

Around 70% of Norway's natural caves are found here in the Saltfjellet region. The Grønli Cave north of ▶Mo i Rana is a famous tourist attraction. The caves were created when the numerous water courses in the mountains dissolved the limestone and marble predominating in the region. In fact, at the edge of the national park the famous Saltfjellet marble is still mined today.

Junkerdal

Beginning at Storjord on the E 6, the RV 77 leads through Junkerdal, a valley as dramatic as it is fertile, all the way to the Swedish border. Hiking in this densely forested landscape is a great way to spot interesting local flora, such as the **Arctic Orchid**, which belongs to a species that normally only grows in more southerly latitudes.

Sulitjelma
Near Fauske on the E 6 turn east onto route 830 and continue to Sulitjelma, where iron ore was mined until 1990. It was one of the Sami locals who discovered a seam here by chance in the 1880s. The **Mining Museum** in Sulitjelma bears witness to a unique epoch in the history of Norwegian iron ore mining. There are also guided walks onto the 1571m/5154ft-high **Blåmannsisen glacier** and ascents of Suliskongen at 1913m/6276ft on offer from Sulitjelma.

* Senja (Island)

— ✵ M 13–15

Region: North Norway

The coastal strips to the west and north of Senja Island are among the roughest mountain regions in the country. Sometimes the mountainsides rise vertically 1000m/3281ft out of the sea. A starker contrast to the flat, white, sandy beaches that can also be found on the island is hardly imaginable.

Treasure island for nature lovers
Norway's third largest island after Spitsbergen and Hinnøya lies between Tromsø and the Vesterålen islands and is a veritable paradise for nature lovers. Steep mountainsides frame deeply cut fjords on the seaboard, while sheltered bays and forested hills characterize the landscape facing the mainland. All routes to Senja lead via Finnsness, where the region's only hotel can be found (airstrip at Bardufoss), and where the ▶Hurtigruten ships also stop. Access to the island is made easy by the 1120m/3675ft-long Gisund Bridge.

History
The island has been inhabited since the end of the last Ice Age. The oldest surviving scripts tell of a nomadic tribe. Loot from one of their raiding trips to Friesland found under a stone by a farmer in 1905 is **Norway's greatest silver treasure** (including a ring with Runic inscriptions). King Ottar of Senja sailed to Nordkapp around 890, and then to England via Bergen and Stavanger. In the 16th and 17th centuries there were many Dutch settlements on the seaboard side of the island. The people lived mostly from whaling and also fitted out ships for polar expedi-

> ! MARCO ⬡ POLO TIP
>
> *Coastal Cognac* Insider Tip
>
> Cognac producer Jon Arne Berthelsen stores his French cognac in Senja with its coastal climate. The fine spirit is believed to develop a completely different – and hopefully even better – taste in the cool Norwegian conditions (www.jonsutvalgte.no).

Senja

INFORMATION
There is no local tourist office; for information see www.visitsenja.noo

WHERE TO EAT/WHERE TO STAY
Hamn i Senja tourist resort £££
tel. 77 85 98 80

www.hamnisenja.no
Hamn is a fishing village that has been restored and turned into a comfortable holiday resort. Traditional north Norwegian food is served at the Storbrygga Spiseri.

tions. Since 1993 the island's cultural emblem has been the 18m/59ft-high **Senja Troll**, the world's largest troll registered in the Guinness Book of Records. The troll is to be found in Berg in the island's north-west. Children especially enjoy visiting the inside of the troll, where exhibitions on Nordic mythology are on display.

The pretty Torsken Church (1773), whose interior was donated by Hanseatic merchants from the northern German town of Lübeck, can be visited in the village of Torsken on the west coast near Gryllefjord.

Torsken Church

The 68 sq km/26 sq mi **Ånderdalen National Park** is in the south of Senja Island. Its has a wealth of flora and bird species, including eagles. There are no footpaths or cabins, so visitors are dependent on their own tents, but mountain hikers really do get their money's worth here. Water sports enthusiasts can go canoeing, diving, and sailing, enjoy relaxing boat trips, and try both freshwater and sea fishing – Senja is a major fishing ground for halibut.

Ånderdalen National Park

❶ June–Aug daily 9am–8pm; 110 NOK; www.senjatrollet.no

✳ Setesdalen

✦ A/B 4

Region: South Norway

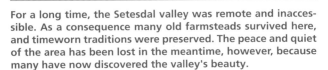

For a long time, the Setesdal valley was remote and inaccessible. As a consequence many old farmsteads survived here, and timeworn traditions were preserved. The peace and quiet of the area has been lost in the meantime, however, because many have now discovered the valley's beauty.

In recent decades, the lovely and deeply forested Setesdal or Sæterdal valley has become the most important road connection between

Over the hills...

the south coast and ▶Bergen and the ▶Hardangerfjord. For centuries, though, the few inhabitants of Setesdalen lived in great isolation and developed their own customs and folk costumes: the women wore black, knee-length skirts with red borders. The railway and the road through the valley were built in the 19th century, but the latter has only been passable all year round since the 1960s.

Setesdalen

INFORMATION
Evje/Setesdal Informasjonsenter
4735 Evje, tel. 37 93 14 00
www.setesdal.com

Hovden/Setesdal Ferie
4755 Hovden, tel. 37 93 93 70
www.hovden.com

LEISURE
Sport and Excursions
During the summer season Troll Mountain offers daily three-hour tours on the Ortra at 11am and 3pm. Also on offer are a climbing wall, canoe and mountain bike hire, and elk and beaver tours (www.troll-mountain.no; tel. 37 93 11 77).
The Klatreskogen climbing forest at Hornnes is an adrenalin pumping attraction for vertigo-free visitors over 1.40m/4ft5″: speedy trips over the river by wire cable, along with plenty of tree climbing (May–mid-June Sat–Sun 11am–4pm, till mid-Aug daily 11am–4pm; www.klatreskogen.no).

Collecting minerals
In Evje in the direction of Vikstøl, mineral collectors can find rare stones in six pegmatite pits.

WHERE TO EAT
Fjellgården Hovden £ £
Hovden, tel. 90 19 07 71
www.fjellgardenhovden.no

The old farmhouse »Den Gamle gaard« offers traditional cooking or just coffee in a cozy room with open fires. Merethe Hjemdahl and Rolf Arne Haugen run the farm shop and also have accommodation.

WHERE TO STAY
Hovden Resort £ £ £
Hovden, tel. 37 93 95 52
www.hovdestoylen.no, 42 rooms.
Glorious mountain setting with modern comfortable cabins, apartments and hotel rooms with wood interiors, close to the ski resort and golf course.

Rysstad Feriesenter £ £ £
Rysstad, tel. 37 93 61 30
www.rysstadferie.no
New and very comfortable cabins of varying sizes in a quiet location right by the water. There are also motel rooms and holiday apartments in the main building, and a cafeteria offering simple dishes. Good fishing, boat rental and a silver workshop.

Neset Camping £ – £ £
Byglandsfjord
tel. 37 93 40 50, www.neset.no
This 4-star campsite is situated on a spit of land at the southern end of the Byglandfjord and offers sites for mobile homes and tents, many of which are right by the water. 20 cabins, a café and supermarket complete the pleasing picture.

WHAT TO SEE IN SETESDALEN

The Setesdal valley lies north of ►Kristiansand on the RV 9. Many   Evje
colourful minerals can be seen and a replica mine visited at the
Setesdal Mineral Park, where there are also minerals for sale. The
wooden Hornnes church, 5km/3mi south of Evjes, is worth a visit.
This octagonal building was erected between 1826 and 1829.
Setesdal Mineral Park: June–Aug daily 10am–4pm/6pm, May, Sep–
mid-Oct usually Wed–Sun 10am–4pm; 130 NOK; www.mineralparken.no

Continuing, the Byglandsfjord (207m/679ft) is soon reached, mark-   Byglands-
ing the end of the Setesdal railway line, which was closed in 1962.   fjord
Today the place is a winter sports resort with chairlifts and downhill
runs. Cruises on the Byglandsfjord on the historic **»Bjoren«** ship also
set off from here. The steamship used to be a continuation of the
Setesdal railway service and continued to ply a regular route across
the water until 1962. The RV 9 – partly blasted out of the rock – now
follows the eastern shore of the Byglandsfjord with the 760m/2493ft-
high Årdalsfjell towering above. A Runic stone dating from 1100 in
front of the wooden church in **Årdal** (1827) is worth taking a look at.
300m/330yd south of the church stands a mighty 900-year-old oak
tree.
Bjoren Ship: July–early Aug daily 4pm; reservations/info via the Hotel
Revsnes, Byglandsfjord, tel. 37 93 46 50.

Rare minerals can be purchased at Evje, but also collected yourself

The road crosses the lake at the Storstraumen bru bridge and continues along the western shore. To the left, the Reiårsfossen waterfall descends. At the northern end of the lake some historic storage barns on stilts (»stabbur«) can be seen. Following the course of the Otra, the road leads around Rustfjell (1070m/3511ft) to the left and continues through a magnificent landscape to **Helle**, a traditional centre for the art of silversmithing in the Setesdal valley.

South of Nomeland, the RV 45 – known as the Suleskardveg here – winds its way up into the mountains, with its highest point at 1052m/3452ft (viewing point). It continues onwards into the **Sirdal** valley and ▶Stavanger. During the drive, the 15m/50ft Hallandsfoss can be seen to the left, with several deep potholes. **Valle** (307m/1007ft) is the main settlement in the valley, and has historic houses and a church from 1844. It is situated where the valley widens. The **Setesdal Museum** with old wooden houses can be reached on a side road (2km/1mi) that turns off by the Flateland farm, 9km/6mi beyond Valle.

Bykle The RV 9 route now travels high above the Otra, which cuts a ravine into the rock here, and continues to the old farming settlement of Bykle, not far east of Bossvatnet. The pretty interior of the 13th-century church was painted with acanthus vines in the 19th century. To the north of the church lies the Huldreheim Museum with wooden houses dating from the 16th century. There are signposted footpaths beginning in Bykle and leading into the mountainous surroundings, many of which are well worth the walk. To the north of Bykle, the valley becomes flatter, though the region takes on an increasingly mountainous character. The Otra is crossed once more at the Berdals bru bridge, where the road continues on the east side of the Hartevatnet lake.

Hovden Located in an attractive position at the mouth of the Otra into the Hartevatnet, Hovden is Setesdalen's most important winter sports resort and mountaineering centre (lifts). At the Hovden **Jernvinne Museum**, visitors are transported back to the time of the Vikings with special effects produced with lighting, sound and smoke. The museum is small but memorable. **Hovden Aqualand**, complete with water slide, sauna and solarium, is the right place to spend a rainy day or take a break (www.hovdenbadeland.no). The lakes of Lislevatn,

Breivatn and Sessvatn are situated along the road north of Hovden. The route reaches its highest point between Kristiansand and Hauke-ligrend here at 917m/3009ft. From Haukeligrend it is possible to drive to Haugesund on the ▶Haukeli Road.

Jernvinne Museum: July–mid-Aug daily 11am–5pm; free; www. setesdalsmuseet.no

Hovden Aqualand: changing opening times (see website); from 135 NOK; www.badeland.com

Sognefjord

✦ C/D 1-3

Region: West Norway

None is mightier: with a length of 204km/127mi and a depth of 1308m/4291ft, the Sognefjord is rightly known as the »King of Fjords«. The mild climate allows walnut and apricot trees to flourish along its northern flank, and famous resorts and cultural monuments, such as the country's oldest stave church, line its shores.

Only the northern shore of the Sognefjord can be reached by car, but there are numerous ferries that penetrate back into even the tiniest nooks of the fjord. Cruise ships sail from Bergen all the way to Ård-alstangen at the eastern end of the fjord. These ships stop off at all major settlements.

Cruises

Furthermore, there are several car ferries in operation: Rysjedalsvi-ka–Rutledal (on the outer Sognefjord, 30mins); Lavik–Oppedal (20mins); Nordeide–Måren–Ortnevik; Leikanger–Vangsnes–Bale-strand–Hella–Fjærland (tourist ferry during summer); Hella–Drags-vik / Vangsnes; Kaupanger–Gudvangen (2hrs 20mins); and finally between Mannheller (south of Kaupanger) and Fodnes (north of Lærdalsøyri).

Car ferries

WHAT TO SEE AT THE SOGNEFJORD

The Sognefjord begins to the west of **Rysjedalsvika** in the midst of numerous skerries and islets that were rubbed smooth by glacial ac-tion in the Ice Age. The environment changes very rapidly, as the rockfaces on either side of the fjord become ever higher and steeper. Lavik is the main centre for the western Sognefjord region and has a pretty magistrate's court dating from 1760, known as Alværen. Near-by is a mission centre with cheap accommodation. 15km/9mi further

Lavik

on, at the Breivik farm, the deepest point of the Sognefjord is reached (1308m/4291ft).

The romantic fjord resort of Balestrand is reached after driving through the 8km/5mi long Høyanger tunnel. It was already a popular holiday destination with English and German tourists at the end of the 19th century. Among its most famous guests were **Kaiser Wilhelm II**, who stayed several times at the magnificent **Kvikne's Hotel**, built in the Swiss style. The hotel festival hall still contains the chair in which the emperor sat in 1914. The resort's famous guest donated the statue of Bele, one time king of the Sogn fylke, that stands to the west of the small St Olav church founded by the English in 1897. The fjord is illustrated with models, films and exhibitions at the **Sognefjord Aquarium**. Relax at the Cafe Fløyfisken next door, where there are also rowing boats, canoes and fishing equipment for hire.

*Balestrand

Sognefjord Aquarium: main season daily 9.30am–5pm.

In order to visit the Hopperstad stave church in **Vik**, it is necessary to cross the fjord on the ferry from Dragsvik to Vangsnes. There is a beautiful dragon portal on the west side of the church dating from 1130. The pergola, roof structure and apse were reconstructed in the style of the ►Borgund stave church.

*Hopperstad stave church

A detour to the Fjærlandsfjord – an approximately 26km/16mi-long side arm of the Sognefjord – to the north of Balestrand, is highly recommended (cruise ship to Mundal). To the north of the idyllic fjord settlement of Fjærland, it is worth visiting the Suphellebreen and Bøyabreen glaciers, both arms of the large ►Jostedalsbreen. To the west of Suphellebreen, it is also possible to hike up to the Flatbrehytta, at a height of 1000m/3281ft. Sogndal to the southeast can be reached via the Fjærlandsvegen and the 7km/4mi-long Frudals tunnel, which passes underneath a glacier.

*Fjærlandsfjord

The RV 55 leads along the serpentine north shore through one of Norway's largest fruit-growing regions before reaching Leikanger and Hermansverk. Even while snow still lies on the mountains **in May, over 80,000 fruit trees flower** along the fjord shore. Due to the influence of the Gulf Stream, even walnuts, apricots and peaches ripen here during the short summer. No surprise then that Europe's most northerly research institute for fruit and berries is stationed in Hermansverk. 14 of the local fruit farms have joined together to become Norway's first »Fruit Route« that offers visitors the chance to sample fresh fruit and berries during harvest time, as well as to shop

Leikanger, Hermansverk

The journey through the Aurlandsfjord, a branch of the Sognefjord, counts as one of the most beautiful in all Norway

Sognefjord

INFORMATION
Sognefjord-Destination Sogndal & Luster
Pyramiden Kontorfellesskap
6868 Gaupne
tel. 97 60 04 43
www.sognefjord.no

WHERE TO EAT
Lindstrøm Hotel £ £ £ – £ £ £ £
Lærdalsøyri, tel. 57 66 69 00
The buffet in the main house of this hotel is particularly generous, especially the selection of cookies and cheese.

Quality Hotell Sogndal £ £
tel. 57 62 77 00
The main Compagniet restaurant serves mostly à la carte dishes; the Dr Hagen offers light meals and refreshments; and the Dolly Dimple has 20 pizzas on the menu

WHERE TO STAY
Kvikne's Hotel £ £ £ £
Balestrand, Balholm
tel. 57 69 42 00
www.kviknes.no, 200 rooms.
Fantastic: a meal or a nostalgic night in this magnificent building from 1894 standing directly on the shore of the fjord, with its own marina and bathing beach. The rooms in the extensions built in the 1960s are however rather disappointing. Wonderful fishing and boat tours are on offer here, as well as sightseeing flights by helicopter over Jostedalbreen.

Munthehuset £ £ £
Ytre Kroken, Skjolden
tel. 57 68 37 25

www.munthehuset.no, 6 rooms.
The Munthehuset lies on the south side of the Lustrafjord, on the way to the Urnes stave church. Accommodation is neither cheap nor luxurious, but the interior is worth seeing.

Skjolden Hotel £ £
Skjolden
tel. 57 68 23 80
www.skjolden.com/skjoldenhotel
55 rooms
Beautifully located hotel at the end of the Lustrafjord, with a well maintained park and very comfortable day rooms.

Balestrand Hotel £ £
Balestrand
tel. 57 69 11 38
www.balestrand.com, 30 rooms.
Quiet hotel on the fjord in the centre of Balestrand. Half the rooms face the fjord and have balconies. There are also panoramic views over the fjord from the hotel terrace.

Marifjøra Sjøbuer £ – £ £
Marifjøra, near Gaupne
tel. 57 68 74 05
www.rorbu.net
Four new, comfortable huts accommodating four people each are lined up directly on the shore of the fjord. Boats and fishing equipment for hire.

Flåm Vandrerhjem £
Flåm
tel. 57 63 21 21
www.hihostels.no
www.flaam-camping.no
This friendly family-run operation right on the Aurlandsfjord in Flåm offers visi-

tors cabins and camping, as well as hostel rooms. Hostelling International voted this business Norway's best youth hostel in 2011, 7th in Europe and 13th globally, from over 2000 accommodations bookable via Hostelling International – a high recommendation. April–Sep.

for homemade products in the local farm outlets. Many also provide accommodation and delicious meals. Ten rare trees, including a 16m/52ft-high walnut tree and a 23m/75ft-high sequoia tree planted in 1980, stand near the parish house and the pretty stone church of Leikanger dating from 1250.
Fruit Route: www.sognfruktrute.no

Sogndal is the largest economic and educational centre of the region, as well as a major transport hub (air strip). Near the old people's home stands an almost 2m/7ft-high runic stone from around 1100 on which is inscribed: »King Olav shot between these stones«.

Sogndal

About 10km/6mi to the southeast, directly on the fjord, lies Kaupanger, an important trading centre in the Middle Ages. The stave church here, dating from around 1185, is worth taking a look at. Even though it was later given windows and an extension, its interior is entirely authentic and includes high, mighty pillars connected by arches (restored in 1862). The remains of two even older churches were found underneath the present building, the oldest dating from 1000. Also worth a visit is **»De Heiberske Samlinger«**, the local Kaupanger museum, named after the teacher Heiberg whose collection formed its foundation. An **open-air museum** contains 30 buildings, including a medieval hut and a modern farmhouse from the 1980s. The museum also has displays of tools and machinery to do with ploughing, hunting, beer brewing and much more. The adjacent **Fjord Museum** near the ferry quay covers all topics on fjords, fishing and ferries.
Kaupanger stave church: June–Aug 10am–5.30pm; 50 NOK; www.stavechurch.com
Fjord Museum: May, Sep daily 10am–3pm, Aug till 5pm, otherwise Mon–Fri 10am–3pm; 70 NOK; www.dhs.museum.no

*Kaupanger

12km/8mi north of Sogndal there is a turning to Svolvorn. Directly below the Walaker Hotel built in 1690, with its own art gallery, a small ship sets off every hour for the ****Urnes stave church** (can also take a few cars). **Norway's oldest surviving stave church**, it was built on a spit of land on the east shore of the 45km/28mi-long Lustrafjord (11th century, ▶MARCO POLO Insight p.178). A climb of around 20mins is necessary to reach the church, whose northern

Wonderful carvings decorate the stave church at Urnes

portal, from 1060, is especially worth seeing: it features lions, dragons and snakes locked in battle, as well as a gorgeous pattern in the so-called Urnes style. Inside the church, which is on the **UNESCO World Heritage List**, the high pillars with their ornate cubiform capitals are especially noteworthy. The Urnes stave church can also be reached from **Skjolden**, located further in the interior of the picturesque Lustrafjord. Coming from that direction, the route follows the east shore and passes the 218m/715ft Feigunfoss waterfall.

❶ May–Sep 10.30am–5.30pm; 60 NOK; www.stavechurch.com

Eastern tip of the Sognefjord **Årdalstangen** lies at the extreme eastern tip of the Sognefjord, where there is a loading station for the Hydro Aluminium smelter located in **Øvre Årdal**, 11km/7mi further north (visits are possible during summer). North of Øvre Årdal extends the **Utladal valley**, from where it is possible to hike from Hjelle through the Vettisgjel ravine up to the Vettishytta and the spectacular 275m/902ft-high **Vettisfoss**. The waterfall is in a protected area. It is another 6hrs to the Skogadalsbøen hut and then a further 5hrs to the Fannaråkihytta near Fannaråki (▶Jotunheimen). The private road (toll payable) from Øvre Årdal to Turtagrø (▶Jotunheimen, Sognefjell) – open during summer only – is worth the trip for its wonderful viewing points and the ice fields alongside the route. Warning: not suitable for mobile homes and caravans.

**Aurlandsfjord Arrival in the Aurlandsfjord – a southern branch of the Sognefjord – on board the ferry from Kaupanger or on a cruise ship is one of the most impressive experiences to be had in the west Norwegian fjord country. In some places the mighty rockface rises vertically out of the water and reaches heights of up to 1500m/4921ft (▶photo p.374). Flåm (Voss surroundings) lies at the southern end of the Aurlandsfjord, from where there is a worthwhile detour to be taken to what is probably Scandinavia's smallest church in Undredal (Voss surroundings). The Aurlands river empties into the fjord at Aurlandsvangen, where one of Norway's large hydroelectric power stations is located (▶MARCO POLO Insight p. 380). It is comprised of five different sectors: Aurland I–III, as well as Reppa and Vangen. All in all, the station produces 1128 megawatt and the median annual production stands at 2869 gigawatt hours. Built in 1969, electricity production began in 1973. The construction was hotly debated at the time and, as a result, the dams, turbines and power cables were implemented according to ecological needs. The plant belongs to E-CO Energi.

The ferry from Kaupanger to Gudvangen (2hrs 20mins) branches off into the imposing Nærøyfjord (►Voss, surroundings and photo p. 442), which is one of the narrowest of the west Norwegian fjords, where the sun becomes invisible for months during winter. With a bit of luck, it is even possible to spot seals from the deck of the ferry. The Nærøyfjord, which is only 250m/820ft wide in some places and framed by almost vertical cliffs, has been on the UNESCO World Heritage List since 2005. A boat trip is breathtaking.

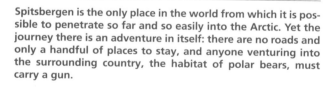

? MARCO ● POLO INSIGHT

Wittgenstein staid at the Lustrafjord

The Austrian philosopher Ludwig Wittgenstein had a cabin near the Lustrafjord. A memorial to the Cambridge scholar stands at a rest stop on the Eidsvatn, shortly after Skjolden, on the way into the Jotunheimen mountains. What remains of his cabin on the other side of the lake can be reached via an incompletely signposted footpath leading from the campsite at the eastern end of the Eidsvatn.

Spitsbergen · Svalbard

✳ C/D 1-3

Population: 2500
Area of the archipelago: 61,022 sq km/23,561 sq mi

Spitsbergen is the only place in the world from which it is possible to penetrate so far and so easily into the Arctic. Yet the journey there is an adventure in itself: there are no roads and only a handful of places to stay, and anyone venturing into the surrounding country, the habitat of polar bears, must carry a gun.

Svalbard, as the Norwegians call Spitsbergen, is just 1300km/8125mi from the North Pole, but the Gulf Stream ensures that the islands' waters are ice free from June to December. The arctic archipelago lies around 700km/440mi north of ►Nordkapp. With a total area of around 61,022 sq km/23,561 sq mi Svalbard is almost twice the size of Belgium, though only around 2500 people live here, spread over four settlements on the main island, Spitsbergen (37,673 sq km/14,546 sq mi), which is characterized by fjords that cut deeply into the land. To the northeast lies the glacier-covered Nordaustland (Nordaustland; 14,443 sq km/5576 sq mi), which is usually cut off by

Twice the size of Belgium

Green Energy

Norway is blessed with its energy resources: it owns half of Europe's entire hydropower capacity. Thanks to high levels of precipitation, the steep mountainsides by fjords, and uninhabited high plateaus, it is an ideal base for pumped storage power plants, which provide Norway with virtually all of its electrical power needs. Its oil and natural gas resources are therefore available for export.

▶ **Power resources in Norway**
In percentages
Hydropower has a long tradition in Norway. Where once the energy produced by water was generated by water mills and hammer mills, there are now hydro power stations producing electrical energy. Neither coal nor nuclear power stations are used.

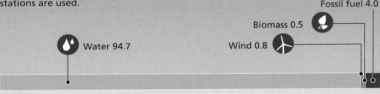

Fossil fuel 4.0
Biomass 0.5
Wind 0.8
Water 94.7

▶ **Mechanics of a hydropower station**
The water source into the upper basin, the drop ratio, and water flow onto the turbine are all key for the productivity of a hydropower station.

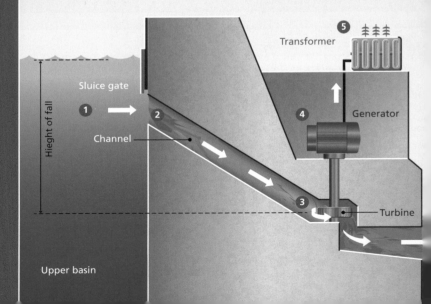

5 Transformer

Hieght of fall

Sluice gate

1

2

Channel

4 Generator

3

Turbine

Upper basin

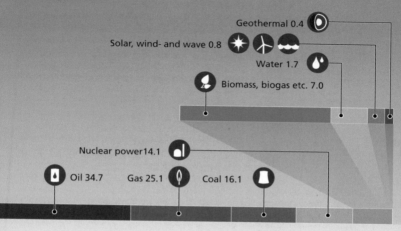

Power resources in the European Union
in percentages (2009)

Geothermal 0.4

Solar, wind- and wave 0.8

Water 1.7

Biomass, biogas etc. 7.0

Nuclear power 14.1

Oil 34.7   Gas 25.1   Coal 16.1

1. Water is gathered in the upper basin

2. When the sluice gate is opened, water flows at high speed and great pressure into the pressure channel

3. Water flows activate the turbine. The kinetic energy of the water is transformed into rotational energy

4. The turbine in its turn activates the generator that transforms the rotational energy into electricity

5. The transformer turns the generator power into high voltage for feeding into the high voltage power network

Norway's most productive hydro power stations

	Average annual production	Gross height of fall
●nstad	3650GWh	450m/1476ft
●illdal	2990GWh	338m/1109ft
●urland I–V	2869GWh	480m/1575ft (Aurland II)
●ma	2728GWh	1152m/3779ft (Lang-Sima)
●kke	2200GWh	394m/1293ft

Lower basin

©BAEDEKER

Spitsbergen

INFORMATION
Svalbard (Spitsbergen) Reiseliv
Postboks 323, 9171 Longyearbyen
tel. 79 02 55 50
www.svalbard.net

GETTING THERE
There are direct flights to Longyearbyen
three to four times a week from Tromsø
as well as from Oslo. Since 2008 the low
cost airline »Norwegian« (www.norwe-
gian.no) has been flying between Oslo
and Longyearbyen on Thur and Sun. Arrival by sea is only possible on private
vessels or cruise ships.

MIDNIGHT SUN
Midnight sun: 19 April–24 Aug. Polar
night: 27 Oct–15 Feb (Longyearbyen).

EVENT
April: Svalbard Skimarathon, (www.sval-
bardturn.no)

TOURS
Trekking, wilderness camps, husky or
snowmobile tours, guided walks with
snow shoes, and boat tours in the Isfjord
are offered in Longyearbyen, for example by:

Svalbard Villmarkssenter
tel. 79 02 17 00
www.svalbardvillmarkssenter.no

Spitsbergen Travel
tel. 79 02 61 00
www.spitsbergentravel.no

Svalbard Wildlife Service
tel. 79 02 22 22
www.wildlife.no

WHERE TO STAY
*Radisson BLU Polar Hotel
Spitsbergen* £ £ £ £
Longyearbyen.
tel. 79 02 34 50
www.radissonblu.com/hotel-spitsbergen,
95 rooms.
The world's most northerly hotel was
built in Lillehammer for the 1994 Olympic Winter Games; afterwards it was dismantled and rebuilt on the island of
Spitsbergen.

Gjestehuset 102 £ £
Longyearbyen, tel. 79 02 57 16
www.gjestehuset102.no, 31 rooms.
Simple guesthouse that used to house
miners.

the frozen pack ice of the Hinlopen Strait. To the southeast lie
Edgeøya (5074 sq km/1959 sq mi) and Barentsøya (1300 sq km/502
sq mi). To the far south lie the narrow long islands of Hopen and
Bjørnøya (Bear Island), with weather stations.

WHAT TO SEE IN SPITSBERGEN

Good plan-
ning required
In the meantime there are a handful of accommodations on the island, including the campsite by Longyearbyen airport, but there are
still **no roads** between settlements. Visitors need to be sufficiently

equipped to take care of themselves without outside help (including bringing items such as tents and sleeping bags). In particular **provisions for hiking tours** should be bought in advance, though it is a good idea to bring your own provisions in all cases. **Mobile phones** only work in Longyearbyen, Barentsburg and Svea. The importation of live **animals** is prohibited due to the risk posed by rabies. Every tour outside the settlements requires a **permit** and must be registered with the Governor of Spitsbergen. This includes tourists who wish to leave the Longyearbyen and Barentsburg area. In addition, every traveller is obliged to take out insurance against potential search and rescue costs. The governor has the right to issue restrictions or even ban tours, depending on individual circumstances, the travellers' level of experience, and the equipment taken. All those undertaking tours beyond the settlements are required to **carry guns**, because encounters with polar bears can happen any time. Weapons can be hired lo-

MARCO ⊕ POLO INSIGHT

? *Seedbank*

Seed samples from 25 international and Norwegian organizations have been kept in a protective seedbank in the permafrost on Svarlbad since February 2008. Layers of rock and ice are designed to protect the reserve's 4.5 million seeds from environmental disasters or epidemics, which was set up by the Norwegian government in conjunction with the Global Crop Diversity Trust (GCDT).

Cruise ships bring visitors to the icy world of Svarlbard in relative comfort

cally. Environmental protection legislation also allows **severe restrictions on shore leave** to be imposed on those travelling by cruise ship.

History   The Vikings reached the archipelago as early as 1194, sending back the message: »Svalbardi fundinn« (»the cold coast has been found«). The Dutch seafarer **Willem Barents** did not discover the group of islands until 1596, another 400 years later, when he named it »Spitsbergen» (Dutch for »jagged mountains«). Instead of the hoped-for trading route to China, he found a wealth of seals and whales living on the edge of the pack ice; shortly afterwards, in the extreme northwest, the **whaling settlement of Smeerenburg** (Transtadt) was founded. The whaling era went into decline after just a few decades,

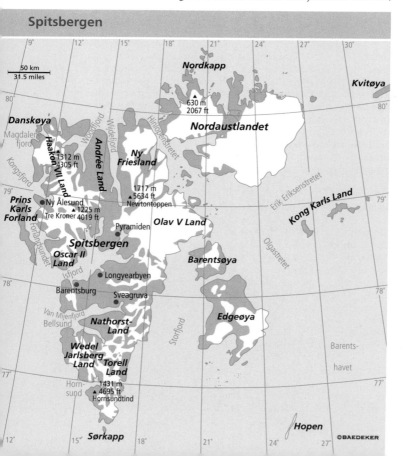

Spitsbergen

50 km
31.5 miles

Nordkapp

Kvitøya

630 m
2067 ft

Danskøya

Magdalene-
fjord

Nordaustlandet

Woodfjord

Wijdefjord

Hinlopenstretet

▲1312 m
4305 ft

Haakon VII Land

Andrée Land

Ny
Friesland

Kongsfjord

Erik Eriksenstretet

1717 m
▲5634 ft
Newtontoppen

Kong Karls Land

Prins
Karls
Forland

Ny Ålesund
▲1225 m
Tre Kroner 4019 ft

Forlandsundet

Pyramiden

Olav V Land

Olgastretet

Spitsbergen

Oscar II
Land

Barentsøya

Isfjord
● Longyearbyen

Barentsburg
Sveagruva

Van Mijenfjord
Bellsund

Nathorst-
Land

Storfjord

Edgeøya

Barents-
havet

Wedel
Jarlsberg
Land

Torell
Land

Horn-
sund

1431 m
▲4695 ft
Hornsundtind

Sørkapp

Hopen

©BAEDEKER

however, as the whales and seals were quickly hunted to extinction. Peace returned to Spitsbergen, and it was only Fridtjof Nansen's polar expeditions at the end of the 19th century that revived interest in the islands. The Norwegian seafarer Søren Zachariassen discovered **rich coal deposits** in 1899 and the first coal mine was duly established in 1906, founded by the American millionaire John M. Longyear. The attached settlement was given the name Longyear City. The Norwegian coal mining company of SNSK then took over the pits and settlement in 1916, and Longyear City became Longyearbyen (byen = place). The rich coal deposits threw up the unresolved question of territorial rights. In the end, the archipelago came under Norwegian sovereignty in 1925, but most of the pits were already closed by the time of the Great Depression. Remaining today are Longyearbyen (pop. 1800), the research station of Ny Ålesund (the world's most northern settlement), and the mining settlements of Svea Gruva (Norwegian) and Barentsburg (Russian).

Thanks to the Gulf Stream, Spitsbergen's average temperatures are substantially higher than those of comparable places, despite its arctic location. However, that does not mean the climate is comfortable! During winter temperatures sink to -8°C/18°F to -16°C/3°F. The record low lies at -49°C/–56°F, recorded in 1917. During July and August temperatures can rise to an average +5°C/41°F (the record high is +22°C/72°F). Frost and snow is possible throughout the year. Almost the entire east coast is covered by glaciers and there are only larger glacier-free zones in the central area. Thanks to the sea it is often foggy or cloudy, but **normally dry**.

Frosty climate

The arctic flora here encompasses 140 species: low growing flowering plants, ferns, mosses and lichen. The animal world is represented by more than 30 species of ocean birds, as well as seals, polar bears, reindeer and arctic fox. Polar bears have been protected since 1973 and their numbers have now reached several thousand. They predominantly inhabit the frozen east coast of Spitsbergen. Nevertheless, it is possible to encounter polar bears on the west coast as well. Hungry bears are very aggressive and often attack without warning – the obligatory weapon rule therefore makes perfect sense. Yet both weapons and the compulsory electronic alarms around campsites can fail, which is just what happened in August 2011, when a bear attacked a British youth expedition in the early hours of the morning, killing a 17-year-old boy and injuring several others.

Beware of the bear!

Almost half of Spitsbergen's environment is protected. Every step taken by a tourist on the permafrost destroys the fragile vegetation for a long period. In these cold temperatures, rubbish takes many years to decompose. In order not to disturb the fragile ecological bal-

Fragile nature

ance of the wilderness here, it is imperative to take all rubbish back home, including from multi-day boat tours.

Hornsund The tourist cruise ships usually only cover the west side of the Svalbard islands. They travel beyond Spitsbergen's Sørkapp (Southern Cape) and through the 15km/9mi Hornsund Fjord that is often thick with drift ice, even in summer. The coast is marked by the alpine summit of Hornsundtind (1431m/4695ft) and the mighty peaks of Sofiekammen (925m/3034ft).

*Isfjord Around 50km/31mi north of the wide Bellsund lies the 100km/62mi-long Isfjord with its several fjord tongues. The northern shore is partly covered in glaciers, but the southern shore features steep mountainsides plunging down towards the fjord. This is where the two main settlements are located: **Longyearbyen** on Advent Bay, and Barentsburg on the Grønfjord. The museum on Spitsbergen, run by the author Bolette Petri-Sutermeister in Longyearbyen, is recommended and will tell you all you need to know about the islands. The little Spitsbergen Airship Museum illustrates the story of the three airships that attempted to reach the North Pole. It is near the church, which is believed to be the most northerly place of Christian worship in the world.

Kongsfjord Those on a cruise along the west coast heading north will see the long, narrow island of Prins Karls Forland with its glacier-covered jagged mountain peaks (Monacofjell, 1084m/3557ft) as they sail up the Strait of Forlandsund. Heading around the northern tip, the Kongsfjord becomes visible, beyond which the pyramids of Tre Kroner (Three Crowns, 1225m/4019ft) tower above a 14km/9mi-long ice front.

Ny Ålesund On the southern shore lies the former mining settlement of Ny Ålesund, where the Ny Ålesund railway can be visited – a monument to the history of mining here. The locomotive dates from 1909, built by Borsig in Berlin. The settlement has the **world's most northerly post office** (special postmark) and a **research station**. This is also where the **landing mast for airships from the 1920s** still stands to this day, from which the Norwegian polar explorer Roald Amundsen (▶Famous People) set off with his airship »Norge« in 1926 (stone memorial). Two years later, the Italian Nobile's »Italia« crashed in the Spitsbergen pack ice and Amundsen disappeared during the rescue operation.

Krossfjord To the north of the Kongsfjord lie the Krossfjord and the Bay of Møller, where the Møller port is located. About 30km/19mi further north, seven icy rivers empty over steep cliffs into the sea. Even further north lies the Magdalenefjord, whose eastern end is formed by the 2km/1.2mi-wide and up to 100m/330ft-high edge of the Waggonway glacier. At the northwestern corner of Spitsbergen nearby, the island of Danskøya (»Island of the Danes«) rises out of the sea. During the 17th and 18th centuries both Danskøya and Amsterdamøya opposite had whaling stations.

* Stavanger

 A/B 2

Region: West Norway
Population: 129,200

Stavanger, Norway's oil boom town, is the most expensive city in the country. Nevertheless, it has many quiet and charming aspects, such as the historic town centre with its white-painted wooden houses. Visits to the Canning Museum and the Oil Museum are also very interesting. Stavanger was »European City of Culture« in 2008.

A picture-book façade hides Norway's most expensive city

Oil! Stavanger is Norway's fourth-largest city and capital of the county of Rogaland. The pretty town on the Byfjord experienced a massive upturn at the beginning of the 1970s, when oil was discovered in the North Sea off Stavanger's shore. In Norway the inhabitants of Stavanger – along with those from Bergen – are considered especially cosmopolitan, not least because of the American, French and British working for the oil companies, as well as the students at the various higher education establishments.

A bronze statue in honour of the poet Alexander Kielland (1849–1906), who was born in Stavanger, stands on the »Torget«, the fish and vegetable market. There are several dockyards in the harbour basin protected by outlying islands. The oil platforms built to service the oilfields of Tor, Ekofisk and Eldfisk, about 320km/200mi to the southwest of Stavanger, are located in the Gansfjord south of the city.

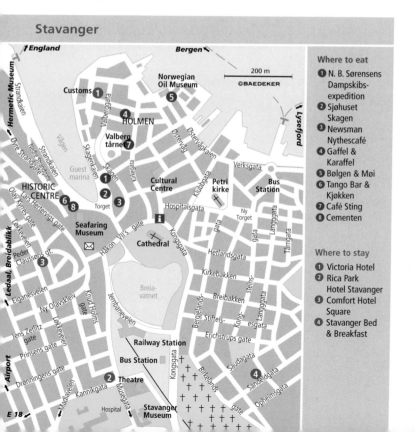

Stavanger

Where to eat
1. N. B. Sørensens Dampskibs-expedition
2. Sjøhuset Skagen
3. Newsman Nythescafé
4. Gaffel & Karaffel
5. Bølgen & Møi
6. Tango Bar & Kjøkken
7. Café Sting
8. Cementen

Where to stay
1. Victoria Hotel
2. Rica Park Hotel Stavanger
3. Comfort Hotel Square
4. Stavanger Bed & Breakfast

200 m
©BAEDEKER

Stavanger played a vital role in the history of the Norwegian empire: Harald Hårfagre (Harald Fairhair) vanquished the minor kings in a battle at the Hafrsfjord to the south of the city and thereby achieved the conditions that allowed Norway to be **united under one monarch** around 872. In memory of this event, **three oversized swords** were rammed into the rock at Harfrsfjord in 1983 (photo p.44). The artist Fritz Røed created the handles of the mighty Viking swords from sword finds discovered in different parts of the country; the crowns represent the Norwegian districts that were involved in the battle. The construction of the cathedral was begun in the year of the **city's foundation, in 1125**. Stavanger quickly developed into an important religious centre. After major herring shoals appeared off the coast in the 16th century, the city also became an important **fishing centre**. However, after the herring stayed away for extended periods and the city suffered several fires, the bishopric was transferred to Kristiansand in 1672. The herring returned at the beginning of the 19th century, and **Norway's first canning factory** was opened in Stavanger in 1873. The last sardine was canned in the 1950s.

History

WHAT TO SEE IN STAVANGER

The approximately 170 lovingly restored white painted wood houses complete with gas lanterns and attractively decorated windows and doors in the lanes of old Stavanger (on the west side of the Vågen harbour) recall the 18th and 19th century, when fishermen, craftsmen and seafarers lived here. Most of the houses on the Øvre Strandgate are listed buildings.

*Gamle Stavanger

Highlights Stavanger

► **Stavanger Domkirke**
One of Norway's most important medieval churches. The magnificent Gothic choir was built in 1272.
►page 391

► **Gamle Stavanger**
This idyll of white wooden houses, cobblestones and gas lanterns lies right on Vågen harbour, a lively district with historic buildings and many friendly bars.
►page 389

► **Oil Museum**
Lots of technology and detail about »black gold« and the oil boom
►page 391

► **Canning Museum**
Everything you always wanted to know about canning sardines
►page 391

► **Prekestolen**
»Pulpit Rock« rising 600m/1969ft out of the Lysefjord
►page 397

Stavanger Cathedral stands above Vågen harbour, on the small urban lake of Breivatnet, and is considered Norway's most important medieval sacred building next to Nidaros Cathedral in Trondheim. The church was designed at the end of the 11th century as a triple-aisled basilica in the Anglo-Norman style and built under Bishop Reinald of Winchester with the help of English craftsmen. Its patron saint was St Swithin. After a fire in 1272, a **magnificent choir** was built in the Gothic style. The rich **interior** dates from the Baroque era and the entire building was renovated in the 19th and 20th centuries. The finely carved pulpit (1658) and the stone baptismal font from Gothic times are worth taking a look at inside. The east window with scenes from the New Testament was designed by Victor Sparre in 1957.

*Stavanger Domkirke

> **! All about Sardines** *Insider Tip*
>
> MARCO⊕POLO TIP
>
> Everything there is to know about sardine canning, which was Stavanger's most important industrial sector until the Second World War, can be discovered at the Canning Museum (Hermetikkmuseet) in the old town at Øvre Strandgaten 88a. On Tuesdays and Thudays during summer, sprats are smoked here (www.museumstavanger.no).

The architecturally striking **Oil Museum** (Norsk Oljemuseum), opened in 1999 on the Kjerringholmen quay north of the city centre, is the place to discover everything about the oil boom in Norway and the creation of natural gas and oil. Children can operate machinery on the replica oil drilling platform or be »saved« by the rescue net. There is a 3D cinema, too and the museum is considered one of the country's best history museums.
❶June–Aug daily 10am–7pm, otherwise Mon–Sat 10am–4pm, Sun till 6pm; 100 NOK; www.norskolje.museum.no

Oil Museum

The Rogaland Museum of Fine Arts (part of the Stavanger Art Museum) near the Mosvannpark, to the southwest of the city centre, has an extensive collection of 2000 Norwegian paintings from 1900 to the present – though it exhibits only a certain number of them at any one time. The collection of the frequently huge landscape paintings by Stavanger artist Lars Hertervig (1830–1902) is unique.
❶ Mid-June–mid-Aug daily 10am–4pm, otherwise Tue–Sun 11am–4pm; www.museumstavanger.no

Stavanger Art Museum

A city stroll inevitably includes an encounter with the London artist **Antony Gormley's** Broken Column permanent installation. It consists of 23 iron statues placed throughout the city, all 1.95m/6ft4in tall and all exact portraits of himself. The first stands by the Art Museum,

Broken Column

Unusual: the Oil Museum in Stavanger

Stavanger

INFORMATION
Destinasjon Stavanger
Domkirkeplassen 3, 4006 Stavanger
tel. 51 85 92 00
www.regionstavanger.com

MUSEUM PASS
If several museums belonging to Stanvanger Museum are to be visited on the same day, a single entry Museum Pass can be purchased for 80 NOK.

ENTERTAINMENT
Those looking for nightlife stream into the Vågen guest harbour and the quarter that adjoins it to the east, where there are any number of bars and restaurants

EVENTS
January: national and international jazz (www.tradjazzweekend.no).
End of July: Gourmet festival (Gladmatfestivalen, http://gladmatavis.no).

WHERE TO EAT
❹ Gaffel & Karaffel £ £ £
Øvre Holmegate 20
tel. 51 86 41 58
www.gaffelogkaraffel.no
Exquisite cuisine in an old townhouse, with an arty champagne bar in the cellar.

❶ N.B. Sørensens Dampskibsexpedition £ £ £
Skagen 26, tel. 51 84 38 20
www.herlige-restauranter.no
Gourmets dine in the »Directionen« on the first floor. More affordable meals are available in the Dampskibsekspeditionen restaurant on the ground floor.

❻ Tango Bar & Kjøkken £ £ – £ £ £
Nedre Strandgate 25, tel. 51 50 12 30
www.tango-bk.no
New dinner menu daily, with a cheaper and equally delicious champagne lunch menu. Closed Sundays.

❷ Sjøhuset Skagen £ £ – £ £ £
Skagenkaien 16, tel. 51 89 51 80
www.sjohusetskagen.no
The maritime interior is entirely appropriate for this old house from 1770 where excellent meals are served. Lunch dishes such as bacalao or bouillabaisse are good value. On Sundays between 2pm and 7pm there is an affordable family menu.

❺ Bølgen & Møi £ £
Kjerringholmen (in the Oil Museum)
tel. 51 93 93 51, www.bolgenogmoi.no
The snacks and delicious cheesecake made by master chef Trond Moi can be enjoyed with a fantastic view onto the harbour at the museum café. In the evening the prices are higher with a menu for the gourmet.

❸ Newsman Nyhetscafé £
Skagen 14, tel. 51 84 38 80
This is a good place for a relaxing read of the Norwegian and foreign newspapers that are provided along with the coffee or a glass of beer. Light snacks from noon until the late evening.

❼ Café Sting £
Valberget 3, tel. 51 89 38 78
www.cafe-sting.no
A cozy inn with tasty Norwegian and international snacks; also has a stage for music events and readings..

❽ Cementen £
Nedre Strandgt. 25, tel. 51 53 41 77
www.cementen.no
A bar for bookworms with collector's
posters on the walls. The live events club
opens around 11pm.

WHERE TO STAY
**❷ Rica Park Hotel Stavanger
££££**
Prestegårdsbakken 1
tel. 51 50 05 00
www.rica-hotels.no
The Rica Park is a first-class, centrally located hotel suitable for business visitors
and families. Voted Norway's best hotel
by Travellers' Choice Awards in 2012; the
rooms are spacious and the service is just
what any visitor would ideally hope for.

❸ Comfort Hotel Square ££££
Løkkeveien 41
tel. 51 56 80 00
www.nordicchoicehotels.no, 194 rooms.

Voted Norway's trendiest hotel, this very
comfortable new hotel in the city centre
boasts street art, modern design and
glowing colours.

❶ Victoria Hotel £££
Skansegt. 1
tel. 51 86 70 00
Fax 51 86 70 10
www.victoria-hotel.no
Venerable hotel in an ideal location,
completely modernized. Rooms are elegant and welcoming and there are value for money weekend prices. The restaurant serves juicy steaks from the grill.

❹ Stavanger Bed & Breakfast ££
Vikedalsgt. 1a
tel. 51 56 25 00
www.stavangerbedandbreakfast.no
22 rooms.
This simple small pension is centrally located and offers fresh waffles every
evening, included in the price.

41m/134ft above sea level. Every additional sculpture is located precisely 1.95m/6ft 4 inches lower down, the last being on the Natvigs
Minde skerry at the entrance to the harbour, partly submerged. Some
are found in rather strange places, such as the municipal swimming
pool, a petrol station, a car park and a small shop.

The Stavanger Museum is on Muségata and contains collections on   Stavanger
natural history and ethnology. The Norwegian Children's Museum in   Museum
the Kulturhus (Sølvberget) covers child cultures and the history of
childhood, with an appealing sector in the adjacent park containing
historic children's games. Meanwhile, the Maritime Museum over on
Nedre Strandgata 17–19, in the historic town centre, illustrates the
200-year maritime history of Stavanger.
Stavanger Museum: mid-June–mid-Aug daily, otherwise only Tue–Sun
11am–4pm; 60 NOK; www.museumstavanger.no
Norwegian Children's Museum: Tue–Sun, during school holidays incl.
Mon 11am–4pm; 60 NOK; www.museumstavanger.no
Stavanger Maritime Museum: Tue–Sun 11am–4pm; 60 NOK;
www.museumstavanger.no

Arkeologisk Museum	Museum of Archaeology Exhibits from 15,000 years of natural and cultural history are shown in the University of Stavanger's **Museum of Archaeology** on Peder Klows gate 30A. ● June–Aug Mon–Fri 10am–7pm, Sat–Sun 11am–5pm, otherwise Tue 11am–8pm, Wed–Sat till 3pm, Sun till 4pm; 50 NOK; http://am.uis.no
Ledaal	The aristocratic Kielland family's Ledaal residence built in the Empire style in 1799 stands at Eiganesveien 45. Today it is the royal residence when the family is in Stavanger. The library on the first floor is in honour of the writer Alexander Kielland who featured Ledaal in his novels as »Sandsgård«.

AROUND STAVANGER

*Beautiful views	The most beautiful view onto the city is offered by the 85m/279ft-high **Vålandshaug** at the southern edge of town, reached via Hornklovesgate. A wonderful view across Stavanger can also be enjoyed from the **Ullandshaug tower** located to the southwest in the municipal forest of Sørmarka; the view from the tower also takes in the flat Jæren landscape, the sea to the southwest, the mountainous Ryfylke region, the Boknafjord in the northeast and the Gansfjord in the east.

! *White sandy beaches...* Insider Tip

MARCO ⊕ POLO TIP

... just like those in southern Europe can be found in the region known as Jæren to the south of Stavanger. Solstranden by the airport, Hellestøstranden 30km/19mi southwest of Stavanger and Orresanden on the Jæren outcrop are among Norway's most beautiful beaches. The information centre by the car park at Orresanden provides information on the efforts to preserve the unique dune landscape from the wind and the weather.

Not far to the west of the tower, the **Iron Age** (AD 350–550) **Jernaldergarden farm** (managed by the Museum of Archaeology) has been reconstructed on its original site, the only such place in Norway. Next door are the remains of a Stone Age settlement, as well as Bronze Age and Viking graves.
Jernaldergarden Farm: mid-June–mid-Aug daily 11am–4pm, end of May–mid-June and mid-Aug–Sep Sun only; bus X60; 50 NOK; www.jernaldergarden.no

Kongeparken leisure park	Kongeparken lies on the E 39 by Ålgård, about 30km/19mi south of Stavanger and includes a miniature car town, a mountain bike track, bob trail, aviary park and horse-riding. ● Mid-April–mid-Sep daily 10am–6pm; from 260 NOK; www.kongeparken.no
Aviation museum	The history of Norwegian aviation since the Second World War is covered by the Aviation Museum near Stavanger Airport, at Sola.

Among other exhibits, it includes 35 historic military and civilian aircraft, models and photos. The building belongs to the regional Jærmuseet.

❶ End of June–mid-Aug Tue–Sun noon–4pm, beginning of May–end of June and end of Aug–end of Nov Sundays only; 70 NOK; www.flymuseum-sola.no

How much does a human brain weigh– Close-up views of Orion, Pegasus and other constellations– All this and more is presented at the Science Factory (Vitenfabrikken) in Sandnes, which is also part of the Regional Jærmuseet. Exhibitions, films, workshops and theatre all serve to make science fun for the whole family in this, Europe's best Technology Museum, according to the 2009 Micheletti Awards.

Sandnes Science Factory

❶ Tue–Fri 10am–3pm, Thu till 8pm, school holidays till 4pm, Sat 11am–4pm, Sun noon–5pm; 100 NOK; www.jærmuseet.no

The island of Mosterøy can be reached from Stavanger via the almost 6km/4mi-long Byfjordtunnel which, at 223m/732ft below sea level, is the deepest underwater tunnel in the world, constructed 45m/148ft underneath the seabed. A ferry also makes the crossing between Stavanger and the Utstein monastery on the island. Since there are hardly any parking spaces in the near vicinity of the monastery, it is best to park the car 1km/0.6mi away and cover the final stretch – through beautiful countryside – on foot. The Augustinian monastery of Utstein was first mentioned in the 13th century and is the best preserved of its kind in Norway. The setting is lovely: high trees and gentle hills with sheep grazing on meadows embraced by the blue sea. During summer, concerts are held behind the monastery's thick stone walls and it also functions as a hotel.

Utstein Monastery

❶ Reservations: tel. 51 72 00 50; monastery opening times: mid-May–mid-Sep Tue–Sat 10am–4pm, Sun noon–5pm, March–mid-May, mid-Sep–Nov Sun noon–5pm; 60 NOK; www.utstein-kloster.no

Hå Gamle Prestegård (Old Vicarage; 1637), one of the most popular excursion destinations around Stavanger, stands right by the open sea near a large Iron Age burial site. There is a small museum, a gallery and a friendly café.

Hå Gamle Prestegård

❶ Mid-May–Aug Mon–Fri 11am–5pm, otherwise till 3pm, Sat–Sun noon–5pm; 60 NOK; www.hagamleprestegard.no

There are four lighthouses in Jæren that are partially still in operation (Friluftsfyret Kvassheim, Obrestad Fyr, Feistein Fyr and Tungenes Fyr) and worth a visit; facilities include cafés, exhibitions and even accommodation, so exploring the coast by car or bicycle is an attractive option. Ryfylke Country Route Another option for discovering the best of Norwegian countryside and rural architecture beyond the main highways is to travel along one of the designated national coun-

Lighthouses

tryside routes (»Nasjonale Turistveger«). They include attractive viewpoints and rest areas and are also suitable for cycle touring, for those with more time. The 183km/114mi Ryfylke Country Route begins south of Stavanger at Oanes, following the coast and leading around lakes until reaching Hårå. The route takes visitors through sweeping agricultural landscapes where the stone walls are listed as cultural heritage, even while they continue to serve their age old practical purpose. The landscape of this panoramic trail includes everything from gentle gardens and fertile regions to rough scree slopes, vertical cliff faces and deep fjords and includes highlights, such as the Lysefjord with its Prekestolen rockface, the Ryfylke Museum in Sand, and the waterfall at Svandalsfossen. Visitors can enjoy this waterfall that drops down the mountain over several ledges close-up, thanks to a dramatic stepped footpath. Additional modern architectural features are planned, including an exhibition space at the former zinc mine in the Allamannajuvet Gorge.

❶ www.nasjonaleturistveger.no

Beyond the Hågsfjord, the Lysefjord, located east of Stavanger (cruise ship from Stavanger), extends 37km/23mi inland: an up to 2km/1mi-wide and 457m/1499ft-deep gash penetrating the mountains. The fjord, of a light green hue, is enclosed by steep, bare walls of rock on both sides that tower up to over 1000m/3281ft high.

*Lysefjord

Prekestolen (**Pulpit Rock**) is a cliff rising almost 600m/1969ft vertically out of the Lysefjord and is without doubt one of the most beautiful and impressive destinations in Norway. Those who suffer from vertigo should on no account venture onto this platform above the abyss that was created by a frost break around 10,000 years ago. The Prekestolen can be reached from Stavanger via the RV 13 as far as Lauvvik on the Hågsfjord, from where the ferry departs for Jøssang. At Jøssang a road branches right for the Prekestolhytta, from which the cliff can be reached in about two hours on foot (good walking shoes required). There are several narrow stretches. The Norwegian tour company Fjord Tours is the first to offer day trips to the Prekestolen entitled »Lysefjord in a Nutshell«. A bus sets off from Stavanger, followed by a stop at the 1000m/3281ft high Ørneredet viewpoint (Eagle's Nest), before continuing to Lysebotn, where a boat is taken over the Lysefjord to see the Prekestolen. The return journey to Stavanger is by bus from Lauvvik.

**Preke-stolen

❶ www.norwaynutshell.com

One of the most breathtaking experiences for drivers in Norway is the route near **Lysebotn** with 27 hairpin bends. Southwest of Lyse-

Lysebotn

For the vertigo-free only: the Prekestolen 600m/1969ft abyss

botn, the **Kjerag** cliff towers 1000m/3281ft into the sky, a popular destination for base jumpers (the riskier version of sky diving). The car park is near Øygardstøl (the challenging mountain tour takes approx. 5hrs there and back).

Sunndalen

✳ E 5/6 ●

Region: Mid and West Norway

The romantic Sunndalen valley with the river Driva flowing through it begins at the winter sports resort of Oppdal and extends west all the way to the industrial town of Sunndalsøra. The adjacent mountains are extremely beautiful areas for hiking, especially the Trollheimen mountains to the north.

The salmon's decline   The Driva was once one of the best salmon rivers in Norway, but the legendary salmon stocks were destroyed by a parasite. Attempts are being made at present to reintroduce the fish with newly bred stock. Those who wish to benefit from the fruits of that labour need a fishing permit.

Casting out on the Sunndal valley, popular for its salmon

WHAT TO SEE IN THE SUNNDALEN VALLEY

The RV 70 leads from **Oppdal** down the valley of the Driva, past a burial site from Viking times, to Oppdal church (1651), whose pointed spire can be seen from quite a distance away. The interior of this pretty church with old paintings dates from the 17th and 18th century. A road branches off to the Gjevilvasshytta, a listed building, located 22km/14mi away near **Vognill**. It stands on the northern shore of the Gjevilvatnet at an elevation of 700m/2297ft. From here, it is possible to reach the Trollheimshytta to the northwest in 8–9hrs on foot. The mountains of Trollhetta

Sunndalen

INFORMATION
Sunndal Aktivum
Mongstugata 2
6600 Sunndalsøra
tel. 71 68 99 80
www.sunndal.com

WHERE TO STAY
Sunndalsfjord Camping £ £
On RV 62 between Sunndalsøra and
Eidsvåg
tel. 71 23 31 12
www.hut.no
On offer are two large and comfortable cabins right on the fjord with
pleasant interiors. Ideal for fishermen.
There is also a small campsite on the
property.

(1614m/5295ft; 7–8hrs there and back with a guide) and Snota
(1668m/5473ft) can be climbed from there – these are the highest
summits of the Trollheimen mountains (reached in 8–9hrs there and
back with a guide).

The old Gravaune farm has an interesting collection of old tools and   Gravaune
weapons. Near the Lønset Handel a footpath branches off for the   farm
Storfallet waterfall in Lønset. The **Storlidal** valley is also beautiful.
There are several places to stay the night along the route leading
north from Lønset, including the Storli farm that makes a good starting point for hikes into the Trollheimen.

After crossing the county border the winding path continues down-   Detour into
wards (viewing points) to Gjøra. To the left, a side road leads through   the Grøvudal
the Jenstadjuvet ravine with the impressive 156m/512ft-high Svøu-   Valley
foss waterfall cascading into the Grøvudal valley, a beautiful hiking
region with catered huts and interesting flora. From Romfo to the
Sunndalfjord The octagonal **Romfo church** (1820) has a beautiful
carved altar panel and a medieval sculpture of St Olav, and to the west
of it lies the Driva Power Station, inside the mountain. The villages of
Fale and Grøa are popular bases with salmon fishermen. An exhibition on the first English salmon fishermen who lived in the Elverøy
House in the 19th century can be visited in the Sunndal
Bygdemuseum, located 400m/438yd away from **Elvererhøy** bridge.
Next to the school there is a large burial site dating from the Ice Age.

Sunndalsøra lies at the end of the Sunndalfjord, surrounded by snow-   Sunndalsøra
covered mountains. The large Aura Power Station and an aluminium
works – the largest industrial employment centre in the county of
Møre og Romsdal – are of economic importance.

*Aursjøen Lake Aursjøen located approximately 39km/24mi south of Sunndalsøra (first 2km/1.2mi in the direction of Molde and then turning due south) is reached via the steep cliffs of the Litledal and then the Torbudal valley, whose highest point lies at 900m/2953ft. The Aursjøhytta is here, along with one of Norway's largest dams.

✳ Telemark

—————————————————— ✳ B 5/6

Region: South Norway

The birthplace of modern skiing is in the county of Telemark, where the »Telemark turn« was invented. Today, there are excellent ski resorts here. Those who visit during summer quickly discover that the forested central highlands have far more to offer than a trip on the Telemark canal.

Hustle and bustle or relaxation Telemark covers a great area: the county stretches from the Skagerrak Sea to the south up to the south Norwegian highlands. There are numerous holiday cabins and pretty coastal towns with white-painted wooden houses along the jagged coast with idyllic **skerries**. During summer, Telemark's **marinas** are often overrun. Those looking for peace and relaxation find it in the mostly hilly forested landscape of the interior, as well as by hiking on the barren highland plateau of Hardangervidda to the north, with its crystal clear **mountain lakes** and streams.

WHAT TO SEE IN TELEMARK

Skien The capital of the county of Telemark and a lively industrial town, Skien (pop. 52,500) calls itself the »Ibsen town« because this is where Henrik Ibsen (▶Famous People) was born in 1828, at StockmannsGården on the Torget. The building no longer exists, as it was destroyed in the town's large 1886 fire. Seven years later, the family moved to Venstøp farm (museum 5km/3mi north of Skien) with its famous loft that inspired the setting for the play Wild Duck. Finally, the Ibsen family moved to the Snipetorpgate (IbsenGården) quarter, with its pretty 18th-century wooden houses. There is also more to discover about the famous playwright in the **Telemark Fylkesmuseum**, which is the local museum set in the English garden style Brekkepark to the east of the town centre (restaurant and summer theatre). The open-air section of the museum contains several historic Telemark farms.

Telemark

INFORMATION
Telemarkreiser
Nedre Hjellegate 18
3724 Skien
tel. 35 90 00 20
www.visittelemark.com

WHERE TO STAY
Hotel Dalen £ £ £ £
Dalen (near the Bø Sommarland leisure park)
tel. 35 07 70 00
www.dalenhotel.no, 76 rooms.
This hotel is an architectural jewel on the Telemark canal. The Swiss, Dragon and Romantic style combine in perfect symbiosis in this wooden palace – it is no surprise that several royals have stayed here. Even those who don't stay the night should at least indulge in tea and cake on the terrace, with its panoramic view of the extensive park.

Gaustablikk Høyfjellshotell £ £ £
Rjukan
tel. 35 09 14 22
www.gaustablikk.no, 91 rooms.
The modern and spacious mountain hotel built in wood in the Norwegian style lies at the foot of Gaustastoppen and includes a swimming pool, saunas, tennis courts and a large sun terrace. Skiing region nearby.

Quality Lifjell Hotel £ £ £
Bø i Telemark
Lifjellvegen 375
tel. 35 95 33 00
www.lifjellhotel.no, 150 rooms.
This very comfortable family hotel with indoor and outdoor swimming pool lies very centrally in the Telemark region. Nice tours to the Telemark canal and the Heddal stave church can be made from here.

Tuddal Høyfjellshotell £ £ £
Tuddal
tel. 35 02 88 88
www.tuddal.no, 23 rooms.
Hotel with a century of tradition. Elsa and Rune Gurholt ensure personal service and make good use of the historic furniture and antiques. Traditional Norwegian cuisine is served in the restaurant.

Sandviken Camping £ – £ £
Tinn Austbygd
tel. 35 09 81 73
www.sandviken-camping.no
Small campsite with a familial atmosphere on the northern shore of the Tinnsjø, containing 12 simple huts, some of which are right on the sandy beach with views onto the lake.

Without doubt one of Telemark's finest attractions is a journey on the 110km/69mi-long Telemark Canal, also known as the Bandak Norsjø Canal. During summer, one of the historic motorboats, either the Victoria (1882), the Henrik Ibsen, (1907) or the Telemarken, departs Skien each morning at 8.30am, arriving in the evening at the small settlement of **Dalen**, 110km/69mi away. Dalen is located on the west side of the Lake Bandak and surrounded by steep mountains up to 700m/2297ft high. The boat then quietly glides over Lake Norsjø to

*Telemark Canal

Telemark Skiing and Slalom

Telemark skiing played an important role in the development of skiing. Sondre Norheim, the father of modern skiing, first demonstrated how you could make elegant turns down the mountainside with a heel binding on skis, in Christiania (Oslo), in 1868. In the meantime, the inhabitants of Morgedal had also discovered that skis could be used to jump over small ramps.

In fact, these developments were 4000 years in the making, since the people of Scandinavia, where plentiful snow cover often stays for a long time, were forced to construct travelling aids for getting through the snow to pursue their hunting way of life. Various archaeological finds in moors and on rock paintings indicate that oval and long stepping aides were made of woven birch, birch rind or planks of wood. The word »skid« for describing these winter travelling aides grew from the old Nordic expression for wood plank or board. Linguistic research has unearthed that snow shoes were brought to Europe by Finns and Sami People coming from their original Asian homelands.

Kings on Boards

Skiing is mentioned in the very earliest written records. For example, both Kings Olav Trygvasson and Harald Hårdrade (11th and 12th century) are praised for being good skiers. The Telemark turning technique proved to be positively

Fun in the snow

amazing. Talented skiers were now able to swing down the mountainsides and negotiate tight slalom curves at high speed. The breakthrough for skiing to become a popular sport received its main impetus from the two polar explorers Fridtjof Nansen and Roald Amundsen. Nansen, who considered skiing the best of sports, traversed Greenland on skis in 1888, while Roald Amundsen reached the South Pole on skis, in 1911.

Trendsetting Telemark

Important centres of Nordic skiing soon evolved in the Telemark region, where an early skiing industry was established, and also in the mountains around Oslo and Lillehammer, as well as in the Gudbrandsdal area. The top Norwegian skiing mountain is the Holmenkollen, one of the venues for the Winter Olympics. In 1994, world class skiers attended the 17th Winter Olympic competitions in Lillehammer. Spreading out from Norway, the »new« winter sport of skiing quickly caught on elsewhere and the first skiers were already enjoying themselves in the southern Black Forest and in the Alps around Arlberg, as early as the 1890s. Norwegian immigrants also brought skiing to North America and were instrumental in the foundation of ski resorts such as Lake Placid, Aspen and Vail. Typically Nordic disciplines are cross-country skiing, slalom (»slalåm« = track on the mountain) and ski jumping over a ramp. Cross-country skiing (or Nordic skiing) and ski jumping together form the Nordic Combined sports discipline.

The telemark turn is a Norwegian invention

Ulefoss, where the striking blue dome of the small Empire castle of **Ulefoss HerreGård** (1807), Norway's seminal example of Napoleonic architecture and open to the public, stands on the north side of the Eidselva. In the immediate vicinity lie the 11m/36ft-high **Ulefoss locks**. The most impressive lock, the Vrangfoss sluser, actually contains a total of six chambers. While the boat surmounts a height difference of 23m/75ft, passengers can disembark and take photographs from the steps or the bridge over the canal. From **Lunde**, passengers can either return to Skien by bus or on another boat. Alternatively they can slowly chug across the lakes of Flåvatn, Kviteseidvatn and Bandak. At the northern shore, near Dalen, a road winds up to the 13th-century **Eidsborg stave church** (small open-air museum nearby). The west portal displays glorious vine ornamentation and capitals with standing lions.

! *Adrenalin rush* Insider Tip

MARCO POLO TIP

The quickest way from Dalen to Åmot is via route 38, but a small detour on a partially unpaved road running parallel leads to the Ravnejuvet Gorge, which is worth seeing. A panoramic view over the whole valley opens up after following a short footpath, and it is also possible to take a careful look over the cliff.

❶ Tours: Telemarkreiser, tel. 35 90 00 20; www.telemarkreiser.no

Bø Sommarland
There's fun in the water for children and adults alike at theBø Sommarland aqua park near Bø. The park has developed into one of Telemark's major attractions and offers more than 20 different water activities for young and old – including a giant waterslide, the largest artificial surf wave in the world, and Europe's largest water helter skelter.

❶ mid-June–mid-Aug daily 10am–5pm/7pm; 359 NOK (high season); www.sommarland.no

**Heddal stave church
The stave church at Heddal (Hitterdal) to the west of the small industrial town of Notodden, 50km/31mi north of Skien on the E 134, dates from the 12th and 13th century. It was reconstructed in 1849–51, and has been restored several times, but it is the largest surviving stave church in Norway (▶MARCO POLO Insight, p.406).

❶ mid-June–mid-Aug daily 9am–6pm, mid-May–mid-June and mid-Aug–mid-Sep daily 10am–5pm; 60 NOK; www.heddalstavkirke.no

*Gaustatoppen
About 16km/10mi west of Heddal stave church, a road turns off to the north into the romantic Tuddalsdal valley and on to Rjukan. Beyond **Tuddal** with its pretty wooden church (1796), the occasionally steep road winds its way up to the 1275m/4183ft pass, with wonderful views along the way, and onwards to the foot of the mighty Gaustatoppen (hiking and skiing region) that, at 1883m/6178ft, is the highest summit south of the Bergen railway. From the car park right next to the

road a marked footpath leads almost as far as the summit, from which there is an awe-inspiring **view over Hardangervidda**. An easier and more spectacular option is to take the Gausta train to the summit, travelling via the shaft built into the mountain. Originally for military purposes, it now serves to transport visitors from the base station at the Rjukan Ski Centre to the summit, in 15 minutes flat.

❶ Return ticket: 350 NOK; www.gaustabanen.no

Directly below Gaustatoppen, the industrial town of Rjukan (pop. 7500) lies in a deep and long valley whose inhabitants have to make do without sun for several months a year. Rjukan was designed and built at the beginning of the 20th century, when the large Vemork hydroelectric power station and the sodium nitrate factory were built in 1911. The »Krossobanen« cable car leads up into the mountains from the town centre. Norway's first cable car was built in 1928 by Norsk Hydro so that workers could enjoy sun and fresh air at the weekends. A popular cycle touring route to the Kalhovd mountain cabin begins at the top of the Krossobanen line. The return to Rjukan is by bicycle or by bus (information and cycle hire from the tourist office).

Rjukan

> **MARCO POLO INSIGHT**
>
> *Long wooden staircase*
>
> The power station by Mår near Rjukan contains the world's longest wooden staircase. You have to be quite fit to make the descent down the 3975 steps leading to the ventilation chambers from the electricity hall.

The Mår power station 5km/3mi east of town (Dale junction), whose construction was begun by the Germans during the Second World War, produces 1 billion kWh annually and has three dams. There are beautiful hiking and skiing regions around Lake Møsvatn above Rjukan and in the area around Rauland (RV 37). Rjukan became notorious during the **Second World War** when the Germans showed a special interest in the deuterium oxide (heavy water) that was being produced there. Several sabotage efforts were carried out by the Allies – among others, the sinking of the Hydro ferry on Lake Tinnsjøen that was loaded with heavy water, so as to prevent the valuable water reaching Germany for the production of atomic bombs. More about the battle for the heavy water can be found along the **Sabotage Trail** and in the nearby **Norwegian Industrial Workers' Museum** (incl. old BBC films) housed in the Vemorker hydroelectric power station, which was the world's largest of its kind at the beginning of the 20th century. The mighty interior with its giant turbines is impressive.

Mår power station

Krossobanen line: www.krossobanen.no

Norwegian Industrial Workers Museum: mid-June–mid-Aug daily 10am–6pm, May–mid-June and mid-Aug–Sep daily 10am–4pm, Oct–April Tue–Fri noon–3pm, Sat–Sun 11am–4pm; 80 NOK; www.visitvemork.com.

A Masterpiece of Wood Architecture

Heddal church – the »cathedral« of Norwegian stave churches – stands right next to the E 134, to the west of Kongsberg and Notodden. Building began in 1147, and the church was dedicated to the Blessed Virgin Mary in 1241. The pillar stave church with its striking three-tier roof is a masterpiece of wood architecture.

ⓘ ▶p.404

❶ Nave

Heddal is Norway's largest stave church: built of pine, it is 24m/79ft long, 14m/46ft wide, and 26m/85ft high Stave churches are not stone churches in wood, but an original form with a mighty central area which is presumed to recall Nordic royal halls. The interior of Heddal contains, among other things, a carved 12th-century bishop's throne with scenes from the Sigurd Saga. Sigurd and King Gunnar set off to bring the Nibelungen Ring to Brunhild. The altar by an unknown artist is from 1667.Renovation works in the 19th century changed parts of the building. This was revised in the 1950s and 1960s in order to restore the mediaeval character of the church

❷ The »staves«

A frame of square planks lies on a square stone foundation, on which staves (»stav« in Norwegian), vertical masts or posts, were erected. At the base they are set in the wooden frame and at the top they are held in place by an additional square frame that also carries the gable. This perfect wooden construction has survived 850 years.

❸ St Andrew's Crosses

The diagonal St Andrew's Crosses are typical of stave churches. Fixed at the height of the first roof section, they ensure additional stability..

❹ Sval gallery

A roofed gallery runs around the church (»svalgang«), where men once had to leave their weapons before attending religious services.

❺ Roof shingles

Scale-like overlapping shingles cover the five roof tiers. Half of the shingles at Heddal were replaced between 1998 and 2004. Handmade shingles based on the medieval model were used. In addition, the church needs tarring at regular intervals to preserve its ability to withstand the weather. As scaffolding is not allowed to be fixed to the church, mountaineers do that job.

❻ Church spires

Like the roof, Heddal's spires are also on several levels. The towers are empty, as the bell tower stands apart from the church.

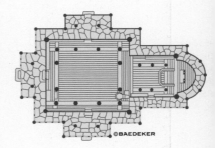

©BAEDEKER

Covering an area equivalent to around 100 football pitches, the **world's northernmost zoo** 25km/15mi south of Bardu offers bears, elks, wolfs and their ilk a home from home in the authentic wilderness of the Salangstal valley. Information on the specific fauna of the polar region is available.

Polar zoo

❶ June–Aug daily 9am–6pm, otherwise Mon–Fri 9am–4pm, Sat–Sun 11am–3pm; 215 NOK; www.polarzoo.no

WHAT TO SEE IN TROMS

Leaving Narvik on the E 6 in the direction of Tromsø, take the secondary road leading to the Målselvfoss waterfall east of Andselv, shortly after the junction with the RV 87. The 140km/87mi-long Målselv river is the largest waterway in Troms and reaches from the Lille Rostavann lake to the Målsnes headland and on as far as Malangen. In addition to trout and char, this is predominantly a river for salmon fishing. In 1910, a salmon ladder was built near the 600m/1969ft-long **Målselvfoss waterfall** that allows the salmon to travel an additional 70km/44mi upriver, until they are stopped by the waterfall of the Divi river. The best time for salmon fishing below the waterfall is from the end of June to the end of July, while mid-July to 20 August is the ideal period for fishing above the waterfall.

Salmon fishing on the Målselv river

Following the Målselv upriver as far as Øverbygd, a side trip into the densely forested Dividal is an option. One of Europe's last wildernesses, and a wealth of plants and animals, can be found here. The Øvre Dividal National Park covers an area of 750 sq km/299 sq mi and is easily accessible to all who wish to stay in the cabins provided by the Troms Turlad hiking association. Guides are available to lead expeditions into rough terrain and territories inhabited by beasts of prey such as **wolves and bears**. The guides can also provide horses or dog sleds, as well as Sami tents. Adventurous visitors can also arrange guided canoe and rafting tours (May–June) in Rundhaug and Øverbygd along the RV 87.

*Øvre Dividal National Park

The region around the Rohbunborri mountain range, reaching the Swedish border to the south, is the country's newest protected landscape. The 571 sq km/220 sq mi Rohkunborri National Park is characterised by a mountainous region with dense pine forests, damp alpine meadows and valuable freshwater reserves. It is also home to large predators, including lynx, wolverine and brown bear. Many of the native inhabitants, such as the mountain fox, gyrfalcon and snowy owl, are threatened by extinction and are intended to get better protection by the establishment of this new national park. The area is also used by Sweden's and Norway's Sami People for reindeer keeping.

Rohkunborri National Park

Mollisfoss   En route from Tromsø to Alta, the E 6 follows the shoreline of the broad ►Lyngenfjord. At Storslett, the RV 865 leads into the pretty Reisadal. It is possible to travel upriver on the Reisa, for example, as far as the Mollisfoss in the Reisa National Park. This waterfall has not been regulated by human intervention of any kind and its 269m/883ft free falling flow makes it **Norway's second highest waterfall**.

Kvænangs- **The** E 6 continues along the coast and reaches a height of 402m/1319ft
fjell on the Kvænangsfjell mountain plateau. During summer there are
Sørstraumen numerous Sami tents to be seen here and the view onto the Kvænangenfjord is impressive. A short while later the road descends steeply down to the fjord. The Sørstraumen bridge crosses the tidal strait of Sørstraumen, which is rich in fish. At Burfjord, the Kvænangstindan (up to 1175m/3855ft) mountain range can be seen to the west; its north face has still to be scaled.

Troms

INFORMATION
www.visittroms.no
Tourist offices:
►Tromsø und Harstad

GETTING THERE
Train stations: Narvik and Fauske.
Airports: Tromsø, Bardufoss, Sørkjosen and Harstad (in Evenes)

RAFTING, FISHING
Permits for salmon fishing in the Målselv river can be purchased in Andselv. The river is also ideal for rafting and kayaking (Målselv Turistkontor, tel. 77 18 10 97).

EVENT
Early July, a single fish draws fishermen from all over the world to Salingen in Tromsø. This tagged »millionfish« wins one lucky person a million Norwegian Krone (about US$134,000). In the meantime, an entire festival lasting several days has developed around this event (www.millionfisken.com).

WHERE TO EAT
Vollan Gjestestue
Nordkjosbotn
At the junction of the E 6 and E 8
tel. 77 72 23 00
www.vollangjedtetue.no
The meat balls here are especially popular: 15,000 portions are sold annually. The menu also features nettle soup, herring soup, fish balls, cod tongues and a whale meat terrine.

WHERE TO STAY
Skjervøy Fiskekamp AS
Skjervøy Fiskekamp AS
Skjervøy
tel. 90 72 45 55
www.skjervoy-fiskekamp.com
The Fiskecamp is a veritable paradise for fishermen, set on the Island of Skjervøy. It has several well appointed cabins, as well as boats and equipment for rent. Reached via a branch road off the E6, in the direction of Arnøy.

* # Tromsø

 M 15

Region: North Norway
Population: 69,100

Tromsø likes to refer to itself as the »Paris of the North«, and rightly so, because the pretty port city surprises visitors with a very lively cultural and restaurant scene, vibrant nightlife included. It also has something that Paris cannot offer: the midnight sun during summer and a magical arctic light during winter.

Tromsø is located between Narvik and Hammerfest on a small island connected with the mainland by the striking 43m/141ft-high Tromsø Bridge, at one end of which the impressive white Arctic Cathedral

Gateway to the Arctic

Tromsø is known as the »Gateway to the Arctic«

Tromsø

INFORMATION
Turistkontor
Kirkegata 2
9253 Tromsø
tel. 77 61 00 00
www.visittromso.no

GETTING THERE
The Hurtigruten ships arrive in the port daily. During summer Tromsø is also the final destination for Spitsbergen cruises. There are flights to Longyearbyen/Spitsbergen, Oslo and other larger cities. Troms is not connected to the railway network. The nearest stations are Narvik and Fauske. Airports are at Tromsø, Bardufoss, Sørkjosen and Harstad (in Evenes).

FESTIVALS
International Film Festival
Every year during the third week in January, Norway's largest film festival takes place here (www.tiff.no).

Northern Lights Festival
The Northern Lights Festival at the end of January concentrates on innovative music, in particular, especially crossover music with traditional music styles (www.nordlysfestivalen.no).

Barents Jazz Festival
High karat jazz with artists from northern Scandinavia comes to Tromsø in November (www.barentsjazz.no).

SPORT
Polar Night Half Marathon (Mørketidsløp)
This unique winter race is held in Tromsø during the first weekend in January.

Start and finish lines are in the city centre. The distance to be covered is either 10km/6mi or a half marathon(www.nrk.no).

Tromsø Ski Marathon
Tromsø invites participants to the Ski Marathon at the beginning of April. The cross-country route lies in truly beautiful landscape outside the city and is 40km/25mi long.
This, the world's most northerly marathon, is held in mid-June; information at www.msm.no.

MIDNIGHT SUN
From 21st May to 23rd July

EXCURSIONS
Take the Fjellheisen cable car to the 420m/1378ft-high viewing point at Storsteinen. Timetable: May–Sep 10am–5pm; in fine weather also from 9pm–12.30am.

WHERE TO EAT
❷ Compagniet Restaurant £ £ £ £
Sjogata 12
tel. 77 66 42 22
www.compagniet.no
Early reservations are recommended, given this is supposed to be Northern Norway's best restaurant. Excellent cuisine in a beautiful setting. Closed Sundays.

❹ Arctandria Sjømat Restaurant £ £ – £ £ £
Strandtorget 1
tel. 77 60 07 20
There are no less than three restaurants here: the Vertshuset Skarven awaits

guests with simple but exotic small dishes; the Arctandria is a highly praised fish and shellfish restaurant with regional and Sami specialities; and the Skarvens Biffhus serves up juicy steaks in varying sizes.

❸ Blå Rock Café £ _Insider Tip_
Strandgata 14/16
tel. 77 61 00 20
www.blarock.no
An institution in Tromsø and probably the world's most northerly rock'n'roll café. Lots of little cosy rooms on several floors with authentic interiors from around the world. DJs ensure a great atmosphere at the weekends. Occasionally there is also live music.

❶ Kaffe å Lars £
Kirkegata 8
tel. 77 63 77 30
This miniscule café on the second floor of Emm's Drømmekjøkken opposite the

cathedral serves breakfast as early as 7am. In the evening there is often live music, especially jazz. Light meals at affordable prices make this a popular meeting place, including at lunchtime.

WHERE TO STAY
❶ Scandic Hotel £ £ £
Heiloveien 23, tel. 77 75 50 00
www.scandic-hotels.com, 147 rooms.
This hotel, opened in 1986, offers a high level of comfort and houses three renowned attractions with its Måken restaurant, Pelikanen bar and Pingvinen nightclub.

❷ Hotell Nord £ £
Parkgata 4
tel. 77 66 83 00
www.hotellnord.no, 22 rooms.
This small hotel near the centre has been offering clean and affordable rooms for years. Simple breakfast. Special prices for students; advance booking essential.

stands. The city that emerged around the site of a 13th-century church and received its municipal charter in 1794 is known as the »Gateway to the Arctic«. Once the first fishing boat had successfully been sent into the Arctic Sea in 1820, **seal hunting** quickly established itself as the most important economic sector for the city. Furthermore, it was from Tromsø that Fridtjof Nansen, Roald Amundsen (►Famous People) and other **polar explorers** set off on their great expeditions. A memorial on the harbour breakwater recalls Amundsen's flight with the water plane Latham, on which he set off in search of Umberto Nobile in 1928. Student town During the 19th century, numerous rich businessmen lived in Tromsø, whose continental lifestyle and tastes acquired during their journeys abroad brought the city the fashionable moniker of the »**Paris of the North**«. Today, it is the over 9000 students that enrich the lively restaurant and nightlife scene. Tromsø is northern Norway's largest city, capital of the county of Troms and a significant fishing centre.

During summer, the temperatures can reach 25°C/77°F, so that the vegetation is positively exuberant. The front gardens of houses are

Tromsø palms

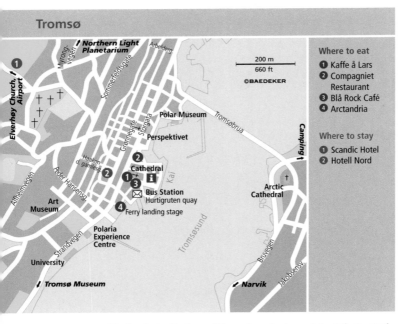

Tromsø

Where to eat
1. Kaffe å Lars
2. Compagniet Restaurant
3. Blå Rock Café
4. Arctandria

Where to stay
1. Scandic Hotel
2. Hotell Nord

©BAEDEKER

200 m
660 ft

notable for their displays of flowering plants, and 2m/6ft–3m/10ft-high »Tromsø palms« are common in the city. This sub-species of Heracleum sibiricum (eltrot) has stands with broad pinnate leaves (hence »palm«) and white blossoms, and can grow up to 10cm/4in per day; this flowering plant of the Umbelliferae, or carrot family, can occasionally snap under its own weight after two months of growth.

WHAT TO SEE IN TROMSØ

*Arctic
Cathedral

Still on the mainland, right next to the Tromsø Bridge, stands Tromsdalen church, otherwise known as the Arctic Cathedral. This architecturally interesting building was designed by Jan Inge Hovig in 1965 to symbolize the dark time of year and the Northern Lights. The Return of Christ is symbolized by Norwegian Victor Sparre's wonderfully colourful 23m/75ft-high stained glass window with a total of 86 panes. The organ with 42 registers was installed in 2005.

❶ June–mid-Aug 9am–7pm, Sun from 1pm, mid-Aug–mid-Sep and second half of May 3pm–6pm, otherwise 4pm–6pm, June–July daily organ concert at 2pm, June–mid-Aug daily 11.30pm midnight sun concert; 35 NOK, concerts 70–140 NOK; www.ishavskatedralen.no

The municipal museum has exhibits at three locations. In the city centre (Storegata 95), there is an exhibition on the city's history and youth culture. At the **Folkeparken** open-air museum in the south of the city, 13 different farms and mansions are exhibited, and there is a fascinating display on the Lofoten fishing industry. The **Straumen Gård** on the island of Kvaløya (see below, p.416) houses 19th-century farms.

Perspektivet

Perspektivet Museum: June–Sep Tue–Sun 11am–5pm; free; www. perspektivet.no Folkeparken open-air museum: June–Sep daily, depending on the weather; www.perspektivet.no

Located on the fjord, the Polar Museum is well worth seeing and includes items from Amundsen's South Pole Expedition.

Polar Museum

❶ Mid-June–mid-Aug daily 10am–7pm, otherwise 11am–5pm; 25 NOK; www.polarmuseum.no

To the southwest of the ships' landing area in the city centre of Tromsø stands the 1861 cathedral with attractive stained glass windows. King Håkon Håkonsson had the first church built here in 1250, around which a settlement gradually developed. Today the Lutheran cathedral is Norway's largest neo-Gothic wooden church.

Cathedral

The Tromsø Museum is 2km/1.2mi further to the southwest, past the university. Located in a park, its natural and cultural history collections focus on Sami culture and arctic nature, and also provide extensive information on Lapland's traditional music, such as the Sami joik, which visitors can listen to on headphones. Archaeological finds testify to the fact that people were already living by hunting and fishing in the Troms region as much as 10,000 years ago.

*Tromsø Museum

❶ Mid-June–mid-Aug daily 9am–6pm, otherwise Mon–Fri 10am–4.30pm, Sat noon–3pm, Sun 11am–4pm; 50 NOK; www.uit.no/tmu

Elverhøy church (1802) to the west of the city centre served as Tromsø's Lutheran cathedral from 1803 to 1861 and was moved here in 1975. The interior of this wooden church contains a noteworthy altar and a medieval Madonna, also made of wood.

Elverhøy church

Close to the world's most northern brewery with its own beer cellar (»Mack« on Storgata), lies the north Norwegian museum of art (Sjøagata 1), with works by north Norwegian artists from the early 18th century to the present day, as well as changing exhibitions.

Nordnorsk Art Museum

❶ Mon–Fri 10am–5pm, Sat–Sun from noon; free; www.nnkm.no

Opposite the Nordnorsk Art Museum, at Hjalmar Johansgata 12, visitors to the Polaria Adventure Centre, built to look like stacked ice blocks, can discover everything about life in the arctic. A panoramic

*Polaria Adventure Centre

film carries spectators off to the islands of Svalbard, while bearded seals provide the main attraction walking through the glass tunnel of the aquarium. Be sure to watch the training and feeding sessions at 12.30pm and 3pm.

❶ Mid-May–Aug daily 10am–7pm, Sep–mid-May 11am–5pm; 120 NOK; www.polaria.no

*Nordlys Planetarium

At the world's northernmost planetarium (Northern Lights Planetarium) on the university campus in Breivika, visitors can experience a variety of meteorological phenomena, including the Northern Lights, on the big screen.

Screenings: Mon–Fri 3.15pm, Sat–Sun hourly from 12.15–3.15pm; 50 NOK; www.nordnorsk.vitensenter.no

Catholic church

At the Stortorget, the »Large Market«, reached via Skippergata and Havnegata, stands the 19th-century Catholic church. The Norwegian Catholic diocese was established in 1843 after Catholicism was banned during the Reformation.

AROUND TROMSØ

*Storsteinen viewing point

The base station of the Fjellheisen cable car route up the 420m/1378ft Storsteinen is located in a side street behind the striking Arctic Cathedral. In fine weather, there is a fantastic view from up here, and it is also a good place to experience the midnight sun. The »Fjellstua« mountain restaurant is there for hungry souls.

Cable car hours: May–Sep 10am–5pm, by good weather up to 9pm–12.30am; tickets 120 NOK

Hikes

Mountain hikers can ascend the 1238m/4062ft-high Tromsdalstind east of Tromsdal, as well as explore the Tønsvikdal valley. There are three cabins offering accommodation: Skarvassbu, Nonsbu and Blåkollkoia. During winter, there are several cross-country skiing routes. More information is available from the Tromsø tourist office.

Kvaløya Island

The island of Kvaløya (»Whale Island«) lies to the west of Tromsø and its moist meadows facing the Sandnessund Strait can be reached via the Sandnessund Bridge that leads across it. Near the RV 862 at the southern end of the island, the 2500–4000-year-old Skavberg **rock paintings** are worth seeing; as is the pretty village of Hella, located right by the tidal waters of the Rystraumen, where there is a small open-air museum with several beautiful historic houses from Tromsø. Hillesøy church (1880) at the far western side of the island has two German altar panels dating from around 1500. In the fishing village of **Hillesøy,** further north, there is also a wonderful view of the sea. Kvaløya Island is connected to its northern neighbour of **Ringsvassøy** by the Kvalsund Tunnel (1630m/1783yd). Deep-sea fishing tours set off from Hansnes on Ringsvassøya, which is about an hour's drive from Tromsø. Those interested in a closer encounter with Sami culture can book reindeer-drawn sleigh tours or a traditional meal, or even a night in a typical Sami tent. Information via the Tromsø tourist office.

** Trondheim

F 7

Region: Central Norway
Population: 179,600

Norway's third largest city boasts a picturesque location on a southern bay of the Trondheimfjord. Trondheim was the country's first capital. St Olav died here, and the Nidaros Cathedral, Scandinavia's most magnificent church in which Norway's monarchs are crowned, was built over his grave.

Trondheim's old town is bounded by the Nidelv river and is therefore a peninsula that is only connected to the mainland in the west. All the sights are easily reached on foot. The capital of the county of Sør-Trøndelag is also the seat of both the Protestant and Catholic bishops. The favourable temperatures (average January temperatures rarely fall below -3°C/27°F) always leave the fjord **free of ice** and allow a wealth of flora to grow. Trondheim is not only an important industrial city (engineering, food industry and fish processing), but has also made a name for itself as a centre of university research and learning. Norway's largest technical college is here, as well as a university and **Scandinavia's largest technological research centre** SINTEF.

City on a peninsula

Originally Trondhjem, Trondheim was once the name for the entire region around the Trondheimfjord, which is considered the cradle of the Norwegian empire. This is where Norwegian monarchs were chosen by the Øreting. Olav Tryggvason (or Tryggvesson) had the **royal residence of »Nidarnes«** built as early as 997, but the real founder of the city, in 1016, is considered to be **St Olav**. From then until the 16th century, the city was known as **»Nidaros«** (mouth of the Nid). After St Olav's death in 1030, hordes of pilgrims came to see the shrine of the canonized king and it was through this cult that Trondheim became the largest and **richest city in the land**. Apart from the cathedral, another nine churches and five monasteries were

History of a royal town

Insider Tip

The Middle Ages brought to life

The best time to visit Trondheim is during the St Olav Days at the end of July/beginning of August, when a variety of churches and public buildings host numerous concerts, exhibitions, and music and theatre performances. A medieval market held in the courtyard of the Archbishop's Palace (Erkebispegård) includes demonstrations of traditional trades and Norwegian crafts, such as ceramics, candles and carvings are sold.

built. The Reformation put an end to the pilgrimages; the saint's shrine was carried off to Denmark and destroyed there, and the body was buried at an unrecorded spot inside the cathedral. The number of churches and monasteries declined, and Trondheim's heyday came to an end.

After repeated fires – the last in **1651, when the entire old city was destroyed** – the Luxembourg general Caspar de Cicignon was given a contract by Christian V to design a new city. Inspired by **Versailles,** he built broad boulevards that led off in all directions from the market square. He also built the **Kristiansten fortress,** which was to withstand several Swedish attacks. The increase in wood trading at the beginning of the 17th century resulted in an upswing for the city and numerous rich Swedish families settled here. The population increased fourfold within 100 years and, by the beginning of the 19th century, Trondheim's 9500 inhabitants made it just as large as Christiania, today's Oslo. The city received a further boost in growth when it was connected to the rest of the Norwegian and then the Swedish **railway network**, in 1877 and 1881 respectively.

WHAT TO SEE IN TRONDHEIM

Torget

The heart of Trondheim is the Torget market square where the two main roads of Kongensgata and Munkegata converge. A tall octagonal pillar with a statue of Olav Tryggvason (1923) stands on the square. In the paving stones below the memorial, it is possible to see the four points of the compass (N–V–S–Ø).

Arts and Crafts Museum

The Arts and Crafts Museum (Nordenfjeldske Kunstindustrimuseum), founded in 1893, exhibits historic furniture and domestic items dating from the 16th century to 1930 (including, among other things, 17th–18th-century Trondheim silver), objects from the Arts and Crafts Movement of the turn of the 19th century, an art nouveau collection, Scandinavian design (1950–65), tapestries by Hanny Ryggen, folk costume and a Japanese collection.

❶ June–mid-Aug Mon–Sat 10am–5pm, Sun from noon, otherwise Tue–Sat 10am–3pm, Thu till 5pm, Sun noon–4pm; 80 NOK; www.nkim.no

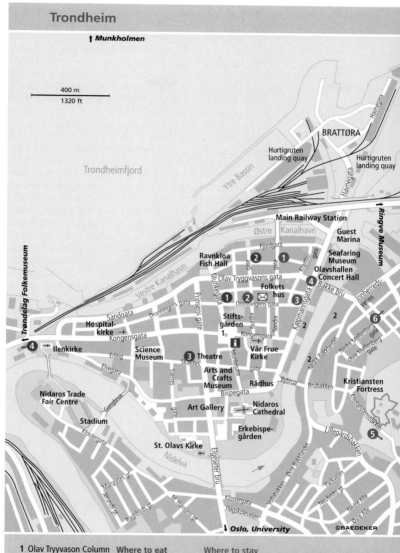

Trondheim

↑ *Munkholmen*

400 m
1320 ft

Trondheimfjord

BRATTØRA

Hurtigruten landing quay

Hurtigruten landing quay

Ytre Bassin

Main Railway Station

Østre Kanalhavn

Guest Marina

Fjordgata

Ravnkloa Fish Hall

Seafaring Museum

Olavshallen Concert Hall

Olav Tryggvasons gata

Folkets hus

Vestre Kanalhavn

Prinsens gata

Dronningens gata

Stifts-gården

Nordre

søndre

Bakke bru

Kongensgata

Sandgata

Hospital-kirke

Kongensgata

Vår Frue Kirke

Ilenkirke

Science Museum

Theatre

Skakkes

Nedre Møllenberg gate

Øvre Møllenberg gate

Erling

Elvegata

Sverres

Arts and Crafts Museum

Rådhus

Bybrua

Brubakken

Kristiansten Fortress

Nidaros Trade Fair Centre

Bispegata

Art Gallery

Nidaros Cathedral

Lillegårdsbakken

Stadium

Klostergata

Gangbruar

gate

Erkebispe-gården

St. Olavs Kirke

Nidelva

Elgeseter bru

Ringve Museum

Innherreds-veien

Havnegata

Havnegata

Kjøpmannsgata

Krambu gata

Munkegata

Trøndelag Folkemuseum

Parkveien

Neufeldts gt.

Nedre Allé

Øvre Allé

Margretes gt.

Jernbanebru

Råghilds gt.

M. Hansens gt.

Klostergata

Høgskoleveien

Volbakken

Øvre Bakklandet

Nedre Bakklandet

Kristiansteinsbakken

↓ **Oslo, University**

©BAEDEKER

1 Olav Tryyvason Column
2 Historic warehouses

Where to eat
1 Palmehaven
2 To Rom og Kjøkken
3 Persilleriet
4 Vertshuset Tavern

Where to stay
1 Thon Hotel Gildevangen
2 Britannia Hotel
3 Clarion Collection Hotel Grand Olav
4 Radisson SAS

Royal Garden Hotel
5 Singsaker Sommer-hotell
6 Vandrerhjem Rosenberg

**Nidaros Cathedral

Nidaros Cathedral (Nidarosdomen) was founded **on the site of St Olav's grave** by King Olav Kyrre (1066–93), and substantially extended in 1151 after the establishment of the archbishopric of Nidaros that encompassed all of Norway. The building complex and its artistic execution make it the most magnificent church in all of Scandinavia and Trondheim's most important sight (photo p.56). The transept, chapter house and the splendid early Gothic octagonal dome are characterized by a **late Romanesque transitional style** influenced by Anglo-Norman thought at the time. The cathedral's building material was the blue-grey soapstone from the area around Trondheim. The **long choir** with its beautiful south portal was built in the early 13th century, the mighty **nave** and spire in the Gothic style in 1280. After several fires, the western section, starting with the transept, was left in ruins. But the nascent national consciousness of the 19th century saved the cathedral from oblivion: **reconstruction** began in 1869 and on 28 July 1930, in time for the 900th centenary of St Olav's death, the church was reconsecrated. The **organ**, with its Baroque styling built by Steinmeyer from Oettingen in Swabia in 1930, was moved to stand below the window rosette in 1963. The west wall was restored in the period 1914–68; the cathedral's **west façade** is very beautiful with its statues of Norwegian kings and bishops, along with biblical figures. The cathedral served as the final royal resting place in the 11th and 12th centuries. Several kings were crowned here in the 15th century and, since 1814, it has been constitutionally set that Norwegian kings must be crowned in Trondheim's cathedral. On entering the cathedral, the ceremonial atmosphere immediately impresses the visitor. The only sources of light are the colourful stained glass windows (1913–34) by Gabriel Kielland and the luminous blue and red tones of the glass rosette above the organ. 14

Nidaros Cathedral Trondheim

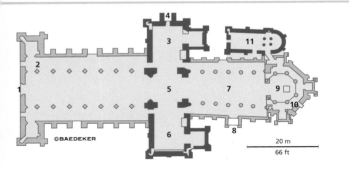

©BAEDEKER

20 m
66 ft

■ Romanesque
▢ Gothic

1 West portal
2 Coronation insign
3 Northern transept
4 North portal
5 Crossing
6 Southern transept
7 Long choir
8 Southern choir po
9 High choir
   (octagonal dome)
10 St Olav's well
11 Sacristy
   (chapter house)

pillars separate the 43m/47yd-long and 20m/22yd-wide nave from the aisles. The octagonal dome in high Gothic style rises above the high choir, where the 26m/28yd long choir with its exquisite baptismal font adjoins.

❶ Mid-June–mid-Aug Mon–Fri 9am–6pm, Sat till 2pm, Sun till 5pm, otherwise Mon–Fri 9am–2pm, Sat till 3pm, Sun till 4pm; 70 NOK; combined ticket with the Archbishop's Palace (see below) and the royal coronation insignia 140 NOK; www.nidarosdomen.no

Next door stands the Archbishop's Palace (ErkebispeGård), a medieval stone building that once served as home for the bishops. It is northern Europe's oldest secular building. Originally it was encircled by thick walls; after the Reformation it served as an aristocratic seat for the Danish overlords and, from 1660, it housed military munitions. The magnificent **Knights' Hall** (1180), used for official occasions and celebrations by the city of Trondheim, is open to the public. The storage buildings of the bishops' seat burnt down to their foundations

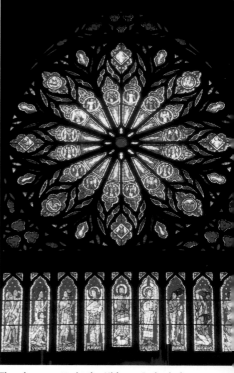

The glass rosette in the Nidaros Cathedral is by Gabriel Kielland

in 1983 and valuable collections were destroyed. Today a large **museum centre** is housed here with interesting exhibitions on the history of Norway and Trondheim, a weapons collection, the royal coronation insignia, and the Museum of the Resistance (1940–45).

Archbishop's Palace & Museum: June–Aug Mon–Fri 10am–5pm, Sat 10am–3pm, Sun noon–4pm, otherwise Tue–Fri 11am–2pm, Sat till 3pm, Sun noon–4pm (royal insignia Sat–Sun only); museum only 70 NOK; combined ticket with cathedral and coronation insignia 140 NOK; www.nidarosdomen.no

The Jewish Museum at Arkitekt Christies gate 1 has two permanent exhibitions: one on Jewish life in Trondheim and another on the impact of the German occupation during the Second World War.

Jewish Museum

On Bispegate, northwest of the cathedral, stands the **Art Association** (Kunstforening) which has a picture gallery and changing exhibitions.

❶ Tue, Wed, Fri, Sun noon–4pm, Thu till 6pm; free; www.tkf.no

Art Association

There is an attractive view towards several 18th–19th century **old warehouses** (largely restored) set **on posts** from the **Bybrua**, a red wooden bridge (1861) that crosses the Nidelv to the northeast of the cathedral. Today there are several **good fish restaurants** here. Olav Tryggvason had the first warehouses built by the Nidelv on Øvre Elvehavn about one thousand years ago, but they quickly burnt down again. On the east side stand historic, mostly restored, wooden houses that were once workers' apartments.

Old warehouses

The Norwegian Museum of the Deaf is housed in a former boarding school for deaf children at Bispegata 9. Touch screens offer an unusual insight into the world without hearing, using both sign language and standard sound and text.

❶ Wed, Thu 11am–3pm, Sat from noon; 55 NOK; www.norsk-dovemuseum.no

Norwegian Museum of the Deaf

The family-friendly Folk Museum at Sverresborg Allé 13, is an open-air museum with 80 historical buildings and exhibitions chronicling everyday life, including maritime culture, from the past 150 years.

❶ June–mid-Aug daily 9am–2pm, otherwise Tue–Fri 9am–2pm, Sun noon–4pm; 55 NOK; www.sverresborg.no

Folk Museum

The Kristiansten fortress, built in the European Baroque style by General Caspar de Cicignon in the 17th century, can be reached by walking across the Bybrua and up through the suburb of Bakklandet onto the hill, from where there is also a panoramic view of the city. The view is most beautiful during the early morning or at sunset.

Interior: June–Aug daily 11am–3pm

Kristiansten fortress

A wonderful view of Trondheim and the fjord landscape can also be enjoyed from the 80m/262ft-high rotating restaurant inside the Television Tower (Tyholttarnet; 124m/407ft), to the east of the city centre.

Television Tower

North of the market square, on Munkegata, stands the mighty yellow wooden house of the Stiftsgården, built in 1770, whose approximately 140 rooms serve as the royal seat when the Norwegian king visits Trondheim. When the widow **Cecilie Schøller** commissioned this building – one of the largest wooden buildings in northern Europe

*Stiftsgården

The Gothic nave of the Nidaros Cathedral dates from around 1280

Trondheim

INFORMATION
Turistinformasjon
Torget, 7411 Trondheim
tel. 73 80 76 60
www.trondheim.com

EVENTS
March/April: International Film Festival
(www.kosmorama.no).
May: Jazzfest (www.jazzfest.no).
End of July/beginning of August:
Trøndersk Matfestival, gourmet festival
with regional specialties (www.oimat.no/
tronderskmatfestival).
End of August/beginning of September:
Jewish cultural festival (www.jkfest.no).
September: Trondheim Chamber Music
Festival (www.kamfest.no).

WHERE TO EAT
❶ *Palmehaven* £ £ £ – £ £ £ £
Dronningens gate 5
tel. 73 80 08 00
Very fancy restaurant in the Britannia
Hotel. Stylish atmosphere among the
palms and fountains.

❷ *To Rom og Kjøkken* £ £ £
Carl Johans gate 5
tel. 73 56 89 00
www.toromogkjokken.no
Stylish restaurant in an old wood house
in the city, whose delicious dishes make
up for the occasionally slow service.
Book ahead!

❹ *Vertshuset Tavern* £ £
Sverresborg allé 7, tel. 73 87 80 70
This establishment next to the Trondelag
Folk Museum has been in business since
1739. Rustic home cooking from Grand-
mother's recipes.

❸ *Persilleriet* £
Erling Skakkes gate 39
tel. 73 60 60 14
www.persilleriet.no
Market fresh vegetarian cuisine in a quiet side street – the place to be for a
meat-free lunch.

WHERE TO STAY
❸ *Clarion Collection Hotel Grand
Olav* £ £ £ £
Kjøpmannsgt. 48,
tel. 73 80 80 80
www.choicehotels.no, 106 rooms.
First-class hotel in the busy city centre
with popular and outstanding gastro-
nomic services (restaurant, café, bar,
night club).

❷ *Britannia Hotel*
£ £ £ – £ £ £ £
Dronningensgate 5
tel. 73 80 08 00
www.britannia.no, 247 rooms.
First class comfort is offered here, as well
as the Palmehaven restaurant, a piano
bar, a cellar restaurant and an English
pub.

❹ *Radisson SAS Royal Garden
Hotel* £ £ £
Kjøpmannsgt. 73
tel. 73 80 30 00
www.radissonblu.com, 297 rooms.
This modern hotel with giant lobby has
architectural appeal as well as a beautiful location on the river, not far from the
harbour.

❶ *Thon Hotel Gildevangen*
£ £ £
Søndre gt. 22b

tel. 73 87 01 30,
www.thonhotels.no, 165 rooms.
Neogothic and contemporary style: mid-range hotel dating from 1908, with modern and comfortable interiors.

❺ *Singsaker Sommerhotell* £ £
Rogerts gate 1
tel. 73 89 31 00
www.sommerhotell.singsaker.no
103 rooms.
The value for money alternative is a sim-
ple hotel in a very quiet location on a hill near the Kristiansten fortress (mid-June–mid-August).

❻ *Vandrerhjem Rosenborg* £
Weidemannsveien 41
tel. 73 87 44 50
www.trondheim-vandrerhjem.no
53 rooms.
Slightly out of town new building with a great view over the town and fjord.

– she intended to outshine her rivals who lived in the urban mansions of HornemannsGården and Harmonien. Sure enough, this small palace became Trondheim's finest building. The coronation celebrations for kings Karl XIV Johan (1818), Karl XV (1860), Oscar II (1873), Håkon VII (1906), Olav V (1958) and latterly Harald V (1991) took place here. The building can only be visited during the one-hour guided tours.

❶ June–mid-Aug Mon–Sat 10am–4pm, Sun from noon; 80 NOK; www.nkim.no/stiftsgarden

On Bispegaten 7b, west of the cathedral, the Trondheim Kunstmuseum contains Norway's third largest public art collection, including Norwegian art from 1850 and several works by Edvard Munch. Also worth seeing is the Danish art collection.

Trondheim Kunstmuseum

❶ Tue, Thu–Sun noon–4pm, Wed till 9pm; 60 NOK; www.tkm.museum.no

The Trøndelag Centre for Contemporary Art is at Fjordgata 11, and also features video art in its »Black Box«.

Trøndelag Centre

❶ Tue–Sun noon–5pm; www.samtidskunst.no

Norway's first museum of pop and rock was opened in an old warehouse in 2010 and contains six floors of exhibits on Norwegian musical and cultural history since the 1950s. Included are internationally famous artists, such as A-ha, Lene Marlin and Marit Larsen, as well as nationally popular musicians, such as the New Jordal Singers, Alf Prøysen, and Bjørn Eidsvåg. You can even record your own sound or learn some insider's tricks on the guitar from Ronnie Le Tekrø, guitarist with the rock band TNT. The museum has already won several prizes and includes a concert hall on which Norwegian newcomers as well as established legends give concerts.

Rockheim Museum of Pop and Rock Music

❶ Tue–Fri 11am–7pm, Sat–Sun till 6pm; 100 NOK; www.rockheim.no

Science
museums

A little way outside the centre, several buildings belonging to the University of Trondheim on Erling Skakkes gata house divers collections, including an important library with ancient manuscripts and an exhibition of sacred art. There is a mineral, botanic, zoological (incl. bird diorama) and archaeological collection. A particularly well executed exhibition is »Medieval Trondheim«, housed in a former warehouse from 1843. The visitor is taken through the city's history during a tour complete with audio effects, beginning with the Vikings, continuing with the foundation of the city in the 10th century by Olav Tryggvason, and through to the 17th century. Everyday life from that era is made real with the help of archaeological finds as well as reconstructed workshops and domestic interiors. The museum was voted Norway's »Museum of the Year« in 2010.

❶ Tue–Fri 10am–4pm, Sat–Sun 11am–4pm; 75 NOK; www.ntnu.no/vitenskapsmuseet

Folklore
Museum

On a hill in the southwest of the city, where King Sverre's (1177–1202) Sverresborg once stood, there is a huge area with a fine view

Old warehouses and the Nidaros Cathedral define the Nidelv waterfront

that is now the Folklore Museum (Folkemuseet). There are farms from the 18th to the 20th century from the district of Trøndelag, as well as the 12th century Haltdalen stave church and buildings from Trondheim's old town.

❶ June–Aug daily 11am–6pm, Sep–May Mon–Fri 11am–3pm, Sat–Sun noon–4pm; 125 NOK; www.sverresborg.no

AROUND TRONDHEIM

The island of Munkholmen lies in the Trondheimfjord and can be reached by boat from the Ravnkloa fish market at the northern end of Munkegata (hourly, 10mins). There was a place of execution here during the reign of Olav Tryggvason. The round tower of the Benedictine Nidarosholm monastery built at the beginning of the 11th century can still be seen on the island. From 1658 onwards, a fortress and prison stood here, but times change: today there is an open-air swimming pool and a restaurant.

Munkholmen

❶ www.munkholmen.no

Following the E 6 out of the city centre in the direction of Narvik and then taking a left turn after about 2km/1mi (signposted), drivers reach the Ringve Gård farm where the bold sea hero and adventurer Tordenskjold grew up in the 17th century. The Ringve farm is surrounded by a lovely botanical garden and has served as a museum for a noteworthy **collection of musical instruments** since 1952. Furnished true to their time, the interiors of the rooms of the composers Chopin (including the composer's death mask), Edvard Grieg (original photos), Beethoven and Mozart are worth taking a look at. The presentations on the historic instruments by the museum guides enhance the exhibition's impact. A particular attraction is also the music history museum opened in the hay loft in 1999, which has a collection of keyboard, wind and string instruments from all around the world, as well as a representative collection of Norwegian folk music instruments. Examples of diverse music styles ranging from classical to jazz and contemporary pop underline the museum's educational appeal.

**Ringve Museum

❶ June daily 11am–4pm, July–Aug daily 11am–6pm, from mid-Sep Tue–Sun 11am–4pm; 100 NOK; www.ringve.no

A pleasant excursion is to Fjellseter (skiing region, ski jump) on the Fjellsetervei and then to Fjellseter chapel 8km/5mi west of the city. From there, a footpath (15mins) can be taken to the summit of Gråkallen (556m/1824ft) and the incredible views over the Trondheimfjord and onto the Trollheimen mountains. It is also possible to take the **Gråkall railway** from Trondheim (departures from St.

Excursion to Gråkallen

Olavsgate) or a bus from the city's Dronningensgate to Lian (30mins) and walk via Fjellseter and Skistua to ascend Gråkallen – a beautiful walk that takes 2.5hrs there and back.

Rock art by Hegra

Hegra is reached on the E 14. About 2km/1mi beyond Hegra a country path turns off to the left, signposted »Bergmuseet«, to Leirfall, one of northern Europe's largest sites containing Bronze Age (1500–500 BC) rock art. At the site, for example, is a group of 13 people that walk behind each other, as in a **procession**. The figure at the forefront and the three smallest ones represent »masked men« who were probably responsible for encouraging plants to grow. Furthermore, ships, sun symbols and a group of horse riders (approx. 600 BC) can be seen at Leirfall. Also near Hegra are the remains of the 1911 Hegra fortress, where 200 Norwegians held out for 27 days during the Second World War before capitulating to the Germans.

Steinkjer

Steinkjer lies 125km/78mi northeast of Trondheim on the E 6. The town on the Breistadfjord was already an important trading centre in ancient times, but lost its historic buildings in two devastating fires. Today it is the unspectacular administrative centre for the region of Nord-Trøndelag. The **Steinkjer church**, consecrated in 1965, is located on the former farm of Steinkjer. Its unusual stained glass windows and frescoes are by the locally born artist Jakob Weidemann. The modern »**Dampsaga**« cultural centre, created from three old sawmill buildings and a modern annex, is located on the Sagmestervegen, to the north of the Steinkjerelva river. Further north lies the appealing **Egge open-air museum** which has 11 historic farms and also the Eggevammen burial mounds on both sides of the E 6, where finds from AD 200 up to the Viking era testify to the fact that there was a lively trade with England and other countries here.

! MARCO●POLO TIP

Battle re-enactment Insider Tip

Norway's largest open-air stage is in Stiklestad. Each year on 29 July – the anniversary of Olav Haraldson's death – 5000 spectators relive the Battle of Stiklestad at close quarters, with 300 actors taking part. Visitors to the Stiklestad Nasjonale Kulturhus can also follow the course of the battle along a walkway where they are inundated with violent light and sound effects.

Bardal

Around 400 rock paintings at Bardal, 11km/7mi northwest of Steinkjer, show images of hunting scenes (human figures, elk and reindeer) from the Stone Age, and also sun symbols from the Bronze Age. The site of perhaps the most famous rock painting of hunting scenes (c3000 BC) in Scandinavia is located about 30km/19mi north of Steinkjer (RV 763), near the southeastern shore of the idyllic Snåsavatn: the life-sized »**Bøla Reindeer**«.

33km/21mi south of Steinkjer lies the Stiklestad national cultural centre, with an open-air museum and the Stiklestad hotel in the middle of the historic site. The annual St Olav's summer music festival also takes place here. At the spot where the altar of the Stiklestad church (1128, with interesting chalk paintings) now stands, the national patron saint King Olav, alias **Olav Haraldsson** (995–1030), received a fatal shot from his arch enemy Tore Hund on 29th July 1030. Olav's body was later taken to Trondheim.

About 10km/6mi south of Stiklestad lies the little town of **Levanger**, where people have been meeting at the popular **»Levangermartan«   Levanger market** every August since the early 15th century.

* Valdres

✦ C/D 5-7

Region: East Norway

Farms and green meadows characterize the scenery of the Valdres valley, in the vicinity of which are several stave churches. The open-air museum, with its many historic houses from the region, in the main settlement of Fagernes is among the most notable sights here.

Valdres

INFORMATION
Valdres Destinasjon
Jernbanevegen, 2900 Fagernes
tel. 61 35 94 10
www.valdres.com,

FESTIVAL
The fermented trout dish (Rakfisk) has its very own festival in November, during which this local delicacy is eaten in large quantities, alongside enjoying concerts and other cultural events (www.rakfisk.no).

WHERE TO STAY
Valdres Mountain Lodge £ £ – £ £ £

Danebu Kongsgaard, Aurdal
tel. 61 35 76 00
www.valdreslodge.no, 32 rooms.
Very close to all sporting opportunities, this historic lodge enjoys great views and has hosted royals among its guests. Traditional Norwegian cuisine.

Fagernes Camping £
In the centre
tel. 61 36 05 10
www.fagernes-camping.no
Not just for those under canvas: at this campsite with a pretty and central lakeside location, simple and value-for-money cabins can also be rented.

The fertile Valdres landscape of southern Norway extends on both sides of the Begna river that comes from the southern Jotunheimen mountains and empties into Lake Tyrifjord near the Hånefoss waterfall.

WHAT TO SEE IN THE VALDRES VALLEY

*Hadeland glass works

Norway's most famous glass works is located at the southern end of the Randsfjord, at Jevnaker about 23km/14mi northeast of Hånefoss. Hadeland Glassverk was founded as early as 1762 and is Norway's oldest industrial firm. Visitors can watch glass-blowers at work, purchase glass products, take a journey through history and design in the exhibition sites, and admire the artfully designed glass products.
❶ Mon–Fri 10am–5pm, Sat till 4pm, Sun 11am–5pm; www.hadeland-glassverk.no

*Hedalen stave church

North of Hånefoss travelling up the valley, the E 16 runs along the eastern shore of the 23km/14mi-long Lake Sperillen. The RV 243 turns off to Hedalen (25km/16mi) after the church and village of **Nes** at the northern end of the lake, not far from the mouth of the Begna. The oldest stave church in the Valdres valley stands here (not to be confused with the similarly-named Heddal stave church; see p. 406). Built in the 12th century, it was remodelled in 1738 and restored in 1901. A **bear skin** in the church recalls the rediscovery of the church in around 1500, when it is said that two hunters pursued a bear into the church and killed it there. Before that the church had stood empty ever since an outbreak of plague 150 years earlier. The **valuable interior** includes a Madonna statue and a medieval reliquary shrine.

> **!** MARCO ⊕ POLO TIP
>
> *Delicious rømmegrøt* Insider Tip
>
> The Nystøga café in the Valdres Folkemuseum is housed in a 250-year-old building that once served as an inn for travellers to the Filefjell. Traditional Norwegian fare is served here, such as alpine pancakes and sour cream waffles. »Rømmegrøt«, Norway's calorie-heavy sour cream porridge is definitely worth tasting here. The farmer's plate of ham, dried leg of lamb and dried sausage is also a regional delicacy (opening times: mid-June–mid-Aug; tel. 61 35 99 00).

Bagn

The E 16 follows the Begna through forested landscape to Bagn, a pretty, drawn out settlement. Take a look at the 18th-century wooden church here. Near Bagn a secondary road turns off to the small 12th-century stave church of Reinli, from which there is a marvellous view.

Fagernes

Fagernes, also popular with fishermen, lies picturesquely between forested hills at the mouth of the Neselv river that forms beautiful waterfalls here as it empties into the Strandefjord. In Fragernes it is worth visiting the **open-air folk museum** with its numerous historic farm buildings from the Valdres region complete with historic domestic items, textiles, musical instruments, and hunting weapons. From Fragernes, the RV 51 leads north to the famous Jotunheimen mountain massif.

❶ July–Aug daily 10am–4pm/5pm, otherwise Tue–Fri 10am–3pm; 90 NOK; www.valdresmusea.no

It is worth paying a visit to the 13th-century stave church at **Lomen**, which lies on the E 16 en route to **Lake Vangsmjøsa**. **Vang**, where the local church is equally interesting, lies along the southern shore of the 19km/12mi-long lake. Once upon a time there was a stave church here, but it was carried off to Silesia in 1841 and replaced by the white wooden church seen today. The runic stone in front of it carries the inscription: »Gose's sons erected this stone for Gunnar, their brother's son«. In **Øye** – at the west end of the Vangsmjøsa – stands a stave church that was rebuilt from the remains of a 12th-century building.

Lomen, Vang

Varanger Peninsula

✳ N 26

Region: North Norway

The peninsula of Varanger is a treeless expanse of scree, blasted by arctic storms. Travellers break their journey here at Vadsø, the administrative centre for Finnmark, or in Vardø, where the world's most northerly fortress stands.

The Varanger peninsula is separated from the mainland by the Tanafjord and the Varangerfjord, the latter of which has tidal waters that have a differential of up to 4m/13ft during full moon and a new moon. Norway's most easterly point lies on the island of Hornøya near the town of Vardø. At 31° 10' eastern latitude, its location is further east than St Petersburg or Istanbul. During the 19th century, so many Finns moved to Vadsø, on the northern coast of the Varangerfjord, that the fishing settlement was also known as the »Finnish capital« in Norway. In 1875, over 60% of the population in the administrative centre for the county of Finnmark spoke Finnish. For centuries there was a lively trade along the coast of the Barents Sea between Russians, Norwegians and Sami, which only came to an end with the onset of the Russian Revolution. This so-called »**Pomor trade**« – the word comes from the Russian phrase for the coastal inhabitants – involved the bartering of fish, grain and wood between

Finnish enclave

Varanger Peninsula

INFORMATION
Destinasjon Varanger
Ishavssenteret, 9840 Varangerbotn
tel. 78 94 04 44
www.varanger.com

Turistinformasjon Vardø
Havnepromenaden
tel. 78 98 69 07

GETTING THERE
Hurtigruten ships arrive daily in Vadsø
and Vardø. There are flights to Kirdenes
and Båtsfjord from Svartnes Airport
4km/3mi outside Vardø. There are also
daily bus connections to the rest of Finnmark.

FESTIVALS
The Varanger Jazz Festival, the largest of
its kind in the high north, is held at Vadsø in mid-August. It is followed by the
King Crab Festival in October, during
which all the events revolve around the
king crab www.highnorthhighend.no).

MIDNIGHT SUN
The midnight sun shines from 16 May to
29 July. From 23 November to 21 January, on the other hand, there is no sun
at all.

WHERE TO EAT
Nordpol Kro £ – £ £
Vardø, Kaigt. 21
tel. 78 98 75 01
www.nordpolkro.no
Northern Norway's oldest inn is near the
quay. It does not look like much from
the outside, but it is an atmospheric
English pub with lots of local colour. The
live concerts in the Nordpol are renowned.

WHERE TO STAY
Rica Hotel Vadso £ £ £
Oscarsgate 4
tel. 78 95 52 50
www.rica.no, 68 rooms.
Friendly hotel with light, modern rooms.

northern Norwegians and Russians from the White Sea region. Since
the dismantling of the Soviet Union these old trading relationships
of the high north have been revived – and are duly celebrated in July
on the Varanger peninsula during the **Pomor Festival**, with numerous cultural events and attractions.

WHAT TO SEE ON THE VARANGER PENINSULA

Vadsø   Vadsø (pop. 6000) is the administrative centre of the county of Finnmark. It was fortified by the Germans during the Second World War
and almost entirely destroyed by Allied bombs. This is where the expeditions by Umberto Nobile and Roald Amundsen, the first man to
reach the South Pole (Famous People), set off in 1926 with the inten-
tion of reaching the North Pole with their airship, the Norge. Two
years later, Nobile set off on a North Pole journey once again. When

he did not return, Amundsen went in search of him, also never to return. The anchor mast for the two airships remains on the island of Vadsøya, a memorial to the tragedy. The architect Magnus Poulsson called the Vadsø church of 1958 the **»Arctic Ocean Church«**. Its two spires are meant to represent icebergs.

Varanger's most interesting attraction is the **Vadsø Museum** with the Tuomainen building, which mostly focuses on the history of Finnish immigration; the Danish Norwegian aristocratic mansion of EsbensenGården, a merchant house dating from 1850 and the only building of its kind in the county of Finnmark, is also worth a visit.

Vadsø
Museum

❶ 20th June–20th Aug daily 11am/noon–5pm; 50 NOK; www.varangermuseum.no

The idyllic fishing settlement of Ekkerøy lies around 14km/9mi east of Vadsø (turn-off from the E 75). There is the grave of a woman here that dates from Viking times. The »bird mountain« of Flåget offers the chance to see arctic birds, such as auks, puffins and kittiwakes.

Ekkerøy

Vardø – one of Norway's easternmost settlements – lies just off the coast on an island in the Arctic Ocean that is connected with the mainland via a 3km/2mi-long underwater tunnel. Until the October Revolution of 1917, there was a lively trade with the Pomors of the Kola Peninsula (▶Finnmark). During the Cold War, Vardø played an important role in NATO's early warning system. Today, though, the domes that dominate the town's picture also serve civilian interests. Two thirds of the town was destroyed during the war years between 1942 and 1944, but it has now been rebuilt. **Vardøhus fortress**, the world's northernmost fortress, was originally built in the 14th century and redesigned in 1734–38 in the form of an eight-pointed star by Denmark's King Christian. When the long, dark, polar night of winter is over and the sun rises over the horizon again around the 22 January, the fortress cannons are fired and children get a day off school. The **Vardøhus Museum** dates from the time before the Second World War and contains the only surviving port in Finnmark. Norway's most carefully cared for tree must surely be the mountain ash at the fortress that soldiers wrap up in protective layers in October and unpack in April.

Vardø

A **memorial** in Vardø recalls one of the darkest eras in northern Norway's history: 91 people (77 women and 14 men) were accused of witchcraft and burnt at the stake here in the 17th century. The striking monument is the joint work of the Swiss architect Peter Zumthor and the French artist Louise Bourgeois, who died in 2010. A cube of dark glass designed by Zumthor contains an installation by Bourgeois in the form of a chair with burning gas flames, surrounded by seven oval mirrors that reflect and magnify the light of the fire. Another building houses the museum. 125m/410ft long, the construction is illuminated by 91 light bulbs and 91 small windows and contains tablets dedicated to each and every victim of the witch hunts. The memorial is part of the Varanger Norwegian Landscape Route that follows the coast for 154km/96mi along the Barent Sea coast, between Gornitak and Hamningsberg.

Vardøhus Museum: mid-April–mid-Sep 10am–9pm, otherwise 10am–6pm; www.nasjonalefestningsverk.no

* Vesterålen

✳ L 11-13

Region: North Norway

The Vesterålen islands to the north of Lofoten are rather unfairly overshadowed by their famous neighbours. Of particular interest is an excursion to Andenes, the islands' northernmost settlement: on the famous whaling tours that set out from here, there is a near guarantee of sperm whale sightings.

Picturesque landscape
The Vesterålen mountains are not as rugged and mighty as those of Lofoten, but rather covered in green meadows up to quite high elevations. However the landscape of the islands is very appealing and definitely worth a visit. The island group consists of Andøya, Langøya and Hadseløya, as well as parts of the islands of Hinnøya und Austvågøya.

WHAT TO SEE ON THE ISLANDS OF VESTERÅLEN

Hinnøya
The many sections of Hinnøya combine to make it Norway's second largest island after Spitsbergen. The main settlement on the island is ▶Harstad. The route that runs right along the water to the west of Harstad is also known as the »Midnight Sun Route«. The 1266m/4154ft-high Møysalen in the south of the island is **Vesterålen's highest summit**. It offers an appealing panorama over Vesterålen and Lofoten, the view extending all the way to the mountains in the direction of Sweden. The ascent can be made from Kaldjord, at the end of the RV 822; there and back 9hrs). From Lødingen in the south of the island (RV 85), it is possible to catch a ferry to Bognes and the E 6.

Andøya
The old trading settlement of **Risøyhamn** perches on the middle of a bare cliff right next to the sound. The Andøy Museum, with numerous cultural and historical objects, is located here. The fishing village

of **Andenes** lies at the northern tip of the island and has a 2.5km/1.5mi-long jetty. A polar and fishing museum is located in one of the historic homes. You can find out everything you need to know about whales at the Whale Centre in Andenes or, alternatively, live during a whale safari (Whale safaris, p.436), where you come face to face with 20m/66ft-long sperm whales – as well as smaller species.

The fishing village of Bleik and the sugarloaf bird island of Bleikøya a short distance from the coast (boat tours) are also worth a visit. Puffins, guillemots, shags and kittiwakes live on the island.

Bleikøya

Langøya and its many peninsulas and fjords forms the largest section of west Vesterålen. **Sortland** is an old trading settlement and harbour for the Hurtigruten ships. Around 20km/13mi west of Sortland, the breathtaking needle-like peak of Reka reaches to the sky. Its steep 607m/1992ft-high southwest face has never been climbed. Around a century ago, **Nyksund**, in the north of Langøya, was one of Vesterålen's largest settlements, a canning factory providing employment. The place then fell into steady decline, however, and became a ghost town. In the meantime, a little life has returned to Nyksund; accommodation is available, a café has opened and, in summer, a few tourists are attracted to the place. One of northern Europe's largest bird

Langøya

On the island of Andøya you could almost imagine you were in the Caribbean – if it weren't so chilly

Vesterålen

INFORMATION
Sortland / Vesterålen Reiselivslag
Kjøpmannsgt. 2, 8401 Sortland
tel. 76 11 14 80, www.visitvesteralen.com

GETTING THERE
Thanks to bridges and tunnels from the mainland, all the Vesterålen islands can be reached by car. The Hurtigruten ships dock at Stokmarknes, Sortland, Risøyhamn and Harstad.

FESTIVALS
An international cultural festival with concerts and theatre performances is held at Melbu on Hadseløya in July each year (www.sommermelbu.no).

MIDNIGHT SUN
The midnight sun shines from 16th May to 29th July; from 23rd November to 21st January there is no sun at all.

WHALE SAFARIS
A special attraction: whale safaris out of the former whaling station of Andenes from June to mid-September (reservations at least two days in advance; Andøy Reiseliv, tel. 76 11 56 00, tour 5hrs). Tours are accompanied by employees of the whale research institute and the World Wildlife Fund (WWF). They can also be booked in Stø on the island of Langøya.

WHERE TO EAT/WHERE TO STAY
Strand Hotell Sortland £ £ £
Strandgata 34, Sortland

tel. 76 11 00 80
www.strandhotell.no, 37 rooms.
This small hotel where Knut Hamsun wrote »The last pleasure« in 1911/12 in the centre cannot be missed due to its striking blue colour. Several of its rooms were designed by the Norwegian Academy for Interior Decoration, so the hotel has an original character. The Spisestua restaurant serves arctic fish and meat dishes and has made a name for itself with north Norwegian cuisine.

Sjøhus Senteret £ £ £
Ånstadsjøen, Sortland
tel. 76 12 37 40
www.lofoten-info.no/sjohussenteret
Seven comfortable wood cabins right by the water, with two bedrooms each. The large wooden hot tub can be fired up on request. The main building has the Sjøstua restaurant, which offers a beautiful view of the midnight sun as well as freshly prepared fish dishes.

Holmvik Brygge £ – £ £
Nyksund, tel. 76 13 47 96
www.nyksund.com
Simple, value for money accommodation in an old fisherman's house in Nyksund.

Nyksund Ekspedisjonen £ – £ £
tel. 76 13 27 00, www.nyksund.biz
Clean and value-for-money single or family rooms. The restaurant, with a view of the harbour, serves up regional dishes.

colonies can be found near Nykvåg on the Fuglenyken and Måsnykas cliffs facing the open sea to the west. Vesterålen also boasts northern Europe's largest numbers of sea eagles who still find plenty of food here, though they suffer greatly from nest robbers. Swimmers will enjoy the 800m/875yd-long sandy beach at Fjærvoll, south of Føre. The writer Knut Hamsun (►Famous People) was a police assistant in this area for two years, until he tried his luck as a teacher and storyteller.

Stokmarknes on the island of Hadseløya is an economic centre with an important merchant fleet and also serves as departure point for cruises into the Trollfjord (►Lofoten), one of the most beautiful fjord cruises Norway has to offer. The Hurtigruten Museum was founded in honour of the shipping line's founder Captain Richard With (►MARCO POLO Insight p.247). Hadsel church (1824), south of the town centre, is also worth seeing: it contains an altar panel from around 1500. The port of **Melbu**, where an important fishing fleet is based, lies in the south of the island. The historic Melbu Hovedgård (1830) with its beautiful warehouse (»stabbur«) is notable, as is the 200-year-old Rødgården, where changing exhibitions are held during summer. There is a wonderful view of the islands from **Husbykollen** (513m/ 1683ft), and there are also beautiful views of the sea and islands from the road that runs along the west coast from Melbu back to Stokmarknes. There is a lovely **sandy beach** near Taen, where swimmers can enjoy the midnight sun.

Hadseløya

Fishing boats in the harbour of Nykvåg, on the west side of Langøya island

Whale Hunting

Whaling has played a role in the economic foundation of Norway since time immemorial. This is particularly true for the settlements of the north Norwegian coast. After stocks of all large whale species were substantially decimated throughout the world due to overfishing, the International Whaling Commission (IWC) banned whale hunting and the export of whale meat in 1986. Norway does not recognize this ban and continues whaling.

A telltale blast of condensed water vapour shoots out of the sea. The ship will now pursue the whale for as long as it takes to have it in front of its bow, so that it can be killed by the harpoon cannon. Once the harpoon has embedded itself in the body of the ocean-going mammal, a small grenade explodes inside the animal at a depth of around 60cm/24 inches. On average, the animals are dead within three minutes, but sometimes the battle with death can also take up to an hour. The cadaver is then brought alongside the ship with the harpoon rope before being heaved on board where it is immediately quartered. The whale, a resource for humans for generations, supplies not only oil and blubber but also the raw materials for industrial products such as perfume, cosmetics, shoe polish, cod liver oil, glue, gelatine, fertilizer, animal feed and hormone pills. Norway and Japan are among the few nations that still hunt whales.

Norway Swims Against the Tide

When, in 1993, the Norwegian government decided to permit once more the hunting of up to 800 minke whales annually, and despite the fact that the real quota lay well below that figure, a cry of outrage rang out among the international animal protection community. Foreign firms answered with a boycott of Norwegian products. European politicians saw the countrys membership application for the EU endangered. The Norwegian government insisted, however, that whaling was not only a matter of economic interests, but also a matter of principle: Norway must be allowed to administer its ocean resources independently and responsibly. Meanwhile, the International Whaling Commission (IWC) added further restrictions to the 1986 prohibition of commercial whaling in 1993. A limited number of whales may be hunted for research purposes. This loophole allows the Japanese to kill 440 minke whales annually, supposedly for research purposes.

What is the Purpose of Whaling?

Norway returned to whaling with the justification that minke whale stocks are not endangered, since there are around 750,000 animals of this species found throughout the world. The country is the only one that is not tied to the decisions

Prized mammals: whaling tarnishes Norway's otherwise positive ecological image

of the IWC, because it exercised a veto against the whaling ban. Furthermore, the kill quota clearly lies below the rate of reproduction. The hunting of the larger and rarer species of whale, such as sperm whale, blue whale, fin whale and humpback whale continues to be strictly forbidden in Norway, just as in the rest of the world. Despite these figures, which are basically accepted by Greenpeace, it was of all countries Norway – normally considered advanced in ecological matters – that suffered a severe blow to its image due to its decision to recommence whaling. From a strictly economic point of view, whaling makes no sense in a country that has become rich from North Sea oil. The profits from whaling are estimated to be over 4 million pounds annually and no more than 100 people still work in the business, many of them second-jobbers. In spite of decreasing

demand for whale meat the Norwegian government allows up to 1052 minke whales to be killed annually – although the actual figure for each of the hunting seasons of 2006 and 2007 was less than 600 animals.

Whale Hunts Once Took Months

The era of widespread whale massacres had already come to an end in the 1960s, simply because it was no longer economically viable: only a few hundred individual animals of the large whale species remained in Antarctic waters. Even today, there are still only a few thousand of the up to 40m/131ft-long blue whales, when once there were 250,000. Parts of the whaling fleets from all the industrial nations, with Norway leading the way, had moved out of their coastal waters to the Arctic and Antarctic oceans by the turn of the 19th century, in order to hunt down the animals that supplied so many raw materials during expeditions that took many months. But the range of products produced by the synthetic industries eventually made these gruelling whaling journeys pointless. What is hunted today is the relatively small minke whale (10m/33ft). However, due to the violent protests and occasionally militant obstruction efforts mounted by foreign »whale kissers« – as fishermen disparagingly call them – the relations between whalers and animal rights activists have become strained. This is the reason there is probably no chance that any tourist would succeed in coming along on a whaling ship.

Whale Safari

In order to enjoy the majestic ocean animals first hand, a bloodless »whale safari« is recommended, such as those offered from the small port of Andenes on the Vesterålen island of Andøya. As with the inhabitants of California, the

locals have discovered the financial benefits of whale tourism as an alternative to hunting. Not far north of Andøya the flat continental shelf meets the deeper waters of the Atlantic. Warm and cold ocean currents meet here, which draws ocean life of many different species, among them the 20m/66ft sperm whales that can be observed rising from the deep to breathe. During summer, these large whales leave their territories near the equator and migrate to Norways coast to eat their fill there. Sperm whales have teeth, so their diet includes fish, as well as plankton. A whale safari costs around £70 and lasts several hours, requiring appropriate clothing for the weather and good sea legs. Some people may suffer many hours of sea sickness on the small former whaling craft before a whale is seen. The sight of such a giant is compensation enough, though, for any hardships suffered; which explains the growing number of whale watching fans.

Bloodless exploitation: whale watching near Andøya

★ Voss

✦ C 3

Region: West Norway
Population: 14,000

Architecturally, Voss has little to offer due to its many plain post-war buildings, but its location is unique. Located on the shores of Lake Vangsvatn and surrounded by high mountains, the town is an ideal base for active holidays.

Voss is not only a significant industrial town and transport hub on the Bergen railway line, but also a busy tourist and winter sports resort with a large selection of hotels and guesthouses. Above the railway station, a cable car leads up the approximately 700m/2297ft-high Hangursnolten mountain. The town is an excellent base for excursions to the ▶Sognefjord and the ▶Hardangerfjord.

Good base for excursions

WHAT TO SEE IN AND AROUND VOSS

One of the few buildings to survive the German aerial bomb raids of 1940 unscathed is the early Gothic **Vangs church** dating from 1277, situated in the centre of Voss. The formerly late Gothic altar cupboard received a Baroque restyling in the 17th century to create an altar panel that was painted by Bergen-born Elias Figenschoug, a pupil of Rubens. The chandelier in the choir comes from Holland and dates from 1614. The stone Olav Cross was erected to the southeast of the church to recall the region's Christianization during the 11th century. Norway's oldest secular wooden building, the **Finnesloftet** guild hall built in 1250, is located

Voss

> **!** | *Breathtaking views* | Insider Tip
>
> MARCO ⊕ POLO TIP
>
> At Vinje it is worth making a side trip to Stahlheim and one of Norway's most famous viewing points. There is a breathtaking view of the Nærøy valley, 550m/1804ft down below, from the terrace of the Stahlheim Hotel (open access), which once inspired J.C. Dahl to paint his famous picture Stahlheim (1842) that hangs in the National Gallery in Oslo.

15mins walk from the centre, to the west of the railway station, at Finnesveien. The open-air museum is set in a wonderfully panoramic location to the north of the railway station. The 16 wooden buildings of the Mølsterhof reflect the traditional building arts of the 17th to the 19th century, as well as the people's way of life in the fjord regions. The internationally renowned wood carver **Magnus Dagestad** (1865–1957) established a museum that exhibits much of his work.

Voss Folkmuseum: May–Aug daily 10am–5pm, otherwise Mon–Fri
9am–3pm, Sun noon–3pm; 70 NOK; www.hardangerogvossmuseum.no
Dagestad Museum: June–15th Aug Tue–Sat 11am–2pm, Gjernes,
Helgavangen.

Gudvang The Nærøyfjord, a southern arm of the Sognefjord (Sognefjord, surroundings), can be reached via the E 16 from Vinje. There
are also buses running between Voss and Gudvangen, which lies at
the southern end of the fjord. A visit to the Magic White Caves at
Gudvangen is an amazing experience that is made truly memorable
by the light show and classical music inside the labyrinth. The only
other place where the anorthosite rock of this mountain is found is
the moon.
❶ www.gudvangen.com.

**To the west, the Sognefjord splits into a number of narrow arms,
such as the Nærøyfjord surrounded by perpendicular cliff faces**

The Aurlandsfjord, another branch of the Sognefjord, lies east of the Nærøyfjord (Sognefjord, surroundings). This gash in the mountains, less than 2km/1mi wide, is flanked by rockfaces 900m/2953ft–1200m/3937ft high. **The region's oldest stone church** (around 1200) is in Aurlandsvangen, the administrative centre for the district of Aurland.

Aurlands-
vangen

At the southern end of the Aurlandsfjord lies the tourist resort of Flåm (don't miss a tour with beer tasting at the new Ægir Microbrewery), at the exit of the Flåmdal valley, south of Aurlandsvangen. This is the end of the Flåm railway line, a branch line of the Bergen railway that leads to Mydal station, to the east of Voss. This is probably **Norway's most spectacular railway line**. Built between 1920 and 1940, the route has the distinction of being the world's steepest railway line to run without the help of rack-wheels. There are 22 tunnels on the route and an elevation differential of 864m/2835ft over a distance of just 20km/13mi is covered during the 50-minute journey from Flåm to Mydal (connections to the Bergen line). The views change con-

*Flåm
railway

Voss

INFORMATION
Destinasjon Voss AS
Vangsgata 20, 5700 Voss
tel. 40 61 77 00
www.visitvoss.no

LEISURE AND SPORT
The tourist office in Voss can provide info on white-water rafting, sea kayaking, rafting, riding on fjord horses, fishing and skiing. One of Norway's top alpine ski centres is at Bavallen (cable car) to the northwest of Voss, where there are opportunities for cross-country skiing, alpine skiing, biathlons and trick skiing.

WHERE TO EAT
Ringheim Kafe £
Vangsgata 32
tel. 56 51 13 65
www.ringheimkafe.no
Baguettes, pizza, pasta, a typical Norwe-

gian Smørebrød and homemade cake are served here.

WHERE TO STAY
Fleischer's Hotel £ £ £ £
Evangervn. 13
tel. 56 52 05 00
www.fleischers.no, 110 rooms.
The Belle Epoque façade dating from 1889 has lost something of its beauty because of the modern annex. Nevertheless, this hotel built in the Swiss style is still one of the town's architectural jewels.

Tvinde Camping £
12km/7mi north of Voss
tel. 56 51 69 19
www.tvinde.no
This campsite by the 150m/492ft-high Tvindefoss also rents out cabins and holiday apartments of varying levels of comfort.

A Train Through the High Mountains

*It is only 470km/294mi long and its highest point lies at just 1301m/
4269ft, yet the Bergen railway route that connects Bergen with the capital city of Oslo is considered one of the most fascinating rail journeys in
Europe.*

The Bergen railway, which also stops in Voss, is largely famous thanks to the fantastic route it follows, which passes through almost all the types of landscape that Norway has to offer: forests and lakes in the east, the cultivated land of the Hallingdal valley, the high mountains and plateaus of Hardangervidda, and the fjords to the west.

Leisurely Tempo

The entire journey takes nearly seven hours – hardly a record-breaking time in this era of high-speed trains. The most beautiful section runs through the high mountains. The train travels above the tree line, which in southern Norway lies at around 900m/2953ft, and is exposed to the whims of nature while crossing a barren highland plateau on a 100km/63mi stretch between

Ustaoset and Myrdal. In the area around the small village of Finse (only accessible by train) in particular, storms and snow with up to 15m/49ft drifts make life difficult for the railway staff during the dark season of the year. Here, at the watershed of the damp western Norwegian climate and the drier one of the east, it can snow hard, even during the summer months. The creation of the Bergen railway line is thanks in great part to interested parties in western Norway at the end of the 19th century, who sought a definite cross-country connection to the capital of Kristiania. Enthralled by the technological innovations of the time, they were convinced the train was the answer. Fifteen years was spent building the route, during which engineers created a logistical masterpiece: the route was designed in such a way that neither superfluous stone materials were left over nor additional material brought in. All the required shoring up was achieved using rock from tunnel excavations. The inaugural journey in January 1908 was the first to fall victim to the vagaries of nature: the train got stuck in snow on the fjell and it took tremendous effort to rescue the passengers. Half a year later they tried again – and this time passengers were safely conveyed from the Oslofjord to Bergen in 21 hours.

stantly, from snow-covered mountains to wild waterfalls and green meadows. An intermediate stop is made very close to the mighty Kjosfossen waterfall. Groups should book ahead as demand is always very high. ❶ During summer the railway runs about ten times a day, otherwise around four times a day; time table and discounts at www.visitflam.com

> **MARCO ⊕ POLO TIP**
>
> **!** *The Rallarvegen* Insider Tip
>
> A beautiful hike can be made from Mydal down into the Flåmdal valley along the Rallar footpath. The first section is especially spectacular, with 21 hairpin bends and a slope of 15%. The mountains rise up almost vertically. After about 2.5hrs of walking, Berekvam station is reached, where the next Flåm train can be caught.

A worthwhile detour from Flåm is to the tiny settlement of **Undredal**, with Scandinavia's tiniest still operational church. This stave church, originally built in 1147 and rebuilt in around 1700, is less than 4m/13ft wide and has 40 seats. The hamlet is just a short distance from Aurlandsvangen, the administrative centre for the Aurland region. Also noteworthy is the outstanding goat's cheese produced in Undredal, which has its own festival, held every two years. Another good spot for cheese is Vik, on the southern shores of the Sognefjord, north of Vik, which also has a cheese festival dedicated to its Gamalost cheese each June.
❶ www.gamalostfestivalen.no

About 11km/7mi southeast of Voss, the RV 13 leads in the direction of the Hardangerfjord at the southern end of the Opelandsvatnet. It passes through the Skjervedal valley enclosed by mighty rock faces. This section of road, about 3km/2mi long, was built as early as 1863–70; this is where the Skjervefoss waterfall, formed by the Granvinelva, cascades down into the valley.

*Skjervet

PRACTICAL INFORMATION

What means of transport works best in Norway? When is the best time to go? What are the pitfalls? Find out here – ideally before you leave!

Arrival · Before the Journey

ARRIVAL

By air Flights from the UK to Norway tend to operate to the capital Oslo, but there are also direct connections to cities along the country's North Sea coast. For the no-frills, **low-cost flights**, Ryanair (www.ryanair. com) and local budget airline Norwegian (www.norwegian.no) are the carriers to check out. Prospective travellers in the north of England may also be interested in the low-cost airline Jet2's (www.jet2. com) service to Bergen from Newcastle Airport. Ryanair flies direct to Haugesund Karmoy and Oslo Sandefjord Torp airports from London Stansted. There are also daily Ryanair flights from Newcastle to Torp. The budget airline also flies to Oslo from Glasgow Prestwick, Liverpool and London Stansted airports, as well as operating flights between Stansted and the western Norwegian city of Haugesund. Norwegian offers direct flights from Stansted to Oslo, Rygge, Bergen, Trondheim, and Tromsø, from Gatwick to Oslo and Stavanger, and from Edinburgh to Oslo. The routes Stansted to Stavanger, and Edinburgh to Bergen, Bodø, Stavanger, Tromsø, and Trondheim, require a stop in Oslo. **British Airways** (www.ba.com) flies direct from Heathrow to Oslo, and **SAS Scandinavian Airlines** (www.flysas.com) also offers direct flights to Norway: from Gatwick to Bergen, from Heathrow to Stavanger, and from Newcastle to Stavanger. There are **bmi** flights (www.flybmi.com) between Heathrow and Stavanger too, as well as a direct connection between Oslo and Heathrow.

Oslo's Torp Sandefjord airport is 130km/80mi from the city centre. A shuttle bus brings passengers free of charge to the railway station to board the regional train for the lengthy journey into the capital. **Oslo Gardermoen airport** is 47km/29mi from the city, but the high-speed »Flytoget« train carries passengers to the centre within 20 minutes. For internal flight connections: ▶Transport.

By car Since the opening of the 16km/10mi-long **Öresund bridge** between Copenhagen and Malmö (Sweden), it is possible to reach Norway overland. The bridge toll is €47 for cars, €94 for mobile homes (2015); www.oresundsbron.com. Those driving from the UK can use the Eurostar service through the Channel Tunnel or make the crossing by car ferry, either across the Channel or to the western coast of Denmark (see below).

By ferry Due in part to rising fuel costs, DFDS Seaways announced the complete withdrawal of its historic Newcastle to Norway ferry routes as of September 2008. For the first time in a century, there is currently

FERRY FROM UK TO DENMARK
Harwich – Esbjerg (»M/S Dana Sirena«)
DFDS Seaways, 19hrs

FERRIES FROM DENMARK
Frederikshavn – Oslo
Color Line, 9–14hrs (»M/S Color Festival«)
Stena Line, 9–14hrs (»M/S Stena Saga«)

Hanstholm – Egersund/ Haugesund/Bergen
Fjord Line, 8hrs to Egersund, 13hrs to Haugesund, 18hrs to Bergen
(»M/S Atlantic Traveller«)

Hanstholm – Kristiansand
Master Ferries, 2hrs (Mastercat)

Hirtshals – Larvik
Color Line, as of May 2008: 4hrs (Super Speed 2)

Hirtshals – Kristiansand
Color Line, 4.5hrs or 6hrs (M/S Christian IV) and 3.5hrs (Super Speed 1)

Hirtshals – Stavanger/Bergen
Color Line, approx. 12hrs to Stavanger, 18–20hrs to Bergen (»M/S Prinsesse Ragnhild«)

Copenhagen – Oslo
DFDS Seaways, approx. 16hrs (»M/S Crown of Scandinavia«)

FERRIES FROM GERMANY
Kiel – Oslo
Color Line, approx. 20hrs (»M/S Color Magic«, »M/S Color Fantasy«)

Puttgarden – Rødby (Denmark; Fugleflugtslinien)
Scandlines, approx. 1hr

Rostock (international port) – Gedser (Denmark)
Scandlines, 2hrs

FERRIES FROM DENMARK TO SWEDEN
(Copenhagen–) Helsingør – Helsingborg
Scandlines, 1.5hrs

Frederikshavn – Göteborg
Stena Line, 2–3.5hrs

Grenå – Varberg
Stena Line, 4hrs

FERRY COMPANIES
Color Line
www.colorline.com
tel. +47 (0) 22 94 42 00

DFDS Seaways
www.dfdsseaways.co.uk
tel. 0871 522 9955

Fjord Line
www.fjordline.com
tel. +47 (0) 815 33 500

Kystlink
www.kystlink.no
tel. +47 (0) 815 56 715

Master Ferries AS
www.masterferries.com
tel. +47 (0) 815 26 500

Scandlines
www.scandlines.com
tel. +49 (0) 381 5435-0

Stena Line
www.stenaline.com
tel. +46 (0) 31 85 80 00

For journeys on the Hurtigruten line
Hurtigruten Ltd. 3 Shortlands, London, W6 8NE tel. 020 88 46 26 66
www.hurtigruten.co.uk

NO FERRY CONNECTIONS FROM UK
The historic DFDS Seaways Newcastle to Norway route was scrapped in September 2008.

no ferry service from the UK to Norway. However a DFDS Seaways ferry, »M/S Dana Sirena«, does sail every other day from Harwich in Essex to Esbjerg in the Ribe region of western Denmark. Those in continental Europe can travel easily to western Norway from Hirtshals at the northern tip of Denmark; Kristiansand is just a short ferry journey away. There is also a ferry connection to Bergen from Denmark's Hanstholm. These routes are heavily frequented during the high season – make sure you book well in advance.

By rail   It is of course possible to travel from London to Oslo by rail. Take the Eurostar through the Channel Tunnel to Brussels, board a connecting Thalys or Deutsche Bahn ICE train to Cologne, and then to Hamburg (IC train) to catch a ICE to Copenhagen. From here, there is a high speed Linx train to Gothenburg (3hrs 30mins), from which Oslo is another 4hrs 15mins away. A good source of information for those who wish to take the train is www.seat61.com.

By bus   National Express coaches leave London Victoria coach station for Oslo three to five times weekly. The journey takes around 32hrs, with half-hour waits in Brussels and Copenhagen (www.eurolines.co.uk).

TRAVEL REGULATIONS

Travel documents   Though not a member of the EU, Norway has signed the Schengen Agreement which is intended to do away with border controls within the European Union. The UK and Republic of Ireland apply the Schengen provisions regarding police and judicial cooperation, but have not ended border controls with EU states, so UK and Irish nationals, as well as those from outside the EU, will need a valid **passport**. Those wishing to remain in Norway for over three months or to seek employment there must apply for a residency permit. **Driving licence** National driving licences and vehicle registration documents of European Union nationals are recognized in Norway. In the case of traffic incidents involving damage to vehicles, the **international green car insurance card** is required. All cars must display the blue European Union sticker or the oval European national stickers.

Healthcare Healthcare needs should be covered by private travel and health insurance. European Union citizens should also remember to bring their **European Health Insurance Card** (EHIC) which replaced the E111 form in 2004 (see www.ehicard.org).

Dogs and cats can be brought to Norway as long as they have been vaccinated against rabies and have been issued with a pet passport. A period of six months should be planned for required vaccinations. See www.pettravel.com or contact the Norwegian tourist office for more precise information (▶Information).

Pets

CUSTOMS REGULATIONS

The following **alcoholic beverages** can be imported duty free: 1.5 litre/0.39 US gal of wine, 1 litre spirits (minimum age 20) and 2 litres/0.5 US gal of beer; or 2 litres of wine and 2 litres of beer. 200 cigarettes or 250g/9oz of tobacco (minimum age 18) can be imported, along with gifts to a value of £600/6000 NOK. Duty can be paid to import an additional 4 litres/1 US gal of wine or spirits, or 10 litres/2.6 US gal of beer and 400 cigarettes. The minimum age for importing spirits is 20; it is 18 for wine.
The importation of **hunting weapons** is governed by special regulations. The importation of drugs, poisons, weapons, ammunition and explosives (with the exception of hunting materials), fishing nets and lobster and crab catching equipment is **prohibited**.

Arrival

Travellers returning to the UK from Norway, a non-EU country, can bring the following quantities duty free for personal use: 200 cigarettes (or 100 cigarillos, 50 cigars or 250g/9oz tobacco); 2 litres/0.5 US gal of still table wine, 1 litre/0.26 US gal of spirits with more than 22% alcohol content or 2 litres/0.5 US gal of fortified wine, sparkling wine or other liqueurs, 60cc/2 fl oz of perfume, 250cc/8.5 fl oz of eau de toilette, plus goods to a value of £145/1400 NOK.

Returning to the UK

MOSQUITO PLAGUE

The plague of mosquitoes during the warm seasons particularly affects Norway's damp and lower-lying regions. Myriads of insects, including the ones that bite, buzz and whirr through the air in the river valleys, along lakes and especially in the high north, where the sun never sets for almost half the year. It is therefore imperative to pack insect repellent and even mosquito nets. Salt water is unattractive for mosquitoes, so those travelling near the sea and the fjords should escape torment.

Insect repellent a must!

Electricity

220 volt The Norwegian mains supply is generally 220 volts. Visitors who are not from mainland Europe are advised to take an **adapter**.

Emergency

GENERAL EMERGENCIES
Emergency doctor
tel. 113

Fire services
tel. 110

Police
tel. 112

Automobile Association
tel. 00 44 8705 33 22 11

Cega Air Ambulance (worldwide service)
tel. +44(0)1243 621097
www.cega-aviation.co.uk

Call centre for members of Norwegian automobile clubs
tel. 81 00 05 05, www.theaa.com

US Air Ambulance
tel. 800/948-1214 (US; toll-free)
tel. 001-941-926-2490
(international; collect)
www.usairambulance.net

Etiquette and Customs

Reserved people
Part of a successful holiday is making an effort to avoid misunderstandings that can otherwise spoil the atmosphere. Norwegians may appear somewhat reserved, even unfriendly, but as a rule this is not the impression your hosts wish to give. Instead it is typical of many a Norwegian's characteristically **reticent nature**. Conversely, Norwegians value tactful and discrete behaviour. Shaking hands is not common in Norway and a short »hei« is normally sufficient when greeting a local. Another Norwegian phrase that is essential is **takk – thank you**. Without »takk«, nothing gets done in this country. The modest Norwegians do not make much of their titles or honours: no one here would ever think of introducing themselves as »Dr. Knudsen«, for example.

Potential blunders
Remove your shoes before setting foot in someone's house: it is considered the height of bad manners to enter a home with street

shoes on. This also goes for many mountain huts, where walking boots should remain outside. There are really only two conversation topics that are risky: **patriotism and whaling**. As regards the former, Norwegians are proud of themselves and their small country and show national pride unreservedly. It is quite normal to hoist the patriotic Norwegian flag outside the summer home and to celebrate national holidays with the royals accompanied by much flag waving and the donning of traditional dress. If you dare to broach the subject of whaling in the far north, it will quickly become clear that Greenpeace sympathizers are few and far between in this region.

The increasing number of foreign mobile homes and camper vans has become a problem. **Rubbish** in the countryside and dirty toilets have led to a prohibition of overnight camping on the open road almost everywhere, including popular areas such as the Jotunheimen mountains. The **right of public access** (generally free access to land – fenced or not – and permission to camp at least one night) typical of Scandinavia that existed before mass tourism was only really intended for hikers. In fact, there are already those demanding drastic restrictions on this historic right. To encourage a continuation of this almost limitless freedom of the open road in Norway for the future, it is a good idea to follow the local example and ensure no damage is done to the sensitive Norwegian environment, and to leave no traces of your visit (for more information see 'Right of Public Access' on the official Norway website: www.norway.org.uk). **Limits on freedom**

Norwegian nightlife cannot be compared with that in central Europe and the Mediterranean, not least because of the **extremely restrictive laws on the consumption of alcohol and tobacco**. Bar opening times and drinks licences are highly regulated. The most highly developed nightlife so far is found in Olso, where there are countless nightclubs and bars. Night owls will also find nocturnal entertainment in Bergen, Stavanger, Tromsø and Bodø. **Norway by night?**

In recent years, the Norwegian government has continuously refined the laws directed against tobacco consumption. There is a strict no-smoking policy for all public buildings and transport, in restaurants, cafés and bars. In urban areas smoking while driving is prohibited. The minimum age for buying tobacco is 18. **No smoking!**

Those providing standard services do not normally expect a tip in Norway, although it is worth remembering that although prices are high in Norway, salaries in the service sectors are certainly not. For many city and tour guides, for example, tips represent a significant portion of their income. In restaurants it is customary to round up the final bill, and taxi drivers also receive a small tip for their services. **Tipping**

Health

Medical care
In Norway initial medical care and emergency care normally take place via the hospitals (sykehus, sjukehus) or emergency surgeries (legevakt) and only rarely at private doctors' practices. As virtually every Norwegian is familiar with this system, it is easy to get information on the nearest hospital. The **phone numbers** for doctors are on page 2 of Norwegian phone books (search under »Legevakten« for doctors, »Tannleger« for dentists).

Health insurance
The European Health Insurance Card is acceptable for medical consultations in Norway (▶p.451).

Pharmacies (apotek)
There are numerous pharmacies located in all cities and major settlements in the country. They are open during normal shop opening hours, and there are also emergency pharmacies that open at other times in the towns. Medication can only be purchased by presenting a Norwegian doctor's prescription in a pharmacy.

Information

USEFUL ADRESSESIN THE UK AND REPUBLIC OF IRELAND
Innovation Norway (Norwegian Tourist Board)
5th Floor, Charles House
5 Lower Regent Street
London SW1Y 4LR
tel. 020 7389 8800
www.visitnorway.com

IN THE USA
Norwegian Tourist Board
655 Third Ave
10017 New York
tel. +1 212 885 9700
Fax +1 212 885 9710
www.visitnorway.com

IN CANADA
Tourist information provided by the Norwegian Embassy
See embassy contact information
www.emb-norway.ca/travel/ or
www.emb-norway.ca/faq/tourism/

IN AUSTRALIA AND NEW ZEALAND
Scandinavian Tourist Board
Contact: Carpe Diem
Level 1, 16 Foster Street
Surry Hills, NSW 2010
tel. + 61 (0) 2 9212 1332
www.visitscandinavia.com.au

EAST NORWAY
A/L Gudbrandsdal Reiseliv
Vinstra Skysstasjon,
N-2640 Vinstra

tel. 61 29 47 70
www.gudbrandsdalen.no

Hedmark Reiseliv BA
Grønneg 11, N-2317 Hamar
tel. 62 55 33 20
www.hedmark.com

SOUTH NORWAY
Telemarkreiser AL
Nedre Hjelleg. 18, N-3724 Skien
tel. 35 90 00 20, fax 35 90 00 21
www.telemarkreiser.no

Vest-Agder Fylkeskommune
Tordenskjoldsgate 65
N-4614 Kristiansand
tel. 38 07 45 00, fax 38 07 45 01
www.vaf.no

WEST NORWAY
Fjord Norge AS
P.O. Box 4108, N-5835 Bergen
tel. 55 30 26 40, fax 55 30 26 50
www.fjordnorway.no

Hordaland Reiseliv
Strømgaten 4, Pb. 416 Marken
N-5828 Bergen
tel. 55 31 66 00, fax 55 31 52 08
www.visithordaland.no

Møre og Romsdal Reiseliv
Fylkeshuset, N-6404 Molde
tel. 71 24 50 80, fax 71 24 50 81
www.visitmr.com

Sogn og Fjordane Reiseliv
P.O. Box 299 N-6852 Sogndal
tel. 57 67 23 00, fax 57 67 28 06
www.sfr.no

CENTRAL NORWAY
Trøndelag Reiseliv
P.O. Box 65, N-7400 Trondheim

tel. 73 84 24 40, fax 73 84 24 50
www.trondelag.com

NORTH NORWAY
Nordland Reiseliv
P.O. Box 434, N-8001 Bodø
tel. 75 54 52 00, fax 75 54 52 10
www.visitnordland.no

Finnmark
Finnmark Reiseliv
Sorenskriverveien 13 N-9511 Alta
tel. 78 44 00 20, fax 78 43 51 84
www.visitnorthcape.com

NORWEGIAN EMBASSIES
In the UK
25 Belgrave Square
London SW1X 8QD
tel. 020 7591 5500
emb.london@mfa.no

In the Republic of Ireland
34 Molesworth Street
Dublin 2
tel. +353 1 662 1800
emb.dublin@mfa.no

In the USA
2720 34th Street, N.W.
Washington, D.C. 20008
tel. 202 333 6000
washington@invanor.no

In Canada
150 Metcalfe Street, Suite 1300
Ottawa, Ontario K2P 1P1
tel. (613) 238 6571
emb.ottawa@mfa.no

In Australia
17 Hunter Street
Yarralumla ACT 2600
tel. +61 2 6273 3444
emb.canberra@mfa.no

A listing of Norwegian embassies and consulates is available at www.embassies.mfa.no.

EMBASSIES IN NORWAY
British Embassy
Thomas Heftyes gate 8
N-0244 Oslo
tel. 23 13 27 00
www.britishembassy.gov.uk
The British Embassy also handles Australian consular affairs.

Irish Embassy
4th Fl, Håkon VII's gate 1

N-0212 Oslo
tel. 22 01 72 00

United States Embassy
Drammsveien 18
N-0244 Oslo
tel. 22 44 85 50
www.usa.no

Canadian Embassy
Wergelandsveien 7
N-0244 Oslo
tel. 22 99 53 00
www.dfait-maeci.gc.ca

Language

In many places in Norway it is perfectly possible to communicate in English, but in remote areas, especially in central and north Norway, it is useful to know the most important words and phrases. The following explanations and vocabulary offer just the basics. For a deeper understanding of the Norwegian language, the purchase of a language guide is recommended.

Indo-Germanic language

Norwegian belongs to the North Germanic or Scandinavian language group. It has a curious proclivity to suffixes, as shown in the added on articles and in the formation of the passive, for example: veien = the path, huset = the house, hjelp søkes = help needed. In the Norwegian alphabet, æ, ø and å follow on from z.

Two languages

The Norwegian language today is split into the Danish-rooted Bokmål and Nynorsk (new Norwegian), which was borne of various dialects and which was also known as Landsmål until 1929. The increased national consciousness of the population inspired by independence from Denmark in 1814 led to a rediscovery of the old Norwegian language. While Nynorsk is predominantly spoken in the southwest and west of the country, Bokmål is spoken in the country's east and in the cities; both languages have equal status.

Pronunciation

Norwegian pronunciation presents a challenge to native English speakers. Vowels have a long and a short version, so that a can be pronounced like the u in cut or like the a in father; å is either like the o in pot, or the aw in law; e or æ is short as in bet or long as in the British received pronunciation of day; i is either like the i in police or the double-e in seethe; o is pronounced short like pot or put, or long as in zoo or or; ø is like the e in her; u is like the u in put or the double-o in soon; and y is spoken as if saying ee with pursed lips. As for consonants, d is usually silent before s, after n and l, also as the final consonant after r; g is spoken as in go unless before ei, i, j, øy, or y when it is like the y in yard; j is always like the y in yard; egn is pronounced as the ine in fine; ng is like the ng in sing; r is normally trilled as in Spanish, while in southwest Norway it is like the r in the French word rien; and s is like the s in so, except when sk is followed by ei, i, j, øy, or y, when it becomes a sh sound, making the Norwegian pronunciation of ski more like she.

Norwegian Language Guide

At a glance

Yes/No	Ja./Nej.
Maybe	Kanskje.
Thanks / Please	Takk / Vær så snill.
My pleasure (answer to thanks)	Ja takk!
My pleasure	Det var da så lite.
Sorry	Unnskyld!
What did you say?	Unnskyld!
I don't understand you	Jeg forstår deg ikke.
I only speak a little …	Jeg snakker bare litt …
I like that (not)	Det liker jeg (ikke).
Do you have …?	Har dere/du …?
How much is it?	Hva koster det?
What time is it?	Hvor mye er klokka?

Greetings

Good morning	God morgen!
Good day	God dag!
Good evening	God kveld!
Hallo!	Hallo!/Hei!
My name is …	Navnet mitt er …
What is your name?	Unnskyld, hva var navnet?
How are you?	Hvordan har du det?
Thanks. And you?	Takk, bra. Og du?
Goody bye	På gjensyn!
See you soon	Vi sees!

Travel information

left/right	til venstre/til høyre
straight ahead	rett fram
near/far	nær/langt
Excuse me, where is ...?	Unnskyld, hvor ligger ...?
Railway station	hovedstasjon
Metro	T-bane
Airport	flyplass?
I want to rent...	Jeg ville gjerne leie ...
... a car	...en bil
... a bicycle	...en sykkel

Breakdown

I have broken down	Jeg har en skade på bilen.
Where is there a car mechanic workshop near here?	Fins det et verkstedi nærheten?

Petrol station

Where is the next petrol station please?	Unnskyld, hvor er nærmestebensinstasjon?
I would like ...liters.	Jeg skal ha ...liter ...
... petrol.	...normalbensin.
...premium petrol.	...super.
...diesel.	...diesel
...unleaded/leaded.	...blyfri/ ...blyholdig
Fill it up, please	Full tank, takk

Accident

Help!	Hjelp!
Watch out!	Se opp!/Forsiktig!
Please quickly call ...	Vær så snill og ring etter ...straks.
...an ambulance.	...en sjukebil.
...the police.	...politiet.
...the fire brigade.	...brannvesenet.
Please give me your name and address.	Kan jeg få navnet og adressendin.

Eating/Entertainment

Where is there ...	Hvor er det ...
...a good restaurant?	...en god restaurant?
...an affordable restaurant?	...en ikke altfor dyr restaurant?
Cheers/To your health!	Skål!

| The bill please | Kan jeg/vi få betale! |
| The meal was very good. | Maten var utmerket. |

Shopping

Where do I find …	Hvor finner jeg…?
pharmacy	apotek
bakery	bakeri
photographic shop	fotoforretning
department store	varehus
provisions shop	dagligvareforretning
market	marked

Accommodation

Can you please recommend…?	Kan du anbefale meg …?
…a hotel	…et godt hotell
…a guesthouse	…et pensjonat
I have booked a room with you.	Jeg har reservert et rom hosdere.
Do you still have a room?	Har dere noe ledig rom?
a single / a double	et enkeltrom / et dobbeltrom
with shower/bath	med dusj/bad
for one night/week	for ei natt/uke
How much is the room with breakfast?	Hva koster rommet medfrokost?
…half board?	…halvpensjon?

Doctor

| It hurts here. | Jeg har vondt her. |

Bank and post office

Where is there …	Unnskyld, hvor finner jeg …
…a bank?	…en bank?
…a foreign currency exchange booth?	…et vekslingslkontor?
I would like to change …into Krone.	Jeg ville gjerne veksle… ikroner.
How much is …	Hvar koster …
…a letter …	…et brev …
…a post card …	…et postkort …
to England?	til England?

Days of the week

| Monday | mandag |
| Tuesday | tirsdag |

Wednesday	onsdag
Thursday	torsdag
Friday	fredag
Saturday	lørdag
Sunday	søndag

Numbers

0	null
1	ehn/ett
2	to
3	tre
4	fire
5	fem
6	seks
7	sju (syv)
8	åtte
9	ni
10	ti
11	elleve
12	tolv
13	tretten
14	fjorten
15	femten
16	seksten
17	sytten
18	atten
19	nitten
20	tjue (tyve)
21	tjueen
22	tjueto
30	tretti (tredve)
40	førti
50	femti
60	seksti
70	sytti
80	åtti
90	nitti
100	hundre
200	tohundre
1000	tusen
2000	totusen
10 000	titusen
1/2	en halv
1/4	en fjerdedel

Spisekart/Meny (Menu) Frokost (Breakfast)

svart kaffe	black coffee
kaffe med melk	coffee with milk
koffeinfri kaffe	decaffeinated coffee
te med melk/sitron	tea with milk/lemon
urtete	herbal tea
sjokolade	chocolate
fruktsaft/juice	fruit juice
blødkokt egg	soft egg
eggerøre	scrambled egg
egg og bacon	egg and bacon
brød/rundstykke/ristet brød	bread/roll/toast
horn	croissant
smør	butter
ost	cheese
pølse	sausage
skinke	ham
honning	honey
syltetøy	jam
mysli	muesli
yoghurt	yoghurt
frukt	fruit

forretter og supper (starters and soups)

tøndersodd	meat broth with vegetables and meat balls fromTrøndelag
ertesuppe	pea soup
fersk suppe	soup with fresh meat andvegetables
fiskesuppe	fish soup
gravlaks	salt and sugar cured salmon
kryddersild	spiced herring
rekecocktail	prawn salad in mayonnaise
røkelaks	smoked salmon
rømmegrøt	cream porridge with high fat content (35%);also served as main dish
speket reinsdyrkjøtt	pickled reindeer meat
salater	salads
tomatsild	tomato herring

Kjøttretter (meat dishes)

elgsteik	roast elk
fårikål	mutton and cabbage casserole
flesk	pork

ferskt kjøtt	boiled beef with vegetables and a light sauce
hjortesteik	roast stag
kalkun	turkey
kjøttkaker	meat balls in brown sauce
knackpølse	knackwurst sausage
kylling	chicken
lammefrikassé	fricassee of lamb
lammekoteletter	lamb cutlet
lammesteik	roast lamb
oksesteik	roast beef
rådyrsteik	roast deer
reinsdyrsteik	reindeer roast
spekemat	cold pickled or dried smoked meat
svinekotelett	pork cutlet
svinesteik	pork roast
vilt	game
wienerpølse	wiener sausage

Fisk og skalldyr (fish and shellfish)

ål	eel
blåskjell	mussel
fiskeboller	fish dumplings
fiskepudding	fish pudding
gjedde	hake
hummer	lobster
kreps	river crab
kveite	halibut
laks	salmon
makrell	mackerel
ørret	trout
rødspette	plaice
sei	coley
sik	vendace
spekesild	pickled herring
steinbit	spined loach
torsk	cod

Grønnsaker (vegetables)

agurksalat	cucumber salad
bakte poteter	baked potatoes
blandet salat	mixed salad
blomkål	red cabbage

champignon	mushrooms
erter	peas
gulrøtter	carrots
hodekål	white cabbage
kål	green cabbage
kantarell	chanterelle mushrooms
løk	onions
potet(mos)	mashed potatoes
rødkål	red cabbage
salat	salad
sopp	mushroom
steinsopp	porcini mushroom

Smørbrød (open sandwiches)

egg og ansjos	bread with boiled egg and anchovies
fiskekabaret	bread with fish and vegetables inaspic
karbonade	bread with meat balls
leverpostei med syltede agurker	bread with paté andpickled gherkin
patentsmørbrød	bread with fried egg and bacon
rekesmørbrød	bread with prawns in mayonnaise
roastbiff	bread with roast beef
svinesteik	bread with roast pork

Bakverk (pastries and cakes)

boller	sweet rolls with raisins
bløtkake	torte
eplekake	apple cake
julekake	raisinbread
lefse	soft, thin patty made of potatoe andflour
rulade	biscuit rollade
småkaker	biscuits
vannbakkels	cream puff
wienerbrød	Danish pastry

Dessert (desserts)

fruktkompott	stewed fruit
fruktsalat	fruit salad
is	ice
sjokolade	chocolate
jordbær	strawberry
vanilje	vanilla

jordbær med fløte	strawberries and cream
karamellpudding	caramel pudding
moltekrem	cloud berries and cream
osteanretning	cheese plate
riskrem	rice pudding with cream and red sauce
rødgrøt med fløte	red jelly with cream

Vinkart (wine list) Alkoholholdig (alcoholicdrinks)

akevitt	aquavit
fatøl	draught beer
hvitvin / rødvin	white wine / red wine
likør	liquor
øl	beer

Alkoholfritt (non-alcoholic drinks)

alkoholfri vin	alcohol-free wine
brus	lemonade
kaffe	coffee
kakao	cacao
melk	milk
saft	fruit juice
juice	fruit drink
sjokolade	hot chocolate
te	black tea
med sitron	with lemon
vann	water

Media

Newspapers & magazines

The top selling newspaper in Norway is the daily Aftenposten. As a rule the major newspapers and magazines in English are available in the larger towns one day after publication.

Radio

During the summer months, as a service for tourists, Norwegian Broadcasting (NRK) provides news programmes on the radio in English between 10am and 11am. The **BBC World Service** can be received on short wave or cable FM. Offering regular news bulletins as well as cultural and entertainment programmes, it broadcasts on 9410 kHz on the 31m waveband and on 6195 kHz on the 49m waveband. Full details can be found at www.bbc.co.uk/worldservice. Voice of America is also available on short wave (www.voanews.com).

Norwegian television usually transmits films and series in the original language with subtitles in the local language. The weather report at the end of the evening news is of no little interest; the symbols used are internationally recognizable, high and low pressure weather fronts being indicated by »H« and »L« as appropriate.

Television

Money

The national currency is the Norwegian krone (1 NOK = 100 øre). There are 50, 100 and 1000 krone notes, and coins to the value of 50 øre, as well as 1, 5 and 10 krone.

Currency

The import and export of both national and international currency is unrestricted, though the export of more than 25,000 NOK must be declared by filling in a customs form. There are no limits on travellers' cheques.

No restrictions

Credit cards The standard international credit cards such as Mastercard, American Express, Visa and Diners Club are accepted almost all over Norway. Travellers' cheques can normally be used without problems. Occasionally, however, transaction fees are imposed. ATM machines at all the important tourist destinations allow cash withdrawals using a bank card in conjunction with the PIN.

Credit cards

EXCHANGE RATES
1 NOK = £ 0.08
1 £ = 11.5 NOK
1 NOK = 0.13 US$
1 US$ = 7.4 NOK
1 NOK = €0.11
1 € = 8.8 NOK

LOST OR STOLEN CARDS
The following numbers can be used to report and stop lost or stolen bank and credit cards:

American Express
tel. +44 1273 696 933

MasterCard
tel. +44 20 7557 5000

Visa
tel. +1 410 581 9994

Diners Club
tel. +44 1252 513 500

HSBC
tel. +44 1442 422 929

Barclaycard
tel. +44 1604 230 230

NatWest
tel. +44 142 370 0545

Lloyds TSB
tel. +44 1702 278 270

Loss of bank cards and credit cards

If bank cards or cheque and credit cards should get lost, you should call your own bank or credit card organization to make sure they are immediately stopped. It is a good idea to make a note of the telephone number on the back of the card.

Bank opening times

Norwegian banks are open at the following times: Mon–Fri 8.15am–3.30pm, some also Thu 8.15am–5pm.

National Parks

Protected Areas

Norway has officially protected 43 regions and cultural areas of special significance, of which 36 are on the mainland and seven are on Svarlbard (Spitsbergen). Another three national parks were added in 2009, and another in 2011. The **Lomsdal Visten National Park** (1115 sq km/430 sq mi) protects the sub-arctic biosphere between fjords and fjells. In the **Breheimen National Park** (1794 sq km/693 sq mi), in the districts of Oppland and Sogn og Fjordane, the roots of its cultural heritage reach back into the early Stone Age (www.jostedal.com). The **Ytre Hvaler National Park** (www.ytrehvaler.no) is part of the inter-regional park project administrated jointly by Norway and Sweden, which includes Swedish Kosterhavets National Park. The maritime landscape in the **Oslofjord** off the south coast of Norway and the southwest coast of Sweden is home to over 6000 different species, of which 200 are endemic. This area is also where the world's largest known cold water coral reef is located among the skerry landscape. The **Sjunkhatten National Park** (417.5 sq km/161 sq mi) spreads out from sea level to an altitude of 1185m/3888ft) and is particularly intended to encourage children, youths and families to enjoy nature. The **Rohkunborri National Park** was established in the province of Troms in 2011, and covers an area of 572 sq km/221 sq mi. The varied landscape in the southeastern region of **Sørdalen** and its surrounding mountains is predominantly characterised by deciduous forests, wetlands and moors. The park also contains the larger lakes of Geavdnjávri and Eartebaalijárvi. Norway is home to Scandinavia's first UNESCO Geopark – the **Gea Norvegica Geopark** (www.geanor.no). Located near Skien and Larvik on the Fylke Vestfold and Telemark coast, the park protects 1500 million-year-old formations marking where ancient Scandinavia meets the younger continent of Europe.

All plants and animals are protected. Fishing is allowed according to certain rules. Mushrooms and berries can be picked, depending on local regulations. Motorized traffic is prohibited. Walkers should stick to marked footpaths and in the period between 15 April and 15 September it is strictly prohibited to light fires in the open.

Sights from A to Z describes the following national parks: Ånderdalen (see Senja), ►Dovrefjell-Sunndalsfjella, Femunden (see Femundsmarka), ►Hardangervidda, ►Jotunheimen, ►Jostedalsbreen, Ormtjernkampen (see Gudbrandsdal), Øvre Dividal (see Troms), Øvre Pasvik (see Finnmark), Rago National Park (see Bodø), Rondane (see Gudbrandsdal), Saltfjellet–Svartisen (see Saltfjellet), and on ►Spitsbergen the national parks Nordvest Spitsbergen, Forlandet and Sør Spitsbergen.

National Parks in this guide book

Post and Communications

Stamps can be purchased in all post offices, from machines, from many kiosks and in stationary shops. Letters and cards up to 20g within Norway cost 9.50 NOK; for destinations within Europe (clearly mark your letter »A - priority«) 13 NOK; elsewhere 15 NOK; www.posten.no.

Stamps and postage

All phone numbers have eight digits and there are **no local codes**. Coin operated telephones work with 1, 5, 10, and also 20 krone coins. Telephone cards (telekort) can be bought at kiosks and in post offices.

Telephone

Even remote areas of Norway have good mobile phone coverage. Owners of mobile phones will automatically be redirected to Norwegian service providers via their roaming facility. In contrast to landlines, there is no need to input the first double zero for international codes. As in other countries, car drivers in Norway are only allowed to telephone with hands-free equipment while driving.

Mobile telephones

TELEPHONE DIRECTORY SERVICES
National: tel. 180
International: tel. 181

INTERNATIONAL DIALLING CODES
Dialling codes to Norway
from the UK and Republic of Ireland:
tel. 00 47
from the USA, Canada and Australia:
tel. 00 11 47

Dialling codes from Norway
to the UK: tel. 00 44
to the Republic of Ireland: tel. 00 353
to the USA and Canada tel. 00 1
to Australia: tel. 00 61
The 0 that precedes the subsequent local area code is omitted.

Prices and Discounts

Norway is an expensive country. Here more than anywhere it pays to be on the look out for discounts. In border regions, it is worth shop-

Norway Card and City Card

ping in Sweden, where all goods are 10?20% cheaper. Norwegians themselves do it and spend over 10 billion NOK across the border each year. With Color Line's **Norway Card**, holidaymakers get between 10% and 60% discount at more than 60 Norwegian tourism companies. Oslo and Bergen offer a City Card with which parking is cheaper and entrance to museums is free or reduced (for more information see the relevant sections on ▶Bergen and ▶Oslo).

Accommo-dation

Accommodation is expensive in Norway, but many hotels offer weekend discounts. To take advantage of the hotels' **special offers**, it is often necessary to buy a hotel pass or a hotel cheque which gives discounts on accommodation, usually with breakfast included. Many discount cards, such as the Fjordpass (www.fjordpass.no), the Nordic Hotel Pass, the ProScandinavia Cheque or the Scandic Holiday Card, are valid in all Scandinavian countries. The hotel cheques have to be bought prior to your journey.

The Norwegian Trekking Association, the DNT (De Norske Turistforenig), maintains 420 cabins in Norway and those with a DNT Card can stay the night at much reduced rates. More information at www.turistforeningen.no.

Railway

Travelling by rail is a pleasure that doesn't come cheap in Norway. Discounts of 25% are available for groups of at least ten people (15% from June to August) and discounts of 50% are available for seniors from age 67. The ScanRail pass was discontinued at the end of 2007, meaning that European nationals must use the InterRail pass to get cheap rail travel in Norway (www.interrailnet.com). Three, four, six and eight-day passes can be purchased for between 181 and 311 Euros for second class tickets, and between 258 and 436 Euros for first class tickets. Non-Europeans can purchase the Eurail Scandinavia pass, which is almost identical to the old ScanRail pass (www.eurail. com).

Flights

Substantial discounts on domestic Scandinavian flight routes are available for those who use the **SAS Visit Scandinavia Air Pass**. Travel agents and SAS representative offices can supply the latest conditions. Travellers from the age of 18 have the option of taking part in the **SAS EuroBonus Programme** which offers air miles for multiple flights. Furthermore, participants gain discounts or air miles when checking into SAS hotels, as well as when hiring cars with Avis and Hertz. The Norwegian airline company Widerøe, which serves over 35 airports in the country, offers a **Explore Norway Ticket**, which offers unlimited flights within one or two chosen zones of Norway, or the entire country, during a period of 14 days. Extension weeks are available (zone 1: 2775 NOK; zone 2: 3375 NOK; all of Norway: 3975 NOK; www.wideroe.no). Carriers of the Braathens

SAFE airline operate from Kristiansand in the south as far as Tromsø and Spitsbergen in the north of the country, and serve 15 airports. For travellers resident outside Norway, discounts are available via the **Visit Norway Pass**, which is valid for one month.

Time

Central European Time (CET; GMT + 1hr) applies in Norway. From the end of March to the end of October the Central European Summer Time applies (CEST; British Summer Time + 1hr).

Winter and summer time

Transport

DRIVING IN NORWAY

Even though Norway is almost entirely mountainous, the road network is very well developed. In the south and on the major tourist routes during the holiday season, motor traffic is on a par with other European countries. However, the occasionally narrow **mountain roads**, often with limited visibility, require driving skill and a relatively disciplined attitude. Drivers heading uphill always have priority on difficult tight bends or on narrow stretches. Some mountain roads are only passable in one direction at a time. Travellers with mobile homes and camper vans would do well to make enquiries with an automobile club or at the »Vegdirektoratet« in Oslo before choosing routes. Certain stretches of road in the southern Norwegian mountains and in northern Norway are only passable from June to mid-October, due to the long winter season. Many bridges, tunnels and private roads charge tolls (»bompenger«). Some **minor roads** are unpaved gravel or sand roads.

Road network

There are around 50 toll roads in Norway, of which half are integrated into the AutoPASS system where you can no longer pay in cash. A credit card and car registration number must be registered in order to use the AutoPASS, whereby you can register online up to two weeks after passing the first toll station. Each time a vehicle passes a toll booth, the number plate is photographed and the fee is automatically deducted from the credit card associated with it. Vehicles up to 3.5t must register a 300 NOK credit on their AutoPASS; vehicles over 3.5t must register 1000 NOK credit. Whatever is unused is refunded. All toll stations also have video surveillance. Those who don't have

Toll Roads

Norges Automobil Forbund (NAF)
Østensjøvejen 14 N-0609 Oslo
tel. 085 05, www.naf.no
www.naf.no

Breakdown service of NAF
tel. 175 (inland)
81 54 89 91 (from abroad)

Vegmeldingstjenesten
(Road maintenance)
tel. 175 (within Norway) or
81 54 89 91 (from abroad)

Statens vegvesen / Vegdirektoratet
tel. 02030 (inland) or
91502030 (from abroad)
www.vegvesen.no

their credit card details registered online can also pay by the next petrol station – just follow the signs for »KR-Service«. Those who don't pay receive a bill in the post within three weeks, with no additional charges. Vehicles registered outside Norway are traced and owners billed via Euro Parking Collection (EPC) in London.

National tourist routes
In 2007, Norway's new national tourist routes received the Norwegian Prize for Cultural Heritage. There are five such routes: along the northern coast of Helgeland; along the Sognefjell Road high in the Jotunheimen mountains; along the Strynefjell Road, which is more than a hundred years old; the route through Lofoten; and the route through Hardanger. A particularly popular route is the » **Adventure Road**« (Eventyrveien; www.eventyrveien.no). Stretching 500km/ 310mi from Oslo to Bergen, the route passes through some of the most spectacular landscapes of the north, including the Hallingdal valley, Hardangervidda, Europe's largest mountain plateau, and the world famous fjords of western Norway, as well as the country's two largest metropolises. By 2018 there will be a total of 18 national tourist routes, including one along the over 100-year-old Trollstigen pass to the famous Geirangerfjord.

Kilometres or miles?
As a rule, distances are indicated in kilometres (km). Locals, if asked about distances, however, often still respond with an account of distances in Norwegian miles (mil). One Norwegian mile equals 11.3km or 7 British miles.

Main roads
The major routes are divided into European roads, state roads (»riksveg«, RV for short), rapid transit roads (»motorveg«) and, around major cities, motorway style highways. All important county roads (»fylkesveg«) also have numbers.

Road signs
International road signage applies in Norway. In addition though, there are signs that are unknown elsewhere. For example, a white M on a blue background signifies a passing place; »Innkjøring forbudt«

means access prohibited. A stylized castle in a blue frame indicates a cultural heritage site (such as a castle or rock art).

The network of petrol stations in the densely populated areas comes up to European standards. While planning routes, it is a good idea to remember that the number of petrol stations in Norway declines as you move further north. **Petrol prices** are somewhat above the European average, but it is difficult to give a reliable guide to prices. The following fuel is sold: 97 octane leaded, 98 octane leaded, premium unleaded (Super blyfri, 95 octane), Super Plus, unleaded (blyfri, 98 octane), and diesel.

Petrol

Rules concerning right of way are the same as standard European rules. Trams always have priority. Seatbelts are obligatory both on the front and back seats. The **alcohol limit** for drivers is presently set at 0.2%. Those caught behind the wheel with more than 0.5% alcohol in their blood will receive a fine 1.5 times the sum of their monthly gross income, those caught with 1.5% alcohol in their blood can expect a prison sentence. **Parking** is prohibited on all main roads. Parking within larger urbanized areas is only permitted at signed and (normally) fee-paying sites. **Dimmed headlights** are also **obligatory during the day**. Chains are officially required to be carried and mounted in good time during winter and spring in the mountains. **Spiked winter tyres** are permitted from 1 November to 1st Sunday after Easter (in northern Norway from 15 October to 30 April).

Traffic regulations

In urbanized areas: 31mph/50kmh. Outside urbanized areas: 50mph/80kmh. On motorway style roads: 56mph/90kmh, sometimes 62mph/100kmh. Buses: 50mph/80kmh. Vehicles with non-breaking trailers or caravans: 37mph/60kmh.

Speed limits

There are frequent speed traps and traffic controls all over Norway. Speeding is very expensive! By particularly grave offences, driving licences can be confiscated or even a prison sentence passed without possibility of parole or remission.

Speed traps

On-the-spot fines are issued by the police who have the right to impound vehicles until the full fine has been paid.

Fines

All over Norway there is a heightened **risk of collisions with wandering game**, especially during dusk and in particular on wide roads, as the animals prefer them for the light breeze that keeps the insects off. **Elk** may have thin legs, but they are very large and can weigh up to 800kg/1764lbs. During a collision between a car and an elk, the heavy body usually smashes the windscreen. If an animal is

Collisions with game

hit on the road, the accident site must be clearly marked and the **police contacted**. They will contact the agency responsible for wild game (Viltnemnda), who will ensure the animal is killed. Even animals that are already dead have to be reported to the Viltnemnda and it is absolutely prohibited for the driver to remove the animal from the scene: as reindeer always have an owner, it is even possible to be accused of theft. The police simply make a record of the accident. Damages are not payable by the driver; the reindeer's owner can apply to the state for payment. Fleeing the site of an accident generally carries very serious consequences and is highly inadvisable.

Car hire Local car hire firms offer their services alongside the international car hire firms, but their fees are no lower. Those wishing to rent a vehicle must be 21 or over (in some places even 25) and hold a valid EU/EEA driving licence. Those without a credit card have to leave a hefty deposit. Unfortunately there is no central address for the rental of mobile homes and camper vans in Norway. One firm, Bodø Bobilutleie, in the north of the country offers this service.

RAIL TRAVEL

Slow progress The rail network of the Norwegian state railway (**NSB Norges Statsbaner**) is relatively limited. The main routes lead from Oslo to Stavanger (via Kristiansand), Bergen, Åndalsnes, Trondheim (via Dombås or Røros) and Bodø (the NSB's most northerly station with connections for the Norway Bus to Kirkenes). Travel on the express trains is relatively comfortable, though slow, as three quarters of the network is along tracks with high gradients. A journey from Oslo to Bergen during summer takes just under seven hours. During the winter there can be delays of many hours. Reservations must be made on Norwegian night trains, but on other services it is no longer necessary to reserve a seat, though this is strongly recommended for long-distance routes. Rail Europe's Norway Pass allows unlimited train travel on 3–8 days within any given month (www.raileurope.com). A large number of vintage trains are lovingly maintained – a selection of the most attractive vintage rail routes is given on p.474.

BUS OR COAST TRAVEL

The long-distance bus network is quite extensive in Norway. The various bus companies are very well coordinated with each other, so that rapid headway can be made. Here, too, there is a broad range of discounts and special offers.

HIRE CARS
Avis
Reservations in UK:
tel. 0844 581 0147, www.avis.com

Budget
Reservations in UK: tel. 0844 581 2231
www.budget.co.uk

Europcar
Reservations in UK:
tel. 0845 758 5375
www.europcar.com

Hertz
Reservations in UK:
tel. 08708 44 88 44
www.hertz.com

Bodø Bobilutleie
Armbakken 2, N-8023 Bodø
tel. 75 56 01 68, fax 75 56 00 26

TRAIN INFORMATION
Norges Statsbaner (NSB)
Prinsensgt. 7 – 9, N-0048 Oslo
tel. 81 50 08 88, www.nsb.no

ATTRACTIVE RAIL ROUTES
Bergen route
Oslo – Bergen
Journey time around 6.5hrs

Dovre route
Oslo – Trondheim
via the Dovrefjell (6.5hrs)

Flåm route
Myrdal – Flåm (just under one hour)

Northern lands route
Trondheim – Bodø (approx. 11hrs)

Ofot route / Lappland route
Narvik – Kiruna (Sweden)

Rauma route
Dombås – Åndalsnes
Journey time: 1hr 20min

Sørland route
Oslo – Kristiansund –
Stavanger Journey time approx. 7.5hrs

VINTAGE TRAINS
U.H.B.
Urskog – Høland train
(»Tertitten«); Sørumsand station
(40km/25mi west of Oslo)

Krøder Line
Vikersund – Krøderen
(Midt-Buskerud)

Thamshavn Railway
Thamshavn – Løkken; stations at Løkken, Svorkmo, Fannrem

Setesdal Railway
from Grovane or Beihølen

Voss Railway
Garnes – Midttun (Nesttun); stations at
Garnes or Midttun

Rjukan Railway
Rjukan – Mæl and Tinnoset – Notodden
along with rail and steamship ferry Am-
monia (Rjukan station)

Rauma Railway
Åndalsnes – Bjorli (Trolltindane); station
at Åndalsnes

BUS INFORMATION
NOR-WAY Bussekspress
Karl Johans gate 2
N-0154 Oslo
tel. 81 54 44 44
www.nor-way.no

TRAVELLING BY FERRY

The inland ferry connections play a vital role in the national transport network. In Norway the car ferries servicing the numerous

FERRY COMPANIES
Bornholm Ferries
Service Center Havnen
DK-3700 Rønne
tel. 56 95 18 66
Fax 56 95 57 66
www.bornholmferries.dk

Color Line
PO Box 1422, Vika
N-0115 Oslo
tel. +47 22 94 42 00
Fax +47 22 83 04 30
www.colorline.com

DFDS Seaways
Scandinavia House
Refinery Road, Parkeston
Essex CO12 4QG
tel. 0871 522 9955
Fax 0191 293 6245
www.dfdsseaways.co.uk

Fjord Line
Skoltegrunnskaien
N-5003 Bergen
tel. +47 55 54 87 00
Fax +47 55 54 87 01
www.fjordline.com

Scandlines
Hochhaus am Fährhafen
D-18119 Rostock
tel. +49 1805 11 66 88
Fax +49 381 5435 678
www.scandlines.com

Silja Line
Jernbanetorget 4A
N-0154 Oslo

tel. +47 23 355750
Fax +47 73 884136
www.tallinksilja.com

TT-Line
Zum Hafenplatz 1
D-23750 Lübeck-Travemünde
tel. +49 4502 801 81
Fax +49 4502 801 407
www.ttline.com

Viking Line
Lönnrotinkatu 2
FIN-00100 Helsinki
tel. +358 9 12 351
Fax +358 9 647 075
www.vikingline.fi

OSLO AIRPORT
Oslo Lufthavn AS
P.O. Box 100
N-2061 Gardermoen
tel. 64 81 20 00
www.osl.no

DOMESTIC AIRLINES
SAS Norway Hotline
tel. 81 52 04 00 (in Norway)
Hotline tel. (00 54 00) 32 32 68 00
www.flysas.com (international)

Norwegian Air Shuttle
Reservations and enquiries:
tel. 815 21 815
www.norwegian.no

Widerøe's Flyveselskap ASA
Langstranda 6, 8001 Bodø
tel. 81 00 12 00
www.wideroe.no

fjords complement the road network. Coastal and fjord cruises are also popular. From Bergen, the **Hurtigruten** (►MARCO POLO Insight p.247) postal boats service the Norwegian west coast as far as Kirkenes, travelling there and back in eleven days.

During June and July the **ice breaker »Kapitan Dranitsyn«** travels from Kirkenes to Spitsbergen and to the islands of Franz Joseph Land, which are surrounded by thick pack ice (►address box).

DOMESTIC AIR TRAVEL

In a country with about 50 airports and airstrips, the aeroplane is a good way to cover long distances in a short time, and to reach even remote destinations.

Norway's hub for air traffic is Oslo, while significant regional airports are at Bergen, Trondheim, Stavanger, Kristiansund, Bodø, Tromsø and Alta (for Nordkapp tourists).

The national airlines are SAS (Scandinavian Airlines System), Norwegian, Coastair and Widerøe.

Travellers with Disabilities

Good provision Norway is exemplary in its provision for disabled travellers. Many hotels offer specially adapted rooms. All public facilities have disabled toilets. Pavements and street corners are often adapted for wheelchair access and wheelchair lifts are common. Traffic lights give sound signals for those with impaired vision or hearing. Rapid and express trains have disabled access. Campsites also have appropriate sanitary facilities.

INFORMATION IN UK
RADAR
12 City Forum, 250 City Road,
London EC1V 8AF
tel. (020) 72 50 32 22
www.radar.org.uk

INFORMATION IN USA
SATH (Society for the Advancement of Travel for the Handicapped)
347 5th Ave., no. 610
New York, NY 10016:

tel. (21) 4 47 72 84
www.sath.org

INFORMATION IN NORWAY
Norges Handikapforbund
Schweigaardsgt. 12
Postboks 9217
Grønland
N-0134 Oslo
tel. 24 10 24 00
Fax 24 10 24 99
www.nhf.no

Five region-typical climate stations

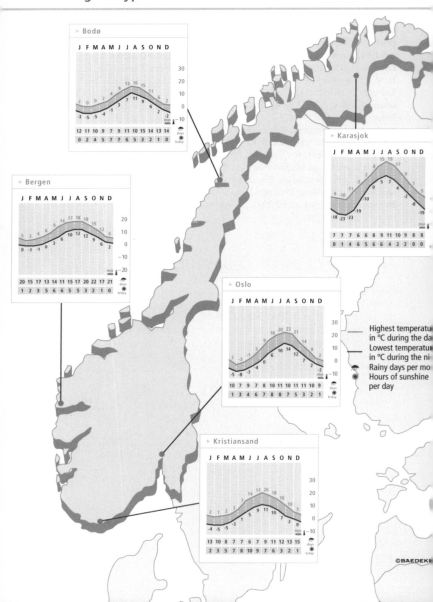

Bodø

J F M A M J J A S O N D

Karasjok

J F M A M J J A S O N D

Bergen

J F M A M J J A S O N D

Oslo

J F M A M J J A S O N D

Kristiansand

J F M A M J J A S O N D

Highest temperature
in °C during the day
Lowest temperature
in °C during the night
Rainy days per month
Hours of sunshine
per day

©BAEDEKER

When to Go

The best times to travel to southern Norway is May to June; for northern Norway, mid-June to mid-August is best. After those months, the weather gets noticeably worse all over the country. The best time to visit the west coast is April to May, when the least rain falls. Those who put a high premium on warm summer weather with lots of sunshine and little rain are best served by the southeast of the country, between Kristiansand and Oslo, or the eastern interior. The latter is also attractive for winter sports enthusiasts because of guaranteed snow. During the drive up to Nordkapp, winter driving conditions can still be expected in Lapland in June.

The ideal time

For cruise journeys, the months of April to June are recommended for the best chance of clear views and lots of sunshine. The best opportunity for experiencing the fjords in sunshine occurs during April and May. March and April are especially suitable for winter sports, because the days get longer then. More on climate ▶ p.18.

Index

List of Maps and Illustrations

Photo Credits

AKG p. 49, 69 (2 x), 72, 75

Bilderberg/Christophe Boisvieux p. 407 (below right)

Bilderberg/Rainer Drexel p. 219

DuMont Bildarchiv p. 168, 173, 271, 440

DuMont Bildarchiv/Modrow p. 8, 13, 58, 221, 246, 260, 316, 402, 421, 422

DuMont Bildarchiv/Nowak p. 1, 4 (left), 5 (left), 6, 26, 50, 70, 83, 94, 118, 119, 144, 147, 149, 158, 164, 179, 183, 187, 195, 204, 207, 210, 212, 215, 228, 230, 233, 236, 239, 250, 276, 301, 334, 347 (below left), 348, 354, 358, 371, 374, 380, 387, 390, 398, c2

DuMont Bildarchiv/Ola Roe p. 44 (right), 64, 101 (below), 116

Feltes-Peter p. 12, 63, 170, 177, 178, 274, 408

Feltes-Peter/The Munch-Museum p. 74

gettyimages/Dorling Kindersley p. 100 (left)

Hans Klüche 396

Huber (BA)/Damm p. 46

Huber (BA)/Gräfenhain p. 281, 314, 319, 383

Huber (BA)/Picture Finders p. 360

Huber (BA)/Schmid p. 2, 199

Hurtigruten p. 222, 292

IFA-Bilderteam p. 294

Interfoto p. 66

iStockphoto p. 127

iStockphoto p. 53, 323

laif p. U3 (above), 35, 84, 193, 263, 411

laif/Arcticphoto p. 106

laif/Toma Babovic p. 96, 366, 446

laif/BODY Philippe/hemis.fr p. 426

laif/Simon Descamps/Hemis.fr p. 10

laif/Fautre/Le Figaro Magazine p. 3 (below), 78, 128

laif/Max Galli p. 3 (above/2) 304, 326, 435

laif/Reiner Harscher p. 92

laif/Hemispheres p. 80

laif/Frank Heuer p. 7, 249

laif/Bernd Jonkmanns p. 115

laif/Chr. Kaiser p. 43

laif/Keystone Schweiz p. 21

laif/Markus Kirchgessner p. 110

laif/Sanna Lindberg/PhotoAlto p. U3 (below), 100 (right)

laif/Andre Luetzen p. 14

laif/Joerg Modrow p. 3 (above), 112, 333

laif/Hardy Mueller H. p. 95

laif/Christopher Olsson p. 45

laif/Pool BENAINOUS/DUCLOS p. 57

laif/Quidu/Le Figaro Magazine p. 5 (above right), 152

laif/Berthold Steinhilber p. 336

laif/Wallet/Le Figaro Magazine p. 105

mauritius images p. 4 (above right), 191, 254, 437

mauritius images/age p. 217

mauritius images/CuboImages p. 108

mauritius images/ib/Christian Handl p. 101 (above)

mauritius images/Trond Hillestad p. 309

mauritius images/jose fuste raga p. 142

mauritius images/Bard Loken p. 4 (below right), 197

mauritius images/Tsuneo Nakamura p. 366, 442

mauritius images/Uwe Umstätter p. 86

McHugh,T./Okapia p. 28

Nowak p. 289, 290, 320, 321, 327, 407 (above right), 407 (below left), 439

picture alliance p. 350

picture alliance/akg-images p. 347 (above left), 347 (above right), 347 (below right)

picture alliance/Duval Cyril p. U4, 403

picture alliance/Härtrich/Transit p. 444

picture alliance/Huber/Gräfenhain p. 214, 225

picture alliance/Rpe-Albert Nieboer p. 44 (left)

Piper Verlag/Felbert, Peter von p. 65

Cover: huber-images/Gräfenhain

Publisher's Information

1st Edition 2015
Worldwide Distribution: Marco Polo
Travel Publishing Ltd
Pinewood, Chineham Business Park
Crockford Lane, Chineham
Basingstoke, Hampshire RG24 8AL,
United Kingdom.

Photos, illlustrations, maps:
170 photos, 39 maps and and
illustrations, one large map
Text:
Christian Nowak, Hans Klüche, Odin
Hug, Andrea Mecke, Robert Fischer
Editing:
Kathleen Becker, Rainer Eisenschmid
Translation: Kathleen Becker, Barbara
Schmidt-Runkel, Natascha Scott-Stokes
Cartography:
Franz Huber, Munich; MAIRDUMONT
Ostfildern (city map)
3D illustrations:
jangled nerves, Stuttgart
Infographics:
Golden Section Graphics GmbH, Berlin
Design:
independent Medien-Design, Munich

Editor-in-chief:
Rainer Eisenschmid, Mairdumont
Ostfildern

Printed in China

Despite all of our authors' thorough
research, errors can creep in. The pub-
lishers do not accept any liability for thi
Whether you want to praise, alert us to
errors or give us a personal tip Please
contact us by email or post:

MARCO POLO Travel Publishing Ltd
Pinewood, Chineham Business Park
Crockford Lane, Chineham
Basingstoke, Hampshire RG24 8AL
United Kingdom
Email: sales@marcopolouk.com

FSC
www.fsc.org
MIX
Paper from
responsible sources
FSC® C011918

MARCO ⊕ POLO

HANDBOOKS

MARCO ⊕ POLO
TRAVEL HANDBOOK
ANDALUCÍA

MARCO ⊕ POLO
TRAVEL HANDBOOK
BARCELONA

MARCO ⊕ POLO
TRAVEL HANDBOOK
BERLIN

MARCO ⊕ POLO
TRAVEL HANDBOOK
BUDAPEST

MARCO ⊕ POLO
TRAVEL HANDBOOK
DRESDEN

MARCO ⊕ POLO
TRAVEL HANDBOOK
FLORENCE

MARCO ⊕ POLO
TRAVEL HANDBOOK
FLORIDA

MARCO ⊕ POLO
TRAVEL HANDBOOK
GRAN CANARIA

MARCO ⊕ POLO
TRAVEL HANDBOOK
ICELAND

MARCO ⊕ POLO
TRAVEL HANDBOOK
LONDON

MARCO ⊕ POLO
TRAVEL HANDBOOK
MADEIRA

MARCO ⊕ POLO
TRAVEL HANDBOOK
NEW YORK

MARCO ⊕ POLO
TRAVEL HANDBOOK
NORWAY

MARCO ⊕ POLO
TRAVEL HANDBOOK
PARIS

MARCO ⊕ POLO
TRAVEL HANDBOOK
ROME

MARCO ⊕ POLO
TRAVEL HANDBOOK
SRI LANKA

MARCO ⊕ POLO
TRAVEL HANDBOOK
VENICE

MARCO ⊕ POLO
TRAVEL HANDBOOK
VIETNAM

www.marco-polo.com

Norwegian Curiosities

Northern Europe is also home to some oddities. In Norway, for example, people are convinced they discovered America, are bi-lingual, and have their very own measurement for the mile.

►One country, two languages
The country may be small, but it has two official languages. In the west, Nynorsk is the predominant language, while in the east and in cities, Bokmål reigns.

►The capital of rain
Bergen is Europe's rainiest city, where it rains an average of 248 days a year and the locals distinguish between more than two dozen types of rain. But don't worry, it rarely actually rains all day.

►Expensive fuel
Norway has long had the most expensive petrol and diesel in Europe, even though the country is one of the largest oil exporters.

►Swedish jokes
The Norwegians spent a long time under Swedish hegemony, so there is a certain rivalry between these Scandinavian neighbours and the Norwegians enjoy telling jokes at Swedes expense. They are also pleased when the Swedes loose at football or win less medals at the Olympic Games.

►The land of lakes
Finland normally reserves this title for itself, even though it 'only' has 60,000 lakes, compared to Norway's approximately half a million lakes.

►Norwegian miles
Distances are normally indicated in kilometres, but the locals often think in terms of Norwegian miles, whereby one Norwegian mile is equal to 11.3km/7mi.

►The discovery of the Americas
Most Norwegians are thoroughly convinced one of their own was the first European to set foot on the Americas, namely the Viking Leif Eriksson, despite the fact that he was unarguably born in Iceland.

►Driver education
Exceeding the speed limit in Norway by just 10km/6mi per hour results in fines of several hundred Euros. Those driving faster can even land in jail. On the other hand, if a junky is caught with a small amount of drugs, the fine is usually smaller.

►Buying sex is illegal
Men are not allowed to pay for sexual services in Norway, but prostitutes are not criminalised for their activities.